Sailing
FOR
DUMMIES®
2ND EDITION

by JJ and Peter Isler

WILEY

Wiley Publishing, Inc.

Sailing For Dummies®, 2nd Edition

Published by
Wiley Publishing, Inc.
111 River St.
Hoboken, NJ 07030-5774
www.wiley.com

WILEY

About the Authors

JJ and Peter Isler have been sailing for most of their lives. JJ grew up around boats in San Diego, California, learning to sail in a little 7-foot dinghy called a Sabot. Peter started out loving powerboats and fishing (boys can be so strange!), but took up sailing after his family moved to Connecticut when he was 13 years old.

The Islers are well known throughout the world of sailing as top competitors and teachers. They both have taught sailing to people of all ages and experiences. Peter played an important, early role in developing US Sailing's educational program. He also coached at the Olympic level and helped found the American Sailing Association, which accredits sailing schools and certifies sailors and instructors.

Peter has twice won the America's Cup, serving as navigator aboard *Stars & Stripes* with Dennis Conner in 1987 and 1988. An accomplished small-boat sailor, Peter was Intercollegiate Sailor of the Year while at Yale University. He was the top-ranked U.S. sailor on the professional match-racing circuit for five years and has won many of the world's major ocean races, including the Bermuda Race and the Transpac (where he navigated *Morning Glory* to an elapsed time record in 2005).

Peter has also been very active in the media. In the 1990s, he shifted his America's Cup energies to television, where he was a featured analyst in ESPN's Emmy Award–winning Cup coverage in 1992 and 1995. More recently, he covered sailing for the Outdoor Life Network (OLN), including its coverage of the 2003 America's Cup. He is the author of several books on the sport and is presently Editor at Large of *Sailing World* magazine. In his spare time, Peter enjoys playing guitar and keyboard with his band, The Water Brothers.

JJ is the only American female (so far) to have won two Olympic medals in sailing, and she is the first female inductee in the *Sailing World* Hall of Fame. With crew member Pamela Healy, JJ won the Bronze Medal in the Women's 470 class in the 1992 Olympics in Barcelona, Spain. In the 2000 Olympics in Sydney, Australia, she and crew member Pease Glaser won the Silver. JJ is a four-time Rolex Yachtswoman of the Year (in 1986, 1991, 1997, and 2000) and has won three World Championships and numerous national titles. She was the first female to compete in a number of events on the international match-racing circuit. And in 1995 she was the tactician and starting helmsman for the *America³* Women's America's Cup team. She graduated from Yale University where she was captain of the sailing team and a collegiate All-American.

The Islers reside in San Diego with their two daughters, Marly and Megan, their two cats, two chickens, five fish, eight boats, numerous sailboards, and a lot of miscellaneous sailboat parts that Peter plans on using someday.

Dedication

To our daughters, Marly and Megan.

Authors' Acknowledgments

We first want to thank our two daughters who were so patient (and helpful) through this revision — and thanks to the wonderful Francis Parker School that is teaching them to enjoying learning about so many things. Our friend (and famous author of several *For Dummies* titles and lead guitarist in Peter's band) Peter Economy encouraged us to do this second edition revision and provided plenty of advice along the way. Josh Adams and John Burnham helped us find our great illustrator, Michael Boardman. Mike Dorgan provided his experience and insight in the process of buying a boat (see Chapter 20). And Urban Miyares shared his expertise on sailing with disabilities. Harry Munns stepped up to provide his services as technical editor. Harry has the qualifications to write any book about sailing, so we're really lucky to have his help here. And our friends at IMG Literary have remained consistently professional and ever helpful since day one, when we wrote the proposal for the first edition.

We are very proud of the first edition of *Sailing For Dummies* and the success it achieved, but we want to thank Tracy Boggier, Joyce Pepple, our project editor Chad Sievers, and the rest of the Wiley's *For Dummies* team that worked so hard on helping us produce this new-and-improved second edition.

One of the things we're most pleased of in this second edition is the new art-work and photographs. And we definitely needed a little help from our friends to get the photos that we wanted. So in no particular order, our heartfelt thanks go to Mike Boardman of Boardman Designs (for the updated illustra-tions); Andy Burdick and the team at Melges Performance Boats; Tim Wilkes, Keith and Nigel Musto, and their team at Musto Performance Clothing; Glenn Bourke and his team running the Volvo Ocean Race; Tom Carruthers and Whit Batchelor of J World San Diego; Lew Newlands and Offshore Challenges; Craig Leweck of *Scuttlebutt* (for loaning his camera to Peter when the perfect shot appeared one day while they were out sailing); Christine DeSimone and Sunsail; Nick White and his Expedition Software; and last but not least, up-and-coming sailing star, Emily Bohl. And finally, this book (and especially the first edition) never would have happened (at least not anywhere close to deadline) without the carpool and childcare support from JJ's parents and our next-door neighbors, Jane and Tom Fetter.

We still appreciate the efforts of many people whose help with the first edition still shines through in this edition, including Brad Dellenbaugh; Sally Samins, who shot the photos (and helped us find the ones we couldn't shoot); and Jeff Johnson, who helped immensely, as did our neighbor Aine McLean (a great capsizing-photo model). Other people and organizations who helped with the first edition are Pat Healy, Doug Ament at H&S Yacht Sales, Geri Conser (for that great aerial photo of JJ and Pam), Billy Black, Kristen Lawton, Doug Skidmore, and Matt Miller — the folks at Hobie Cat, Jason Campbell, Tom Leweck, Cam Lewis, Skip Novak, Mark Reiter, Marty Ehrlich, Rich Roberts, Katie Poe, Dennis Conner, the San Diego Yacht Club, and the American Sailing Association.

People who have played a key role in Peter's education as a sailor and a teacher include his mother, Marilyn Isler Brunger; Ted Jones, who bent some rules at Norwalk (Connecticut) Yacht Club so Peter could join the junior sailing program; Kendrick Wilson; Tyler Keys; Tom Whidden; Richard Hokin; Stan Honey; Steve Benjamin; Dave Perry; Lenny Shabes; Robert Hopkins; Gary Jobson; and John Rousmaniere.

JJ would like to thank her sailing instructors — Jack Wood, Mark and DeAnn Reynolds, and Dave Perry — for instilling an early and lasting love of the sport. Also, thanks to Pease Glaser, Pamela Healy, the U.S. Olympic Sailing Committee and her Olympic coaches, and Bill Koch for giving her the opportunity to take her sailing to a higher level.

Finally, we would like to thank you for your interest in "our" sport. May the wind always be at your back, and if it must come from ahead, may your sails be well shaped and trimmed in tight!

Peter and JJ Isler

La Jolla, California

Publisher's Acknowledgments

We're proud of this book; please send us your comments through our Dummies online registration form located at www.dummies.com/register/.

Some of the people who helped bring this book to market include the following:

Acquisitions, Editorial, and Media Development

Project Editor: Chad R. Sievers
(*Previous Edition: Rev Mengle*)

Acquisitions Editor: Tracy Boggier

Copy Editor: Melissa Wiley
(*Previous Edition: Christine Beck and Michael Simsic*)

Editorial Program Coordinator: Hanna K. Scott

Technical Editor: Harry Munns

Editorial Manager: Michelle Hacker

Editorial Assistant: Erin Calligan

Cover Photos: © Southern Stock/Getty Images

Cartoons: Rich Tennant
(www.the5thwave.com)

Illustrations: Mike Boardman
(www.boardmandesign.com)

Production

Project Coordinator: Tera Knapp

Layout and Graphics: Carl Byers, Andrea Dahl, Stephanie D. Jumper, Lynsey Osborn, Alicia B. South, Julie Trippetti

Proofreaders: Leeann Harney, Christy Pingleton, Techbooks

Indexer: Techbooks

Photo Credits:

All photos by Sally Samins, except for the following:

J World, San Diego, Figure 2-2

Tim Wilkes, www.timwilkes.com, Figures 11-4(b) and 13-3

Oskar Kihlborg/Volvo Ocean Race, Figures 7-2 and 13-5

Rich Roberts, Figure 13-4

Sunsail Sailing Vacations, www.sunsail.com, Figures 17-1 and 17-2

Benoit Stichelbaut/DPPI/Offshore Challenges Sailing Team, sidebar in Ch. 13

Peter Isler, Figures 3-1(c), 5-6, 8-7, 8-9, 9-5, sidebar in Ch. 9, 11-5, 15-6, 21-1, 21-2

Skip Novak, Figure 10-9

Hobie Cat Co., Figures 11-9 and 11-10

Geri Conser, Figure 13-2

Bob Grieser, sidebar in Ch. 16

Publishing and Editorial for Consumer Dummies

Diane Graves Steele, Vice President and Publisher, Consumer Dummies

Joyce Pepple, Acquisitions Director, Consumer Dummies

Kristin A. Cocks, Product Development Director, Consumer Dummies

Michael Spring, Vice President and Publisher, Travel

Kelly Regan, Editorial Director, Travel

Publishing for Technology Dummies

Andy Cummings, Vice President and Publisher, Dummies Technology/General User

Composition Services

Gerry Fahey, Vice President of Production Services

Debbie Stailey, Director of Composition Services

Contents at a Glance

Table of Contents

Introduction

· ·

There is nothing — absolutely nothing — half so much worth doing as simply messing about in boats.

—Water Rat to Mole, Kenneth Grahame, The Wind in the Willows

*W*hat gives sailing such enchanting prospects? Water Rat certainly had a piece of the puzzle. Messing about in a boat — any kind of boat — is great fun. You escape the cares and stresses of everyday life, conveyed on a craft powered solely by the forces of nature. The spell that the wind casts onto the sails of a boat is bewitching to behold.

Maybe the best part of sailing is the part that your imagination can latch onto, conveying your mind to places you've never been, promising experiences yet untold. And no matter how experienced you become or how much water passes beneath your keel, sailing still has more to offer. The sport is so vast that no one can experience all of sailing's facets in a single lifetime.

But enough generalizing. After all, you wouldn't have picked up this book if you weren't already at least intrigued by the allure of sailing.

About This Book

In this book, you can find all the information you need to go sailing. This book is a textbook, user's manual, and reference book all in one. We start with basic sailing skills and move on to cover more advanced topics for when you widen your horizons to activities such as chartering a boat and going cruising. You get to practice tying knots, and we talk about what to wear on a boat. (You can skip the blue blazer and captain's hat, but soft-soled shoes are a must.) You find out how to sail such diverse crafts as a sailboard and a catamaran, how to forecast the weather, and how to find a boat that's right for you. You even discover the basics of sailboat racing. We cover all you need to know to be safe on the water, and we make the whole process easy and fun!

Conventions Used in This Book

Have you ever listened in on the conversation of two sailors? Sailing has so many specific words that sailors can sound like they're speaking a foreign language. But don't let the jargon turn you off. The language of sailing has an old and rich tradition, and as you become more comfortable in a sailboat, you gradually pick up more and more of the language and become a part of the sailing tradition yourself.

In this book, we try to avoid sailing jargon as much as possible, but we can't get around it completely because some of the terms are very important for safety. When the skipper plans a maneuver that requires a coordinated crew effort, using and understanding the exact sailing term allows everyone on the boat to know what's happening and what to do.

We use the following conventions to help you understand everything that we're discussing and to stay consistent:

- ✔ We *italicize* boat names and new terms and follow them with an easy-to-understand definition. We also list most of the italicized terms in the glossary so you can brush up on sailing terminology.

- ✔ We **bold** important keywords in bulleted lists as well as the action parts of numbered lists.

- ✔ We use `monofont` for all Web addresses.

Finally, in this book we simply refer to *boats* or *sailboats*. We sometimes further differentiate between bigger sailboats with keels *(keelboats)* and smaller sailboats with centerboards *(dinghies)* as needed for the subject we're covering. (In the United States, a yacht is the snobby cousin of the boat, but in New Zealand and much of the current and former British Empire, the word *yacht* has no snob connotations. You can use *yacht* safely, without giving away anything about yourself, in place of *boat* or *sailboat*.)

What You're Not to Read

We love telling sea stories — and we include our favorites in this book. But if you're looking for just the purely instructional information, you can skip the places where you see the Peter Says or JJ Says icons (see "Icons Used in This Book," later in this Introduction, for other icons used).

Sidebars are the shaded boxes that appear occasionally. We use the sidebars to go off on a *tack* (a basic sailing maneuver where you turn your boat and sail in a different direction) and go into more depth on a topic or give you a bit of interesting information that isn't strictly essential. So you can skip side-bars, although we hope you come back to them someday.

Foolish Assumptions

The most foolish assumption we made when we wrote the first edition of this book was that only our parents and a few close friends would ever read it. We've been overwhelmed by the positive responses to the first edition, and we hope you enjoy all the new information we've crammed into this book. We assume one or more of the following about you, our reader:

- You've been given this book as a gift by a friend who wants to take you sailing.
- You get dragged out on the water by your sailing-loving family, and you don't really know what to do.
- You've always been intrigued by the sea.
- You may have had a bad experience on the water, but now you want to give sailing another try.
- Your child has been bitten by the sailboat-racing bug, and you want to figure out what you're watching.
- You love the water and enjoy powerboats, but now with the world's oil reserves dwindling, a sailboat seems better for the environment (and cheaper).
- You're staying at a friend's beach cottage, and you picked up this book because you just finished your trashy romance novel.
- You discovered the basics of sailing at summer camp and you haven't sailed since then, but now you want to charter a boat in the Caribbean.
- You already enjoy sailing and want a good, complete reference book and ideas to explore some new directions in the sport.

We wrote this book to lure you into the sport that we love — no matter how you came to turn that first page.

How This Book 1s Organized

Unlike a novel, this book isn't designed for you to read it from cover to cover. Depending on your familiarity with sailing, you may want to begin by reading Chapter 1 or Chapter 5 or Chapter 15 — the choice is up to you. If we write about something important that we cover in more depth elsewhere, we tell you where to turn. Simple? We think so.

Part 1: Before You Get Your Feet Wet

The four chapters in this section ensure that your first experience on the water is comfortable and fun, even if you've never been on a sailboat before.

Chapter 1 takes a broad overview of the sport, looks at the different types of sailboats and some of their basic parts, and introduces the basics of sailing. Chapter 2 covers your options of where to go to discover sailing. And as you're preparing for that first day on the water, Chapter 3 answers that age-old question, "What should I wear?" (which on smaller boats should always include a life jacket). In Chapter 4, you step aboard a boat and prepare the sails and gear for your first adventure afloat, powered by the force of the wind.

Part II: Casting Off and Sailing Away

This section is the meat of the book for the new sailor. Chapter 5 is the big kahuna, covering the principles of sailing: how to get your boat from point A to point B (and back again). Chapter 6 wraps up the basics by showing you how to sail away from a dock or mooring and how to launch your boat from a trailer, ramp, or beach. Chapter 7 discusses safety, because you need to be prepared when you're out on the water. We show you where the safest spots are to enjoy your ride, how to rescue a man overboard, and how to get going again if your boat tips over. Chapter 8 is great for anyone interested in weather (which, by the way, includes all sailors). Identifying the weather helps you know whether those dark clouds on the horizon are going to dump rain on you, bring wind, or both. And Chapter 9 covers navigation, including how to read charts, plot your course, use a compass, and find your position while at sea (without having to stop at the nearest gas station for directions). Chapter 10 focuses on anchoring. Even powerboaters need to know the information in Chapters 7 through 10 before heading out on the water.

Part III: Sailing Fast — Taking Your Sailing to the Next Level

We intend the first two chapters of this section to be most helpful for intermediate and advanced sailors who have at least a season of sailing under their belts. Chapter 11 provides plenty of tips to sailing faster, including surfing waves and sailing catamarans — those speedy boats with two hulls. Chapter 12 introduces you to the subtleties of adjusting the shape of your sails. This chapter also shows you how to use a *spinnaker* — that colorful sail for going fast downwind. Chapter 13 acquaints you with our favorite world of sailboat racing.

Part IV: Sailing Away for a Year and a Day

This part helps you with special circumstances you may encounter, no matter if you're out for a day cruise or for a much longer time. Chapter 14 covers what to do on an unlucky day: when you run aground, break something, or have to abandon ship. In Chapter 15, we introduce you to the basics of maintenance — keeping your ship in shape. Chapter 16 helps you enjoy sailing with children, because you get to go sailing more often if your family enjoys the sport, too. Chapter 17 introduces you to the great world of *chartering* (renting) sailboats and going cruising. Affordable boats are available for charter in exotic locations around the world. Chapter 18 focuses on how to sail a sailboard — those surfboards with sails that we love and you've always wanted to try.

Part V: The Part of Tens

No *For Dummies* book is complete without this section. Sailboats always have plenty of rope, and Chapter 19 reminds you how to tie those knots you practiced in Girl or Boy Scouts and tells you which one to use when. Chapter 20 poses ten questions to help you find the right boat for you. Chapter 21 has a list of ten of our favorite things about sailing.

Part VI: Appendixes

Appendix A has a glossary with all the sailing lingo you need to impress your friends and sound like a yachtie. Appendix B covers first aid afloat — from what to have in your first-aid kit to how to handle the most common medical problems at sea. Finally, in Appendix C we cover how a sailboat moves for those technical types who always want to know "how" and "why."

Icons Used in This Book

You may notice icons, or cute little pictures, in the margins of this book. Those icons do more than just break up the white space; they tell you something about that particular paragraph.

This symbol helps you avoid common mistakes while you're just starting out and alerts you to potential dangers. As a sailor, you need to have a healthy respect for the power of the wind and the sea.

Our many years of sailing have resulted in some wonderful memories and some unusual stories. This icon indicates a story from JJ's own experiences.

Peter also has a few stories to tell, and we use this icon to point those stories out.

This icon points out information that we don't want you to forget. Store it in your brain for quick recall at a later time.

This icon, shaped like one of the life jackets you read about in Chapter 3, highlights advice to help keep you and your loved ones safe.

In sailing, because you're letting the wind do the work, the easy way is the right way. These tips can help you find the easy way.

Where to Go from Here

Where you start is up to you. If you're brand new to the world of sailing, just turn the page and start with Chapter 1. If you've been around boats before, browse through the table of contents and pick a chapter that interests you.

But do start somewhere. The faster you start, the faster we can share our love of sailing with you. While cruising, we've explored some of the most remote and beautiful parts of the world. While racing, we've had the chance to challenge ourselves in international competitions and make friends around the globe. Who knows? Maybe on one of our future voyages, we'll even get a chance to meet you.

Part I
Before You Get Your Feet Wet

The 5th Wave — By Rich Tennant

"Take a starboard tack at the next exit!"

In this part . . .

Some people think that sailors are incredibly snobby rich people who hang out at the yacht club all day sipping gin and tonics, wearing blue blazers, and talking without moving their jaws (kind of like Thurston Howell III in *Gilligan's Island*). If this intimidating vision has kept you from beginning to sail, this part is for you. We formally introduce you to a sailboat and then show you where you can take sailing lessons — from regular people and with regular people. We also dispel those blue-blazer myths and answer that incredibly important question that mankind ponders every morning — what to wear? Finally in this part, we look at what you need to know before you leave the dock.

Chapter 1

Ready, Set, Go: Time to Start Sailing

In This Chapter

▶ Exploring the essentials of beginning sailing

▶ Dissecting the parts of a sailboat

▶ Answering basic sailing questions

▶ Describing where sailing can take you

> *It is an interesting biological fact that all of us have, in our veins, the exact same percentage of salt in our blood that exists in the ocean, and therefore, we have salt in our blood, in our sweat, in our tears. We are tied to the ocean. And when we go back to the sea, whether it is to sail or to watch it — we are going back from whence we came.*
>
> —John F. Kennedy

Water covers nearly three-quarters of the planet. Over the course of human history, the oceans (as well as lakes and rivers) have served as pathways upon which trade and civilization have developed. Getting away from shore, you feel a link to those ancient mariners who set off for undiscovered lands. When you're flying across the water, you're harnessing the same forces of nature that powered the early explorers.

Why are humans drawn to the sea? President John F. Kennedy had a poetic answer. Generations before you have felt the call of the wind and waves, beckoning to accept their offer of unknown possibilities — adventure and serenity.

Even in today's high-tech, fast-paced world, sailing regularly rates high on pollsters' lists of desirable activities. So if you ever find yourself dreaming of packing it all in and setting sail over the horizon or of simply having your own boat to sail near home on a warm, breezy afternoon, you're not alone. And this chapter shows you that getting out on the water is easier than you think.

What You Need to Start Sailing

Starting sailing is a little different than starting most sports. In basketball, you can start to learn the basic moves like dribbling and shooting without worrying about the "playing field" — the court boundaries or the height of the basket. But the sailor's "playing field" — the wind and the water — is constantly changing. The wind changes strength and direction while waves and/or current change the water conditions. Sailing is harnessing the power of Mother Nature, and sailors need a healthy respect for her power. So in this section, we cover some important weather and safety considerations you need to know before you start sailing.

Also in this section, we encourage you to begin your sailing career by taking lessons from a qualified instructor — we both did — so you can focus on learning the basic moves while the instructor makes sure the conditions are suitable for learning.

Taking lessons

You can find sailboats near almost every body of water. And where you find sailboats, you can find sailing schools and/or a sailing club with experienced sailors looking for crew. Most boats longer than 15 feet (5 meters) are meant to be sailed with more than one person, and the average 30-foot (9-meter) sailboat is best sailed with at least four crew members. So go down to the local marina, check out the bulletin board, and ask around. The offers you get to go sailing may pleasantly surprise you.

Although having friends to take you sailing can make practicing and progressing easy, we strongly recommend taking lessons from a sailing school with certified instructors before you head out on your own. For a variety of safety reasons, we don't recommend sailing alone while learning the basics. In Chapter 2, we help you find the right sailing course for any experience level.

Location, location, location

You can probably guess that the weather and water conditions in a given area affect the sailing possibilities, and that most sailors put away their sailing clothes in wintertime in the snowy latitudes whilst Southern Californians can sail year round. But even snow and ice can't stop some die-hard enthusiasts who sail ice boats on frozen northern lakes. Not to be outdone, adventurous sailors in dry, desert areas blast around on "land yachts" or "dirt boats" with wheels. Assuming that you plan to go sailing on regular, salt or fresh, non-frozen water, then your main concerns are twofold: the water conditions (waves, currents, depth, and water temperature) and the wind conditions (wind strength and changeability). Some areas have very consistent conditions during a particular season, and others are more variable. In some places, a typically windy spot and a calm location may be less than a mile apart due to some geographic feature.

That's why knowing the local conditions can be invaluable to any sailor. We encourage new sailors to start out, if possible, in steady light-to-medium winds and protected (calm) waters — and a sailing school knows where and when to find those conditions in your area. But as you gain experience, you can enjoy sailing in more challenging conditions — such as windy Chicago or San Francisco in midsummer, cruising in foggy Maine, or blasting down the Molokai Channel in Hawaii.

Feeling the wind

You probably know that a sailboat doesn't move unless it has wind. (Yes — you can start up the engine, get a tow, get out a paddle, or swim along pulling your boat — but we're talking about "sailing" using the power of the sails, right?) The wind rules a sailor's universe — it's the sailor's alpha and omega. To become a sailor, you need to raise your awareness of the weather, starting with the importance of feeling and finding the wind's direction.

Look around for a nearby flag and use its direction as a clue. In Chapter 5, we show you how to develop your feel for sensing the wind direction and staying aware of any shifts (without having the local weatherman on your speed dial). Knowing the wind's direction is crucial because you get your boat to move by adjusting the angle of the sails relative to the wind's direction. When the wind direction changes or you change course, you need to change your sail *trim,* or the angle of your sails to the wind, as you see in Chapter 5.

No matter how constant the weather seems on shore, the wind is frequently shifting both speed and direction. Staying aware of these changes is important for your safety and comfort while sailing. Sensing the wind's speed is important too so you avoid going sailing when the wind is too strong or blustery and so you can avoid getting *becalmed,* unable to sail if the wind dies. Listen to the local marine forecast before a day of sailing to help you avoid getting caught in unpleasant (and potentially dangerous) conditions on the water — such as thunderstorms or thick fog. (You can also check out Chapter 8, which discusses important weather-related information you need to know before heading out.)

Considering safety

Before going out on the water, you need to consider some safety issues and be prepared with basic safety gear, especially life jackets. In Chapter 3, we give you plenty of tips for what to wear and bring so you're comfortable and safe on the water. Chapter 7 covers other essential safety information, such as safely recovering a person who falls overboard and getting a capsized dinghy upright and sailing again.

Looking at a Sailboat

Sailboats come in all sizes, shapes, and types. The beauty of sailing is that you can't help but find a boat (or two or three) that's just right for you. All sailing craft, big or small, have at least one (and sometimes more) of the following components, which we outline in the following sections: a hull, an underwater fin for steering control and stability, a mast to hold up the sail or sails, a sail, and plenty of rope.

What floats your boat?

Have you ever sat in a boat and wondered how in the heck it doesn't sink? Well you don't have to wonder anymore.

Your boat floats because it's less dense than the water in which it sits. *Density* is expressed as mass per unit volume. The density of freshwater is 62.2 pounds per cubic foot (1 gram per cubic centimeter). Saltwater is denser at 64 pounds per cubic foot, so a given object can float better (or higher) in saltwater than in freshwater. In saltwater, a boat floats if it's less dense than 64 pounds per cubic foot, including everything on board: mast, sails, and people. For example, if the density of a boat in saltwater is 32 pounds per cubic foot (½ gram per cubic centimeter), the boat floats half in and half out of the water.

The weight of a boat is also called its *displacement,* because the boat displaces (or pushes aside) a volume of water equal to its weight. An object with a very light displacement, such as a surfboard, lies on top of the water like a leaf. A boat with a heavy displacement sits lower in the water, displacing more water to stay afloat.

Here's the amazing part. You can build boats of nonbuoyant (denser-than-water) materials, such as steel or concrete, as long as you design them with enough volume so that their total density is less than the density of the water. As proof of that principle, consider that an empty aluminum soda can floats, but the same can sinks if you flatten it and decrease its volume. (Of course, don't try this experiment on the water — you'd be littering.)

All sailboats have a hull

The hull is (ideally) the floating body of a boat, and it can be made of a wide variety of materials, including wood, fiberglass, metal, plastic — even cement. The hull can be as small as a surfboard or more than 100 feet (30 meters) long.

You can get a good idea about how fast a boat is by how it looks. Just as you can tell that a sports car will be faster than a golf cart, you can tell that a big, heavy, wide boat with a short mast is a good cruiser but won't break any speed records on the water. Sailboats fall into three basic types based on their hull shape, as Figure 1-1 illustrates.

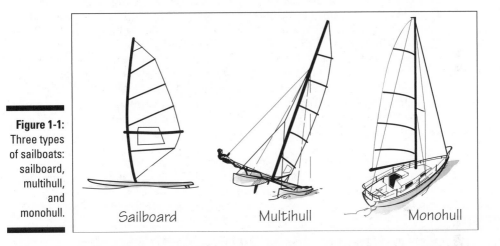

Figure 1-1: Three types of sailboats: sailboard, multihull, and monohull.

Sailboard   Multihull   Monohull

✔ **Sailboards:** These boats are basically surfboards with a sail. They come in many different sizes and shapes, depending on their intended use and the skill level of the rider. Sailboarding is a great way to enjoy the sport with equipment that you can throw on the roof of your car. For fun, recreational sailing (as opposed to racing), we love sailboarding more than any other aspect of our sport. For those of you who doubt the aerobic benefits of the sport of sailing, try windsurfing for an afternoon. We promise that every muscle in your body will be tired afterward. For more on sailboarding, check out Chapter 18.

✔ **Multihulls:** Multihulls are boats with more than one hull (makes sense, doesn't it?). A boat with two hulls is called a *catamaran;* a boat with three hulls, a *trimaran*. Multihulls, especially small, light ones, can be thrilling to sail — with a little wind, one hull lifts out of the water, and you feel like you're flying across the water. (You can find out more about sailing a small catamaran, often referred to as a *cat* [without the fur] in Chapter 11.) Bigger multihulls (more than 30 feet, or 9 meters) can be great cruising boats. Because of their width, they're very stable and have a tremendous amount of space for their length. Multihulls are fast, too, because they're very light and don't have heavy *keels,* or as much surface area underwater, as *monohulls* (boats with one hull) of the same size. Check out "All sailboats have an underwater fin" to find out more about the *daggerboards* used on most multihulls instead of a keel. Huge, 120-foot- (37-meter-) plus multihulls compete in races across oceans and hold most of the point-to-point, long-distance sailing speed records, including sailing nonstop around the world in 50 days! (For more on the fast world of offshore racing, see Chapter 13.)

✔ **Monohulls:** These sailboats are the most common type of boat, and they have one hull (still makes sense, right?). Most of the world's sailing and racing takes place in monohulls, broadly classified as either dinghies or keelboats, as the next section explains. Most sailing schools teach their basic sailing classes in monohulls — either dinghies or keelboats (although some specialty schools, often in tropical climes, teach sail-boarding skills). For more on learning how to sail, including types of boats and where to find a good school, check out Chapter 2. The typical marina is full of monohull keelboats of all shapes and sizes. And if you're the type of person who likes to ask "What kind of boat is that?" turn to Chapter 20 on recognizing boat logos and Appendix A (otherwise known as the glossary) on how to identify different monohulls, such as a *ketch,* a *catboat,* and a *sloop.*

If you compare these water-based crafts to their land-based cousins, sail-boards are the skateboards, dinghies are the bicycles, and keelboats are the cars. And multihulls? The fastest ones are airplanes!

All sailboats have an underwater fin

Hanging underneath the back end of most sailboats (except sailboards) is a rotating fin called a *rudder.* The rudder does just what you think it does — it steers the boat. Underneath the middle of most sailboats is a second, larger, fin called a keel or centerboard.

Comparing keelboats and dinghies

The primary purpose of both keels and centerboards is to keep the boat from skidding sideways from the force of the wind and to provide lift so your boat can sail closer to the wind. (When sailing, your sails and the underwater fins act like wings. If your physics teacher explained wings when you weren't paying attention, see Appendix C for a quick review.) Although a few exceptions exist, if the fin is fixed (not movable) and made of a heavy material like lead, it's usually a keel. And if the fin is lightweight and retractable, it's usually a *centerboard.*

✔ **Keelboats:** Keelboats have a *keel,* a fixed, heavy lead fin for ballast hanging under their hull, as Figure 1-2 shows, providing stability against the wind's force. The smallest keelboats are model (sometimes radio-controlled) sailboats, but keelboats that carry human passengers are usually more than 20 feet (6 meters) in length.

Figure 1-2:
Keels and rudders come in different shapes and configurations. The photo at left is common, while the right photo has twin rudders and a canting ballast fin and bulb.

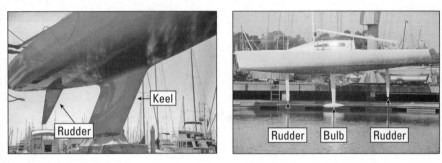

✔ **Dinghies:** Dinghies are nimble, small sailboats that are typically more responsive than their ballasted cousins sporting keels. But watch out — dinghies can *capsize,* or tip over. Instead of that ballast weight in the keel, they have a lighter fin called a centerboard that's retractable. The centerboard may also be called a daggerboard if it retracts vertically (see Figure 1-3), depending on its position and movement (or a leeboard if it's mounted on the side of the boat). Most dinghies range in length from 8 to 20 feet (2.5 to 6 meters).

Figure 1-3:
Two dinghies: (left) with a centerboard and (right) with a dagger-board.

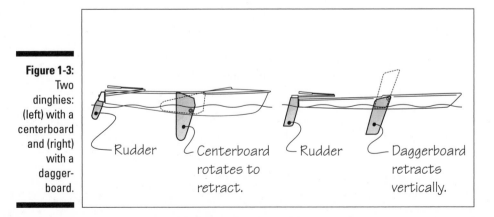

Comparing tillers and wheels

So how do you drive (or *steer,* in sailor speak)? Well, those rudders shown in Figures 1-2 and 1-3 are connected to either a *tiller,* a long lever arm that allows you to turn the rudder, or a *wheel,* which is attached to cables that turn the rudder. Generally, smaller boats have tillers, and bigger boats have wheels, because bigger boats have greater force on the rudder and would require an enormous lever arm.

A boat with a wheel steers just like your car — turn left to go left, right to go right. But you push a tiller to the right to turn left and to the left to go to the right. (Check out Chapter 4 for more on steering.) Steering sounds trickier than it really is — a tiller is quite responsive, and you quickly develop a "feel" for the correct way to turn.

All sailboats have a mast

The mast is the vertical pole that supports the sails, as the dinghy shows in Figure 1-4. Although most modern sailboats have just one mast, some sailboats have several masts that can carry many sails. (Remember the pictures of the *Nina, Pinta,* and *Santa Maria* in your history textbook?) You may have heard of *square riggers, schooners,* or *yawls.* These types of sailing craft are named for the number and position of their masts and the profile of the sails. If you want to know how to identify these cool, usually older, antiquated sailboats, check out the glossary.

Although older boats have wooden masts, most modern boats have masts made of aluminum, which is easier to mass-produce into a lighter and stronger pole. For the ultimate in strength and light weight, the fastest racing boats use carbon fiber. On bigger boats, an array of wires usually supports the mast. These wires are called the *standing rigging* (see the *forestay, backstay,* and *shrouds* on the keelboat in Figure 1-5).

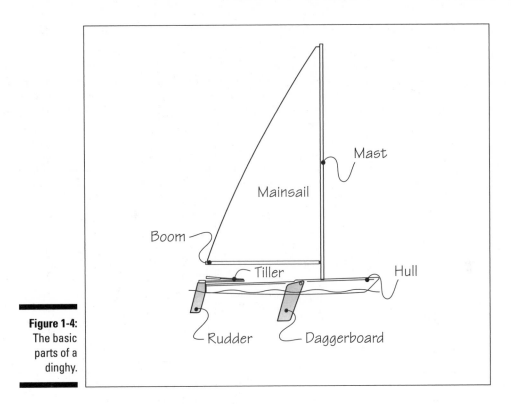

Figure 1-4:
The basic
parts of a
dinghy.

All sailboats have sails

The mast (and standing rigging) supports the third and most common feature
of sailboats — the sails. A sail is simply a big piece of fabric that catches the
wind, enabling you to use its force to move the boat. The sails are your
engines — their power or fuel comes from the wind. The *main*, or *mainsail*,
sets along the back edge of the tallest mast. Some boats carry only a mainsail, while others have a *headsail* as well. A headsail sets in front of the mast.
Headsails come in different types, but the most common is a *jib*. See Figures
1-5 and 1-6 for the basic parts of a dinghy and a keelboat.

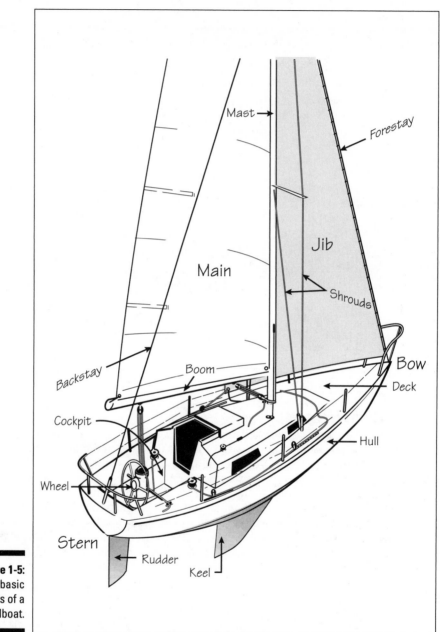

Mast

Forestay

Jib

Main

Shrouds

Backstay

Boom

Bow

Deck

Cockpit

Hull

Wheel

Stern

Rudder

Keel

Figure 1-5:
The basic
parts of a
keelboat.

You can use one of many types of specialty sails to make a boat go as fast as possible at different angles to the wind. A common specialty headsail is the *spinnaker* — a big, colorful, parachute-like sail used when sailing *downwind* (going with the wind), which you can see how to fly in Chapter 12.

Not all sails are created equal

Back in the old days of square riggers, sails were made out of cotton. They were heavy and very stretchy. Today, most sails are made out of a polyester fiber called Dacron. But high-tech racing boats have sails made out of exotic, lightweight, yet strong materials, such as Mylar, carbon fiber, and Kevlar (the fabric in bulletproof vests). In the 1988 America's Cup, I sailed aboard *Stars & Stripes,* a 65-foot (20-meter) catamaran. Instead of "soft" sails, this boat had a "hard wing" — very similar to the wing of a passenger jet. Constructed out of carbon fiber and other very strong and light materials, this hard wing was really a mast and sail all wrapped up in one. Because of its three-dimensional wing shape and innovative shape controls, it was extremely fast — and we won the Cup! But at the end of each day of sailing, the boat had to be carefully tipped on its side (using a huge hydraulic contraption) to hide the wing from any swirl of wind behind a wall. Because you can't just lower and fold up a hard wing after a day on the water, this type of sail isn't very practical for everyday sailors . . . but it sure is fast!

All sailboats have lots of rope

When a sailboat is *rigged* (prepared and ready to go sailing), all the ropes used to raise and adjust the sails can look like spaghetti. This pasta is all part of the boat's *running rigging.* Even the simplest sailboat has several adjustment ropes, and each has its own name. For example, the rope running up mast that's used to pull the sails up is called the *halyard.* Just to make everything more confusing, the "proper" names for ropes on a sailboat, when they have a purpose and use, are *lines,* as in "Throw me a line." But most sailors use the terms interchangeably without confusing their crews, and they are equally acceptable (and we use both terms in this book).

When you're starting out, understanding what the lines do is more important than worrying about what to call them. So the only line that you need to know to start sailing is the *sheet* — the primary line that adjusts the sail *trim* (the angle of the sail to the wind), referred to with the sail it adjusts (for example, *mainsheet* and *jib sheet*).

Depending on the wind strength and the size of the sails, pulling in the mainsheet (and most of the other lines) can be a tough job. Most boats use a system of *blocks,* or pulleys, to make pulling in the lines that carry a lot of load easier. So you don't have to hold that mainsheet with your teeth when your arms get tired, the typical mainsheet system also has a conveniently located cleat.

In a sailboat, the wind is your fuel, and the sail is your engine. So the gas pedal is the sheet (shown in Figure 1-6), the rope that pulls in the sail and harnesses the power of the wind.

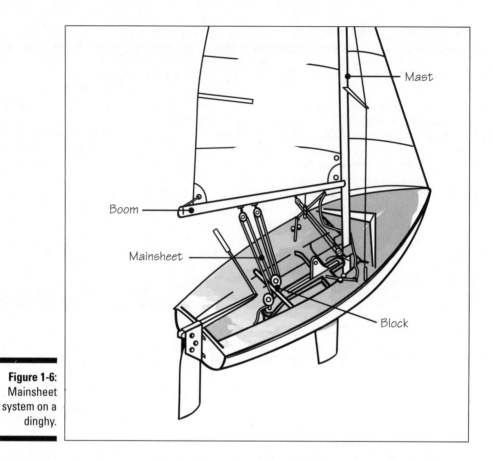

Mast

Boom

Mainsheet

Block

Figure 1-6:
Mainsheet
system on a
dinghy.

Tackling Some Basic Sailing Maneuvers

Now that you know the basic components of a sailboat, you may have some basic questions. Earlier in this chapter we cover "How do you drive this thing?" (with the wheel or tiller connected to the rudder) and show you the gas pedal, or mainsheet (see the previous section). If you're a responsible driver, your next question may be "Where's the brake?" (or "How do you stop this %#$@ thing?"). In this section we also answer a few basic questions you may have, including "Can you sail anywhere?" and "Where to go next?"

Coasting to a stop

So you want to find the brake pedal? Unfortunately, sailboats can't stop on a dime (unless you run them into something hard like land, throw out an anchor, or take other drastic measures). Essentially, a sailboat has no brake. But when you let out the sheet and let the sail *luff,* or flap in the wind like a flag, you've taken your foot off the gas pedal, and your boat can coast to a stop. Heavier boats take longer to slow down (because of momentum).

Some new sailors get nervous when the sails start *luffing,* or flapping — the sails are loud, and the sheets attached to the sails can start whipping around if conditions are windy. But relax. Luffing sails produce no power, and the boat gently decelerates. So just stay low and out of the path of the flapping sail (and that hard *boom*), as Figure 1-7 shows.

Figure 1-7: Beware of getting hit in the head with the boom when the sail luffs.

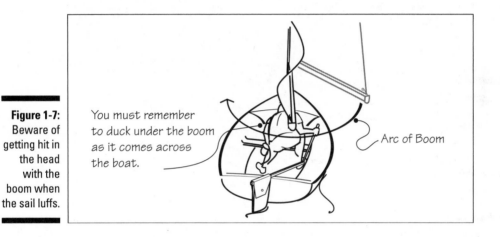

You must remember to duck under the boom as it comes across the boat.

Arc of Boom

Sailing into the wind

You may wonder if you can sail anywhere. Our answer is yes, you *can* sail anywhere! You can even sail to a point directly into the wind, but not by just steering straight there. If you try steering your boat directly into the wind, your sails luff, and you slow down and come to a stop. So to sail to a point directly upwind, you must take an indirect zigzag route, as Figure 1-8 shows. First, the zig: Pull in your sails (with their sheets) as hard as you can and then steer a course as close as you can to the wind direction without having the sails flap. Halfway to your destination, the time comes to zag and perform the basic sailing maneuver of tacking. (Check out Chapter 5 for more about tacking and other basic maneuvers.)

A *tack* entails about a 90-degree course change. In a tack, as you begin the turn, your sails start to luff, or flap (because you're steering directly toward the oncoming wind). But as you continue your turn, the sails refill with the wind now blowing across the opposite side. If you time your tack correctly, you're now steering directly toward your initial destination.

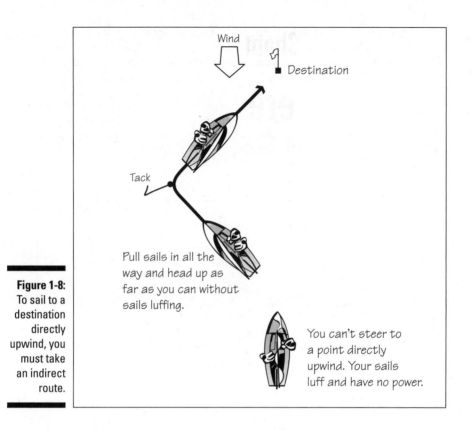

Wind

Destination

Tack

Pull sails in all the way and head up as far as you can without sails luffing.

You can't steer to a point directly upwind. Your sails luff and have no power.

Figure 1-8:
To sail to a destination directly upwind, you must take an indirect route.

Where You Can Go with Sailing

You can enjoy the wonderful sport of sailing in so many different ways. This book shows you some of sailing's amazing diversity. Sailing has taken us all over the world. We probably wouldn't have met, fallen in love, and had two beautiful daughters if not for sailing (cue the soft violin music). Sailing has romance, travel, excitement, and moonlit nights in secluded coves with the sounds of the waves lapping against the hull. Of course, our seaborne romance also brought diapers, college saving funds, book deadlines, and mortgage payments — ah, yes, sailing has brought so much to our lives. And it can bring wonderful adventures to your life too — if you just turn the page.

Chapter 2

Knowing Where You Can Learn: Classes and Sailing Schools

There be three things which are too wonderful for me,

Yea, four which I know not:

The way of an eagle in the air;

The way of a serpent upon a rock;

The way of a ship in the midst of the sea;

And the way of a man with a maid.

—Old Testament, Proverbs 30:18,19

Suppose that you don't know how to sail but want to learn. (A good guess, because you're reading this book, right?) Sailing is a very accessible sport if you know where to begin. Believe it or not, plenty of people would love to introduce you to the joys of sailing. Depending on where you live, how old you are, and who you know, you may have any number of options.

This chapter answers some key questions you may have, such as where you can go to get started in sailing and what type of boat to start on. We highly recommend attending sailing school, and we help you choose the right one for you. This chapter looks at all your options for finding out about this great sport.

Where You Can Go to Learn

So you're interested in sailing but don't know where to start. The following list provides a few different ways you can start discovering more about this great sport, but we strongly recommend that beginners take classes from a certified sailing school:

- ✔ **Through friends.** Some of Peter's friends introduced him to sailing in his teens. Your first taste of the sport may be aboard a friend's boat. But unless your friend is a certified sailing instructor with plenty of free time to dedicate to your education, you should probably just enjoy the ride and plan on getting your first formal training from a professional sailing instructor.

- ✔ **By reading books and magazines.** Many books have been written on all aspects of sailing — from sailing basics to classic sea adventures. Chapter 16 lists some of the books that inspired us. A number of great sailing magazines offer a combination of instruction, entertainment, and feature stories for the sailor. Our favorite is *Sailing World* because it focuses on the racing aspect of the sport (and Peter is the editor at large). Some other great national magazines in the United States are *Cruising World, Sail, Yachting,* and *Sailing.* Like many sports, sailing is part mental and part physical. You can study its theories from an article, a book, or in a classroom, but you can only discover some things with the wind in your face and your hand on the tiller or ropes.

- ✔ **On your own.** Purchasing (or borrowing) a boat and teaching yourself to sail is entirely possible. After all, sailing isn't nuclear physics. However, we don't recommend teaching yourself (in fact, we totally discourage it) because it may be downright dangerous. When you leave the shore behind, you're in the hands of Mother Nature — and she can be a harsh taskmaster on occasion. We devote an entire chapter of this book to safety afloat (Chapter 7) and provide safety tips throughout all the other chapters too. Practice on your own, but learn the basics from a qualified instructor first.

- ✔ **In a formal class from a professional instructor.** Have an idea of where we're heading? We feel very strongly that despite all the options, you should get your education from a pro. See "Choosing a Sailing School," later in this chapter, for more detailed advice.

What Kind of Boat You Should Learn On

Not only can you choose where and how to start your sailing studies, but you may have a choice of what kind of boat to start on. We both started on dinghies, and so did Dennis Conner, Ted Turner, and most other "famous" racing sailors. But then again, we started as kids, and almost all junior sailing programs use dinghies. Dinghies are smaller boats (usually under 20 feet, or 6 meters, long) with a retractable centerboard; they can also tip over. Keelboats are usually longer than 20 feet with fixed keels that provide extra stability.

The bottom line: Consider the pluses and minuses of dinghies and keelboats we outline in this section, and then go take lessons from the best instructor you can find!

Dinghies

Many sailing schools and junior programs instruct beginners in small (10- to 14-foot, or 3- to 4-meter, long) one-person boats; others use larger two- or three-person dinghies, as Figure 2-1 shows. Ideally the boat has a relatively stable hull shape (not too tippy) and a conservative amount of sail area. No need to break any speed records on your first sail!

Figure 2-1: At left, kids on a 420 trainer dinghy; at right, a single-handed Optimist dinghy next to an E-22 keelboat.

© J World, San Diego

Pros

The following are the advantages to using a dinghy for your training:

- ✔ **They're responsive.** Due to the boat's light weight, changes in helm, weight position, and sail trim give instantaneous feedback. You can really feel the boat sail.

- ✔ **The helmsman trims a sail.** On most dinghies (especially the single-person variety), the helmsman must do more than just steer, providing you with a more complete understanding of how everything works.

- ✔ **They're inexpensive.** Therefore, they're favored by many programs that have limited budgets.

- ✔ **Their smaller size makes them less intimidating.** Would you rather take your driver's education class in a compact car or a minivan?

Cons

Starting to sail on a dinghy does have the following disadvantages:

- ✔ **They can capsize.** You can argue that the possibility of capsizing is a "pro," especially because we think that everyone who sails a dinghy needs to know how to right a capsized boat. (We cover that subject in Chapter 7.) Finding out how to right a flipped boat, however, isn't a priority if you start on a keelboat.

- ✔ **They're wet.** Typically, you sit lower to the water in a dinghy than on a keelboat, and being wet can be uncomfortable. But, hey, if water hurt, sailors wouldn't go sailing (at least not as often). Check out Chapter 3 for some clothing ideas to stay more comfortable in the inevitable dampness of sailing.

- ✔ **The instructor doesn't ride with you.** Having the instructor with you is an option, but some small dinghies get pretty cramped with two people on board. Often, the instructor follows you in a motorboat, shouting advice as needed.

Keelboats

Most commercial sailing schools that cater primarily to adults use small (20- to 28-foot, or 6- to 9-meter) keelboats as their introductory training vessel. Ideally, the boat has a large, open cockpit area capable of holding a class of one to four students plus an instructor, as Figure 2-2 shows. A boat that doesn't have a cloud of sail area is easier for the neophyte crew to handle.

Figure 2-2:
A good sailing school boat has space for the instructor to observe and teach without getting in the students' way.

Pros

Advantages to starting off on a keelboat include the following:

- ✔ **The instructor and other students are on board.** Getting instant feedback is nice. Plus, studying with other students on board can be fun.

- ✔ **You can focus on one skill at a time.** On a keelboat with several crew, one person can drive while another adjusts the sail.

- ✔ **You won't capsize.** Removing the constant distraction of possibly capsizing enables students to concentrate on sailing.

✔ **They're more comfortable to sail.** On a dinghy, you must pay constant attention to where you're sitting in order to keep the boat from tipping over too far. One of the decisions you have to make when figuring out how to sail on any boat is where to sit (see Chapter 4). On a keelboat, however, you don't affect performance very much if you're a little slow to react or are out of position by a foot or two. Plus, keelboats are drier — although you don't get any guarantees that a big wave won't come right over the side and land on your lap!

✔ **They can use an engine.** If the wind dies, or if no wind is in the harbor, you can start up the engine and make your way to the good sailing water more quickly.

Cons

If you choose to start your sailing career on a keelboat, remember the following disadvantages:

✔ **They're "duller instruments."** Keelboats are heavier and less responsive to the subtle changes in sail trim and steering that are immediately apparent on dinghies. This fact can make "feeling" the boat, which is such an important part of sailing, more difficult.

✔ **Everything pulls harder.** The heavier the boat, the bigger the sails and the more load on all the control ropes. So the boat may be rigged with devices like winches to provide mechanical advantage.

✔ **They may steer with a wheel.** Steering wheels are normally used on larger (more than 40 feet, or 12 meters, long) keelboats, and some smaller ones have them too. But tillers provide a much better feel of the boat and the water flowing past, so you probably have more fun sailing on a boat with a tiller.

Keeping It Easy the First Time

Here are the ideal conditions for learning to sail, in order of priority:

✔ **Light to medium winds (6 to 12 knots) that are very steady in direction:** For more on wind strength, see Chapter 8.

✔ **Smooth water:** Ideally stay in an area protected from surf, swells, and wind-blown waves.

✔ **An uncrowded, open area with minimal obstructions and room to sail in any direction:** Not having to contend with other boats when you're learning can enable you to focus on the task at hand.

✔ **Warm air and water:** Air and water temperatures higher than 70 degrees Fahrenheit (21 degrees Celsius) are nice; temperatures in the 80s Fahrenheit (upper 20s to low 30s Celsius) are sheer paradise!

Sailing for everyone

Thanks to some big developments in assistive technology, people with all kinds and levels of disabilities are getting out on the water and taking sailing lessons. Personal lifts give wheelchair users a needed boost from the dock onto the boat, as the following figure shows. Boats also have special modifications: "Sip and puff" systems allow quadriplegics to steer and adjust the sails, and fiber-optic technology allows even those individuals with catastrophic disabilities, such as those on ventilators, to steer and trim the sails of a boat. Counter-balanced swivel chairs are available for people with limited mobility, and talking compasses and GPS systems allow the sight impaired to navigate. In our hometown, a nonprofit group, Challenged America (www.challengedamerica.org), has trained sailing crews with disabilities who have competed in distance races like the big Transpac race from Los Angeles to Hawaii. Sailing has been a full medal sport in the Paralympics since 2000. Thanks to many great organizations around the country that provide access to the water for the differently abled, when we say sailing is for everyone and anyone, we really mean it!

Of course, if you live in Stockholm, you may have to wait a long time for the air and water temperatures to get that warm. So as long as you dress warmly (see Chapter 3 for ideas), the key conditions are the first three: light to medium winds, smooth water, and plenty of room to sail. If the wind is constantly shifting or so light that the sails don't fill, getting in the groove and feeling what's happening can be difficult. In contrast, too much wind is a bad thing for beginners. The waves throw the boat around, the sails flap so loudly that you can't hear your instructor, and everything happens way too fast. In short, you have a very difficult time understanding what's happening and why.

Choosing a Sailing School

Now that we've strongly recommended that you start your sailing career with some lessons, we want you to find the right school. Children and teens may have some options, such as summer camps and junior programs at clubs, that aren't available for adults, so we discuss tips for kids later in this section in "Picking a sailing school for the kids."

Exploring your options

If your community has sailboats and sailors, you probably have a choice between a community sailing program or a commercial sailing school or two. Yacht clubs, universities, and some charter-boat rental companies may also offer instruction. Of course, you can always search the Internet for "Sailing Schools" or look in the Yellow Pages under "Schools" or "Sailing" or "Boating Instruction." You can ask a sailor or someone at a marine business for recommendations, and a boat show can be a good source of information too.

In the United States, two organizations oversee national educational programs that certify instructors and provide schools with curriculum and standards. You can contact each of them to receive a list of accredited schools.

✔ **The American Sailing Association (ASA):** Founded in 1983 (Peter was one of the founders and remains on the board of directors), the ASA (phone: 310-822-7171; Internet: www.american-sailing.com) has certified more than 7,000 sailing instructors and 300,000 students. This educational system is highly regarded in the field of sailing education, and major charter-boat companies recognize ASA certification. More than 270 commercial sailing schools are affiliated with the ASA and offer student certification to the multilevel ASA program, which begins with Basic Keelboat Sailing (many accredited schools also offer instruction in dinghies).

✔ **US Sailing Association:** US Sailing (phone: 800-877-2451; Internet: www.ussailing.org) is the national governing body for the sport of sailing. Its primary role for more than a century has been to oversee the racing side of the sport, including the U.S. Olympic Sailing Team, which JJ was on in 1992 and 2000. US Sailing is the U.S. representative to the International Sailing Federation, the organization that produces the racing rules and represents the sport of sailing in the International Olympic Committee. US Sailing has long been involved in yacht club junior-sailing programs due to its focus on racing. More recently, US Sailing has developed certification systems similar to the ASA's; its Keelboat Certification System starts beginners with the Basic Keelboat standard. US Sailing also has an instructor-certification program.

Taking lessons while on vacation

Why not take sailing lessons during your vacation to an exotic (and warm) waterfront location? Such vacations are a great way to find the time in your busy schedule to get out on the water and figure out which way the wind is blowing. You can use the same sources we mention earlier in this chapter in "Exploring your options" to find sailing schools at your vacation destination. Our favorite sailing school in paradise is the Bitter End Yacht Club (www.beyc.com), a resort in the British Virgin Islands with a large and well-maintained fleet of boats and well-qualified sailing instructors ready to teach you how to sail everything from sailboards to dinghies, multihulls to keelboats.

Thousands and thousands of more experienced sailors take sailing vacations by chartering (renting) boats. We cover that sort of ultimate vacation in Chapter 17. Many sailboat charter companies offer a more advanced course designed to introduce an intermediate sailor to the joys of bareboat chartering (chartering a boat "bare" means without hiring a skipper or crew), and some have programs for beginning sailing courses as well.

Looking outside the United States

Some countries have a national authority like ASA or US Sailing that promotes a standardized educational system. The International Sailing Federation (www.isaf.org) provides a list of countries with national entry-level sailing programs. National sailing organizations should be able to provide you with a list of accredited schools. You can also find a list of schools at the International Sailing School Association (www.sailingschool.org). Otherwise, you can always ask for recommendations from local sailors or marine businesses.

Interviewing a potential school

If you decide to go to a school, you need to pick the right one for you. Besides asking the obvious question about how much it costs, you want to find out as much about the prospective school as possible. This short section provides you with some factors to consider about different sailing schools during your selection process:

✔ **Curriculum:** Does the introductory course offer certification to a national standard? Don't settle for an answer like, "Our program is better than ASA or US Sailing certification," unless you have some inside info on the program. Just because a school doesn't offer certification doesn't mean that its course is deficient; the course may be great, but if it doesn't comply with some standard other than its own, how do you know?

Also ask how long the class is. The typical beginners' course at a commercial sailing school takes place over four days, often two weekends, and combines classroom and on-the-water training.

✔ **Instructors:** Are the instructors certified? If only some of them are, make sure that your instructor is certified to one of the national standards.

✔ **Boats:** What kind of boat does the school use? Dinghy or keelboat? Wheel or tiller? (Check out Chapter 1 for more information on these boat specifics.)

✔ **Class size:** How many students will be on the boat? Can you take private lessons? Having other students on the boat with you has advantages and disadvantages. In order to get enough time at each position, you probably don't want more than four students (including yourself) on the average 25-foot (8-meter) keelboat. The typical dinghy is sailed alone or with one other student while the instructor follows behind on a powerboat.

✔ **Bad weather/makeup days:** How much wind is too much for the entry-level course? What is the school's policy for making up blown-out days?

✔ **Safety:** Ask about the school's safety record and any special safety procedures. Does it have any swimming requirements?

✔ **Equipment:** What do you need to bring? Most schools provide life jackets but not foul-weather gear.

✔ **Post-class sailing:** Does the school have a boat(s) available for graduates of the basic sailing course to take out to build sailing experience? If so, do any special policies apply to its use?

✔ **Higher education:** Does the school have further classes that you can take after you build some experience?

Finding the right sailing instructor

In addition to selecting a potential school, you need to look for the following desirable features in a beginning sailing instructor. Look for someone who is

✔ **Certified:** With certification, you know your instructor has made an effort to be trained and to measure his skills and knowledge against a national standard.

✔ **A good teacher:** No matter how good a sailor the instructor is, communication and teaching skills matter most.

✔ **Patient:** Instructors need this quality in spades the 50th time someone asks them to explain something.

✔ **Congenial:** After all, you're sailing, not doing something serious like tax preparation. The more fun the students have, the better they can grasp the key concepts.

✔ **Able to anticipate potential problems:** This quality has everything to do with experience. When the boat is all the way downwind in a narrow passage with rocks on each side, it's too late.

✔ **Able to communicate well:** Your instructor must be able to make complex things perfectly understandable — sort of like the *For Dummies* series of books!

Picking a sailing school for the kids

Many areas have specific programs for kids. They're most commonly located at a yacht club, sailing club, or camp, or through some community program, and are conducted during the summer months. Don't be put off by the fact that you're not a club member, a student at the university, or whatever. Most private yacht club junior programs welcome nonmembers (thankfully, or Peter would still be playing baseball today). Check out the registration process in the winter months to make sure that the class doesn't fill up before your child is on the list.

If you find more than one potential program in your area, ask your child to help make the decision. Nine times out of ten, the best class is with her friends. I kept sailing mainly because all my friends sailed. If it's fun, your child is more likely to stick with it!

JJ SAYS

Sailing instruction just for women

Some great T-shirts are available for sailing couples. Hers says, "Don't yell at me. I'm doing the best I can," and his shirt says, "I'm not yelling." If these slogans describe your sailing relationship, you (assuming you're a female) may want to look into sailing instruction specifically for women. You can find many programs around the United States. One program run by Womanship (based in Annapolis, Maryland) has specific classes for women, including Sail Yourself Safely Home, a two-day clinic designed to help a less experienced spouse feel confident in her ability to get back to shore in case of an accident. Mother-daughter classes are available as well, and Womanship offers classes around the country as well as instructional vacations in the Caribbean and Europe. For more information, contact 800-342-9295 or www.womanship.com.

Keep the following factors in mind when checking out a youth sailing program:

- ✔ **Schedule:** Some programs run for two months, others in biweekly increments. Advanced groups may meet in the afternoon and beginners in the morning. Make sure that you know the number of hours your child will be sailing per day. What about lunch? Hungry kids don't learn as well as kids on a full stomach.

- ✔ **Type and availability of boats:** Find out what type of boat beginners sail. Do you need to own a boat, or does the club provide one? In some programs, if you don't own the boat, you have to crew. Crewing is fine for intermediate sailing, but beginners need to know how to steer the boat too.

- ✔ **Grouping criteria:** Most programs divide students into groups by age, which can create a small problem if your child is starting a few years late like Peter did. Ask the organizers how they solve this problem.

- ✔ **Curriculum:** Some programs (especially yacht clubs) may stress racing (which we love) over recreational sailing. This approach is okay, but having a balance is nice, and the best programs have a high fun factor.

- ✔ **Instructors:** What is the ratio of instructors to students? What certifications do the instructors have? Often instructors are college students; find out how many have previous teaching experience. A school rehiring an instructor for the next season is a good sign.

- ✔ **Safety:** Has the program had any problems in the past? What sort of special equipment, safety procedures, and insurance does it have? What are the age and swimming requirements?

- ✔ **Equipment:** What equipment does your child need? Does the school provide life jackets, or must you provide your own?

Sailing at summer camp

The American Camping Association's Web site (www.aca-camps.org) includes a search feature to help you find camps that offer sailing instruction. Your child will probably have a great time keeping cool on the water because any camps with sailboats are probably located on a beautiful lake or on the beach.

If you can't talk your child into a sailing camp, try finding a camp where your child is exposed to a wide range of water sports. In our opinion, any activities around the water are great activities. An interest in swimming, kayaking, and canoeing this summer may lead to an interest in sailing next summer.

Practicing: The More, the Better

After you graduate from your first course in sailing, practice all those new-found skills and build your experience level. Although many schools offer classes in higher education, don't rush it. Spend a season or more just building your skills before you embark on the next level of education. Your new skills and knowledge fade quickly if you don't keep practicing.

We may discourage learning to sail from friends, but after you master the basic skills in a class, having friends who are sailors is great. Sailboat owners are often happy to find eager crew. You don't have to be a lifelong friend; just let people around the docks know that you're willing to help with sailing duties and make a few sandwiches. Crewing for someone more experienced is a great way to build your own knowledge.

You can also take advantage of the opportunity to try out other types of boats. If you learned in a keelboat, find someone to take you out on a dinghy, or vice versa. Sailing different boats can be a great way to expand your horizons, because each boat is different in the way it's rigged and handled.

Unless you live on a body of water where you just absolutely have to have your own boat, you probably should rent or borrow boats (if you have generous friends) for the next phase of your education in the sport. That way, you can try out different kinds of boats and avoid sinking all your funds into a boat that may not be right for you. We discuss the considerations involved in picking out your first boat in Chapter 20.

Many commercial sailing schools also have sailing clubs or charter/rental operations, and they love to get repeat business from their recent graduates. Renting is a great way to get sailing time without the joys (and hassles) of owning a boat. You may even want to hire an instructor for an afternoon just to refine those basic skills that you're practicing.

If you're not one of its students, a boat rental company may want to see proof of your experience level before it lends you one of its boats, which is one reason why you want to take your course at a facility that offers national certification. The rental company may also require one of its staff to check you out on a particular boat before renting to you, no matter how experienced you say you are.

Just because you've taken one course in sailing doesn't mean that you're ready for an around-the-world cruise. Avoid sailing in wind and sea conditions beyond your ability. These experiences come with time, and now is the time for gaining confidence in mild conditions.

Taking Advanced Classes

After you spend a season or so refining your basic sailing skills, you're ready to take the next step in your education. If you're interested in cruising and recreational sailing aboard keelboats, then you should head to the next levels of certification, such as those the ASA or US Sailing offers. For example, the ASA's progression of keelboat standards is as follows:

- Basic Keelboat Sailing
- Basic Coastal Cruising
- Bareboat Chartering
- Coastal Navigation
- Advanced Coastal Cruising
- Celestial Navigation
- Offshore Passage Making

How far you go within the structure of an educational system depends on what kind of sailing you want to do and what other opportunities you have for gaining experience and practical education. After you've taken three or so levels of education over a couple of years, you may be comfortable enough to stop there. Or you may enjoy the challenge of moving up the certification system.

The U.S. Coast Guard may offer classroom courses in your area on subjects such as safety, seamanship, basic rules of the road, navigation, knots, and weather. Some of these courses are oriented for powerboaters, but most of the classroom subjects pertain equally well to sailing. Check out the Web site (www.uscgboating.org) for details.

If you're more interested in racing, then you have to find a boat on which you can race. Spread the word that you're an eager and willing crew member. We know of no better way to begin racing than to get out there and do it. For more on the world of racing sailboats, read Chapter 13. During the off-season, you may consider taking one of the sailboat-racing classroom courses offered in your area; find class information through your local sailmakers. We have both taught at a national racing seminar series called North U. Who knows? Maybe we'll see you there!

Chapter 3

Planning Ahead: What to Wear and What to Bring

Hoist up sail while gale doth last,
Tide and wind stay no man's pleasure.

—Robert Southwell

*F*ace up to the fact that you're going to get wet on a sailboat. Maybe just a bit of innocuous spray will come aboard, but at some point, you're likely to face a big wave that wants nothing more than to jump down your collar and soak you and all your clothes. If the water is a 90-degree Fahrenheit (32-degree Celsius) Gulf Stream soup on a hot day, a douse is welcome. But on a blustery, cool day, you want to stay as warm and dry as possible — and staying dry means wearing some sort of waterproof outerwear.

Even more important than staying dry is staying safe. This chapter lists the essential safety gear to have on board: Item No. 1 is a life jacket. Even if you can swim the English Channel in your sleep, always make sure that each person aboard has a life jacket before going sailing. Nowadays you can find U.S. Coast Guard (USCG)–approved life jackets that are comfortable and not confining. Furthermore, on a wet, windy day, a life jacket can be a welcome additional layer of clothing!

In addition to selecting the right life jacket, this chapter helps you find the right clothing as you venture out on the open water and lists necessary safety equipment. Keep reading so you know everything you need to take with you before you set foot on a sailboat.

Staying Safe with Life Jackets

The most important safety item you need on a boat is a life jacket. Wearing a life jacket increases your chances for survival in the water — that's why they're called *life* jackets. (About 80 percent of boating-related deaths are from drowning.) In the United States, USCG–approved life jackets (called *personal flotation devices,* or PFDs) are required on board all boats. How many and what type depends on the size of your boat and the number of people on board. Keep in mind the following requirements for the number of life jackets you need:

- ✔ For boats shorter than 16 feet (5 meters), USCG regulations require one wearable life jacket for each person on board.

- ✔ For boats longer than 16 feet, you must have one life jacket for each person *plus* one throwable flotation device, which must be immediately accessible. Each life jacket must be USCG approved, in good and serviceable condition, of appropriate size for the intended user, and readily accessible.

Most boat owners and sailing schools keep the required number of life jackets on board all the time, but you should double-check and ask before you leave the dock.

Many states have additional regulations. You can get information about the federal and state requirements at your local marine store or by contacting the USCG at 800-368-5647 or on the Web at www.uscgboating.org.

If you're sailing outside the United States, check with the local authorities to be certain that you're abiding by their laws; the USCG regulations, however, are highly respected standards in the international boating community.

Choosing the right jacket

To ensure your safety, you need to wear the right life jacket for you. Life jackets are sized by the weight or chest size of the person intending to wear them; user chest size or weight information should be clearly marked on the inside label. The Coast Guard classifies life jackets based upon their use and performance.

- **Type I** is a bulkier jacket that floats the wearer face up even when he or she is unconscious.

- **Type II** is shown in the safety icon in this book — this type is quite common because it's the cheapest life jacket. It's safe, just not as comfortable as the next type.

- **Type III** is a comfortable vest that you can easily wear all day. If you're going to buy a life jacket for your own personal use, this will likely be the one — we both own one of these and wear it more than any other type. They're best suited for use on dinghies and for day sails on bigger keelboats in protected waters.

- **Type IV** is the throwable life ring or float that you should keep on deck (on boats longer than 16 feet) to throw to a person in the water.

- **Type V** is an inflatable life jacket with a compressed air canister. Many offshore keelboat racers wear this type of life jacket because it's the least bulky of all.

Using life jackets correctly

When wearing your life jacket, you want to ensure that it fits properly. You put on most life jackets like a vest. A snug fit is the most comfortable and safest, so always zip them up and tighten any adjustment straps. The following list provides some important safety tips to help you:

- Always wear a life jacket on a dinghy, because the dinghy can capsize.

- Wear a life jacket on a keelboat any time you feel the conditions warrant it.

- As with all safety equipment, make sure that everyone knows where the life jackets are stored before you set sail.

- Children, nonswimmers, and anyone requiring extra assistance should always wear a life jacket on any boat.

- If your life jacket is waterlogged or damaged, replace it.

- Make sure that the life jacket fits, especially for children. Don't put an adult's jacket on a small child — it may slip off in the water. Children's life jackets are always sized by their weight.

Children and life jackets

Life jackets don't guarantee your children's safety around the water — you still must watch them vigilantly and know where they are at all times. Making sure that the life jacket fits properly and that the child feels comfortable wearing it are very important. Most states have regulations that require children under 13 to wear a life jacket when underway unless in an enclosed cabin or down below deck. For more on sailing with children, see Chapter 16.

Staying Warm + Dry = Having Fun

We recommend that you go sailing several times and find out your favorite aspect of sailing before you spend money on special sailing gear. Planning what to wear for a day on the water is similar to preparing for a long hike or going skiing. You need to consider whether you'll still be comfortable if you get damp or wet.

In this section, we assume that you're not going sailing right after the first thaw, and we take a look at what clothing you can bring for a typical day sail in light or moderate winds in the summer months.

Sizing up your sailing wardrobe

Although a wide range of sports-specific clothing is available, you don't need to be in any rush to spend large amounts of money as long as you can find clothing in your current wardrobe that works. After you identify the type of boat and sailing you prefer, you may consider heading to the marine store. If the speed and thrills of a sailboard attract you, a wet suit may be your big clothing purchase (see the left photo in Figure 3-1). Or you may decide to go dinghy sailing and wear the gear shown at center in Figure 3-1. Or you may find that your greatest love is coastal or offshore keelboat sailing, and you want to invest in foul-weather gear for wet days (see the right photo in Figure 3-1).

Figure 3-1:
From left, JJ in windsurfer gear; JJ and Peter dressed for dinghy sailing; and Peter in foul-weather gear rounding Cape Horn.

Ultimately, your clothing depends on three factors:

- ✔ The weather
- ✔ The water temperature
- ✔ The size of the boat

Weather and water temperature considerations are fairly obvious: If you head out to sail on lovely (and chilly) Lake Ontario in the early springtime, you definitely need to bring more layers than your friends who decide to go to Key West for a "learn-to-sail" summer vacation (they'll probably get by with a few T-shirts and swim trunks).

The boat's size plays a role in deciding what to wear and bring, too. Aboard a small boat with a centerboard (dinghies and catamarans), you're very close to the waves — and when the weather is windy, plenty of spray comes aboard. Plus, you always have the chance of capsizing and taking an unexpected swim, so you want to dress to stay warm even if you get wet. On a larger boat, you sit higher off the water — with the benefit being a drier ride. Also, bigger sailboats (keelboats) don't capsize, so your clothing needs are different.

When I started racing, I didn't have any special sailing clothing and couldn't afford to buy any. Sure, I got soaking wet and cold a few times, but at least I was out there having fun. Hey, a little water never hurt anyone, especially when a hot shower and a change of clothes are waiting back on shore.

Layering

When getting dressed to go sailing, keep in mind that the temperature on the water varies much more than it does on shore. One minute the wind is light, and you're basking in the sun with your shirt off; the next minute the wind comes up across the cool water, and you want your jacket in a hurry.

Bring clothes that you can wear in layers so that you can vary your attire depending on your comfort needs. Layering is an efficient way to stay toasty when the air is cold, because the air trapped between the layers warms up and acts as extra insulation. When the temperature rises, you can strip off layers until you reach your comfort zone.

Staying dry on top

The best way to keep warm on the water is to stay dry. This advice may sound pretty basic, but staying dry while on the water requires a little forethought — especially about your top layer. We recommend that your outside layer be a windbreaker-style jacket.

No matter where I go sailing, the first item I pack into my sea bag is a wind-breaker (with a lining if the weather's cool). In all but the wettest conditions (or the tropics), this jacket is my outside layer when sailing.

You probably already have a windbreaker in your closet. Most any nylon-shell jacket works just fine for 90 percent of your sailing requirements. A wind-breaker that's a little oversized is nice, so that you can wear a sweater or a couple of layers underneath. Good pockets to keep your hands warm (and that you can zip closed so you can store stuff) are nice features, too.

Preparing Yourself for Getting Wet

Any time you're sailing a dinghy in summertime conditions expect to get wet. You have more fun when you aren't too concerned about staying dry. This section contains some important clothing tips for dinghy sailing, and many also apply for keelboat sailing on windy, wet days:

- **Bring a towel and a change of clothes and leave them on shore.** Nothing's worse than having to drive home in wet, salty clothes.

- **Consider leaving the gear bag on shore.** You probably have only enough room on board a dinghy for a bottle of water, a tube of sun-screen, and a jacket (which may get soaking wet, too).

- **Leave your cellphone, car keys, and wallet in a safe place on shore, too.** (Don't ask Peter how many cellphones he's killed in the water.)

- **Wear a bathing suit underneath your clothes.** That is, unless your hobby is being a finalist in wet T-shirt contests.

- **Choose wool or modern fabrics instead of cotton.** Cotton is great for keeping you cool on hot days, but it doesn't retain heat when it's soak-ing wet. Wool does a much better job of retaining heat while wet, but modern polyester fleece materials are the best underlayers when condi-tions are really wet and chilly, because they wick water away from the innermost layer so that your skin stays drier.

- **Wear the appropriate shoes.** Because you're always sitting down on a dinghy, the nonskid tread on your shoes is less important than on a keel-boat. Wet suit booties may be the most comfortable. (Check out "Picking the Right Shoes," later in this chapter.)

- **Reapply sunscreen often if you're getting wet.** Even supposedly "water-proof" sunscreens need to be reapplied. While sailing, you can easily get sunburned because of the double-whammy of the sun's reflected rays off the water.

- **Don't forget to wear a life jacket!** See "Staying Safe with Life Jackets," earlier in this chapter, on why wearing a life jacket is so important.

Choosing Foul-Weather Gear

Whether on a dinghy or a keelboat, if you decide that you really don't want to get wet (even in nice weather), you want to make sure you choose the appropriate foul-weather gear. When looking for *foulies* — foul-weather gear — keep the following points in mind:

- ✔ **Style:** Separate chest-height overalls and a jacket are the most versatile and warmest combination. (Check out "Layering," earlier in this chapter, for the importance of wearing layers.) Plus, the jacket can be a stylish addition to your shoreside attire. Paddling or kayaking tops with neck seals that keep water from going down your neck are popular with small-boat (dinghy and catamaran) sailors, and you can even wear them in combination with a wet suit. In colder weather, dinghy sailors favor one-piece *dry suits* with elastic cuffs at the neck and wrists.

- ✔ **Material:** Many manufacturers offer several different lines of foul-weather gear. Lighter weight is for active, small-boat racers in temperate conditions, and heavier, "bulletproof" gear is for cold-weather offshore sailing. If you have to have the best, invest in breathable gear made from a high-tech fabric that allows water vapor to escape from the inside, minimizing the clammy feeling you get from most waterproof clothing.

- ✔ **Room to move:** Make sure that you still have a full range of motion, even with your warmest layers underneath and your life jacket on top.

- ✔ **Construction:** To minimize leakage, make sure that tape seals the seams on the inside. Look for extra fabric on the seat and knees — these areas can wear out from the rough deck surfaces on a boat.

- ✔ **Hood:** A built-in hood that you can fold away under the collar is invaluable when it starts to rain.

- ✔ **Pockets:** Make sure that the overalls as well as the jacket have pockets — bigger and more are better.

- ✔ **Color:** Choose bright colors so that you stand out in a crowd — and especially so that someone can see you if you fall overboard. Avoid white or blue outerwear, because you may be hard to find in the water.

- ✔ **Safety:** With all this cool gear, don't forget that you might be wearing it in the water. Give your attire the float test and jump in a swimming pool while wearing the maximum cold-weather layered look. The float test may further encourage you to wear your life jacket.

Picking the Right Shoes

Sailing barefoot may seem like a good way to get in touch with nature, but running around without shoes is an open invitation for a stubbed toe — or worse. On any bigger boat where you're going to walk on a wet, slippery deck, nonslip shoes are required equipment. Pick shoes that are nonmarking, like the shoes you wear on a tennis or basketball court. You probably own a pair of sneakers or soft-soled athletic shoes that are fine for your first season of sailing.

For years, I wore sneakers aboard big race boats because they were so much more comfortable than leather boating shoes and because they provided plenty of grip on a slippery foredeck. Then, shoe companies came out with athletic shoes with a true, nonslip sole made for boating. Now I wear those shoes until the weather's so wet that I have to break out my *sea boots* (high, waterproof boots).

Some shoe treads work great on boats (we find that soft rubber soles with plenty of grooves to grip the deck are best). If you find yourself slipping around the deck in your regular shoes, you may want to buy a pair of special sailing shoes. You can usually purchase them at a marine store for anywhere from $50 to $80, depending on what features you want.

Packing What You Need

When going out on the water, you want to make sure you're prepared. Nothing is worse than leaving the dock and then having to turn back around after you've forgotten something important. Remember, in a dinghy (or if your keelboat looks like a really wet ride), you may want to leave the gear bag ashore. Use the following checklist to make sure you have everything you need in your gear bag:

- ❑ **A life jacket for each person:** (Check out "Staying Safe with Life Jackets," earlier in this chapter, for more information.)

- ❑ **Jacket or foul-weather gear and/or a bathing suit and wool cap:** Now you have all weather extremes covered.

- ❑ **Nonslip, rubber-soled shoes:** Don't go offshore without them. (Refer to the previous section for the lowdown on picking the right shoes.)

- ❑ **Sun stuff — sunglasses, hat, and sunscreen:** The glare of sunlight (even on an overcast day) reflecting off the water and sails makes sun stuff essential. Make sure that you have a string or some sort of retainer for your sunglasses and your hat. We've proven beyond a doubt that sunglasses sink. An extra hat and pair of $5 sunglasses can make you very popular with your forgetful sailing friends.

When we're going to be on the water all day, we put good sunscreen (SPF 15 or higher) on first thing in the morning, when we brush our teeth, because sunscreen is most effective when it has time to soak in. (But be careful not to confuse your sunscreen with your toothpaste.) Then we reapply sunscreen (everywhere the sun can see us) before going out on the water, and we try to remember to add another layer a couple more times during the day.

I always wear a long-sleeved shirt when I sail, and even in the tropics I wear lightweight, long pants every few days, just to give my skin a rest from the sun.

- ❑ **Gloves:** Sailing gloves are a good investment, unless your other hobby is rock climbing and your hands are well calloused.

- ❑ **Hair band:** Keep long hair in a ponytail or a braid. Loose hair can get caught in the lines and blocks and then pulled out in big chunks. (That's painful even to think about — ouch!)

- ❑ **Water:** Drinking plenty of water is crucial on hot days to prevent dehydration, so throw an extra bottle in your bag.

- ❑ **Snacks:** Having an extra apple or orange (skip the fruit that can get squashed), a granola bar, or an energy bar can make you pretty popular if an intended short sail turns into a three-hour tour.

- ❑ **Sailor's choice:** We're divided on this one. On anything but a dinghy, JJ wants a cellular phone (such a Californian) stored in a plastic bag, but Peter opts to bring a knife (a sailor's best friend). Your choice? Fill in the blank.

When to break out the blue blazer

If someone with a roman numeral in his name asks you to go sailing with several dozen of his closest friends on his yacht, chances are good that the boat is a powerboat, not a sailboat, and you should wear a blue blazer. Other than that, you're rarely expected to wear the traditional blue blazer on the water. The only times we've ever worn blazers and cocktail party attire on the water were for a wedding, a boat christening, or some other really formal party. One top international sailor we know doesn't even own a blue blazer. But before you head off to lunch at the New York Yacht Club (which, by the way, is in midtown Manhattan, not on the water), throw on a coat and tie.

Even at formal parties on large yachts, wear soft-soled shoes and leave the spike heels at home. If someone invites you to go sailing on a fancy yacht, especially an antique wooden boat, be forewarned that you may be asked to take off your shoes to prevent damage to the wooden decks. So make sure that you have trimmed your toenails (and your date's — always more embarrassing) in the last year and that your socks are presentable.

What to leave on shore

Leave the jewelry at home — you don't want to lose your grandma's pearls overboard. Take off your rings, too, because you have to grip ropes with your hands, and rings can pinch your fingers (or worse). Any item of clothing or equipment (such as a camera) that water can ruin should stay on shore. (If you must bring it, at least put it in a sealed plastic bag.) We say it again — sailing is a wet sport, and even a big boat can get wet down below.

Stowing your stuff

Carry your extra clothes and spare gear in a small duffel bag or backpack that closes securely. Ideally, your bag is waterproof — or at least water-resistant. Leave your nice leather bag or suitcase at home and bring only what you need — most boats are tight on space. If the boat is big enough to have a cabin down below deck, go ahead and put your gear bag down there, preferably off to the side on a bunk or in a cubbyhole so that people don't step on it. Make sure your bag is securely wedged in and won't fall on the floor (where it can get wet) when the boat *heels* (leans or tips to one side).

Our final piece of advice for the eternal question of "What should I wear?" is to ask the people with whom you're going sailing. They have the best idea of what gear works well on their boat.

Checking Your Safety List

The following checklist of boating safety equipment is for a typical big keel-boat around 30 to 50 feet (9 to 15 meters) in length, sailing in coastal waters (not across the ocean, but along it). Starred (*) items we also recommend for a smaller keelboat or dinghy:

❑ Life jackets* (just in case you forgot, they're USCG–required equipment)

❑ Drinking water and food*

❑ Sunscreen*

❑ Sunglasses, hats, extra clothing*

❑ Paddle* (smaller boat only)

❑ Sufficient engine fuel and spare parts

❑ Binoculars

❑ Chart

❑ Compass*

❑ Bucket with a retrieval line (can bail water or be used as an impromptu toilet)

❑ Boat hook

❑ All USCG–required equipment for the boat*

❑ Sound signals. Usually a whistle* and/or fog horn for larger boats.

❑ Fire extinguisher. See Chapter 15 for more on fighting fire on board.

❑ Visual distress signals. You can also use signals such as flares or a flashlight* at night to signal distress by using the international Morse code "SOS" distress signal (••• — — — •••). And remember spare batteries.

❑ Navigation lights. All boats are required to display navigation lights (also called *running lights*) at night (including dusk and dawn) and whenever visibility is reduced (such as in fog, heavy rain, or haze). See Chapter 9 for more on navigation lights and sailing at night.

❑ Anchor and anchor rode (chain and line)

❑ Extra line (for repairs, heaving, mooring, and anchoring)

❑ Fenders

❑ VHF radio (see Chapter 7 on using your VHF) and cellphone

❑ First-aid kit and manual (see Appendix B and don't forget any personal medicines)

❑ Tool kit (or a multipurpose tool for a dinghy)*

❑ Knife*

❑ Lifesling or other man-overboard recovery equipment. For more info, see Chapter 7.

❑ Spare parts for the boat

❑ Adequate bilge pump(s)

❑ Radar reflector

At most marine stores or any USCG station, you can pick up a copy of the *Federal Requirements and Safety Tips for Recreational Boats* pamphlet. The USCG's Boating Safety Hotline (800-368-5647) or Web site (www.uscgboating.org) can provide all sorts of boating safety information, including courses in your area, and can link you to the Coast Guard Auxiliary and U.S. Power Squadron, which provides free vessel safety checks.

Chapter 4

Before You Leave the Dock

And biased by full sails, meridians reel
Thy purpose — still one shore beyond desire!
The sea's green crying towers a-sway, Beyond.

—Hart Crane

Climbing aboard a sailboat can be trickier than you think, especially on a small boat. Because you want to maintain your cool image with the crew, pay close attention to this chapter. When you're safely aboard (and hopefully still dry), you need to prepare the boat for sailing. After you complete this process of *rigging* the boat, you're probably ready to *hoist* (pull up) the sails and sail away from the dock. However, in some places, such as marinas with many boats around, you may have to use the engine (if you have one) to motor your boat out into open water before hoisting the sails and having fun.

Most first-time sailors have a sailing instructor or experienced friend put the mast up and *launch the boat* (get it in the water). In this chapter, we assume that your boat is already launched and tied to a dock or *mooring* (a permanently anchored buoy). If you have to put up the mast or launch the boat, see Chapter 6.

In this chapter, we primarily focus on the rigging systems common to a small (20- to 25-foot or 6- to 8-meter) keelboat — an approach that provides an excellent general introduction to the different components involved in the rigging process, no matter what boat you sail. However, every boat is different, and yours may have some steps to rigging that are peculiar to its type. That's why we recommend that you rig the boat with an instructor or someone who knows the boat.

Dissecting a Sailboat: This Part and That Part

Before you climb aboard and rig your boat, we need to briefly introduce you to the names of the parts of a sailboat. Take a closer look at the two basic types of sailboats we discuss in this book — keelboats and dinghies — in Figures 4-1 and 4-2 to see most of these parts (many are common to both keelboats and dinghies).

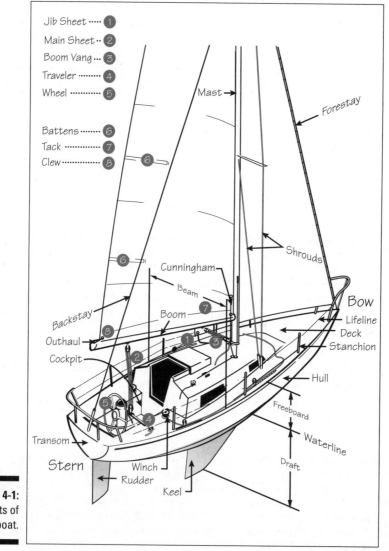

Jib Sheet ····· ①
Main Sheet ·· ②
Boom Vang ··· ③
Traveler ········ ④
Wheel ············ ⑤

Battens ········ ⑥
Tack ············· ⑦
Clew ··········· ⑧

Mast
Forestay
Shrouds
Cunningham
Beam
Backstay
Boom
Outhaul
Cockpit
Transom
Stern
Winch
Rudder
Keel
Draft
Waterline
Freeboard
Hull
Stanchion
Deck
Lifeline
Bow

Figure 4-1:
The parts of
a keelboat.

All sailboats are different, so we can't guarantee your boat has all (or only) the following parts, but this list is a start. This section isn't one of those mission descriptions on Mission: Impossible that self-destructs after the first reading. You can always come back and brush up on your terminology.

The following are the parts of a dinghy:

- **Mast:** The vertical pole that supports the sails.

- **Boom:** The horizontal pole that supports the bottom edge of the mainsail. The boom swings from side to side as the boat turns, so be careful not to get in the boom's way as it swings, or else . . . boom!

- **Tiller:** A lever arm that turns the rudder (thereby steering the boat); commonly found on smaller boats (instead of a steering wheel).

- **Wheel:** On larger boats, the steering wheel that controls the position of the rudder.

- **Bow:** The front of the boat. The direction toward the bow is *forward.*

- **Stern:** The back of the boat. The direction toward the stern (the opposite of forward) is *aft.*

- **Cockpit:** The area where the crew sits to operate the boat.

- **Deck:** The top of the hull.

- **Hull:** The floating part or body of the boat.

- **Lifelines:** Safety line or coated wire that runs around the deck.

- **Stanchion:** Metal poles around the perimeter of the deck that support the lifelines.

- **Backstay:** The support wire that runs from the mast down to the stern.

- **Forestay:** The support wire that runs from the mast down to the bow. Also called the *headstay.*

- **Shrouds:** The support wires that run from the mast down to the edge of the middle of the deck on either side. Sometimes called *sidestays.*

- **Topsides:** The outer sides of the hull above the waterline.

- **Transom:** The outer sides of the stern.

- **Beam:** The width of the boat at any point. The *maximum beam* is the widest point.

- **Waterline:** The water level on the hull.

- **Draft:** Also referred to as *draught,* the distance from the water's surface to the deepest point on the boat. You can also refer to the draft by the verb *draw,* as in "Our boat draws 7 feet."

- **Freeboard:** The distance between the deck of the boat and the water.

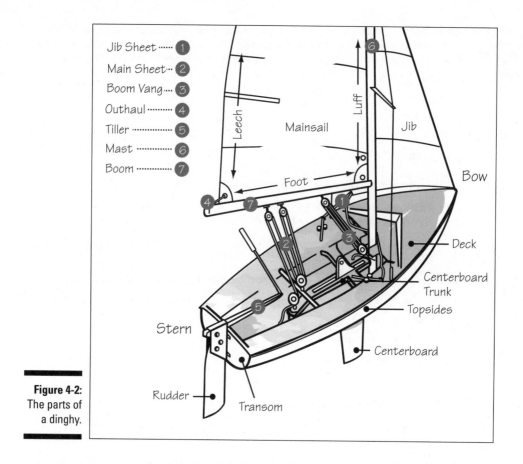

Jib Sheet ······ 1
Main Sheet ··· 2
Boom Vang ···· 3
Outhaul ········· 4
Tiller ············· 5
Mast ············· 6
Boom ··········· 7

Leech

Mainsail

Luff

Jib

Foot

Bow

Deck

Centerboard Trunk

Topsides

Centerboard

Stern

Rudder

Transom

Figure 4-2:
The parts of
a dinghy.

Climbing Aboard

Just as different boats can have different parts, how you climb aboard differs
depending on the boat type. This section has tips for boarding all kinds of
boats. We start with the tippier boats — dinghies — and then cover how to
climb on a bigger keelboat.

Climbing aboard a dinghy

Dinghies, as we explain in Chapter 1, are smaller boats (usually under 20 feet,
or 6 meters) that carry no *ballast* (weight) in their movable *centerboard* (underwater fin). Dinghies can also tip over. Because with this book we want you to
master sailing and not swimming, make sure that your first step into a dinghy is
as near to its *centerline* (an imaginary line that runs down the center of the
boat from end to end) as possible, near the midpoint from *bow* to *stern* (front
to back). (If you're not careful, you may tip the boat and end up in the water.)

If the dinghy has wire rigging *(shrouds)* connecting the mast (near or at its top) to the right and left sides of the boat for support, you may want to gently hold on for balance and to keep the boat near you as you step on board. You may also want to consider starting from a sitting or crouching position on the dock. In any case, keep your weight as low and close to the centerline as possible as you step aboard, as Figure 4-3 shows.

Figure 4-3: JJ shows how to stay dry while climbing into a dinghy.

Putting the centerboard, daggerboard, or leeboard down all the way increases the boat's stability, which makes moving around the boat much easier. Therefore, putting down the fin is the first thing you should do after you climb aboard.

The boat becomes much more stable when it's moving and the pressure of the wind is in the sails. But until you're sailing, keep your weight as low and near the centerline as possible as you rig the boat.

Climbing onto a keelboat

Although keelboats have more stability than dinghies, due to their ballasted keel fin, keelboats can be tricky to board, too. The bigger the boat, the higher the *freeboard,* or distance between the boat's deck and the water. Bigger (more than 25 feet, or 8 meters) keelboats usually have *lifelines,* a wire perimeter around the deck supported by metal poles called *stanchions.* Lifelines help the crew stay on board, but they can be tricky to climb over when boarding.

Some small keelboats don't have lifelines, so you can use the same techniques as we outline for dinghies to climb aboard small keelboats. However, boarding a larger keelboat with lifelines from a dock near water level requires different methods. Maybe some stairs lead from the dock up to an open gate in the lifelines, making you feel like you're boarding the *Queen Mary.* Or, on some boats, an open *transom* (back end) makes boarding a breeze. But if you must navigate up and over lifelines, try to grab a shroud with one hand and then step up on deck and swing one leg over the lifelines, sort of like mounting a horse, as Figure 4-4 shows.

Figure 4-4:
Peter climbs over the lifelines on a keelboat.

Now you know why we suggest in Chapter 3 that you carry your gear in a bag — so that you can easily hand it to someone on board or throw it into the *cockpit* (the inside of the boat, where the crew sits). You need both hands free for climbing onto the boat.

Grab the shroud (if you can reach it) for support; a lifeline or stanchion may not be strong enough to support your weight.

If you're not so athletically inclined, and the lifelines don't have a gate or the transom doesn't have an opening to facilitate your entrance, you can always crawl through the lifelines. Your ego can survive having to crawl on board better than being left at the dock.

Rigging the Boat

You *rig,* or prepare, the boat for sailing by attaching all the necessary parts, including the sails. The best way to find out how to rig a boat is to watch someone else rig it and then try to rig it yourself next time.

Until you're more experienced, always check with your instructor or a knowledgeable sailor to make sure that you rigged everything properly before hoisting the sails.

Even when Peter and I go sailing on a new boat, we always end up asking the owner at least a couple of questions about rigging the boat — questions such as which line to rig where. (Of course, I'm better about asking questions than Peter — just like in our car, he never asks for directions, no matter how lost we are.)

Preparing the sails

As we discuss the process of rigging sails, keep in mind that many variations are possible. For example, on some boats you store the mainsail (folded, or *furled*) on the boom, under a cover to protect it from the sun. In this case, take the cover off and skip to the "Preparing the mainsail" section, later in this chapter.

Each part of a sail has a name, too. Check out the following list for a brief definition of the terms in Figure 4-5:

- ✔ **Head:** The top corner of a sail

- ✔ **Tack:** The front, bottom corner of a sail

- ✔ **Clew:** The back, bottom corner of a sail

- ✔ **Foot:** The bottom edge of a sail

- ✔ **Leech:** The back edge of a sail

- ✔ **Luff:** The front edge of a sail

   Note: Like a few other words in the sailor's dictionary, *luff* has multiple meanings — see the sidebar.

- ✔ **Battens:** Solid slats inserted into pockets along a sail's leech to help maintain its shape

---

Sometimes it's a luffing matter

One of the most common words in sailing is *luff*. The problem for a beginning sailor is that this word has multiple meanings. The forward edge of a sail is called the *luff*. That's the noun. The verb *to luff* defines the flapping motion of sailcloth when a sail is undertrimmed (or not trimmed at all). *Luffing* is also an adjective, as in "A sailboat with luffing sails can't generate any power." Got it?

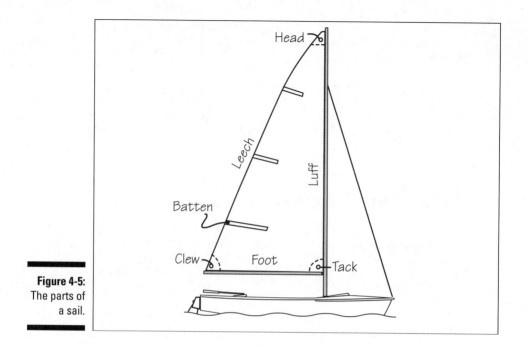

Figure 4-5:
The parts of
a sail.

Sailors also use specific names for the *lines* (ropes with a purpose) used to control the sails. Here are the most common sail controls as shown in Figure 4-6:

- ✔ **Cunningham:** The control line system near the tack of a sail used to adjust luff tension.

- ✔ **Halyard:** The rope running up the mast used to pull the sail up.

- ✔ **Outhaul:** The control line system (mounted on the boom) used for controlling the tension of the foot of the mainsail.

- ✔ **Traveler:** A sail control system that can move the mainsheet attachment point on the boat from side to side.

- ✔ **Boom vang:** The control line system running from the boom to the mast that tensions the leech of the mainsail.

To adjust those ropes, your boat has the following equipment:

- ✔ **Block:** A pulley that provides a mechanical advantage to make it easier to pull a rope.

- ✔ **Cleat:** A fitting used to tie off or secure a line so that it doesn't slip.

- ✔ **Winch:** Larger boats have at least one *winch,* a revolving drum that increases the sailor's power to pull on a rope. (See more about pulling pulleys and using winches at the end of Chapter 5.)

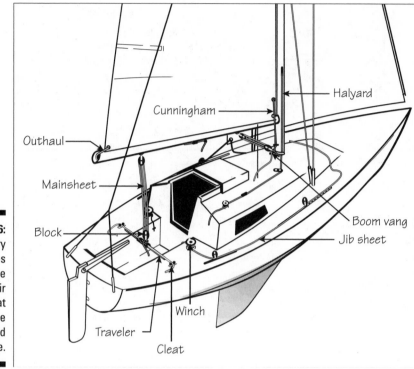

Figure 4-6:
The primary
control lines
(and some
of their
fittings) that
adjust the
sail trim and
shape.

Don't think that you have to memorize all these terms before stepping on a sailboat. Just look them over and acquaint yourself with them, and then put on your sunscreen and get your sails ready.

Preparing the mainsail

The first sail to prepare is the mainsail. You may need to take the sail out of its bag and lay it on the deck lengthwise, still in its folded state, with the leading edge toward the front. Follow these steps to prepare the mainsail:

1. Insert the battens.

Start by checking to see whether the mainsail has empty *batten pockets.* Battens are wood or fiberglass slats that slide into pockets on the sail's back edge, or *leech,* as Figure 4-7 shows. Battens help the sail project its designed airfoil shape and protect it from excessive flapping.

If one end of the batten is more flexible, insert that end first.

Make sure the battens are secure, so that they don't slide out of their pockets when the sails *luff* (flap). Sailmakers use many different systems, such as ties or Velcro, to keep the battens in place.

Figure 4-7:
Insert battens into the pockets along the sail's leech.

2. **Slide in the foot.**

   If you have a *loose-footed* mainsail that only attaches to the boom at the corners, you can skip this step and go straight to Step 3.

   If the *foot,* or bottom edge, of your sail has a rope (sometimes covered by fabric) sewn onto it, then you need to slide the foot of the sail into the track or groove on the top of the boom. Start at the *clew* (the sail's lower back corner) and slide the sail all the way down the boom from front to back, as Figure 4-8 shows. This process usually takes two people — one to feed the rope into the track and the other to hold the sail and help slide it along. Instead of a foot rope, some mainsails have many small plastic or metal slides attached along the foot that you insert into the groove on the boom, similar to the foot rope.

3. **Attach the tack.**

   The *tack* (bottom front corner) of the mainsail usually attaches to a fitting at the front of the boom or to the *gooseneck* (the fitting that attaches the boom to the mast), as Figure 4-9 shows. Preparing the mainsail is starting to sound like ". . . your hip bone attaches to your thigh bone. . . ." But stay with us; it all makes sense when you put it together.

   All three corners of the sail have a *grommet* or a strap loop to enable you to attach them to the proper control lines or fittings. A *grommet* is a plastic or metal ring built into a sail, as Figure 4-9 shows. Quite commonly, you use a *shackle* (a closed metal hook) to connect one or more of the corners to the appropriate fitting. (See Chapter 19 to find out how to tie a *bowline,* the best knot to use when tying a line to a sail.)

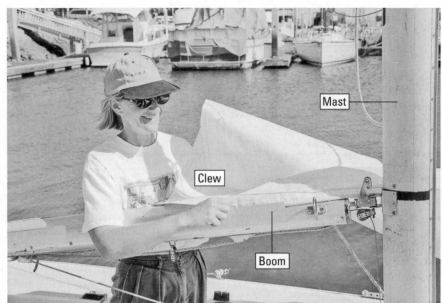

Figure 4-8:
Sliding the mainsail foot rope into the track on the bottom.

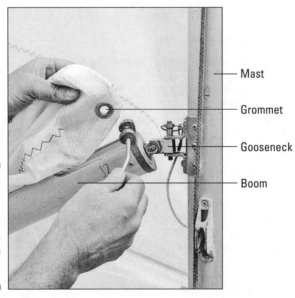

Figure 4-9:
Attach the mainsail tack to the fitting near the front of the boom.

4. **Attach the clew.**

   Next, attach (usually with a shackle) the clew to the outhaul at the end of the boom. The *outhaul* is the control line system, found at the back of the boom, that tensions the mainsail's foot.

   You can launch some smaller dinghies (usually shorter than 16 feet, or 5 meters) with the mainsail already hoisted and luffing (flapping). With these boats, attaching the clew is the last thing you do before leaving the dock. But on most boats, attaching the bottom corners of the main-sail (the tack and the clew) before you hoist is easiest. After you attach the clew to the outhaul, pull the outhaul rope snug and secure it.

5. **Attach the halyard.**

   To hoist the sail to the top of the mast, you use a halyard. A *halyard* is a rope or wire attached to the top corner *(head)* of the sail that's rigged to let you raise the sail to the top of the mast from cockpit level.

   Before attaching the halyard, pull it taut and look up, following the line all the way to the top of the mast. Unwind any wraps or tangles before attaching the halyard to the sail. The halyard attaches to the head of the sail by a shackle or a rope knot, preferably a bowline. You can read all about knots in Chapter 19.

   Always make sure that the halyard is securely attached. Use pliers to tighten a shackle with a screw pin or make sure your bowline is secure.

6. **Prefeed the luff of the main.**

   No, the *luff* (the front edge of the sail) isn't a hungry animal. To *feed the luff* means to slide the top end of the luff (usually a rope) into the groove in the back edge of the mast just above the boom — just like we explain with the foot of the sail. On some boats, you feed the first foot or two of the top of the sail into the mast well before hoisting. On others, you leave the halyard off, keeping the head of the sail down on deck or tied up on the boom, and wait until it's time to hoist.

Preparing the jib

If your boat has a jib, this section can help you prepare to hoist this forward-most sail. (A *genoa* is a large jib. To be perfectly accurate, calling a genoa a jib is okay, but calling a small jib [one that doesn't overlap the mast] a genoa is wrong. For simplicity, we always use the term *jib.*) Follow these steps when preparing your jib:

1. **Take the jib out of its bag.** Set it down on the foredeck lengthwise, with the front edge toward the bow.

   Jibs are attached at the three corners (fortunately, they share the names *head, tack,* and *clew* with the mainsail), plus along the front edge *(luff).*

2. **Attach the tack to the fitting near the bow.**

   Usually you use a *shackle* for this job.

3. **Prepare the luff for hoisting.**

   The system for attaching the jib to the *forestay* (a support wire from the mast running down to the bow, also called the *headstay*) can vary. Some sails attach with snaps or clips *(hanks)* located at intervals along the luff of the sail. Others have a *luff tape,* similar to the foot and luff ropes in a mainsail, which slides into a special, grooved channel built into, or attached onto, the forestay. With this system, one person must feed the tape as another hoists the sail. On a jib with hanks, you clip them onto the forestay (starting at the bottom and working upward) without hoisting the sail, as Figure 4-10 shows.

Figure 4-10: This jib is ready to hoist, with the snaps attached to the forestay.

4. **Attach the halyard to the top of the jib.**

   As with the main halyard, pull the jib halyard taut and look up to ensure that it isn't twisted.

5. **Attach the jib sheets, ensuring that they're fed through the proper *blocks* (pulleys) and cleats on each side of the boat.**

   Many different jib sheet systems are available. A bowline (there's that knot again; check out Chapter 19) or a shackle may attach the sheets (there are two — one for each side) to the sail. The sheets are then run back to the cockpit, where the crew controls them. You must rig jib sheets through a specific path that may include passing through several pulleys. Figure 4-11 shows the jib sheet system on a typical dinghy.

Figure 4-11:
Jib sheet
system on a
420-class
dinghy.

Jib clew

Jib sheet

Fairlead

Cleat

6. Secure the jib.

You don't want it to blow into the water before hoisting, but you must keep it out of the way on deck so you don't slip on it. So do whatever works best: You may just pull it tightly along one side of the deck with a jib sheet or lash it down, but try to avoid crumpling the sail cloth or you'll shorten the life of the sail.

Double-checking before hoisting the sails

Before you hoist the sails, check that everything is ready for you to leave the dock. When you hoist the sails, they begin to flap in the wind — which, although safe, isn't very seamanlike, because the flapping puts extra wear on the sails. Therefore, you want to get sailing as quickly as possible after hoisting. Use the following list to make sure that you're ready to go:

✔ **The boat is in a good position to depart and is pointing "into" the wind.** Trying to raise the mainsail before pointing the bow of the boat toward the wind is a common mistake of new sailors. If the boat isn't pointed into the wind, raising the mainsail may be impossible, because the wind fills the sail when it's partway up, putting too much load on the halyard. After you determine where the wind is coming from (see Chapter 5), think about where you can put your boat so that it points into the wind. A boat secured only at the bow naturally points into the wind (unless affected by strong current). Also look around and plan the path you'll take to sail away from the dock.

✔ **The control lines — especially the main and jib sheets — are properly rigged and have plenty of slack.** Make sure the main and jib sheets are uncleated too.

✔ **Everybody is on board.** Also ensure that everyone knows where to be for getting under way (check out "Knowing where the crew should sit," later in this chapter) and what their special tasks are (trimming sails, storing fenders and dock lines, getting the skipper a cold drink, and so on).

✔ **Life jackets and safety gear are handy.** Check out Chapter 3 for more on the importance of life jackets.

✔ **Loose gear is stowed.** Make sure all bags are put below out of the way and where they will (hopefully) stay dry. Extra hats or jackets should be put away so they don't blow overboard.

✔ **Main and jib are properly rigged and ready to hoist.** Take an extra look to make sure the halyard isn't twisted.

✔ **The rudder (and centerboard if your boat has one) is down and secured.** Secure the rudder so that it stays with the boat if you capsize. Most dinghy rudders have a spring clip or tie-down line to keep them from sliding out if the boat flips. For dinghies with daggerboards, use a restraining line (a shock cord works well) that lets you adjust the daggerboard up and down but keeps it attached to the boat in case of a capsize.

✔ **You have proper clothing and sunscreen on.** Even if you applied sunscreen in the morning, reapply it now.

Before hoisting, make sure enough open water is around so that you can sail away easily. Nothing's more embarrassing than casting off from the dock only to smash right into an adjacent boat. With this warning in mind, you may want to walk your boat down the dock or beach to a less crowded location before hoisting — or if your boat has an engine, you may want to power to an open area before hoisting sails.

Raising the Sails

Now you're ready to raise the sails. The general rule is to hoist the mainsail first, although there are some definite exceptions:

✔ If the dock is oriented in such a way that you can't point the boat into the wind, you may want to hoist the jib first and then sail downwind to an area where you can point the bow toward the wind and raise the mainsail. This maneuver is tricky, though, so don't try it without an instructor or experienced sailor on board.

✔ On some dinghies, you must hoist the jib first, because the tension of the jib halyard keeps the mast secure in the boat.

Most of the time, you can get under way with just the mainsail, saving the excitement and extra responsibility involved with using the jib for later.

Hoisting the mainsail

As we say earlier in the "Preparing the mainsail" section, you must feed the mainsail luff (usually a covered rope or slides) into the mast for hoisting. Unless you're vigilant, the luff invariably gets pinched and stuck as you hoist. On a dinghy, you may have to feed the luff in yourself as you hoist. On a bigger keelboat, assign one person to stand next to the mast to feed the luff into the groove, as Figure 4-12 shows. Someone else (and, if need be, a third person) can then slowly and steadily pull up the halyard.

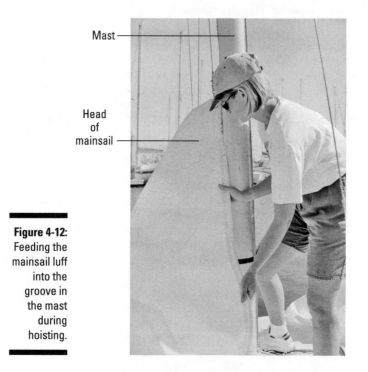

Mast —

Head
of
mainsail —

Figure 4-12:
Feeding the
mainsail luff
into the
groove in
the mast
during
hoisting.

Hoisting the mainsail with a winch

Boats more than 25 feet (8 meters) long may have a winch to help pull up the halyards. A *winch* is a revolving drum that mechanically increases the sailor's power to pull on a rope. See Chapter 5 on how to use a winch.

To raise the main halyard by using a winch, start by putting a couple wraps of the halyard line in a clockwise direction around the winch drum. You want just enough wraps to enable you to hold the line without it slipping. As the load increases (when the sail is partway up), you need to add a wrap or two.

You just have to be different, don't you?

Some boats have the jib permanently rigged on a roller furler, so the jib stays hoisted and rolled up around the forestay even at the dock, as the photo in this sidebar shows. To unfurl the jib, all you have to do is pull on one line!

Some boats (including sailboards) don't even have a main halyard. The mainsail on these boats has a sleeve running along the luff that slides onto the mast like a glove slides onto a finger. Then you attach the mast and sail into the boat together. Chapter 6 covers putting a mast up, and Chapter 18 covers rigging sailboards.

Jib on a roller furler

REMEMBER

Even with a winch, the easiest way to hoist a sail on a bigger boat is usually by *jumping* (pulling on) the halyard at the mast. Have a crew member (the jumper) stand at the mast where the halyard exits (presumably above the jumper's head — otherwise jumping doesn't work). Now he has great mechanical advantage to pull downward on the halyard. As he pulls, another person in the cockpit takes up the slack in the halyard by pulling the halyard that's wrapped around the winch. When the sail nears the top, the load may increase so much that jumping is inefficient. Then you must *grind* (rotate) the winch by turning the *winch handle* (a metal arm placed in the top of the winch) until the sail is up to the top. Pulling the halyard away from the mast like a bow string can also increase your mechanical advantage.

Avoiding certain mistakes

When hoisting a mainsail, you want to stay clear of a few important mistakes that can cause havoc and put a damper on your day at sea. The most common problems when hoisting sails include

- ✔ **Getting the luff rope jammed, which makes the halyard impossible to pull.** If the luff jams, stop pulling the halyard and ease it until the person feeding the sail at the mast can clear the jam and prepare the sail to slide up cleanly again. If you're hoisting the halyard, watch the area where the sail is feeding into the mast so that you know when a problem is about to happen.

- ✔ **Failing to ensure that the *mainsheet* (the sail adjustment rope attached to the boom) has plenty of slack in it and isn't cleated.** If the mainsheet doesn't have enough slack, the sail can fill when it's partway up, a real drag for the person doing the hoisting. Free the *cunningham* and *boom vang* to facilitate hoisting. (See Chapter 12 to discover how these control lines affect sail shape.) If the halyard starts getting really hard to pull, stop and look up — it may be caught on something up high or may not have been led correctly.

- ✔ **Forgetting a step such as attaching the halyard to the head of the sail.** This common (and embarrassing) mistake is sometimes tough to remedy. On small dinghies, you can tip the boat over at the dock to retrieve the errant halyard, but on big boats, you have to climb or hoist someone up the mast to retrieve the lost halyard. (For more on doing the high-wire act up in the rigging, see Chapter 15.)

How high is high enough?

How high should you pull the sail? All the way! The amount of tension you need for optimum sail shape varies (see Chapter 12), but in general, pull the sail up until the sailcloth is taut and just barely begins to show vertical lines of tension when luffing. The windier it is, the more tension you want. The visual aid is the tension in the luff, as Figure 4-13 shows. In the photo on the right, the mainsail is too low — note all the wrinkles along the luff and the gap at the bottom of the mast. In the left photo, the mainsail halyard tension is too tight — note the vertical strain marks just behind the mast.

Cleating off the halyard

After you have the mainsail hoisted properly, you need to make sure your halyard doesn't slip. Secure it with one of the following fittings:

- ✔ **Horn cleat (also called a *t-cleat*):** A common *cleat* (fitting that firmly holds a rope under load) for halyards on dinghies and smaller keelboats. These are simple fittings with no moving parts to break or malfunction.

Figure 4-13:
Mainsail luff
tension: too
tight (left)
and too
loose (right).

To secure a line around one of these cleats, put one complete wrap of rope around the base. This wrap provides friction to keep the line from slipping when cleating or uncleating. Then make a figure eight and finish by twisting it to create a *hitch* on the final turn so that the end is underneath (see Chapter 19 for tying a cleat knot).

✔ **Jammer or rope clutches:** Mechanical fittings with a lever arm that "squish" a rope so tight that it can't slip, even under an intense load (check out Figure 4-14). They're especially common on larger boats, where the loads on ropes are higher. Most jammers enable you to pull the line in when it's closed, but you can't ease it out. Keep the jammer open as you hoist the mainsail so that you can quickly ease the halyard if the sail gets pinched at the feeding point. When the sail is up and the luff is properly tensioned, you simply pull the jammer's lever down to cleat the halyard in position.

Before opening a jammer holding a rope under load, be very careful. Put a few wraps around a winch and then pull snug to take up the tension on the rope behind the jammer so that the rope doesn't burn your hands when it eases out.

Figure 4-14:
Jammers in action —
"jammin'."

Hoisting the jib

Hoisting the jib is similar in many ways to hoisting the main. On small boats, you can hoist the jib while your boat is still tied to the dock and pointed into the wind. Make sure the jib sheets are fully slackened so that the sail can luff freely (and doesn't fill) while being hoisted. You can also hoist your jib while sailing — just make sure the jib sheets are free to run so the sail doesn't fill.

Hoisting a big, overlapping jib (called a *genoa*) on a keelboat is best done while sailing downwind (see Chapter 5 for the points of sail), because if you hoist it while pointing into the wind, it flaps against the mast as you hoist. Plus, by hoisting a genoa while going away from the wind direction, as Figure 4-15 shows, the mainsail protects it from the force of the wind. This system works equally well even if you have only a smaller jib. After the sail is hoisted, save your crew's strength by letting them pull the jib sheet in and cleat it before you turn to your course.

Any time you sail downwind, be careful not to jibe by mistake. If you do, someone could get hurt by the boom (see the "Avoiding danger areas" section at the end of this chapter and find out more about jibing in Chapter 5).

If your jib has a luff rope or tape, a crew member may need to stand on the bow to feed the luff tape into the groove of the headstay. If your jib has hanks (metal clips) or snaps, then you don't need anyone on the bow, because those clips are attached during the rigging process.

Figure 4-15:
Hoisting the
jib while
under way
and pointing
downwind.

Cleaning up all that rope

After you've *hoisted* (raised) your sails, you need to clean up all that spaghetti of rope you create while rigging. Some sailboats have a daunting number of sail control ropes, and ropes left to their own devices have an amazing capability to knot themselves.

As Murphy's Law suggests, after you're sailing, the line that you absolutely have to let out *now* is in a huge knotted mess with every other line on board, including your shoelaces. A good sailor takes the time and effort to clean up the mess and make the ropes as neat as possible. As you see in Chapter 5, keeping lines neat is important from a safety standpoint, too, because being able to let out the mainsheet quickly when a big puff hits can keep you from capsizing.

After you're sailing, you don't commonly adjust certain ropes, such as the halyards, so you can put them away so that they don't tangle with the ropes you need to *trim* (pull in) the sails. You may feed the halyard into a storage bag or coil it in a convenient out-of-the-way area, depending on the boat. To use a bag, start at the very end and neatly feed the halyard into the bag so that it can come out just the way you put it in — with no tangles!

If you don't have a bag for the halyard, coil it, starting a foot or two from its cleat. When you finish coiling, put your hand through the coil and pull part of the line closest to the cleat through the coil, twist it a few times, and loop it over the cleat, as the photo in Figure 4-16 shows, so that you can easily undo the coil.

Figure 4-16:
Left: Storing an active halyard for easy release.
Right: Ropes coiled and finished off securely for storage.

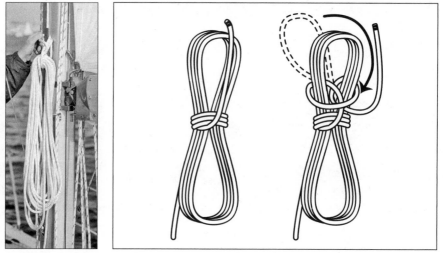

Never tie off a coiled halyard in a way that you can't immediately release it to run freely; you never know when you'll want to lower a sail quickly in an emergency.

Other lines (such as dock lines) that should be put away before sailing are coiled by a different method. Start at one end and make loops of equal size (usually about 3 feet, or 1 meter, in diameter) until you get near the other end. When you have about 5 feet (1½ meters) left, make three or four tight loops around the "throat" at one end of the coils. Then take the doubled end through the top of the coil and pass it over the top as the right drawing in Figure 4-16 shows.

Sitting at the Dock on the Bay

After you hoist the sails, but before you leave the dock, the sails *luff* (flap) in the wind. This flapping is noisy, the boom is swinging back and forth just above your head, and you don't have a clue what to do next. Don't panic. Just sit low enough that the boom doesn't hit you as it swings through its arc, and take a deep breath. You need to feel comfortable with luffing, because you find yourself in this position quite often when you're beginning to sail.

A *luffing* sail flaps because the wind is blowing straight along its surface from front to back. Just like a flag, a luffing sail shows you the wind direction. After you read Chapter 5, you'll know how to *trim in* a sail (by pulling on the mainsheet rope — or the jib sheet rope, as the case may be) to make it stop luffing; you're forcing the sail to lie at an angle to the wind and therefore "fill" with wind. (But if you're in the no-sail zone, your sails luff even if you trim them in.)

When your sails are fully luffing, they don't have any power, so the boat slows down and ultimately coasts to a stop. Luffing sails, then, are your brakes. You apply your "sea brake" by simply letting the sheet out.

Steering (And Riding in) the Boat

All sailboats have a *rudder,* an underwater movable fin that turns the boat. This rudder is attached to either a long stick *(tiller)* or a wheel that you use to steer. In this section, we explain the differences between tiller and wheel steering systems. We also cover where to sit when you drive or crew (on a sailboat, the driver's seat isn't always obvious; it can change when the wind changes) as well as areas to steer clear of when on a sailboat.

Tiller or wheel?

Most sailboats longer than 30 feet (9 meters) are steered with a wheel, just like a car. Through a mechanical linkage, the wheel controls the position of your rudder. When moving forward, turn the wheel left and the boat goes to the left — and vice versa. You may think that we're stating the obvious, but you see why when you compare turning the wheel to the other way of steering a sailboat — with a tiller.

You steer most smaller sailboats by using a tiller. Using a tiller for the first time takes a bit of getting used to, because the boat turns the opposite direction you move the tiller. If you move the tiller to the left, the boat turns right; move the tiller right, and the boat goes left, as Figure 4-17 shows.

"Take the helm, Mr. Sulu"

Although you can refer to the person steering a boat as the "driver," you also hear terms like *skipper* and *helmsman* (or *helmswoman*). *Helm* is another sailing term with multiple meanings. The helm is the rudder or tiller — the steering device. It's also the role of the helmsman on the boat. Helm is also a technical word (refer to Chapter 11) for describing the balance of your boat's rudder when sailing.

Figure 4-17: Move the tiller to one side to turn the boat the opposite way.

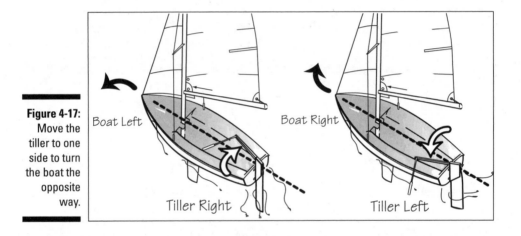

Boat Left   Boat Right

Tiller Right   Tiller Left

 Steering a sailboat is also like a car in that turning becomes more efficient the faster the boat is going (and in the fact that you can't steer when stopped). So when you're going fast, you can turn the tiller or wheel less to achieve the same turning arc. To turn when you're going slow, turn harder and keep the rudder over for a longer time.

 For pure sailing pleasure, I prefer a tiller on any boat up to, say, 40 feet (12 meters). Although a wheel takes up less cockpit space, it compromises the feel of the boat. Because of all the associated parts and connections, wheel steering has much more internal friction. A tiller directly connects you to the rudder, allowing you to feel the water as it flows below the boat, and for me, that sensitivity is preferable.

Knowing where to sit when you drive

One of the easiest ways to spot nonsailors is to see where they sit on a boat. If you're driving, you not only want to be able to steer well, but you also want to look good. The following tips can help:

- ✔ **When steering a dinghy, keep in mind the effect your weight has on the balance of the boat.** Not only should you sit down, but the *windward* side (the side the wind blows on) most likely needs your weight to counteract the *heeling* (tipping) forces of the sails. (In Chapters 11 and 12, we discuss techniques for limiting heel.)

- ✔ **Sit just forward of the end of the tiller so that you can freely move it from side to side.** Most boats have a *tiller extension* or *hiking stick* attached to the end of the tiller that enables you to sit farther out to the side of the boat while steering. Using this extension all the time enables you to sit comfortably while steering — and look cool. Hold the tiller extension in your aft hand so that your forward hand is free to adjust the mainsheet, as Figure 4-18 shows. You also have a better view of the sails on a boat with a jib if you sit farther forward.

- ✔ **On keelboats with a wheel, stand or sit behind or to either side of the wheel.** On keelboats with a tiller, sit on either side, wherever you have the most visibility and feel most comfortable — although keeping your weight on the high side to counteract heeling is important on a smaller keelboat.

- ✔ **If your boat has a blind spot because of a cabin top or the sails, move around occasionally to peek into the blind spot.** Periodically asking a crew member to look for obstructions and other boats never hurts either. It's your responsibility to be aware of everything that may pose a danger to your boat at all times.

Skipper holds tiller extension in "back" hand and mainsheet in "front" hand.

Figure 4-18:
Proper steering position on a dinghy.

Knowing where the crew should sit

On most boats, the crew sits forward of the skipper. The crew members often are responsible for trimming the sails and moving their weight outboard *(hiking)* to keep the boat from heeling. In most conditions, they can sit on the windward side. But if the wind is very light or if the boat's sailing downwind, they may need to sit on the side opposite the skipper to help balance the boat.

On larger boats with several crew members, divide up the jobs so that everyone can feel useful. The skipper usually steers (although nothing says you can't trade around and share the joys of being at the helm). In Chapter 12, you find out about other sail-handling jobs for the crew. As the boats get bigger, your individual weight makes less of a difference in counteracting the heeling forces, but you'll still find staying on the windward side most comfortable, whether operating the boat or just hanging out.

Avoiding danger areas

Certain spots on a boat are safer than others. Before you leave the dock, make sure you know what spots to avoid (or at least be extra careful in) after you're under way. These danger areas include

- **Anywhere in the plane of the boom when it swings across in a jibe or tack.** Don't forget to duck! Along with the boom, be aware of all the associated rigging, including the boom vang and the mainsheet.

- **Anywhere outside of the cockpit where you walk or stand.** Many boats have handrails that make it easier to hold on if you must leave the cockpit.

- **At the bow and the stern.** If you must go to these places, hold on tight, because the motion of the boat is accentuated at the ends.

- **In the path of the jib and jib sheets during a tacking maneuver.** This path runs from the foredeck all the way back on either side to where the jib sheets go through pulleys heading for the cockpit. During a tack (or jibe), when the headsail flaps in the wind, the sailcloth and ropes are like whips.

- **In the "slingshot target zone" of pulleys under high load.** If the block were to break loose, it would go flying.

- **On the leeward side of the boat.** The *leeward,* or downwind, side is especially dangerous if the boat is *heeling* (leaning from the wind); the leeward side is closer to the water, and gravity is pushing you that way.

✔ **Shiny areas, such as varnished wood or plastic hatch covers.** Shiny areas are probably as slippery as they look. Most bigger boats have a *nonskid* (textured) surface on deck to help keep you steady, but look where you step and hold onto something if you can. Sails on deck are also very slippery.

Yes, you figured it out — the safest place in most boats is the cockpit (as long as you stay low and watch out for the darn boom). Check out Figure 4-1 to identify where the cockpit is on a basic keelboat. The deck can be dangerous during maneuvers or in rough seas at any time.

Avoiding Collisions: Rules of the Road

Before you actually set sail and leave the dock, you need to know how to avoid collisions with other boats. Hey, your driver's education teacher didn't let you drive before you knew the basic rules of the road! In bigger harbors, your main concern is staying out of the way of commercial vessels: barges, tugboats, and big ships.

The following are some basic concepts to help you when your course takes you near large vessels:

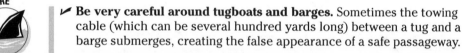

✔ **Be very careful around tugboats and barges.** Sometimes the towing cable (which can be several hundred yards long) between a tug and a barge submerges, creating the false appearance of a safe passageway.

✔ **Large ships and tugboats pushing barges can have a "blind spot" that extends for hundreds of feet in front of them.** If you can't see the pilot house, the pilot or captain probably can't see you.

✔ **Large ships are difficult to maneuver and can't turn at all when stopped.** Stay out of their path; avoid them — don't make them avoid you. Furthermore, the speed of large ships is very deceptive, and stopping can take them more than a mile.

✔ **Large ships can block your wind from a long way away.** This interference can slow you down and make avoiding them difficult.

✔ **Large ships must stay in the channel to avoid running aground.** In confined waters, aids to navigation, usually buoys, mark the channel. You may need to consult a chart to find the channel. (For more information on reading a chart, see Chapter 9.)

✔ **The turbulence in a large ship's wake can throw your boat around.** A heavy ship's wake can create big waves that *swamp* or flood your little boat.

✔ **Understand the whistle blasts.** Five or more short blasts is the "danger" signal. Get out of their way, now!

✔ **Stay away from U.S. Navy ships.** You must stay more than 100 yards (91 meters) from any U.S. Navy ship, and you must slow down to minimum speed within 500 yards (457 meters) under Homeland Security regulations.

If two boats meet, follow these basic rules:

✔ Moving boats must avoid stopped boats.

✔ Sailboats have right-of-way over powerboats, except for fishing vessels and large commercial vessels with restricted maneuverability (that means all big ships, especially in channels).

If you find yourself on a collision course with another boat, even if you have right-of-way, don't be a sea lawyer. Make an early and aggressive course change away from the boat. Don't assume that the other boat sees you or that it will change course. Don't play a game of chicken. Alter your course early to show the other boat clearly your intended new heading to stay out of its way. For tips on steering straight, see Chapter 11. For the basic rules when any two sailboats meet, see Chapter 13.

Part II
Casting Off and Sailing Away

The 5th Wave   By Rich Tennant

"Relax—we're not lost! I have a chart and I know how to read it. Like, right now I can tell you we're in the galley."

In this part . . .

Say that you're standing at the edge of a lake, ready to go for a swim. Are you the type who gets a running start and dives in? Or do you go to the edge and dip your toe in before slowly wading in? If you're the first type, you probably opened the book right to this part — and that's okay, because this part is the most helpful for beginners and introduces the basics of sailing. This part also covers safety, weather, navigation, and anchoring — topics that even powerboaters need to know. Of course, we hope that you're so hooked on sailing that you continue reading (and even go back to what you missed in Part I).

Chapter 5

Going Sailing: Just the Basics, Please

> *It was with a happy heart that the good Odysseus spread his sail to catch the wind and used his seamanship to keep his boat straight with the steering-oar.*
>
> —Homer

*U*nderstanding the important relationship between the wind and your boat and getting yourself, your boat, and your crew ready all lead up to the best part — going sailing! If you have time to read only one chapter of this book before heading out on the water, this is the one.

This chapter covers the basics of sailing and seamanship. *Webster's Dictionary* defines *seamanship* as "the art or skill of handling, working, and navigating a ship." This definition is purposefully vague regarding the size of boat or the wind and sea conditions. This chapter focuses on the skills you need to handle your boat in moderate conditions — which hopefully describes the weather for your beginning sailing trips.

The first part of this chapter shows you *when* to pull in the sails, and the last part shows you *how* to pull in the sails safely. So hoist your sails (refer to Chapter 4 for help) and get out on the water!

Finding the Wind's Direction

The world of sailing revolves around the wind. Your boat can't go anywhere without wind (unless you fire up the engine, which, at this point, would be cheating).

But before you head out to sea, you need to keep safety in mind. Whether you're an old salt or a beginning sailor, being safe on your boat is integral to enjoying the sport. In Chapter 7, we review various safety issues in detail. But remember that no sailor should go out in conditions that exceed his or her ability. A beginner's first sail should be in light to moderate wind conditions in protected waters. Furthermore, as we explain in Chapter 2, the best and safest way to start sailing is to take instruction from an experienced and qualified individual. As you grow in experience, you can expand your limits.

Assessing the wind's direction is of utmost importance to a sailor. The wind's direction is a sailor's North Star, the center of his sailboat's universe. Where he goes, how he trims his sails, whether the ride is wet or dry, fast or slow — all these depend on the wind and its direction.

The wind changes all the time, and your ability to accurately sense changes in the wind speed and direction is the single most valuable skill you bring aboard a sailboat. Increasing your sensitivity and awareness of the wind is the first step in becoming a sailor.

Feeling the wind

The best way to track the wind is simply to feel it. Your body, especially your face, can feel the exact direction of the wind if you just let it. Here's how:

Close your eyes and turn your face until you think that the wind is blowing straight at you. Rotate your head back and forth slightly until you sense that the wind is blowing equally hard across each side of your face, and the "sound" of the wind is the same in each ear.

Practice "feeling" the wind whenever you can. The wind can keep shifting direction and strength. A key to sailing is staying aware of the wind's changes.

Using other clues to find the wind

Besides feeling the wind, you can look around and see clues to the wind's direction. A flag or wind vane on top of a mast can show the wind direction, and so can a flapping sail, which waves in the wind like a flag. On your own boat, short pieces of yarn or cassette tape tied to the *shrouds,* the wire rigging supporting the mast, can provide crucial information about the wind's direction. Also look for sailboats under way or anchored boats that point at the wind (except in strong currents). Another way to see the wind direction is to look at the ripples on the water. Watch the movement of a darker patch of water caused by a puff of wind. Seagulls stand facing into the wind, and cows point their behinds into the wind — but unless you're sailing next to a farm, this bit of trivia is probably useless.

After you gain more experience, you're also able to assess the wind speed by looking at the water. For example, whitecaps generally begin to form on waves at 12 knots of wind speed. (See Chapter 8 for more on wind speed.) Being able to gauge the wind strength is important for safety, because beginning sailors should head for shore if the wind is above 12 knots (unless you have an instructor on board).

If you find yourself getting overwhelmed by which rope to pull and what to call a piece of equipment, *relax* and just feel the wind on your face. A sailor's world revolves around the wind, and you're becoming a sailor.

Identifying the Points of Sail

Figure 5-1 is the big kahuna of sailing, the *points of sail* diagram. As you become a sailor, you can get away with forgetting which side is starboard or which corner of the sail is the tack, but you can't sail without understanding the information in this diagram.

The points of sail diagram looks like the face of a clock, with the wind blowing from 12:00. At the top of the clock face, from about 10:30 to 1:30, is the sector called the *no-sail zone*. It gets its name from the fact that it's physically impossible to sail a boat in this zone. You can call the *no-sail zone* whatever you like — the *can't-sail zone* or the *anti-sail zone* or, if the sun is setting and strange things are happening, the *Twilight Zone*. Pointing your boat anywhere else around the clock face is fair game — with the sails trimmed properly, you move forward. This "sail zone" further divides into three basic *points of sail:*

- ✔ **Close-hauled:** Also called *beating, sailing upwind,* or *sailing to windward,* it's the closest course to the wind that you can effectively sail on the very edge of the dreaded no-sail zone. So close-hauled is right at 10:30 and 1:30.

- ✔ **Reaching:** Anywhere between close-hauled and running.

- ✔ **Running:** The course you're steering when the wind is dead behind. Exactly 6:00 on the clock face if you're a stickler — from 5:30 to 6:30 if you're like us.

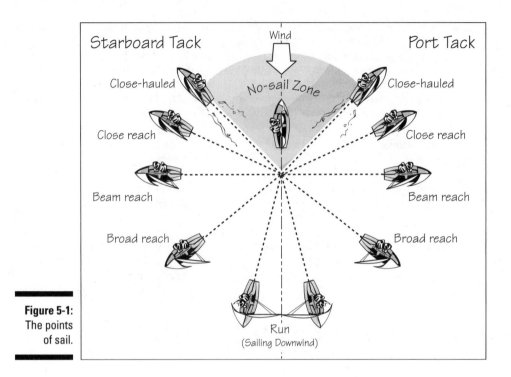

Figure 5-1:
The points
of sail.

More about that darn no-sail zone

The no-sail zone is about 90 degrees wide — about 45 degrees on either side of the wind direction, or from 10:30 to 1:30, if you like the clock. In this zone, a sailboat can't generate power from its sails and will coast to a stop. The problem is that your sails *luff* (flap) even when you pull them in all the way.

As you enter the no-sail zone from the sail zone, the front edge *(luff)* of your sails start luffing a little bit (it looks like the front of the sail is bubbling), and you start to slow down. If you turn to the very middle of the no-sail zone, your sails flap like flags, and your boat quickly coasts to a stop. In fact, if you stay in the no-sail zone too long, the wind blows your boat backward, which is called being *in irons.* Getting *in* irons happens to every first-time sailor. Find out all about getting *out* of irons in the "Ironing out those irons" section, later in this chapter.

But the beauty of sailing is that you have a way around this apparently forbidden territory. To get to a destination directly *upwind* in the no-sail zone (say 12:00), you can take a zigzag route (see Figure 5-2), sort of like hiking up a very steep mountain. This technique involves sailing close-hauled and periodically *tacking* (a maneuver where you turn the boat from 1:30 to 10:30 or vice versa). With this knowledge, you can literally sail wherever you want! (We explain the wonders of tacking in the "Tacking: Turning toward the wind" section, later in this chapter.)

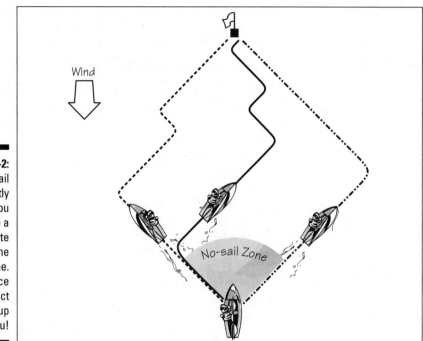

Figure 5-2:
To sail directly upwind, you must take a zigzag route to avoid the no-sail zone. The choice of the exact route is up to you!

You must be very clear on one point: No boat can sail a course directly into (toward) the wind. If you try to do so, the sails start luffing, no matter how tight you try to trim them — like they do when the bow is pointed into the wind at the dock. The boat glides to a stop and eventually blows backward, like any object floating on the water.

Sailing in the zone

Sailing in any direction in the sail zone is as easy as *trimming* the sail (by pulling in on the control rope — the *sheet*). We show you the safest way to pull in ropes in the "Pulling In Lines" section, later in this chapter. Or you can just *cleat* the sail (tie off the control rope so that the sail stays in one place) and turn the boat away from the wind direction until the sail fills. The points of sail diagram shows boats sailing at all different angles to the wind in the sail zone.

To sail fast, trim the sails to the proper angle to the wind. As you can see in Figure 5-1, you trim the sails differently for the various points of sail. You pull the sails in tight when a boat is sailing close-hauled and let them out all the way when on a run. When you're reaching, the in-between point of sail, trim the sails in between. Makes sense, huh?

Why is the no-sail zone 90 degrees?

The size of the no-sail zone is slightly different for each boat. Some racing boats with very efficient sails and keels can sail as close as 30 degrees to the wind. For them, the no-sail zone is around 60 degrees wide (the angle from close-hauled on one side of the zone to close-hauled on the other). The wind strength also affects the size of the no-sail zone. In very light air, all boats go slower, and the *foils* (the keel, rudder, and sails) are less efficient, so you sail a wider angle to the wind than you do in stronger winds.

Keeping your sails properly trimmed is important for maneuverability. Any time your boat slows down, you must be extra vigilant because a very slow boat can lose steerage on any point of sail. Don't just stop in a waterway unless you have plenty of room to regain your forward motion.

Sailing on the edge: Close-hauled

The key to sailing upwind is steering a course just on the edge of the no-sail zone, as physically close to the wind as possible — at about 10:30 or 1:30 on the clock face, depending on which side you're sailing on. Because the wind is never perfectly steady, continuous attention and subtle steering adjustments are required to stay right on the edge. When sailing close-hauled, you must trim your sails in very tight, as Figure 5-3 shows. When they begin to luff, you can't trim them in any more, so you must turn (with the rudder) away from the wind just a tiny bit until the sails stop luffing.

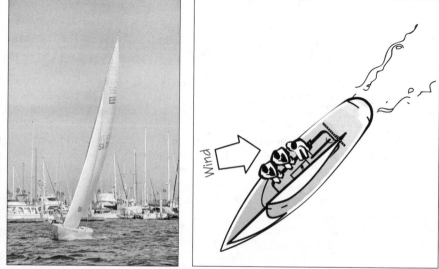

Figure 5-3: Sailing close-hauled with sails trimmed in tight.

When your sails are full, try to turn the boat a little bit toward the wind to see whether you can sail closer to the wind without luffing the sails. See, it really is like sailing on the edge!

Sailing upwind is a modern feat. Columbus sailed across the ocean blue by letting the sails on his square rigger act like a parachute and push the boat along on a reaching or running course. But your boat can sail upwind by efficiently harnessing the lift generated by the sail and the keel or center-board and rudder. Therefore, you can sail much closer to the wind than Columbus ever could. For more on how this "lift" works (if you're the inquiring type), see Appendix C.

Reaching for the gusto

Reaching is a catchall phrase for all points of sail between close-hauled and running. Because it spans such a large range of wind angles, reaching is the easiest place to start sailing. Reaching is also the fastest point of sail.

For your first time on a reach, steer the boat so that the wind is coming from a direction roughly 90 degrees off the bow (blowing across your boat) and trim your sails in until they just stop flapping. Reaching is the easiest point of sail for a new sailor, so try it first and steer the boat to the right and left a little bit to get the feel of how it responds to the tiller or wheel.

If you're reaching on a heading 90 degrees to the wind direction, you're on a *beam reach,* as Figure 5-4 shows. A reach at any heading between 90 degrees and close-hauled is called a *close reach.* If you're reaching at a wider angle to the wind (an angle greater than 90 degrees), you're on a *broad reach.* The expression *broad-reaching through life* applies to happy-go-lucky people who never have to worry about getting upwind.

On a reach, the sails are pulled in just to the point where they're no longer luffing. Although they still look full if you trim them farther in, you give up valuable power when you overtrim the sails.

Sailing with a not-so-patient Joe

One of the great collegiate sailing coaches was longtime Tufts University sailing coach Joe Duplin. Joe was a world-renowned racer, famous for his creativity on the race course and his New England accent but not for his patience with teaching beginning sailing to inexperienced pupils. Joe would sum up all the information in the previous two chapters in two sentences. Pointing to the tiller, he'd say, "This is the steering wheel; pull it this way to turn right and this way to turn left." Then, grabbing the mainsheet rope, Joe would finish the lesson by saying, "This is the accelerator. To speed up, pull it in; to slow down, let it out!" Then he'd push his student's boat off the dock and hope for the best.

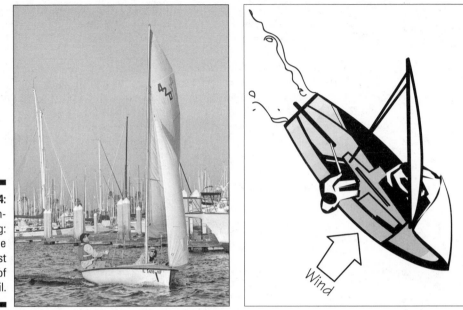

Figure 5-4: Beam-reaching: one of the fastest points of sail.

An important rule for sail trim is *when in doubt, ease it out!* Check the trim of your sails by *easing* (letting out) their respective sheets slightly. If they begin to luff, you were set perfectly, so pull your sails back in to where they were. If they stay full, you were overtrimmed. Check the trim by easing and then pulling back in periodically, as Figure 5-5 shows.

Running with the wind

Sailing with the wind behind you (going the same direction as the wind is blowing) is called *running* (or sailing *downwind*). Sailing with the wind at your back is great — the boat doesn't heel, and because your forward motion reduces the wind blowing across the deck and no spray comes on board, you're warmer. Naturally, you'd like to sail on a run all the time. But unless you're going on a one-way trip, you must, at some point, pay the price by sailing back upwind.

On a run, you need to let the sails all the way out — 90 degrees to the wind so the wind is blowing from directly behind the boat. The sails act like a big barn door rather than an airfoil, so you can't find the proper trim by over-easing the sail until it luffs. The wind is simply pushing the boat along.

You've probably seen pictures of sailboats with big, colorful, balloonlike sails. These specialty downwind sails are called *spinnakers,* and they help you go even faster by catching more wind. You find out how to sail with a spinnaker in Chapter 12.

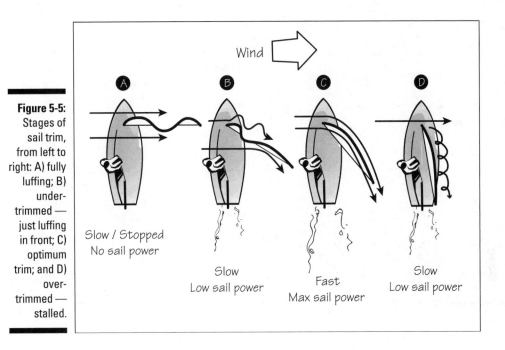

Figure 5-5:
Stages of sail trim, from left to right: A) fully luffing; B) under-trimmed — just luffing in front; C) optimum trim; and D) over-trimmed — stalled.

If your boat has a jib, you may find that it doesn't want to fill when you're on a run because it's in the wind shadow of the mainsail. You can, however, get some extra horsepower by *winging* the jib. Simply pull the weather side jib sheet around until the sail fills on the side opposite the mainsail. Then hold or cleat the jib sheet so that the sail is set approximately 90 degrees to the wind, as Figure 5-6 shows. Running is the only time when your mainsail and jib can set on opposite sides.

Avoiding sailing by the lee

If you're running close to dead downwind (or 6:00), you must be careful that you don't turn a little farther and end up sailing *by the lee* (with the wind coming across the same side of the boat as the boom is on, as Figure 5-7 shows). Changes in wind direction can be tougher to feel when you're sailing on a run, and a wind shift can also force you suddenly by the lee.

You can usually sail 5 or 10 degrees by the lee (compared to dead downwind) without having the boom fly across. But depending on the setting of your mainsail, as you sail farther and farther away from dead downwind on the wrong heading, at some point that wind is going to send your mainsail and boom whizzing across via special delivery.

Sailing by the lee can be very dangerous, especially in stronger winds, because as soon as the wind pushes on the "back" side of the mainsail, it can force the boom across the deck very suddenly and make you jibe accidentally.

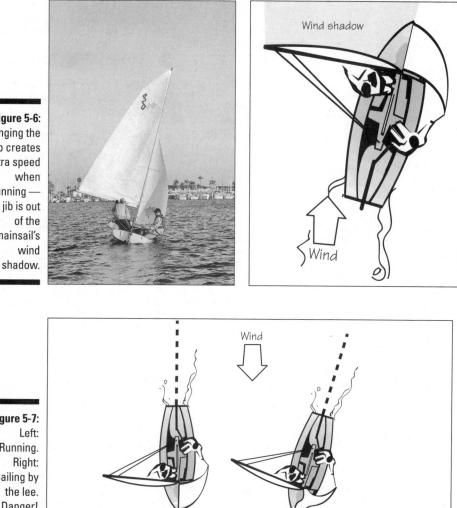

Figure 5-6:
Winging the jib creates extra speed when running — the jib is out of the mainsail's wind shadow.

Figure 5-7:
Left: Running. Right: Sailing by the lee. Danger!

You can prevent sailing by the lee by watching your sails and the wind direction. Some boats have an arrowlike wind indicator at the top of the mast that can help. Also watch the battens; if they're trying to flip over, you're in a trouble zone. Another good indicator that you're close to this trouble zone is when your jib collapses because the main is totally blocking it. Keep asking yourself, "Where is the wind coming from now?"

If the boom does start to come over unexpectedly, be sure to yell "Duck" as loudly as you can to warn your crew to *duck!* Many sailors have suffered bruises or worse from a whack in the head by the boom.

Pointing Out the Basic Sailing Terms

You need to be familiar with some basic sailing terminology before getting into sailing maneuvers. The following section covers *heading up* and *bearing away, port* and *starboard,* and *windward* and *leeward.*

Heading up and bearing away

The two phrases *heading up* and *bearing away* describe any turn on a sailboat. Like almost everything in this chapter, their definitions are also relative to the all-important wind direction. When you make a turn toward the wind, you're *heading up.* When you're steering with a tiller (and sitting in the proper position — on the windward side, facing the sails, as we show in Chapter 4), you push the tiller away from you to head up.

The term *bearing away* is more common than *heading down* or *bearing off,* but they all mean a turn away from the wind direction. You pull the tiller toward you to bear away — assuming that you're sitting in the proper position. If you were to sail in a complete circle, you would, by definition, be bearing away half the time and heading up half the time. Figure 5-8 shows both heading up and bearing away.

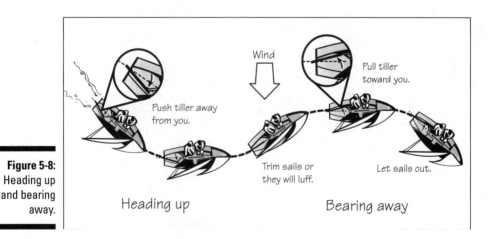

Wind

Pull tiller toward you.

Push tiller away from you.

Trim sails or they will luff.

Let sails out.

Heading up

Bearing away

Figure 5-8: Heading up and bearing away.

Port and starboard tack

Port is left and *starboard* is right (when you're facing the *bow,* the front of the boat). The easiest way to keep these new terms straight is to remember that both *left* and *port* are shorter than *right* and *starboard.* These nautical words for left and right are optional much of the time, because their land-based cousins are equally clear, but using them is important when you're describing whether a boat is on *port* or *starboard tack*.

Like almost everything else pertaining to sailing, the determining factor is the wind. When you're sailing with the wind coming over the left side of your boat, you're on port tack. When the wind is coming over the boat's right side, you're on starboard tack. Whether you're close-hauled, reaching, or running doesn't matter; the determining factor is which side of the boat the wind is hitting first (except if you're sailing by the lee as described in the "Avoiding sailing by the lee" section, earlier in this chapter).

Windward and leeward

The left side of your boat is always the port side, but which is the *windward* and which is the *leeward* side changes depending on the angle of the wind to your boat. The wind always hits the windward side of the boat first. The leeward side, then, is the other side of the boat. You can remember *leeward* because the word comes from *in the lee,* which means "out of the wind." The wind pushes your sails onto the leeward side. If your sails are in the center, then they're luffing and you're *in irons.* (See "Ironing out those irons," later in this chapter.)

Except when you're winging out the jib on a run, you always set your sails on the leeward side. If you get confused about which side is windward and which is leeward, simply let the jib or mainsail luff so that the sail flaps like a flag as Figure 5-9 shows. Whichever side the sail is flapping toward is the leeward side.

When the wind's blowing, docks, buoys, and land also have two sides relative to the wind. The side closer to the wind is called windward, and the side farther away from the wind is called leeward. The windward side of an island can be much wetter as storms hit that side first, while the leeward side is calm and protected.

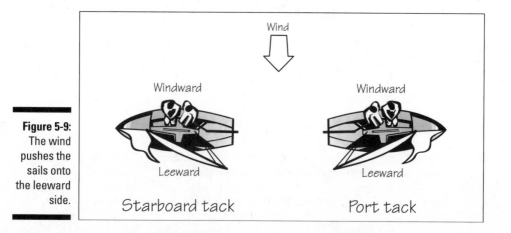

Figure 5-9: The wind pushes the sails onto the leeward side.

Making the Basic Sailing Maneuvers

Imagine that you're sailing along on a nice beam reach, but a long shoreline looms in front of your bow. You can avoid this obstruction by choosing one of the two basic sailing maneuvers:

- ✔ **Tacking,** or changing tacks by turning the boat from one side of the no-sail zone to the other.

- ✔ **Jibing,** or changing tacks by turning the boat away from the wind until the wind blows on the opposite side.

This section also delves into the most common mistake when tacking: getting *in irons* (getting stuck pointing into the wind).

Tacking: Turning toward the wind

Earlier in the "More about that darn no-sail zone" section, we point out that you must use a zigzag route to reach an upwind destination. First, you sail on a close-hauled course on one tack, and then you *tack* (turn the boat through the no-sail zone) and sail a close-hauled course on the other tack. This maneuver of turning the boat through the dreaded no-sail zone, or "through the wind," is called *tacking*.

To get to a point upwind, you can either tack once (assuming that the harbor is wide enough), or you can tack many times — you're the skipper, so you decide! Refer back to Figure 5-2 to see examples of several upwind tacks.

Here are the steps to tacking (see Figure 5-10).

1. **Prepare your crew by calling out "Ready to tack!"**

   Make sure that your crew is ready and in their positions.

2. **Call out "Tacking!" and begin turning the boat toward the wind (heading up), as shown in the top photo in Figure 5-10.**

   Instead of "tacking," some sailors use the term *helm's alee* or *hard alee*, meaning that their helm (the rudder) has been put hard over to the leeward side to initiate the turn. As with most sailing terms, any hail will do, as long as everyone on board understands it.

   As you begin to turn, the sail begins to luff wildly. This step is when most beginners have problems, because if you stop turning at this point, you get stuck in the no-sail zone.

   Don't forget to duck your head as the boom swings across.

3. **Release the old jib sheet and trim the new one as the boat rotates through the no-sail zone.**

Your crew can omit this step if you don't have a jib.

4. **Switch sides (see the middle photo in Figure 5-10).**

You (and your crew, if necessary) switch sides in order to retain visibility and to get your weight to the new windward side. You may find moving across easiest as the boat turns through the no-sail zone — especially on a dinghy where your weight is needed as ballast when the sails fill on the new close-hauled course.

5. **Keep turning the boat until you exit the no-sail zone.**

Slow down your turn as the sails begin to fill on the new side. When you're safely out of the no-sail zone, begin steering straight.

6. **Check the trim of the sails on the new tack (see the bottom photo of Figure 5-10).**

The wind is now blowing across the other side of the boat. Congratulations! You've successfully changed tacks. As you settle in on a close-hauled course and confirm the proper trim of your sails, you may want to cleat the sheets if they're pulling so hard that holding them is uncomfortable.

When tacking, turning all the way through the no-sail zone is important. As the boat turns and the sails flap, your boat is losing momentum. Dally too long in this zone, and you risk losing headway and getting stuck *in irons,* as we discuss in the next section. So make sure that you keep turning until the boat is turned far enough on the other tack that you can trim the sails in without any luffing, and start accelerating. The entire maneuver should take about five seconds on a small keelboat or dinghy.

Ironing out those irons

The most common mistake beginners make when trying to tack is to get the boat stuck in the no-sail zone, dead in the water with no maneuverability. Just like on a car, the steering wheel or tiller has no effect if your boat isn't moving. Being stuck *head-to-wind* in the no-sail zone is called being *in irons.* (Some interesting reason going back to the days of the square riggers must explain why this situation is called "in irons," but that's a story for another day.) You get in irons when you don't turn the boat all the way through the no-sail zone during a tack, or if you turn too slowly during a tack, or when you try to sail too close to the wind direction.

A tack, to tack, on a tack, tic-tack-toe

The word *tack* has many meanings in sailing. The bottom front corner of a sail is the *tack*. The noun *tack* also refers to the boat's heading in relation to the wind (that is, on *starboard* or *port* *tack*). *Tacking* is the act of changing tacks by turning through the wind, entering the no-sail zone from one side and exiting the other.

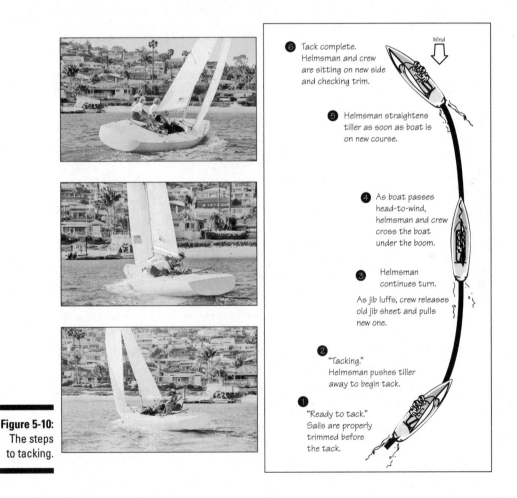

Figure 5-10:
The steps
to tacking.

⑥ Tack complete.
Helmsman and crew
are sitting on new side
and checking trim.

Wind

⑤ Helmsman straightens
tiller as soon as boat is
on new course.

④ As boat passes
head-to-wind,
helmsman and crew
cross the boat
under the boom.

❸ Helmsman
continues turn.

As jib luffs, crew releases
old jib sheet and pulls
new one.

❷ "Tacking."
Helmsman pushes tiller
away to begin tack.

❶ "Ready to tack."
Sails are properly
trimmed before
the tack.

To get out of irons and moving again on a boat without a jib, follow these steps:

1. **Uncleat or release the mainsheet.**

   And keep it released until your boat has turned all the way to a close reach. Your boat needs the mainsheet eased to be able to rotate out of the no-sail zone.

2. **Push the tiller (or turn the wheel) to one side.**

   Keep the helm hard over until the boat backs away to a close-reaching position. Be patient; the boat turns as it starts to go backwards. Basically, you're doing the sailing equivalent of a three-point turn. To speed up the process, you can push on the boom to *back* the mainsail (fill it backwards) and help the boat go in reverse.

3. **Trim the sails and steer straight (don't pinch!).**

   You're off!

Sounds easy, right? But beginning sailors are impatient and tend to steer back and forth as they go backward, remaining stuck in irons. Just leave the helm hard over to one side or the other until you're on a reaching heading.

If your boat has a jib, you have an additional and powerful tool for escaping from the clutches of the no-sail zone. To get out of irons on a boat with a jib, follow these steps:

1. **Pull the jib sheet taut on one side and put the tiller to the opposite side.**

   If you're pointed head to wind, either side works equally well. The jib fills backwards and pushes the bow as Figure 5-11 shows.

2. **Keep your mainsheet loose so that the main doesn't fill until the boat rotates around and is pointed on a reaching course.**

   Keep the tiller hard over on the side opposite the jib. With a wheel, you turn toward the jib.

3. **Release the jib sheet and trim both sails in on the "proper" side as the boat accelerates.**

4. **Straighten out the tiller or wheel to avoid turning back up into the wind when the boat begins to move forward again.**

I can remember the first time I ever soloed a sailboat, when I was about 13 years old. I was halfway out into the harbor when it happened — I got caught in irons. Back then, I had no idea what was going on, except for the obvious fact that the boat wasn't moving at all. My sailing instructor came up to me in a motorboat and said, "Ya know you're doing something wrong," which was, of course, patently obvious. Only later did I realize that I'd been caught in irons. You can't avoid getting caught in irons as a beginning sailor, so be prepared for when it happens!

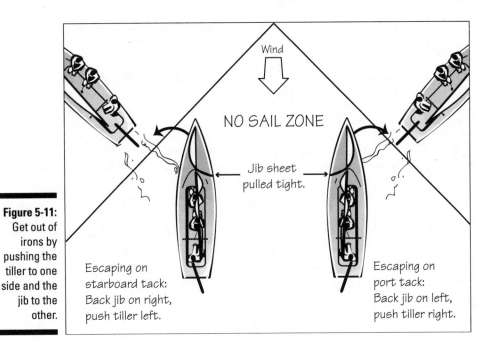

Wind

NO SAIL ZONE

Jib sheet
pulled tight.

Figure 5-11:
Get out of
irons by
pushing the
tiller to one
side and the
jib to the
other.

Escaping on
starboard tack:
Back jib on right,
push tiller left.

Escaping on
port tack:
Back jib on left,
push tiller right.

Jibing: Turning away from the wind

The other method of changing tacks (changing your direction so that the wind is blowing over the other side of the boat) is to turn away from the wind and *jibe*. (Some books spell *jibing* as *gybing,* the British style. We stick with *jibing* [*ji* pronounced as in *giant*].)

Because the downwind side of the points of sail diagram doesn't have a no-sail zone, jibing should be easier than tacking, and, in some ways, jibing *is* easier, because you need to change course by only a few degrees instead of the 90 degrees required when tacking. However, jibing is inherently more dangerous than tacking, because of the force with which the boom swings across the cockpit. Keep in mind that you're on a broad reach or a run before you jibe, so the sails are eased a long way out. Therefore, that boom has a long way to travel across the boat. You can also start jibing from a reach, but doing so requires a bigger turn.

The following steps and Figure 5-12 explain in detail how to jibe:

1. **Prepare your crew for the jibe by calling out "Ready to jibe!"**

   Reminding them to duck never hurts. Given the force with which the boom can swing across, you need to make sure that your crew is ready and in position for this maneuver.

2. **Call out "Jibing!" and start turning the boat away from the wind (bearing away), and begin pulling (or have your crew pull) the main to the other side.**

   The traditional term is "Jibe-ho." Feel free to add "Boom coming across" or "Duck" if you see that someone is in danger of getting hit by the boom.

   You don't need a big or a fast turn, because there's no equivalent to being stuck in irons on this side of the points of sail diagram. Unlike a tack, where you have to keep turning the boat so that you don't get stuck head-to-wind, you may not need to turn the boat at all to jibe if you're already heading straight downwind.

   On bigger boats with several crew members, having a person other than the skipper pull in the mainsheet is safer because of the amount of line to pull in and then release after the boom crosses the boat. (Make sure that crew members keep their feet out of all that mainsheet line.)

3. **As you turn past dead downwind, the mainsail will jibe.**

   As you turn and the wind shifts from one side of the boat to the other, the wind wants to push the mainsail to the other side with tremendous force. If you didn't pull the boom across in a controlled manner (in Step 2), at this point it will come flying across, taking with it everything in its path — so use extreme care not to let this force pull the line through your hands. And keep your head low.

4. **Stop turning and steer straight as you trim the sails on the new jibe.**

   If you have a jib, you can pull it across to the opposite side now.

5. **Switch sides of the boat.**

   On a keelboat you can perform this step whenever you're most comfortable. On a dinghy, you need to switch sides as soon as the boom flies overhead or immediately afterward so your weight keeps the boat from tipping. The entire jibing maneuver takes about four seconds on a small keelboat or dinghy.

   In windy conditions, you may choose to change tacks without jibing. Instead, just turn toward the wind, tack around, and then head down to your new course. Equipment breaks easily when jibing in strong winds, because of the sudden load on the mainsail after it swings across. On the big America's Cup–class boats, we always tacked instead of jibing before the race whenever conditions were windy to minimize the risk of breaking our expensive carbon-fiber battens.

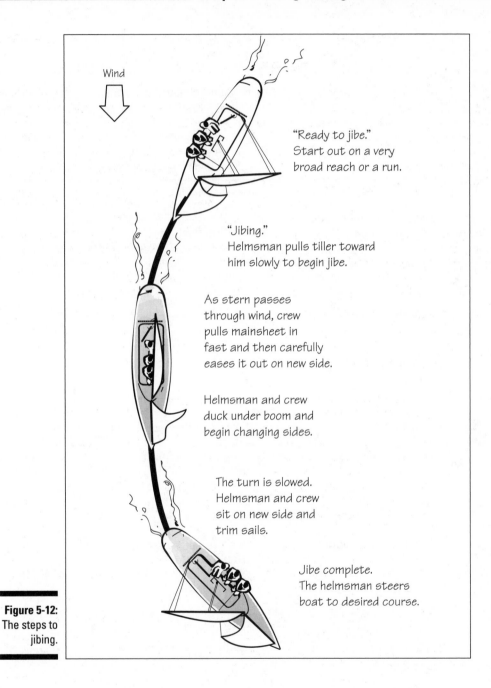

Wind

"Ready to jibe."
Start out on a very
broad reach or a run.

"Jibing."
Helmsman pulls tiller toward
him slowly to begin jibe.

As stern passes
through wind, crew
pulls mainsheet in
fast and then carefully
eases it out on new side.

Helmsman and crew
duck under boom and
begin changing sides.

The turn is slowed.
Helmsman and crew
sit on new side and
trim sails.

Jibe complete.
The helmsman steers
boat to desired course.

Figure 5-12:
The steps to
jibing.

What to say to your crew

As you can probably guess, sailors have many terms for the person who steers the boat — *skipper, captain,* and *helmsman* are three. The one name you don't want to be called is "Captain Bligh" — the horrible captain from *Mutiny on the Bounty.*

An interesting psychological phenomenon can happen when a seemingly normal person gets behind the wheel or tiller of a sailboat — he or she can turn into a power-hungry maniac, screaming orders and treating everyone on board like scum. If you don't want a mutiny on board your boat, make sure that you treat your crew the way you'd want to be treated.

"Tacking!" and "jibing!" are important commands, but the "Ready to tack/jibe!" command is equally important. Your crew needs some time (30 seconds or so) to get in position before you start the turn. If conditions are windy, you may have to yell (nicely) to get them to hear you.

Planning your maneuvers in advance to give your crew time to get ready is a skipper's responsibility. For safety's sake, the skipper should always look to make sure that everyone is prepared and in a safe spot *before* turning the boat. If someone gets hit by the boom, most often the skipper is at fault.

Pulling In Lines

On a windy day, pulling in the boom on a jibe or trimming the sails when close-hauled can be tough work. Some lines on sailboats are lightly loaded, and adjusting them is easy. But others carry tremendous load, especially in strong winds. Trying to pull these lines can result in strained muscles or burned hands. Consider the forces on a line before uncleating it and trying to hold it. "Plucking" the line like a guitar string gives you an indication of the load on it. If the line feels like a steel rod and makes a note like a high G, then don't uncleat it or try to pull it without the help of a mechanical device like a winch, which we cover in this section.

To help use all your strength, make sure that you're in the correct position to pull. You may need to sit down across from the line with your feet pushing against some solid object. Fully extend your arms and grab the line with both hands for maximum pulling power, as Figure 5-13 shows.

If you can't pull the line even when you're in the correct position, don't give up. Sailors of all ages and sizes can operate any boat, because various combinations of pulleys and winches provide the mechanical advantage to enable a wimp to do the work of a hulk.

This may be the most valuable sailing tip in this book: You can make pulling in the lines easier through clever driving and by relying on teamwork. For example, grinding in the jib sheet on a big cruising boat in strong winds can be a real chore. But if the skipper simply heads up slightly toward the wind, the sail begins to luff, and the load decreases. You may even be able to pull in the sheet by hand. Another way to substantially decrease the load on most of the sail control ropes is to turn the boat downwind (bear away) onto a broad reach or run. If your crew has a job to do on the bow, turn the boat downwind. Then the crew can safely go forward and have a flat and dry work space. (Careful — no accidental jibes, please!)

Next time you face a really difficult physical task on a sailboat, ask yourself whether you can do the job more easily by steering the boat at a certain angle. Usually the answer is yes.

Figure 5-13: Aine McLean demonstrates good body position for maximum pulling power.

Using blocks

Mainsheets and most of the other lines on a sailboat run through *blocks* (pulleys). Some blocks just change the direction that the line travels, but when you use several blocks in combination — block-and-tackle systems — they make the line easier to hold and pull. The amount of extra lifting power, called *purchase,* depends on the number of pulleys used and the arrangement. Without delving into the mechanics involved, a *four-part* mainsheet system (also referred to as a *4:1* system) requires only one-fourth the effort to pull in the sail compared to a single rope hanging from the boom (a 1:1 system). The disadvantage of a four-part mainsheet system is that you have to pull in four times as much line to bring in the sail.

A *cascading* arrangement multiplies the benefits, so a 2:1 system used with a 4:1 system provides an 8:1 mechanical advantage, as Figure 5-14 shows. (We talk about the care and selection of blocks in Chapter 15.) No matter what style, purchase systems all have the same purpose: to optimize the mechanical advantage so that the average person can pull the line and sail the boat easily.

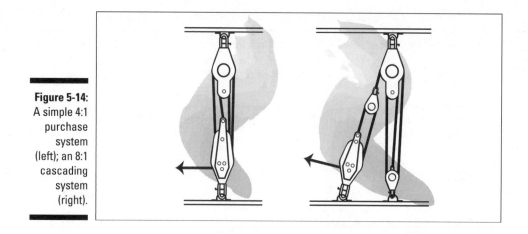

Figure 5-14:
A simple 4:1
purchase
system
(left); an 8:1
cascading
system
(right).

Regardless of the block-and-tackle system you use, you need to keep the line from slipping when you have the rope trimmed where you want it. To prevent slipping, you have two options: Hold onto the rope or cleat it.

Ratchet blocks

Some blocks *ratchet,* which means that they turn freely when you pull the line but don't turn at all in the other direction. This extra friction makes the line easier to hold. Ratchet blocks are common on the mainsheets and jib sheets of smaller keelboats and dinghies. They usually have a button or lever to turn the ratchet action off and let the block turn freely in both directions, which is useful in light wind. The extra holding power of a ratchet block makes hanging onto the mainsheet on a windy day much easier.

Cleats

Most sailboats have more control lines than you have hands. Although certain creative sailors have been known to use their mouths to hold a rope or two (which the American Dental Association doesn't recommend), most control lines have some sort of cleat to hold them.

- **Horn cleats and jammers:** These very secure cleats are best for lines such as halyards that you don't adjust often. (See Chapter 4 for more on hoisting sails.)

- **Clamcleats and cam cleats:** Easier to uncleat, these two cleats are well suited for mainsheets, jib sheets, and other lines that you need to adjust regularly. As you see in Figure 5-15, a Clamcleat has grooves that make it look like the two sides of a clam shell. These grooves help hold a line that's under load. A cam cleat has two movable, notched jaws that use spring action to open and to grasp the line. To uncleat the line, you pull up and toward yourself (sometimes forcefully) to lift it out of the jaws.

TIP

If your boat uses cam cleats or Clamcleats, make sure that the line is all the way down in the jaws so that it stays securely cleated.

Figure 5-15:
Clamcleat
(left) and
cam cleat
(right).

Using winches

Remember the old Charlton Heston movies in which sweaty, ragged sailors pulled in ropes, grunting "Heave, ho," like an ancient tug of war, while a barbaric foreman cracked a whip? Nowadays, you can use a *winch* to pull in that line (and leave your whip at home). You use winches, another way to provide mechanical advantage to adjust ropes under load, mainly on bigger boats, where loads on lines can get really heavy.

REMEMBER

Winches use a system of gears inside a round cylinder called a *drum* to give you the necessary pulling power. Always wrap the line clockwise around the drum, using more wraps as the load on the line increases. Put as many wraps around the drum as you need — the wraps provide the friction so you can hold a heavily loaded line in your hand.

The winch drum spins as you pull the rope wrapped around it if the rope isn't under load. But when the load builds (such as on a jib sheet when the sail fills during a tack), you need to turn the drum with a removable handle called a *winch handle*. This process is called *grinding* (and the folks who do it on big racing boats are called *grinders*).

Grinding

While one person grinds, the other person pulls in (or *tails*) the line that feeds off the drum. One person can do both jobs, but doing so is less efficient. Some winches are *self-tailing,* meaning that they have a built-in mechanism that grips the line and holds it in place so that one person can grind without needing anyone to pull the rope. However, grinding is often a two-person process, as Figure 5-16 shows.

Here are some tips for grinding and tailing properly:

✔ **Choose the right speed.** Many winches have two or more speeds or gears. You change gears by changing the direction you turn the handle so that you can shift speeds if the grinding gets harder.

✔ **Grind in a full circle, using two hands if necessary.** If you can't complete a circle, turn as far as you can and then ratchet the winch handle back to your starting point.

✔ **If you feel the rope slipping, then either you aren't pulling hard enough or you need to add a wrap on the drum.** When you're pulling in a slack or lightly loaded rope by hand, you usually need only one or two wraps. But after the line becomes so loaded that you can no longer pull it by hand and need to grind with the winch handle, you need about four wraps. When you're rapidly pulling in the slack out of a lightly loaded rope, you should add enough wraps for grinding just before the line gets loaded up. This is because when you're rapidly pulling in a lightly loaded line spinning around a winch, having too many wraps may cause a tangle called an *override*. In the next section, we discuss adding a wrap to a loaded winch and avoiding overrides.

✔ **Stand in a comfortable position over the winch.** You can grind a winch sitting beside it (some winches are placed where standing over them is impractical), but you won't be able to grind as hard.

✔ **When you're not grinding the winch, remove the handle and place it in its holder.** These expensive items have never passed the float test, and having the handle already removed is safer if you must quickly release the rope on the winch. You never find winches on dinghies, so you don't have to worry about losing that handle in a capsize.

Figure 5-16:
Jeff
Johnson
grinding a
winch with
Peter tailing.

Adjusting lines safely on a loaded winch

A line under tremendous load can be dangerous to *ease* (let out) or trim. Think first. The last thing you want is to burn your hands as a rope goes whizzing through them. Don't sail with any finger rings because they can get caught on a line. Be especially careful with winches when you're wearing gloves. Make sure that your gloves fit snugly, because extra fabric can get caught and pinched by the line spooling onto the winch drum.

When you need to add a wrap to a loaded winch, carefully hold the line with both hands. Maintain tension on the line as you take both hands all the way around the winch, turning your hands to keep your fingers from getting caught, as Figure 5-17 shows.

Figure 5-17: Keep pulling on the line as you use both hands to add a wrap on a highly loaded winch.

To ease a line slowly and safely, hold onto the line with your right hand and put your left hand on the wraps on the winch. Slowly let the line out counter-clockwise, a couple of inches at a time, keeping some pressure on the line and varying the pressure your left hand applies to the coil of line on the winch.

To take all the wraps off a winch quickly (common in a tacking maneuver on bigger boats that use winches for their jib sheets), pull up on the line with a slight counterclockwise rotating motion. Before you take off the wraps, make sure that the long tail of the jib sheet is free to run, not tangled around your foot (or a body part of your crew!).

When releasing a jib sheet on a winch during a tacking maneuver, wait until the load has just eased on the sheet before removing all the wraps on the winch drum. Watch for the jib to begin luffing as an indication that the helmsman has begun turning the boat. If you cast all the wraps off the winch drum too early, you risk burning your hands as the highly loaded rope runs out. Wait too late, and the jib fills backward and your hands could suffer the same abuse.

At some point, probably when you're already having a bad day, you're going to get an *override* — a misfed line that effectively creates a knot around the winch, shown in Figure 5-18. Overrides can be caused by improper winch placement so the rope feeds on it incorrectly or by having too many wraps when you pull in a slack line.

Figure 5-18:
An override (left) and a properly wrapped winch (right).

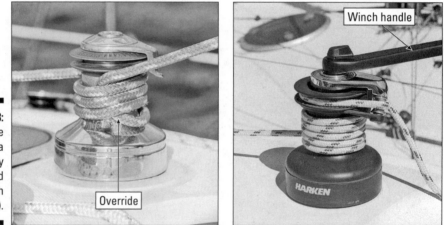

In light air, you may be able to untangle the mess by pulling the rope's end up and around the winch the "wrong" way (counterclockwise). In stronger winds, taking the load off the rope going to the winch and then untangling the mess is usually best.

Before the sail is sheeted hard, you may be able to head up, take the load off the sheet and manually untangle it. Otherwise, to take the load off the override, rig another line to do the same job. Or you can tie another line to the tangled line (forward of the tangle) with a rolling hitch (see Chapter 19) and then tighten the new line so that you have slack in the tangled part. The final option, when danger is imminent or none of the other methods work, is to cut the infringing rope with a knife. Be sure to cut the line near its end (near the clew of the jib on a jib sheet, for example) so that it's still usable (and only a little bit shorter). Avoid cutting a halyard if at all possible, because it requires a major rerigging exercise.

Chapter 6

Leaving the Dock (And Coming Back)

I find the great thing in this world is not so much where we stand, as in what direction we are moving: To reach the port of heaven, we must sail sometimes with the wind and sometimes against it — but we must sail, and not drift, nor lie at anchor.

—Oliver Wendell Holmes

*G*etting under way and getting back safely can be the trickiest part of your day on the water. You're often in a confined area with many other boats (not to mention the shore) nearby, and the rudder doesn't provide much maneuverability while you're at slow speeds and getting the boat going. Plus, all the sailors on the other boats are watching and waiting for you to mess up (not really, but it always feels like it).

We strongly encourage you to get some lessons before sailing (check out Chapter 2). Try to have an instructor or, at least, a knowledgeable friend along on your first few sails to help you get under way and back safely. Most novice sailors practice on boats that already have the mast up and are tied to a dock or a mooring (a permanently anchored buoy). But in case you need to know, the end of this chapter covers the variety of ways to put up the mast and get your boat from land to sea.

Leaving the Mooring or Dock

Casting off means untying and getting under way from a dock or mooring. If your boat has an engine (an *iron headsail* in sailor slang), you can motor away and put the sails up after you're in open water. But knowing how to sail away from a dock or mooring (and back again) under sail is a good idea in case your engine decides not to cooperate some day.

Remember the classic movie, *Caddyshack*? Rodney Dangerfield left his fenders (rubber cushions) dangling over the side while motoring around on his big powerboat. So if you want respect, untie your fenders and dock lines and store them below as soon as you have left the dock.

Using an engine

The biggest concern when using the engine (besides polluting the environment) is keeping lines from getting tangled in the propeller. We discuss that problem and other mishaps in Chapter 14. Make sure that no loose lines are dangling off the side of the boat. And always let go of the *mooring line* (the line permanently attached to a mooring buoy) on the windward side so that you don't run over it as the boat sideslips while building speed.

Some moorings have stern anchors attached so all the boats face one uniform direction. If so, first let go of the stern anchor line (which usually has weights attached), and make sure it sinks out of the way before proceeding.

Leaving the mooring under sail

Leaving a mooring is usually easier than leaving a dock, because the boat is already in relatively open water, but getting the boat turned to an angle out of the no-sail zone is trickier. We're assuming that your boat is tied by the bow with sails already hoisted, and is pointed into the wind. Use the following steps to sail away from a mooring buoy, as Figure 6-1 shows.

1. **Before casting off a dock or mooring, plan your best escape route.**

   Plan out a course so you can sail away on a reach (which gets you up to speed quickly). Make sure the whole crew knows the plan.

2. **The forward crew uncleats the mooring line but continues to hold it.**

   On bigger boats and in strong winds or current, one person won't have the strength to win the tug of war on the mooring line. So keep one full wrap of the line around the base of the horn cleat on the bow (if available) so you can hold on yet be ready to cast off quickly.

3. With the mainsail luffing, back the jib.

Trim the jib on the side opposite the direction that you intend to sail so that the jib *backwinds* (fills with wind backward) and pushes the bow away from the no-sail zone. Make sure that the mainsheet has plenty of slack so that the main can fully luff and won't fill. See Chapter 5 on getting your boat out of irons — it's the same technique.

4. Walk the mooring line back along the windward side to shoot the boat forward.

Have the crew holding the mooring line walk with it toward the stern — on the windward side, so that the line doesn't get caught under the boat. As your crew moves back, your boat is pulled forward, especially on a smaller boat, helping you gain speed and control. On bigger boats, if holding the bow line is too difficult after it's uncleated, just give it a good heave away from the boat when the skipper gives the command.

5. The crew lets go of the mooring and trims in the sails.

Wait until the combination of your steering and the force of the backed jib and fully luffing mainsail rotates your boat onto a reaching course. Then release the backed jib and trim it on the correct side. As the boat begins to gain speed, trim the luffing main and sail away on your desired course.

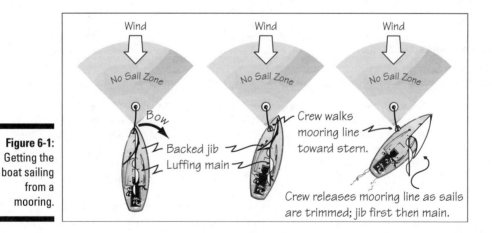

Figure 6-1:
Getting the boat sailing from a mooring.

Leaving the dock under sail

The key to easy arrival and departure from docks is to avoid tying up on the windward (upwind) side of the dock. If you try to leave the windward side of the dock under sail, the boat slips sideways as it gains speed and drags along the dock — not good form! Plus, tying your boat to the leeward side of the dock is better because the wind pushes the boat away from the dock, minimizing the chance of scratching the hull against the dock. If you must tie up on the windward side, ideally you can leave the dock using your engine. Have extra crew on board to help fend off as you leave.

If you want to depart under sail and your boat isn't tied up on the dock's leeward side (such as boats C, D, and E in Figure 6-2), move it. You can usually move boats shorter than 25 feet (8 meters) to a better location by pulling them with the dock lines or by holding onto a *shroud* (one of the wires supporting the mast) and pulling. On a bigger boat, you can use the engine and put the sails up in open water.

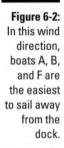

Figure 6-2:
In this wind
direction,
boats A, B,
and F are
the easiest
to sail away
from the
dock.

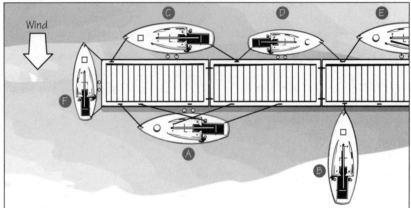

Just like when you leave a mooring, you don't want to let go of the dock until you have the boat turning so that you'll be safely out of the no-sail zone. If you have room at a dock, you can begin to turn the boat by pulling in on the bow line and walking the boat along to generate forward motion so that the rudder is effective. Usually you want to keep the mainsail fully luffing until you're safely into the sail zone, and if necessary, back your jib as described in "Leaving the mooring under sail" to help turn the boat onto the desired course.

If you have plenty of space, you may be able to gain speed (and thus *steerageway* — the speed needed to steer) by having your crew members give a push as they jump on board or by sailing close enough to a nearby boat or dock to push off and get some extra speed.

After you're safely away from the dock, remove any *fenders* (the rubber cushions tied to the side of the boat to keep it from hitting the dock) and store them down below out of the way. Also untie any dock lines, coil them up, and store them out of the way, too.

Getting Back to the Dock or Mooring

Leaving the subject of launching your boat without discussing how to get back to the dock or mooring would be like teaching you to ski and sending you down the mountain without telling you how to stop. In skiing, you can always stop by running into a tree or a big snowbank. The same technique works in sailing, too — you can always run the boat aground or into the dock. But considering how expensive insurance is, we want to give you cheaper and less painful alternatives.

The key to docking or mooring is slowing down at a controlled rate before you get there. You slow down by luffing the sails (see Chapter 5) and letting the boat glide to a stop. The trick is knowing when to start luffing so that you keep enough steerageway to reach the dock without having so much speed that the phrase "ramming speed" becomes applicable.

When in doubt, err on the slow side. If you find that you aren't going to reach your destination, you can always accelerate by retrimming your sails. However, there is a catch: If you slow down so much that the boat is pointed in the dreaded no-sail zone, you're out of luck and in irons, as we describe in Chapter 5. Getting in irons is a big problem when you're in a confined area. So please don't go too slow or too fast!

What if you're approaching too fast and can't kill enough speed? The best solution is to turn the boat around and try the approach again. (Nothing like a practice run to help you judge when to begin luffing your sails on the second try!) In fact, a wise sailor on a new boat always does some practice runs out in the open, next to a buoy or some other floating object, to help judge how the boat maneuvers as it decelerates.

Here are some other tricks that you can use to slow the boat:

- ✔ **On smaller boats, you can kill speed by *backing the main.*** Backing the main is like having a huge air brake. To back the main, push the boom toward the wind (the sail fills backward). Don't try this technique unless you're strong enough to control the boom and smart enough to let it go (and duck) if the boom begins winning the pushing contest.

- ✔ **You can kill speed with the rudder.** If you think you're coming in too fast, make some big turns instead of steering straight so that the boat has more distance to slow down. Make sure that your crew is ready for this maneuver and is holding on.

Coming back to the mooring

Always make a plan before you attempt to make a landing on any object. In the case of a return to a mooring buoy, make sure that the whole crew knows which mooring you plan to pick up. Designate one person to pick up the line attached to the mooring buoy. Grabbing this mooring line may require a *boat hook,* a pole with a hook on the end, to help extend a person's reach. Some mooring lines have a tall stick attached to a float so you can grab the stick to pick up the mooring line. Other crew members should be ready to luff the sails on your command.

Follow these steps when picking up a mooring:

1. **Approach the buoy on a close reach and steer at an imaginary point two to three boat lengths directly downwind from the buoy.**

   Adjust this offset distance based on the coasting or stopping characteristics of your boat. Lighter dinghies slow down very quickly. On heavier boats, the extra momentum makes slowing down take longer.

2. **Depending on the wind strength and your boat speed (and other factors, such as current, which we discuss in Chapter 8), use your best judgment to decide when to luff the sails to begin to kill speed.**

   You may want to luff the jib first and then the main to have more flexibility in adjusting your final speed.

3. **When you're almost directly downwind of the buoy, and if your rate of deceleration appears to be correct, turn in a smooth arc toward the wind and coast up to the mooring pointed directly toward the wind.**

   If you're approaching too quickly, abort the landing and make another try. If you're approaching too slowly, retrim the sails and build more speed. If you can't see the buoy, have a crew member point at it for you. As the bow reaches the buoy, the boat (ideally) comes to a dead stop. On a bigger boat, a boat hook helps the foredeck crew grab the buoy.

4. **Have the crew attach the boat to the mooring buoy.**

   Use a strong line and securely attach it to both the buoy and the boat (a cleat or some other strong object on the bow). Make sure that you inform the skipper when the boat is secure.

5. **Now you can lower the sails to stop their incessant flapping!**

On a boat with main and jib, dropping the jib (and maybe even clearing it away from the foredeck) before making the approach may be best. Doing so gives the crew more room to work up forward, reduces your sail power, and gives you more visibility. The downside is that without a jib, you have less control and ability to get out of irons, so be very careful to keep steerageway.

Coming back to the dock

Docking under sail is often trickier than sailing up to a mooring, because the dock is usually in a more confined space. However, the same basic rules apply:

- ✔ **Plan your approach so that your crew knows what to expect.**
- ✔ **Have your fenders and dock lines tied and ready to go well before you begin your final approach.**
- ✔ **Approach the leeward side of the dock or a side parallel to the wind (any side except the dreaded windward side).**
- ✔ **Approaching slower is better, but don't go too slow.** If you stop, you lose steerageway.

An ideal situation is a long, uncrowded dock with the wind blowing almost parallel along it. Like with the mooring buoy, plan your approach so that the boat has room to coast into position as it decelerates (see Figure 6-3). When the boat is close enough (and going slow enough), have a crew member step from the middle of the boat onto the dock so that she can begin securing the dock line(s). Never yell for someone to jump; let the person who's going to get off judge when the boat is close enough to make her move. With this type of approach (in which the sails are still up), the first line to be secured is the bow line; then you can begin lowering sails and further securing the boat as necessary.

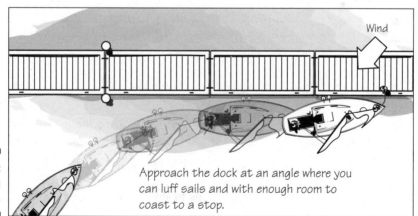

Figure 6-3:
Docking under sail.

Approach the dock at an angle where you can luff sails and with enough room to coast to a stop.

So what do you do if you don't have the ideal long runway? If you're bringing the boat alongside a dock, but you don't have as much space, tie a *spring line* (a line secured at the widest point in the middle of the boat; see "Spring lines," later in this chapter). You still need a bowline, stern line, and fenders all in place and ready to go, but the most important line to secure first is the spring line, because it helps stop the boat, followed quickly by the bow and stern line. When approaching *side on* (as in Figure 6-3), if your crew pulls in on the bow line while you are coasting forward, this action pulls your bow in and swings your stern out. A spring line just stops the boat without turning it, because it's pulling from the middle, widest point.

As soon as your crew is safely on the dock with the bow line secured (see Chapter 19 for the proper knots), you can begin lowering the sails. Depending on the angle of the wind to the dock, you may want to use more lines to tie the boat alongside the dock (see "Tying Up a Boat: Leaving It Secure," later in this chapter). If there is enough space on the dock, you may want to concentrate on dropping the sails and cleaning up the boat before putting the boat in its final resting place.

When helping to stop an incoming boat, the crew member with the dockline should loop her line around the horn cleat on the dock (or around a piling or other secure object) so she has some friction to give her more stopping power than just her body weight. After the line is around the cleat, she can ease it out slightly as the boat's weight tugs on it rather than securing it and causing the boat to stop short.

When a boat is approaching a dock, never put any part of your body between the boat and the dock. Repairing a little fiberglass is easier than repairing your body.

If you must tie up to the windward side of a dock, sail into a position directly upwind of the dock, lower your sails, and let the wind gently push you down to the dock.

Docking under power

Slower is better when docking — including when docking under power. Having an engine doesn't make the boat as maneuverable as your car. In fact, at low speeds, the rotation of the propeller makes the boat pull, or turn easier, to one side. In open water, practice slowing the boat to see how much the propeller torque turns the boat and in what direction, especially in reverse gear. As with docking under sail, the boat's momentum, the wind pushing the hull, and other factors, such as current, also affect your maneuverability. When you discover the maneuvering characteristics of your boat under power, the principles of docking remain the same as those we outline in the preceding section.

Make sure all lines are out of the water before starting your engine. If approaching from upwind (or from an angle where you can't fully luff the sails), you should drop the sails before docking a sailboat under power. Always approach slowly; never rely solely on reverse to slow the boat down. Instead, use a spring line, which we describe later in this chapter in the "Spring lines" section.

Docking between pilings

In many parts of the world, you won't have a nice, protected dock to tie alongside. Often, the sailor's best friends are *pilings* (large wooden poles driven solidly into the bottom. Your array of dock lines depends on the position and orientation of the pilings, and you have to be creative as you plan your strategy to keep the boat from getting banged up no matter which direction the wind or current flows.

One of the most common dock arrangements is a short dock on one side and pilings on the other side. Tie the dock lines from each corner (as well as spring lines) so the boat hangs in the slot without banging into the dock or pilings, as Figure 6-4 shows.

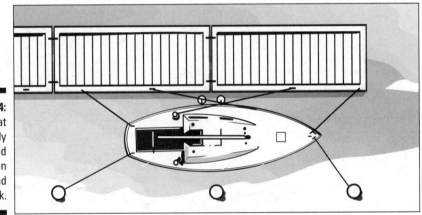

Figure 6-4:
A boat properly secured between pilings and dock.

To keep your boat from getting scratched on pilings or on a rough dock, the marina may use fender boards (long planks of wood with lines at regular intervals). By attaching the fender board to your boat outside your fenders, your boat stays off the pilings as the tide rises and falls.

If you fear that the wind is going to blow really hard, pushing the side of your boat directly into the dock, consider alternative locations to park. If no other locations are available, and no objects such as pilings are on hand to tie off to, you can ease the force of the boat against the dock (and ease your mind) by sending your dinghy out with an anchor directly *abeam* (perpendicular to the centerline of the boat). If this anchor extends into a waterway, do your best to mark it with a fender or other float to tell other boats to keep clear. Chapter 10 shows you how to safely anchor for all situations.

Throwing a Line

Sailing etiquette says that if sailors see a boat approach a dock, they should walk over and offer to help catch a line. So you need to know how to throw a line accurately and far. If you miss your target, you have to pull the soggy line back on board and coil it, and then quickly try again.

The key to proper throwing is to start with a well-coiled line. Put a few coils (up to about 15 feet or 4½ meters) in your throwing hand and hold your other hand (with the rest of the coils) open and pointed at the target so any extra coils can feed out as needed. Then throw (underhand) the coils, aiming slightly above the target. You can see Peter throwing a line in Figure 6-5.

Figure 6-5: Throwing a line: Peter heaves a few coils of rope with a good underhand toss.

Tying Up a Boat: Leaving It Secure

When your sailing day is done and the time has come to return to the rigors of your shoreside life, you want to make sure that your boat is happy until you next get an opportunity to visit it. Temporarily, your boat may be happy to hang from a single bow line (while you're nearby). For more permanent storage, you need several lines. This section discusses how to tie up your boat securely and safely to a dock. The following principles apply to all boats, but they're most useful when you're securing a larger keelboat alongside a dock:

✔ **Always check for *chafed* (damaged) parts of the line.**

✔ **Always use fenders between the boat and the dock or pilings.**

✔ **Always use spring lines (see the "Spring lines" section for more info) —** Peter's favorite dock lines.

✔ **Make sure your docking line is amply strong and thick — at least ⅜ of an inch (1 centimeter) for a 20-foot (6-meter) boat.** Nylon line works well because it's designed to stretch.

✔ **Don't pull the stern and bow lines too tight.** Ideally, the boat lies just off the dock so that it doesn't rub.

✔ **Tie bow and stern lines at about a 45-degree angle away from the boat to hold it secure.**

Spring lines

Spring lines are incredibly effective. Tied from the middle of the boat, they prevent the boat from surging forward or backward and keep it securely positioned so that the few fenders in the middle of the boat are always in the right place. Figure 6-6 shows a boat tied up by a bow line, a forward spring line, an aft spring line, and the stern line. In very rough conditions, you can add additional spring lines and double up all the lines.

Figure 6-6: Spring lines help keep this boat securely cushioned by the fenders.

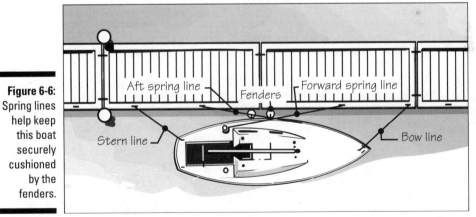

Make sure that you secure dock lines at both ends. For tying off a line on a cleat or tying off to a piling (using either a bowline knot or a clove hitch), see the nautical knots in Chapter 19.

Watch out for that tide!

As you discover in Chapter 8, most large bodies of water have *tidal flow,* thanks to the moon. When tying up your boat, use some common sense. If your boat is going to float up and down on the tide, avoid tying it to something that doesn't float, such as a piling. If you tie your boat incorrectly to a piling or fixed dock at high tide, you may come back to find your boat suspended out of the water at low tide.

If you must leave your boat tied up to a fixed piling or dock in tidal waters, add more angle (and therefore more length) to all your dock lines by tying them to points farther away than the closest part of the dock.

Getting Your Boat into the Water

As we mention at the beginning of this chapter, when you first begin to sail, you probably don't have to worry about launching the boat — the school or the boat's owner more than likely takes care of that. At some point, however, you may find yourself ready to sail, but with a boat that's high and dry. This section goes over how to launch both keelboats and dinghies in the most common situations.

Whether you're launching from a trailer or a dolly or carrying a smaller boat by hand, make sure you're aware of any power lines between the point where the mast is raised and the point where the boat is launched. Fortunately, most yacht clubs, launching areas, and marinas remove overhead power lines, but we want you to be vigilant.

Most boats stored on land have drain plugs. Leaving the drain plug out keeps rainwater from collecting in it. More than a few sailing trips have been ruined by neglecting to put the plug back in before launching, so be sure to check the plug — and note that some boats have several plugs!

Launching a trailerable sailboat

Getting your boat into the water can be an involved process — one that sometimes even includes putting up the mast. Many small keelboats (shorter than 25 feet, or 8 meters) and dinghies are *dry-sailed* — that is, you store them on dry land on a trailer or dolly. Storing a boat on dry land means less maintenance (no barnacles or weeds to scrape off the bottom) and no docking fees. Storing your boat on a trailer makes sailing in many different places quite easy. Keep in mind that objects wider than 8½ feet (2½ meters) may require extra permits to trailer on highways.

Two common methods of launching a keelboat or larger dinghy are by using a *hoist* (crane) or a trailer off a ramp.

Using a hoist or crane

Launching a boat by using a hoist or crane is easy — as long as you have someone to help, the proper lifting bridle, and a boat that weighs less than the maximum allowable weight for the crane. Follow these steps when using a hoist to launch your boat:

1. **Move the boat so that it's underneath the crane.**

   Many cranes have an arc painted on the ground to help guide you in placing your boat. Place the boat so the crane pulls the boat straight up and off the trailer. On boats with a *backstay* (a wire extending from the top of the mast to the back of the boat), you may have to swing the crane's arm over the boat as it's wheeled into place (as Figure 6-7 shows).

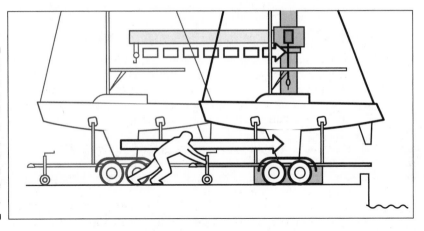

Figure 6-7:
As the trailer is pushed under the crane, swing the crane's arm past the backstay.

2. **Attach the *lifting bridle* — the wire or rope sling arrangement that balances and lifts the boat.**

   Check the lifting bridle (or other lifting device) and attachment points for wear. And never let anyone stand or walk underneath a boat on a hoist.

3. **Attach the bow and stern lines so that the boat can be rotated into position as you lower it into the water.**

4. **Have one person operate the hoist and one hold the lines.**

   Don't try to put your boat in alone; make sure that you have a buddy.

5. **Begin lifting, making sure that the mast and shrouds are clear of the crane's arm.**

   Try to keep the boat perpendicular to the arm as you swing the boat out over the water and begin lowering.

6. **When the boat is in the water, one person can unhook the lifting bridle while the other secures the bow line.**

7. **Before rigging, move the boat and trailer away so that others can use the crane.**

8. **Swing the arm back over shoreside.**

Because the greasy chain or cable from the hoist can mess up your sails (and your hands and anything else), always rig the sails after the boat is in the water and away from the crane.

Launching from a trailer off a ramp

Our two main rules for successfully launching off a ramp are

✔ **Accept that you're going to get your feet wet.**

✔ **Plan ahead.** Stop, get out of your car, and check out the ramp before you back the trailer down. Look at its angle, check for a big drop-off at the end, and plan where you want to position your trailer. Then look at the dock space. When the boat is launched, where are you going to tie up so that you can hoist the sails? How are you going to get to the dock?

When you have a good plan in mind, get in your car and go for it. Backing up a car and trailer is sort of like patting your head and rubbing your stomach at the same time — it can be difficult. Trailers are well-behaved beasts when going forward, but going backward is another story. Oversteering causes the most common malady, jackknifing the trailer. If your boat and trailer are light enough for one person to handle, carefully walk the trailer into the water. But be careful — ramps can be steep and slippery.

Follow these steps to launch your boat from a trailer on a ramp by using a car:

1. **Put the mast up.**

   See the section "Putting up a mast," later in this chapter.

2. **Position your car and trailer parallel to the ramp.**

   Going backward is much easier when you don't have to turn.

3. **Remove all the various lines and straps used to secure the boat, except for a line or cable that attaches the boat to the trailer and a bow line you'll need later to guide the boat to the dock.**

4. **Go slowly down the ramp and correct any tendency to jackknife by turning the back of your car in the same direction the back of the trailer is turning.**

   Make sure you can see or have a person outside your car help direct you.

5. **Back up until the boat is just floating off the trailer, before the wheels (or at least the brakes and wheel bearings) of your car touch the water.**

6. **Make sure that your parking brake is set before getting out of your car to disconnect the boat from the trailer.**

   Saltwater is highly corrosive (as you know from the salt put on the roads after a snowstorm), and even in freshwater, cars can't swim, so don't put your car in the water.

   If the bottom of the ramp has slimy algae, be careful! This stuff is as slippery as ice.

7. **When the boat is afloat, unhook or untie the bow from the trailer.**

   This part is where you get your feet (and maybe your legs) wet. If a dock is nearby, you may be able to take the bow line, walk around to the dock, and pull the boat to you while staying dry, but don't count on it.

   If no dock is available, you may want to consider rigging the sails (but not hoisting them) before you launch, because you probably have to climb in the boat from the water — similar to launching and sailing away from a beach, which we describe in the "Starting from the beach" section, later in this chapter.

8. **After you launch your boat and tie it to the dock, go back and move your car and trailer.**

Launching without a trailer

Dinghies are commonly dry-sailed. Because most are lighter than keelboats, you can often launch smaller dinghies off a dock or ramp or even off a beach without the need of a hoist or a trailer.

You can transport small dinghies on roof racks on top of your car. To get the boat down without damaging it, find several friends and follow these steps:

1. **Find a *dolly* (lightweight trailer for movement by hand) or padding to put the boat on.**

2. **Find enough people so that lifting the boat is easy.**

3. **Slide or lift the boat off the roof and lower it down, carefully setting the edge of the boat (at its widest point) on the padding or on the dolly, as Figure 6-8 shows.**

Never set your dinghy on the ground; you can scratch the hull.

4. **With most of the weight supported on its edge, flip the boat over in the air so that it's right-side up.**

5. **Lift and set the boat on the dolly or padded area for rigging.**

Now, depending on how you're going to launch, you can prepare the boat to go sailing. (See Chapter 4 for more about rigging.)

Figure 6-8:
As you flip your boat, always make sure to set it on padding to protect the hull.

Sliding a dinghy off a dock

Even without a dolly, you can launch lightweight dinghies off the dock — you just need the lifting skills of some friends to get the boat into position at the edge of the dock.

When you have the boat set at the side of the dock, get all the gear ready to sail (see Chapter 4) if you haven't already. Lift the boat on each side and slide it into the water (see Figure 6-9). If the dock doesn't have padding at the edge, place some padding to cushion the hull as you slide it in, or keep lifting so the boat doesn't touch the dock. Then grab the bow line and tie the boat to the dock to further rig it and hoist sails.

Any time you must lift a boat, always ask for plenty of help. Bend your legs and keep your back vertical to avoid injury.

Figure 6-9:
Lift on either side of the boat and slide it in.

If the wind is very light or is blowing from the dock toward the water, you may consider hoisting the sails before you launch, but you usually hoist the sails afterward. Just remember to put the centerboard down when you first get in the boat, or else the boat will be very tippy.

Starting from the beach

Launching off a beach is tricky unless the wind and wave conditions are really mild. Ideally, there are no waves and only a soft *offshore breeze* (wind blowing from shore to water) or *sideshore breeze* (wind blowing parallel to the shore), so sailing straight off the beach is easy.

You can rig boats in any number of ways, so don't be afraid to ask your instructor or the owner for assistance (and see Chapter 4 for how to rig a typical boat). Most beach-launched boats require one or more of these tasks to be done before putting the boat in the water:

- ✔ **Consider hoisting one or both sails while the boat is still on the beach, because hoisting them may be difficult after you launch the boat.** However, doing this makes carrying the boat into the water harder.

- ✔ **If your boat has a *kick-up* rudder (one that rotates up and out of the water), then rig it in the kicked-up position before launching.**

- ✔ **Rig the boat and store all your gear on board.**

Now you're ready to launch the boat off the beach:

1. **Grab as many people as you can and carry the boat into the water.**

   You can't avoid getting your legs wet here! Keep the bow pointed toward the wind if the sails are hoisted. If you have a dolly, you won't need a big gang to get the boat floating in shallow water.

2. **When the boat is floating in knee- to waist-deep water, have someone hold the bow while at least one crew member climbs into the boat to prepare it for sailing.**

The boat is incredibly tippy at this point, because you can't put your centerboard down very far until you're in deeper water — but do put it down partway.

3. **Hoist the sails and lower the rudder (if it's the kick-up variety) at least partway (if the water is very shallow) while someone holds on to the** *bow* **(front) of the boat.**

4. **Have the last person push the boat off on a reaching course and climb into the boat.**

You're sailing!

When you're the someone in Step 2 who is holding onto the boat in the water, keep these safety tips in mind:

- ✔ **Consider wearing shoes — there may be sharp objects underwater.**

- ✔ **If the waves are big, try to keep the boat pointed perpendicular to the waves, just like a surfboard going out through the surf.** This way, the waves have less chance of grabbing your boat and throwing it — and you — back on the beach. This task may be difficult if the sails are up.

- ✔ **In waves, never stand between the boat and shore.** Or else a wave could squish you between the boat and the beach. Always stand on the seaward side of the boat (although doing so may be difficult if the sails are hoisted).

Never leave a boat halfway in the water with the bow pulled up on the beach. Even small waves (or wakes from powerboats) can hurt the boat, or it may float away.

Returning to the beach

Coming back to the beach can be even more difficult than launching. Again, you can't avoid getting wet. Here are the basic steps to bringing a sailboat onto the beach:

1. **Luff your sails and kill your speed a long way out and approach the beach slowly, with the sails fully eased.**

You have to adjust the angle of approach to accommodate the wind direction. If the beach is dead downwind, you may have to briefly turn *head-to-wind* (away from the shore) when you get close and drop your mainsail.

2. **If the water is shallow, pull up your rudder and centerboard partway before the approach.**

3. **When you're close to shore, turn the boat head-to-wind and stop.**

4. **Have your crew jump overboard (you should be close enough to shore that they can stand on the bottom) and hold the boat's bow while you drop sails, fully pull up the centerboard, and remove or kick up the rudder.**

5. **Jump in the water and get the dolly or additional people to help carry the boat onto the beach.**

   Dragging the boat on the sand scratches the bottom, so always carry your boat.

When sailing in saltwater, whether you return from sailing to the beach or to a dock, remember to hose that salt off. For more tips on caring for your boat, see Chapter 15.

Putting up a mast

Some boats are stored with the mast up. Other boats (usually dinghies) require the crew to *step,* or put up, the mast before every sail. You can use a number of different techniques to step a mast, depending on the boat's equipment. Some masts on bigger dinghies and keelboats are so heavy that they require a crane (or some other special lifting device) to help. If this is your first time stepping the mast, make sure that you have experienced help. On smaller boats (up to about 14 feet, or 4 meters, in length), one person can usually lift the mast up and into position in the boat, but having help never hurts.

We need to say it again: If you're putting a mast up on land, first take a good look around (and up) for overhead power lines.

To get the mast from horizontal to vertical, follow these steps:

1. **Have someone push the tip of the mast upward while the base is secure against your foot or other object.**

2. **When the mast is vertical, lift it into position in the boat.**

   You may find that handing the vertical mast to someone sitting in the boat is easier.

   If you get uncomfortable, be sure to ask for help; few sounds are louder than a mast falling over into the parking lot (especially on somebody else's car)!

3. **When the mast is set into its mast step, you can begin to attach all the standing rigging *(shrouds, forestay, and backstay).***

   Often, attaching the standing rigging is a two-person job to make sure that the mast remains vertical during the process (see Figure 6-10).

Figure 6-10:
One person holds the mast while the second person secures the shrouds and forestay.

4. **As you attach the standing rigging, carefully inspect all the fittings that support the mast.**

   Tighten any shackles with pliers, and make sure that the fittings are secure. (Check out Chapter 15 on shackles and other rigging gear.)

Some small dinghies have free-standing masts without any standing rigging. On these boats, you may slide the sleeve on the mainsail luff (the front edge of the sail) over the mast before putting it up, as Figure 6-11 shows.

Figure 6-11:
Rigging a Laser sail by sliding the sleeve over the mast.

Chapter 7

Safety: One Hand for the Boat, One Hand for Yourself

> *There isn't no call to go talking of pushing and pulling. Boats are quite tricky enough for those that sit still without looking further for the cause of trouble.*
>
> —J.R.R. Tolkien

*N*ever underestimate the power of Mother Nature! When you sail on the water, you're her guest, and even on the most relaxing of sailing days, you need to respect her capacity for pure brute strength. Safety on the water comes in many forms and at many levels. On a hot summer day, reapplying sunscreen and remembering to drink enough water may be your primary concerns. If you're out in the open ocean in strong winds, being tossed about by waves that make your boat seem like a toy, the concept of safety takes on a very real meaning of survival.

Although we stress that you should *never* go sailing on a boat or in conditions that exceed your experience and comfort level, expect the unexpected any time you head out on the water. Making sure that you have the requisite skills and equipment to handle whatever happens on your sailboat is the only safe way to approach a day on the water. So in this chapter, we show you how to safely catch a tow and use your marine radio.

Having fun when you sail is easy. In this chapter, we also help you prepare for the not-so-fun situations that can arise, such as handling bad weather, recovering from a capsize, and rescuing a "man overboard" (of course, women, children, and pets can fall in and need retrieving too).

Preparing for Heavy Weather

When the "sheep are in the pasture" (whitecaps all over the water), sailing can be fun or terrifying, depending on your boat, you and your crew's level of competence, where you are, and how windy the weather really is.

Heavy weather and *heavy air* are sailors' terms for a strong breeze. As you find out in Chapter 8, sailors measure wind velocity in units called *knots* and can estimate the speed of the wind by looking at the water's surface. We recommend that a beginning sailor head for home when *whitecaps* (foamy wave crests) become commonplace, or at about 15 knots. But for an experienced sailor (especially on a high-performance dinghy or catamaran), 15 knots of wind is when sailing gets fun.

Sailing in strong winds can be addicting. You get to blast around at high speeds. Pushing your limits and conquering your fears can boost your self-confidence (and you'll sleep well that night). And when you make it back to shore, you have a new appreciation for the simple things in life — like being on dry land.

This section enables you to raise your wind threshold so that you can enjoy and stay safe on those blustery days. We concentrate on windy but sailable conditions, because they're by far the most common. Look at Chapter 14 for tips on surviving a storm, when every sailor should be on shore.

Getting ready in advance

The following list includes some important safety rules you need to remember before you head out on a windy day:

- ✔ **Don't jump too far too fast.** If your limit has been 10 knots, try 12 or 15 knots before going out when the forecast calls for gusts up to 25 knots.

- ✔ **Go out in familiar waters.** If you're in a "new" area, make sure that the wave conditions aren't excessive and that plenty of deep, open water is around. The last thing you want to worry about is going aground.

- ✔ **Go on a familiar boat.** You feel more comfortable in a boat you've sailed before.

- ✔ **Have someone with more experience than you on board.** If you're sailing a one-person dinghy, make sure that a potential rescue boat is nearby with experienced boaters watching you.

- ✔ **Put on a life jacket.** And check the safety list in Chapter 3.

We don't want to scare you from sailing in heavy weather; we just want to tell you a few reasons why you shouldn't exceed your limits. The following are a few of the potential hazards you may face:

- ✔ **The boat may become much harder to handle.** In really heavy conditions, the force of the wind and waves can throw the boat around. Being out of control isn't fun or safe.

- ✔ **You may capsize.** Practice righting your dinghy (check out "Recovering from a Capsize," later in this chapter) until it's routine. However, things can go wrong in rough and windy weather, and you may not be able to right the boat against the force of the wind.

- ✔ **You may lose someone overboard.** The bigger the waves and the more the boat is heeling in the wind, the harder it is to stay on deck. Practice the man-overboard rescue we describe in the "Rescuing a Man Overboard" section, later in this chapter. But remember that in big waves and strong winds, returning and picking up a swimmer can be very difficult.

- ✔ **Strong winds may cause gear to break.** If your boat isn't fully prepared (and sometimes even when it is), things can and do begin to blow apart as Mother Nature's forces increase. We discuss how to deal with potential accidents in Chapter 14 and boat maintenance in Chapter 15.

Preparing when you're already at sea

The wind strength and direction can change quickly, even on cloudless days. So even if you have the best intentions to follow the advice we mention earlier in this chapter to not "jump too far, too fast," chances are that someday you'll find yourself out on the water with the breeze building quickly.

When the sky starts looking ominous, your first plan should be to hurry back to the harbor. This may mean catching a tow (see the "Catching a Tow" section, later in this chapter) or firing up that engine and dropping all your sails (see "Using an engine," later). But if sailing is your only option, adjust your sail trim to reduce power (see Chapter 12) and run through the following list while making haste for home.

Getting your crew and boat ready for strong winds

When strong winds are imminent, do the following tasks right away to get your boat and crew ready:

- ✔ **Point your boat toward the closest harbor.** Ideally this harbor is your home; otherwise, remember the old saying "any port in a storm."

- ✔ **Put on life jackets and warmer clothes.** In Chapter 3, we cover your options of clothing for various conditions. The bottom line: Conditions are going to get wetter and colder, so put the warm and water-resistant clothes on now; otherwise you risk soaking your all-important interior layers of clothing.

✔ **Make sure everything is shipshape.** When the wind comes up, the boat *heels* (tips) more; if you're on a dinghy, you may even capsize. Tie down or securely stow all loose gear. On a dinghy, make sure your key equipment (such as your rudder and centerboard) is always tied into the boat. Now is the time to double-check.

✔ **Make the boat as watertight as possible.** Now is the time to "batten down the hatches." Close any windows or hatches, especially the ones up forward, where the first spray comes on board. Bail out the boat — if it's bound to get wet outside, it's nice to start out dry inside.

✔ **Review safety procedures.** It's time for a quick review of the info in this chapter. Also review the location of safety equipment (see Chapter 3 for a checklist).

✔ **Reduce your sail power.** Reducing your sail power is important because your boat will be easier and safer to handle. Check out "Reducing your sail power," later in this chapter, for more information.

Picking the right course

As the weather gets nasty, you can try to make that trip home easier by picking the safest course: a course that avoids the worst waves, the lee shore, and accidental jibes.

Getting out of the waves

Often the big problem with heavy weather isn't so much the wind but the waves. We've sailed in the Gulf Stream in waves that are so big and steep that the crew calls sailing upwind "condo-jumping," because the boat feels like it's jumping off a condominium with the passing of every wave. Because wave size (and shape) is a function of wind velocity, *fetch* (the distance of open water the wave travels during which it gains height), current, and water depth, you can sometimes plot a course that minimizes condo-jumping. Here's how:

✔ **Plot a course that makes use of the natural breakwater created by land.** For example, if you have a choice of sailing along the windward or leeward side of the island, go to leeward.

✔ **Avoid shallow water.** If you encounter big waves, you could run aground, even where the chart indicates the water is deep enough. Plus, sailing in big waves in shallow water makes for a very bumpy ride, because the waves tend to grow (and even break) as the depth decreases.

✔ **Avoid an upwind destination.** Hey, that sounds pretty simple, but it's easier said than done. If you must sail upwind in big waves, try various angles to the waves to find one that minimizes the bumps in the road.

Sailing in big waves can be fun — like off-roading, except that the road is moving. If the waves are so big that you feel them pushing your boat backward, turn a little bit toward the wave — more perpendicular to the crest just as it reaches your bow. This action minimizes the surface area that the waves can push upon, similar to a surfer paddling out through the breakers. The key when using this technique is keeping your speed — hence, steerageway — up. Bear off and regain speed as soon as your boat is on top of the wave.

Avoiding a lee shore

A *lee shore* is a shoreline to leeward of a boat toward which the wind is blowing. If the shoreline is an island, the lee shore is the island's windward shore. A very important rule of heavy-weather sailing is to avoid getting close to a lee shore. As the wind builds, you always want an escape route of open water to leeward. Then, in a worst-case scenario, you can simply drop your sails and drift until the storm abates. A lee shore forces you to sail close-hauled, the most demanding point of sail, to get away from its dangerous shallow waters and boat busting solid objects.

Watching out for accidental jibes

Accidental jibes are bad, and any jibe in strong winds can be dangerous. When the boom comes crashing to the other side, woe to the person whose head is in the way. Not only does an unintended jibe risk the safety of any crew in the path of the boom or the mainsheet, but it also can put tremendous (maybe even excessive) forces on the mast and boom. You can avoid accidental jibes with vigilant steering and by never letting the boat get near a *dead run* (with the wind straight behind you). Waves can easily throw the boat off course by 10 or even 20 degrees, so in heavy air, keep the boat on a broad reach.

Using an engine

One way to handle your boat in heavy weather is to use the engine. You may even drop all sails and just use the engine alone. You may want to consider using an engine only when you must head on an upwind course. Otherwise, sailing is probably faster and easier on the boat and crew. If you have a reliable engine that's easy to use, consider these pointers before you use the engine in heavy weather:

- ✔ **Consider motorsailing.** When your destination is to windward, the best tactic may be *motorsailing,* in which you keep up a reefed mainsail or small jib and use the motor at the same time. Motorsailing still provides some power from the sail. Plus, if your engine fails, doesn't have enough horsepower, or runs out of gas, the last thing you want to do is try to hoist the sails while wallowing about.

- ✔ **Don't let the boat heel too far.** If you motorsail, the heeling force of the wind may cause the boat to heel so much that the cooling-water intake comes out of the water, which causes the engine to overheat. Other systems on the engine may not like excessive heel either — keep an eye on the engine's vital signs, including the temperature dial and the cooling water coming out of the exhaust.

✔ **Make sure all lines are out of the water before starting your engine.**
And keep those lines out of the water; nothing ruins your day faster than
having a jib sheet or halyard tail get wrapped up in a propeller. For tips
on solving that mishap, see Chapter 14.

Reducing your sail power

The force of the wind increases by the square of the velocity, which means
that at 14 knots, the wind force on your rigging and sails is double the load
on the boat at 10 knots. And that's before you add in the effect of the waves.
Sailboats and their component parts can only stand so much load before
they begin to break. And as we point out earlier in this section, stronger
winds make your boat and sails more difficult to handle. As the wind speed
increases, anything you do to reduce the forces on the boat in strong winds
can make a big difference.

The first way to reduce the load is to depower your sails. We cover that subject in depth in Chapter 12. The next step is to reduce the boat's sail area, or
to *shorten sail*. You can shorten sail in three ways: by dropping a sail, reefing
a sail, or changing to a smaller sail. All three methods have their pros and
cons, depending on the boat and the conditions.

Dropping a sail

Dropping a sail is a pretty extreme tactic on a catboat (which has only one
sail), but sailors commonly use this tactic on sloops of all sizes. Should you
drop the mainsail or the jib? The answer depends on the boat and the conditions. Dropping the jib and sailing with the mainsail alone is appropriate
under the following conditions:

✔ **When the jib is very large.** Dropping a *genoa* (large, overlapping jib) sig-
nificantly decreases your sail power.

✔ **When the boat handles well with the mainsail alone.** For more on boat
balance, see Appendix C.

✔ **When your boat has a roller furler (see Chapter 4).** Rolling the jib partway is really easy; see whether that setting works, and then roll it up all
the way if necessary. Do this as an interim step as the wind builds, and
then plan what your next move is going to be.

Sometimes, however, dropping the mainsail and sailing with the jib alone is
appropriate, as in the following situations:

✔ On dinghies that are rigged in such a manner that dropping the jib
causes the standing rigging to loosen dramatically.

✔ On many boats, the jib has less area than the main, so in extreme conditions, such as squalls, dropping the mainsail may be better because the
reduction in sail area (and thus load on the boat) is more dramatic.

As you lower either sail, keep it under control, bunched up so that it doesn't blow around, until it can either be stuffed down below deck or lashed down on deck securely with ropes so that it can't flog about.

If you must send the crew to the foredeck for a sail change in rough seas, turn the boat onto a very broad reach or run (no accidental jibes, please) to reduce heel. Then everyone on deck can move around on a relatively flat surface. Of course, if your destination is upwind, you'll be going away from it at a pretty fast clip.

Turning downwind can also steady the boat's motion to enable a crew member to work up the mast. Once when I was skippering *Courageous,* Ted Turner's famous 12-Meter in Perth, Australia, the mainsail got stuck at the top of the mast — the crew couldn't lower it. We had to send a crew member 90 feet up in the air to fix the problem. The wind was blowing 28 knots, and the waves were steep and choppy. We knew that he couldn't fix the problem and brace himself from the pounding on an upwind course — the length of the mast accentuated the boat's motion too much. So I had to turn downwind to level the boat and smooth out the ride. Still, he needed nearly 25 minutes to solve the problem; by then we were almost 4 miles farther from home. But at least he was safe!

Reefing

Reefing is a system of reducing a sail's exposed area. Reefing a mainsail requires special equipment on the mainsail and boom. You can reef some jibs by rolling the sail up partway on a roller furler. Most dinghies and many small keelboats don't have the special equipment to reef. When reefing is an option, you perform it as an intermediate step (as the wind becomes stronger) before dropping a sail. An old saying is still as valuable today as it was in the days of the square riggers: "When in doubt . . . reef 'er."

If your sails can be reefed, make sure to rig the lines and equipment used to reef the sails as soon as the breeze starts to pick up or, even better, before you leave the dock if any chance exists that you'll need to reef.

Reefing the mainsail

Reefing the mainsail entails lowering it partway and attaching it by a "new" tack and clew. The reefing system we discuss here is also called *slab, tie-in,* or *jiffy reefing.* Here are the key components, some of which appear in Figure 7-1:

- ✔ **Boom lift:** Also called a *topping lift,* this line or wire holds the boom horizontal when the mainsail is partially lowered. Some boats employ a solid boom vang to keep the boom up instead.
- ✔ **Reefing line:** This strong line is led through a system of pulleys to the back of the boom and up the mainsail leech to the heavily reinforced *clew cringle* (the aft-most reef point).
- ✔ **Reef points:** The mainsail usually has one or more horizontal rows of these reinforced holes built in.

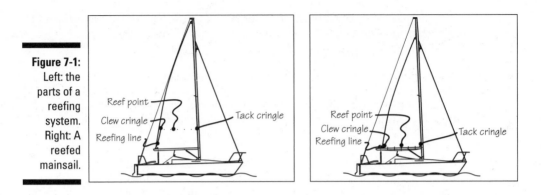

Figure 7-1:
Left: the
parts of a
reefing
system.
Right: A
reefed
mainsail.

Some boats also have a *tack horn,* a strong metal hook, or other means of securing the *tack cringle* (the forward-most reef point) near the gooseneck.

To reef a mainsail, follow these steps:

1. **Ensure that the reef line is properly rigged.**

   Perform this step before you set sail. Feeding the reef line through the clew cringle after the mainsail is hoisted can be difficult.

2. **Have the helmsman steer a steady course.**

   Close-hauled or close-reaching is preferable because the mainsail drops more easily.

3. **Take the slack out of the boom lift and *cleat* it (tie it off securely).**

   This action keeps the boom from falling into the cockpit and causing all sorts of mayhem when you lower the mainsail. If your boat has a solid vang that supports the boom, you can skip this step.

4. **Ease the boom vang and mainsheet until the main is fully luffing.**

   The main should luff throughout the reefing procedure to reduce the pressure on the sail so that you can lower and reef it easily. If possible, conduct all reefing activities from the windward side to minimize the danger of getting hit by the swinging boom.

5. **Partially lower the main halyard — slowly.**

   Gather the dropping luff until the person standing at the mast can secure the tack cringle into the tack horn (or alternate arrangement near the gooseneck) to effectively create a "new" tack for the sail.

6. **Rehoist and tension the main halyard.**

   Feed the luff carefully into the mast and tension it very tightly.

7. **Tension the reef line and cleat it securely.**

   On a boat longer than 20 feet (6 meters) or so, the reef line needs a winch to get sufficient tension. The reef line should pull the "new" clew cringle down to within an inch or two of the boom and aft toward the end of the boom.

8. **Trim the mainsheet to fill the sail and ease the boom lift.**

9. **Tie up the middle of the lowered sailcloth.**

   This step is optional, but it aids in your visibility and makes the boat look neater. We recommend using bungee cord to lace up the middle reef points. Then if the reef line breaks or slips, the sail doesn't shred.

You can see a properly reefed main in Figure 7-2.

Some mainsails have more than one set of reef points. Which set you use is determined by how small you want your mainsail to be. The first step down in size is the *first reef;* the next step down is the *second reef.* Very few mainsails have more than two sets of reef points, unless they're designed for extreme ocean sailing.

Figure 7-2:
Properly
reefed
mains on a
fleet of
Volvo Open
70s.

© Oskar Kihlborg/ Volvo Ocean Race

Reefing the jib

Occasionally, you may find a jib with reef points, just like a mainsail. The most common (and easiest) way of reefing the jib is with a roller furler, but as the sail rolls up, it loses its designed shape. (In Chapter 12, we discuss the importance of sail shape.) So the only racing boats that rely on a roller furler for reefing are the shorthanded round-the-world boats — no one in his or her right mind wants to go up to the bow and change jibs or wrestle a sail back on board when alone in a 60-knot storm in the Southern Ocean.

Changing down

Another way to reduce sail area is to switch to a smaller jib, if your boat has more than one. Most dinghies and small keelboats come equipped with only one jib. But as keelboats increase in size (longer than 25 feet, or 8 meters), many of them have an extra sailbag or two in the cabin. These bags (and the corners of the sails in them) should be clearly marked. On a large race boat, generally, jibs are numbered 1 through 4, with No. 1 for light air and No. 4 for heavy air. The process for changing a jib while under way can be as easy or as difficult as you make it. Here's the easy way:

1. **Turn the boat downwind onto a very broad reach to flatten the boat and make moving around on the foredeck easier for the crew.**

2. **Lower the old, bigger jib and fold it (check out Chapter 15).**

    Bag it and put it down in the cabin.

3. **Rig the new, smaller jib (refer to Chapter 4).**

4. **Hoist the new jib.**

    Crank the halyard good and tight.

5. **Bring the crew back into the safety of the cockpit and then turn onto your desired course, trimming the sheet accordingly.**

For most sailors, sail changes are few and far between. A corollary of the "when in doubt, reef 'er" policy is to err on the side of putting up too small a jib initially — especially in a building breeze.

When reducing sail, reducing too much sail is okay and considered prudent seamanship. Even if you *can* sail the boat in the present conditions with a double-reefed main and a small jib, deciding to lower the mainsail and sail in to shore at half-speed under jib alone is perfectly all right.

Recovering from a Capsize

The main safety concern on a dinghy is *capsizing,* or having the boat flip over. If you're sailing a keelboat, you can skip right to the section "Staying on Board," because that lead keel keeps you from capsizing. For you dinghy sailors, capsizing can be a nuisance, but don't fear it — it can also be fun and should be part of every sailor's introductory dinghy-sailing lesson. Given proper preparation and practice, you can easily handle a capsize.

When the boat flips upside down, all the loose gear in the boat floats away (or sinks), so always make sure that everything is well stowed or tied into the boat — including the daggerboard and rudder.

Centerboard boats fall into two categories with respect to capsizing:

- ✔ Those that the crew can right by themselves *(self-righting)*
- ✔ Those that *swamp,* or fill up with water, and may require outside assistance

The difference is in the design of the boat and whether it has sealed flotation tanks. All modern dinghies are designed to be self-righting — assuming that you drained the flotation tanks and the hull before sailing and made sure that all drain holes were plugged before sailing. Avoid sailing in a boat that swamps when no rescue powerboat is available. Catamarans don't swamp, but they can be tricky to get upright. For tips on getting a catamaran up after a capsize, see Chapter 11.

The anatomy of a capsize

A boat can capsize while sailing by tipping over to leeward or to windward. A leeward capsize is common in strong or puffy winds, where the boat simply heels too much and blows over, as Figure 7-3 shows. A windward capsize, also called a *death roll,* can occur in strong winds when you're sailing downwind. The boat just starts rolling back and forth until, finally — *crash!* Sounds ominous, but you're just going to get wet.

Righting the boat

When sailing a dinghy, the question isn't *if* you're going to capsize but *when.* After you capsize, the sooner you start righting the boat, the quicker and easier the recovery. If you dally, the boat may keep rolling until the mast is straight down. This position is called *turning turtle,* because the hull of the boat looks like a turtle shell. Righting a boat that has turtled is much harder than righting one that's on its side. So the minute you capsize, you need to quickly hustle through the following steps (shown in Figure 7-4):

1. **Ensure that your crew is safe and happy (well, relatively).**

2. **Get weight on the centerboard as quickly as possible, either by climbing over the high side or swimming around.**

   Don't delay, or you may risk making the boat turn turtle.

3. **Make sure that all sheets are uncleated and loose.**

   If you don't loosen the sheets, the sails fill as you right the boat, and you'll probably capsize again. You can lean over the hull to watch and talk to the crew, who should be swimming in the water while performing this step and then waiting in the water to climb aboard (see the next step).

4. **While standing on the centerboard, pull on the *rail* (edge) of the boat and pump your weight to get the mast to come out of the water.**

   By holding onto the hiking straps in the cockpit, your crew can get scooped into the boat as it comes upright. Having their weight in the boat as it comes up also helps prevent capsizing again immediately (a very common occurrence, especially if the mast is to windward).

5. **When you're upright, help each other on board while the sails luff.**

Figure 7-3:
Capsizing to leeward (top) and to windward (bottom) — the death roll.

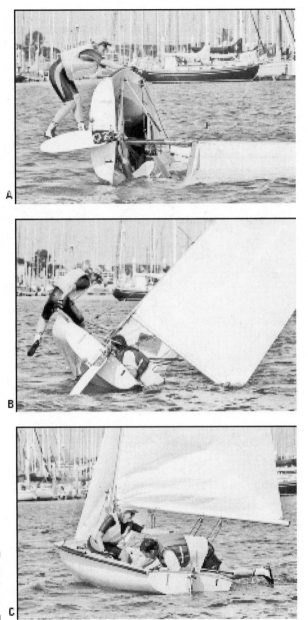

Figure 7-4:
Getting your
boat upright.

Always get all your crew on board the boat as soon as you're upright. Just let
the sails luff; you can worry about getting going again after everyone is safe
and you check over the boat.

Sometimes, especially in wavy conditions, righting the boat is difficult
because the waves keep trying to turtle the boat. One very effective technique

of righting the boat under these conditions is to have the swimming crew hold onto the bow. The boat naturally drifts with the wind until the bow points directly upwind. With this technique, the crew keeps holding onto the bow until the boat is upright.

If you can't pull the boat upright by yourself, get the crew to provide more righting force by climbing up on the centerboard and leaning out together, as Figure 7-5 shows.

Figure 7-5:
Crew members pulling the turtled boat upright.

Rescuing a swamped boat

Dinghies that swamp are much more time consuming to get sailing again, and doing so probably requires outside assistance. So never sail a boat that swamps without other boats around, and always make sure that you have a good bucket, or *bailer,* or two aboard in case you flip. Tie in these bailers so that you don't lose them when the boat rolls.

If you capsize in a swamper, you must first uncleat the sheets and bring the boat upright by pulling on the centerboard. Then climb into the boat over the transom so that the boat doesn't capsize again, and start bailing like mad. If you're fast and you keep the boat upright, you can usually slowly gain on the flood waters and get the boat dry. But be forewarned: A boat half filled with water is very unstable and can flip again easily.

A much easier way to bail out the water is a quick tow from a motorboat. A motorboat with a well-secured tow rope can slowly pull the boat so that the water flows out over the transom. Keep your weight low and in the transom. Soon the water level will be down to a level that you can bail out with your bucket. Some dinghies have cockpit self-bailers that you can open to help drain the water, but they only work if the boat is moving.

If you capsize and can't right the boat, or you find yourself in the water with your boat swamped, *stay with the boat.* The boat is like a huge life ring, and you're much safer with the boat than without it. If the boat has turtled, try to get out of the water by sitting on the overturned hull and wait for help. If you're in the water tangled in lines, stay calm and untangle yourself.

Staying on Board

If you sail long enough, you're probably going to fall overboard sometime. (We both have!) Rule No. 1 for staying on board is to *hold on.* The old saying "one hand for the boat, one hand for yourself" is just as true today as in the days of square riggers. You're responsible for your own safety first, and you never know when a wave or a gust of wind is going to take away your footing.

Here's a basic rule that hopefully scares you into holding on for (shall we say) dear life. The U.S. Coast Guard calls it the 50-50-50 rule — if you're in 50-degree Fahrenheit (10-degree Celsius) water for 50 minutes, you have a 50 percent chance of survival. You lose body heat quickly in cool water, and as the body cools, its functions shut down. The medical term for loss of body heat is *hypothermia,* and it can occur even in 70-degree Fahrenheit (21-degree Celsius) or warmer water. See Appendix B for tips on treating hypothermia.

In order to stay on board, keep the following tips in mind:

✔ **Hold on.** Remember, "One hand for the boat, one hand for yourself."

✔ **Consider safety when deciding where to sit.** The cockpit (if you stay below the path of the boom) is usually one of the safest places. For a review of the danger areas on a boat, see Chapter 4.

✔ **Be ready for anything.** Wind and waves can toss a boat about in any direction, or a boat can come to an abrupt stop if it runs aground.

✔ **Bend your knees for better balance if you must stand.** Doing so lowers your center of gravity and lets your legs act as shock absorbers.

✔ **When moving from the cockpit to the mast or foredeck (or vice versa), take the path along the windward side.** The lifelines or some other solid object, such as a handrail or the shrouds, provide extra support so you adhere to rule No. 1 mentioned earlier in this section.

Lifelines need regular inspection for rust and wear. Relying on a lifeline is convenient but can be risky if they aren't well maintained. If the water is really wavy and rough, use a solid object inboard of the rail for support.

✔ **Never hold onto *running rigging* (lines used to trim sails), whether it's in use or not.** If the line is let out, you lose your hand hold and your balance (and in the worst case, your hand could get sucked into a block).

✔ **Sit down with your feet braced.** This is the best position to work when out of the cockpit (that is, on the foredeck). If the water is too rough to walk around on the deck, you can crawl or even slide on your bottom to move around safely. And if conditions are that rough, definitely wear a life jacket and possibly a safety harness (see Chapters 3 and 14).

✔ **Wear nonskid shoes to provide traction.** However, even with the best shoes, decks can be slippery.

✔ **If you're steering and want to tack or jibe, make sure the rest of the crew is ready for the maneuver before turning the boat.** In strong winds, hearing someone can be difficult if you're at the other end of the boat.

Rescuing a Man Overboard

Obviously, men, women, and children fall overboard, but "man overboard" is the hail that most people remember from the old movies, and it's still the standard hail when someone goes into the drink.

We know that all this talk about falling overboard must sound melodramatic, but going for an unexpected swim is probably the biggest danger facing the sailor. You and your crew need to prepare to deal with such a situation *before* it happens. Waiting until someone is actually in the water is too late.

Avoiding this situation by staying on board is the best advice. Wearing a life jacket can help you if you fall overboard, but the key to your rescue is how the rest of the crew on the boat responds.

Successfully retrieving someone from the water involves four key steps. The following sections discuss each step of a man-overboard drill in detail. The steps assume you're sailing a larger keelboat, but most of the principles apply equally well on any boat.

Each of these steps requires practice so that the crew works together to complete them automatically in an emergency. You and your crew can practice by retrieving a hat. If you get sunburned in the time you take to get your hat back, you probably need more practice (and more sunscreen). For someone heading offshore, we recommend taking the Cruising World or U.S. Sailing "Safety at Sea" courses. You can find courses in your area at your local marine store or www.ussailing.org. For a great review, rent or buy the Annapolis Book of Seamanship series "Safety at Sea" video.

Step 1: Keep the swimmer in sight

If you see someone fall overboard, yell to alert the rest of the crew to the emergency, but don't take your eyes off that person. You're now the designated spotter. If for some reason, you can't perform that job (say, you're driving), make sure that someone else is spotting before you take your eyes off the swimmer. If you lose sight of the person, finding him again in the shadows and reflections of the waves can be very difficult. While you're watching, try to reassure the swimmer by shouting encouragement like, "I see you. We're stopping the boat; don't try to swim to us — we'll be right there." Pointing at the person helps, too (in case you momentarily get distracted). Tell the helmsman how far away and in what direction the swimmer is located. Make sure you tell the helmsman every few seconds using clear terms such as, "three boat lengths, off the starboard quarter."

Many bigger boats carry *Global Positioning System (GPS)* navigation units. If someone is near the GPS when a person falls overboard (many boats have a waterproof unit right on deck), that person should immediately punch the button that saves the present location. Many GPS units have a special *man-overboard button,* which you can push to save the location of the swimmer. The GPS then shifts modes to help you navigate your way back to the victim. For more information on using a GPS, see Chapter 9.

Step 2: Throw the swimmer the life ring

Quickly getting the life ring or other Type IV personal flotation aid to the swimmer so that he can easily stay afloat is crucial (check out Chapter 3 for more on the specific types of flotation devices). If you've gone swimming fully clothed, you know how hard treading water can be, and doing so is even harder in big waves. Often, these life rings have a flag that makes keeping the swimmer in sight easier. Survival Technologies' "Man Overboard Module" (MOM) products have an inflatable life ring, flag, light, and sea anchor all contained in a small package that easily mounts on the lifelines.

Aim your throw slightly upwind of the swimmer so that the float drifts to him. Also, you can probably throw the life ring farther by throwing underhand.

If you're the only person on deck, you must throw the swimmer the life ring while you keep him in sight — another reason why the life ring and safety gear need to be within easy reach.

Even at the relatively slow boat speeds of 4 or 5 knots, every second moves the boat away from the swimmer. If the safety gear isn't readily at hand, launching a nonthrowable personal flotation device or nearly anything with lots of flotation is better than waiting until you're too far away to get something within easy reach of the swimmer.

Step 3: Stop the boat

Stop the boat immediately (as soon as practical) to minimize the distance to the swimmer. Some sailing books and schools teach a time-honored man-overboard procedure called the *figure-eight method* (shown in Figure 7-6), where the boat sails away from the swimmer on a *reach* and then tacks and reaches back to perform the rescue. The best angle to return to the swimmer is a close reach (with the wind forward of 90 degrees). Although this system gives the crew time to calm down and line up for a good approach angle (close reach) back to the swimmer, this system has two shortcomings: the distance you have to sail away and the difficulty for inexperienced crews to judge the proper angle of return and speed of approach.

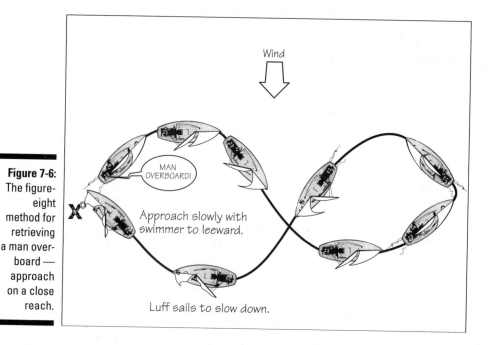

Figure 7-6: The figure-eight method for retrieving a man overboard — approach on a close reach.

Wind

MAN OVERBOARD!

Approach slowly with swimmer to leeward.

Luff sails to slow down.

Another rescue technique, called the *Quick-Stop method,* could be called *Man Overboard For Dummies,* as Figure 7-7 shows. It's an effective technique, even for inexperienced crews, because you just leave the jib cleated and the main luffing. The biggest advantage of the Quick-Stop method is that it keeps the boat closer to the person in the water so that you can keep him in sight more easily — and (hopefully) rescue him more quickly.

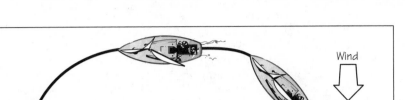

Figure 7-7:
The Quick-
Stop
method for
rescuing
a man
overboard.

Wind

③ Drop jib while
bearing away.

② Immediately
tack and
back jib.

MAN
OVERBOARD!

④ Approach slowly with
swimmer to leeward.

If you have only a main and jib set, here's the procedure for a Quick-Stop rescue:

1. **Yell "man overboard," throw the life ring, and keep the swimmer in sight.**

2. **Immediately tack the boat, leaving the jib sheet cleated so that it backs (fills on the back side).**

   The backed jib helps pull the boat around onto the new tack. See Chapter 5 to brush up on basic sailing skills.

3. **If you have sufficient crew, drop the jib while bearing away so you have one less sail to deal with during the recovery.**

4. **Approach the swimmer slowly, using the mainsail to control your speed.**

5. **Try to stop the boat to windward of the swimmer.**

   The wind blows your boat toward the swimmer, and you can pull the swimmer aboard more easily on the leeward side.

6. **Pull the swimmer aboard.**

   When the spinnaker is set (or any time you're sailing downwind when there is a man overboard), the Quick-Stop method may seem a bit extreme, but on most boats it's still considered the best way to go. The crew eases the spinnaker sheet immediately, and then the helmsman swiftly spins the boat toward the wind, collapsing the spinnaker and then the crew drops it to the deck — the sooner after the splash the better. But the advantage of the Quick-Stop method remains constant — you stay near the swimmer. We strongly recommend practicing this technique with the crew first, because you need teamwork to get the spinnaker cleanly and swiftly stowed away so the boat is ready to make the recovery. The danger in this situation is that the boat travels so far downwind that it's difficult to sail back upwind to the swimmer with just the mainsail set — hence the importance of practice (and the usefulness of an engine).

You can also use the boat's engine, if you have one, to get back to the swimmer more quickly. Just make sure that you pull all lines out of the water before starting the motor, because getting a line wrapped around your propeller stops the engine. When you get close enough to the swimmer to pull him back on board, put the engine in neutral so as not to endanger him with the propeller.

Regardless of the technique you use, practice the man-overboard procedure. These man-overboard routines are designed for larger keelboats, but if you're sailing on a dinghy or small keelboat and drop someone overboard, the general principles still apply. You may not have a life ring to throw to the victim, so getting back to him quickly is crucial.

Step 4: Get the swimmer back on board

In some cases, the swimmer is able to climb aboard and is more embarrassed than anything else. Many times, though, getting the swimmer back on board can be the most difficult part of a rescue, especially if he is injured. You don't want the swimmer to get overly tired trying to swim back to the boat, so always plan on coming to him. Approach the swimmer so that he is to leeward of the boat. This way, if you're a little too cautious (which is better than being a little too daring) and end up too far windward (upwind), the boat simply blows down to the swimmer. Plus, tossing the swimmer a line is easier when you're throwing downwind.

When the swimmer is within range, throw him a rope (preferably with yet another flotation aid attached). After you get him alongside, you probably need a group effort to heft him aboard, grabbing him under the armpits for the big pull. Of course, if you suspect that this lifting motion may aggravate an injury, you may have to get creative to make the retrieval as easy as possible on the swimmer.

Improved man-overboard equipment is constantly being tried and evaluated. One of the best items is the *Lifesling* (a trademarked name for a floating horseshoe-like collar with a polypropylene "tow" line attached). By driving in a circle around the swimmer, towing the Lifesling, you make grabbing hold of the Lifesling easy for him (similar to a fallen water skier grabbing the ski rope — but please keep the speed slow!). The swimmer can put the collar under his arms to facilitate lifting him aboard. If you don't have a Lifesling, you can improvise by tying a large bowline in a loop and throwing that line in the water. The swimmer puts the loop under his armpits, and you can winch him up to the boat or even on deck if you run the take-up line to a halyard. Or you can tie a loop in a line, and the swimmer can use the cleated line as a step up. Then you can haul him on board.

If the swimmer is unconscious or is having trouble staying afloat, you may have to send someone into the water to help with the rescue. But don't double your trouble. Before anyone else jumps in the water, make sure that the second person has adequate flotation and, if practical, a line securing him to the boat.

One good reason to practice man-overboard drills and discuss them with your crew is to decide in advance the best place to get back on board your boat. Don't use the back end *(transom)* of the boat in any kind of rough seas — as the boat bobs in the waves, the transom slams into the water and can seriously injure a swimmer.

Staying Calm If You Fall Overboard

If you fall off a boat, your first reaction may be anger and embarrassment. But you need to stay calm and focused to maximize your rescue chances. We have a friend whose boat sank off the Carolina coast nearly 100 miles offshore. He survived nearly 24 hours afloat, but other crew members didn't. He credits his good fortune to his attitude and mental state. In case you go overboard, even for a few minutes, this section contains some important survival tips.

Conserve energy

The biggest mistake that people make when they fall overboard is exhausting themselves by trying to swim back to the boat. Unless you can *easily* reach a nearby boat, person, or floating object (like a Type IV life ring), try to conserve energy rather than expend it. Swimming toward the wind and waves is very difficult.

Maximize buoyancy

Your first priority, if a floating object is nearby (hopefully the Type IV life ring thrown by your crew), is to swim to it and hold on. Some boating reference books say that your clothing won't affect your buoyancy in the water, and clothing certainly helps keep you warm. But we've seen T-shirts sink in the water, and certain clothing (especially footwear) severely restricts your ability to swim or tread water. So you may want to kick off your shoes and excess clothing. Discard any heavy objects — with the exception of a knife, in case you need to cut away lines, and a waterproof flashlight, for signaling rescuers. A swimming lifesaving course (check with your local YMCA or Red Cross) can provide excellent information on staying afloat.

You can trap air in your jacket or foul-weather pants to help you float. By sealing all but one opening of a waterproof piece of clothing and then holding the one opening wide to catch air, you can turn this gear into a (leaky) balloon that can help provide support.

The first time I ever sailed at night on the ocean was a thrilling but also somewhat scary experience. Because I was worried about falling overboard, I put a waterproof pocket-sized strobe light in my pocket. That way, if I did go overboard, my team would have a better chance of finding me. Even today, I never sail at night without at least a flashlight in my pocket. My friend Cam Lewis, who has raced twice around the world on big high-speed catamarans, has his own pocket EPIRB (an emergency radio beacon that sends an SOS signal out to satellites and airplanes) that he carries in his pocket. (Check out Chapter 14 for more info on EPIRBs.)

Conserve body heat

Because hypothermia is a very real threat, even in moderately cool water, conserving body heat is important. Here are some tips for staying warm:

- ✔ **Get as much of your body out of the water as possible.** At the least, keep your head out of the water.

- ✔ **If you're in the water with other people, huddle together to keep warm.** Huddling also helps keep everyone thinking positively.

- ✔ **Keep your body in a compact shape.** A very compacted shape is the fetal position, also called the "Heat Escape Lessening Position" (HELP). With a life jacket on, you can usually stay in the HELP position with your head out of the water. If this position brings your head under water, try keeping your arms and legs together to conserve as much warmth as you can.

- ✔ **Tighten your life jacket.** A snug fit helps keep you warm.

In Appendix B, we cover basic first aid afloat, including ways to warm hypothermia victims.

Catching a Tow

At some point in your sailing career, you'll probably be forced to accept a tow from a powerboat. But any time you put your boat's fate in the hands of another boater (which is the case in a tow), you take a risk. In order to make your towing experiences as carefree as possible, read the following tips:

- **Don't take a tow unless you need one.**

- **Use a good rope.** An anchor line is an ideal tow line because it's long, strong, and stretchy — all good things for towing. (For more about lines, see Chapter 15.)

- **Attach your tow line securely.** If the loads are moderate (you aren't in heavy weather and you're not aground), tie your tow line to a secure object. The mast is usually best. Tie it as low as possible around the mast, just above the cabin top or deck. If you're concerned about stress and expect extreme loads on the tow line, you can spread the load on the tow line to several places, such as the mast and two cockpit winches, as Figure 7-8 shows. Make sure that the rope isn't chafing anywhere.

- **Use good knots.** Two (or three) round turns around the mast secured with two half hitches are the best. See Chapter 19 for how to tie that knot.

- **Make sure the boat and crew are ready before speeding up.** Ask the tow boat captain not to accelerate until he or she sees a "thumbs up" from you — and then, he or she should increase speed slowly until you give an "okay" sign.

- **Make sure you can get free in a hurry.** If the powerboat captain is a yahoo, you want to be able to free your boat quickly. A sharp knife works (on the line, that is, not on the yahoo). You may be able to untie the round turns and half hitches in a hurry, even when they're under load. So don't use a bowline knot; you won't be able to free it easily.

- **Stay away from the tow line.** The line can break and whip back.

- **Don't tow too fast.** Arrange a comfortable speed with the tow boat ahead of time and fine-tune that speed with hand signals if necessary.

- **Slow down in waves.** Big waves can add tremendous load, so watch for ones that can surprise you, such as the wake of a ship. If practical, the tow boat should slow down and turn toward the wake to minimize its effect on your boat.

- **Adjust the length of the rope to go downhill.** When you get to a comfortable towing speed, you may want to extend the tow rope to its maximum length to make it easier to steer your boat and to let the stretchy tow rope cushion your ride. Fine-tune the rope's length so your bow is pointed downhill, riding on the towing boat's wake, which remains a constant distance from you. This little trick really eases the load on the tow line. In most cases, the longer the tow rope, the better (at least two to three of your boat lengths). The only exception is in confined places where tight maneuvering requires a shorter tow line (and slower tow speed).

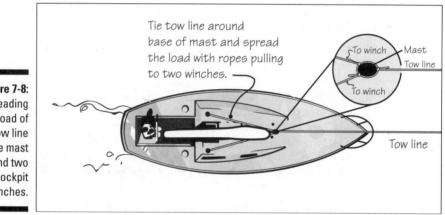

Tie tow line around base of mast and spread the load with ropes pulling to two winches.

To winch — Mast

Tow line

To winch

Tow line

Figure 7-8:
Spreading the load of the tow line to the mast and two cockpit winches.

Communicating via the VHF Radio

Our safety chapter wouldn't be complete without a discussion of how to call for help. You probably want to go sailing to get away from phone calls, faxes, and e-mails, but in an emergency, a communication link can be vital. For coastal sailing, a cellular phone may be your best communication device if it has the range to connect you to shore. But for safety, we strongly recommend that you use a Very High Frequency (VHF) radio because the U.S. Coast Guard and many other boats constantly monitor the VHF (on Channel 16).

VHF radios are simply two-way radios. With a VHF radio, you can get in touch with the USCG, talk to friends on other boats, listen to marine weather reports, and even talk to marinas and yacht clubs to inquire about slip space for your boat. The radio's range depends on the power of the unit and the height of the antenna. A hand-held model has a range of a few miles; a 25-watt VHF radio attached to a masthead antenna on a 40-foot (12-meter) mast has a range of roughly 10 miles. Put a hand-held radio in a waterproof bag to keep it dry, and for extended sails, make sure that you have a supply of charged batteries.

You don't need to register a marine VHF used on a recreational boat in U.S. waters. But a U.S. recreational sailboat traveling elsewhere must register the radio and obtain a user license, called an "FRN," or FCC Registration Number, from the FCC (http://wireless.fcc.gov).

Talking on your VHF

Two people can't talk at once on a VHF radio, so finish your transmission by saying "over," let go of the talk button, and listen for a response. Normal transmissions should not last for more than about 30 seconds.

Here are the common types of radio communications:

- **Radio check:** Once or twice a year and before a major trip, check your radio by tuning to Channel 16 and calling "Any vessel, any vessel. This is the yacht Babbalubba, calling for a radio check. Over." Don't waste the USCG's time with a radio-check request.

- **Ship to ship:** For safety and by law in the United States, every vessel operating a VHF radio must monitor Channel 16 — so when afloat, have your VHF tuned to Channel 16. Doing so makes good sense because, by all listening to Channel 16, everyone can help each other as needed. For general communications, the normal protocol is to first call the other boat on Channel 16 and then switch to another channel as soon as you make contact. Remember, Channel 16 isn't for chatter; make contact with the other boat and then switch to another channel. Channels 9, 68, 69, 71, 72, and 78 are approved for "intership" communication. You can surf to `http://wireless.fcc.gov/marine/vhfchan1.html` for a full list of VHF frequencies and their designated use.

- **Ship to marine telephone operator:** Yes, you can connect to a real telephone by calling the marine operators on Channels 24 through 28 and 84 through 87. They instruct you to switch channels after you make contact. You can call collect or charge your call to your home phone number, but, obviously, we don't recommend giving your credit card number over the radio.

- **Ship to USCG — EMERGENCY:** The Emergency Channel for contacting the USCG is Channel 16. See the next section for the proper procedure during an emergency. Channel 6 is also used for safety and emergency communication, mostly between Coast Guard boats and planes used in rescue operations, but if you're in trouble, make your primary contact with the USCG on Channel 16, and you'll be instructed if they want you to switch.

- **Weather information:** In the United States, marine weather forecasts and warnings are transmitted on special VHF weather channels. Check the radio's instruction book to find out how to tune to those channels, or look for a button that says *Wx*.

Using Channel 16 in emergencies

If you need to make an emergency call on Channel 16 (or SSB Channel 2182, which we discuss later in this section), follow these steps:

1. **If your radio has an alarm signal, press it for 30 seconds (if not, proceed to Step 2).**

2. **Say "Mayday" three times and give the name of your boat three times and your VHF call sign (if you have one) one time.**

    Then repeat "Mayday" and your boat's name once.

    If you need help, but the situation isn't an emergency (for example, you require medical assistance but not emergency evacuation), start your message by saying "Pan-Pan" (pronounced "Pahn-Pahn") three times and then continue with the information we describe in the preceding steps.

3. **Give your location, either by the distance from an object on the chart (for example, "2 miles east of buoy three") or by latitude and longitude.**

4. **Explain your situation as briefly as possible, such as "Swamped and taking on water, in need of tow or rescue."**

5. **Tell how many people are on board.**

6. **Describe the boat's type, color, and any distinguishing features ("30-foot dark red ketch with main and jib hoisted") followed by "over."**

7. **After listening for a short period, repeat these steps until someone responds.**

If you hear a mayday distress call, figure out whether you're close enough to help by writing down the information and computing your distance. If you can help, speak on the radio directly to the boat in distress and give your estimated arrival time. If you can't help, stay off the radio.

If your boat has a VHF, turn it on and keep it tuned to Channel 16, because you never know when you may be able to help somebody else in trouble.

Using SSB and satellite radio

If you're sailing farther offshore (out of VHF range to the shore), you want to have a Single Side Band (SSB) radio. When properly installed and with a well-tuned antenna, you can communicate for thousands of miles to other radios on land and on shore. And with the addition of a modem, you can use the SSB to do very low bandwidth e-mail communication. The worldwide distress frequency for SSB is 2182 kHz. See www.navcen.uscg.gov/marcomms/high_frequency for more information on SSB frequencies. You must register an SSB with the FCC. A marine electronics store can help you, or surf to http://wireless.fcc.gov/uls.

The military alphabet for use on the marine radio

When I was a kid, I memorized the military alphabet — and I'm glad I did. Background noises can make radio transmissions difficult to understand. Maybe this isn't "essential safety info," but the following phonetic alphabet can help you sound really official when talking on your VHF:

A: Alpha	H: Hotel	E: Echo	L: Lima
B: Bravo	I: India	F: Foxtrot	M: Mike
C: Charlie	J: Juliet	G: Golf	N: November
D: Delta	K: Kilo	O: Oscar	U: Uniform
		P: Papa	V: Victor
		Q: Quebec	W: Whiskey
		R: Romeo	X: X-ray
		S: Sierra	Y: Yankee
		T: Tango	Z: Zulu

But just as cellular phones provide a back-up communication option to VHF for boaters close to shore, more boats are heading offshore with satellite radio technology with a growing number of options available. So if you're interested in staying in touch either via satellite phone or Internet when sailing offshore or out of cell range, we recommend heading down to your local marine electronics store to see what's available. For a low-cost satellite communication option for short trips, a number of our friends have had good luck renting satellite phones. For more information on marine communications, surf to www.navcen.uscg.gov/marcomms. But remember, these satellite phones still should be considered a backup to your SSB for offshore sailing safety purposes.

Chapter 8

All about Weather: Red Sky at Night

When it is evening, ye say, It will be fair weather: for the sky is red.

— *Last:Matthew 16:2*

*W*eather is important in many sports — you can't play baseball in the rain, and players abandon tennis courts when snow is on the ground. But sailing, more than any other sport, depends on weather, particularly the wind, for its very existence. Without the wind, you may as well be sitting on a raft. Fortunately, in most parts of the world, enough wind is available to sail much of the time.

In this chapter, we talk about sailing's "playing field" — the wind and the water. We discuss how to estimate the present wind and water conditions and how to predict what's going to happen. Knowing what the weather will do next makes your sail *safer* (so you don't go out when conditions are too windy), *faster* (so you pick the fastest course), and *more fun* (so you get the best wind for your needs).

Figuring Out How Windy It Is

Sailors around the world (whether they use the metric system or not) measure the wind speed in units called *knots* — nautical miles per hour. A nautical mile is equal to one minute of *latitude* — one of the horizontal lines on a chart or globe. (We talk more about latitude in Chapter 9.) A nautical mile is 6,076 feet, or 1,852 meters, 15 percent longer than a statute (regular) mile, so 10 knots of wind equals wind blowing at 11.5 miles per hour. Or if you're used to the metric system, 10 knots equals 5.14 meters per second or 18.52 kilometers per hour.

Most sailors ignore the difference between nautical miles and statute miles and just consider knots to be equal to miles per hour. If you live in a metric-system country, meters per second times two is close to the speed in knots.

Sailors (and weather forecasters) speak of the wind in terms of the *true wind* (the wind that you feel if your boat isn't moving) speed and direction. Be aware that when you're moving, you and your sails "feel" the *apparent wind* (the sum of the true wind and the wind created by the motion of your boat). So even if the wind remains steady, conditions feel windier when sailing upwind than when sailing downwind. (For more about the difference between true and apparent winds, check out Chapter 11.)

Fortunately, you have another way to judge wind speed — by looking at the water. Admiral Sir Francis Beaufort of the British Navy developed Table 8-1 in 1805. He must have been an observant guy (or bored stiff on long sea voyages), and sailors benefit from his perceptions still today. He defined wind speed in terms of a single number — the *Beaufort Force* — which is the first column in Table 8-1. In some parts of the world, weather forecasters still report marine forecasts in these units, although using knots or meters per second is more common. An especially cool feature of the Beaufort Scale is the remarks about the water's surface shown in the "Water-Surface Conditions" column.

Table 8-1		Beaufort Scale		
Force	*Wind Speed (Knots)*	*Description*	*Water-Surface Conditions*	*Dummies Fun Meter*
0	0	Calm	Smooth, like a mirror.	Good time for a nap.
1	1–3	Light air	Small ripples.	Time for lunch.
2	4–6	Light breeze	Short, small wavelets with no crests.	All right! Now the boat's moving!

Force	Wind Speed (Knots)	Description	Water-Surface Conditions	Dummies Fun Meter
3	7–10	Gentle breeze	Larger wavelets with crests.	Hey, this is really fun; great for beginners.
4	11–16	Moderate breeze	Longer, small waves, some with white caps (foamy crests).	Faster is better; time to think about putting on a jacket.
5	17–21	Fresh breeze	Moderate waves with many white caps.	Beginners should head for shelter; experienced sailors dream of wind like this.
6	22–27	Strong breeze	Large waves, extensive white caps, some spray.	Great fun, but this is hard work.
7	28–33	Near gale	Heaps of waves, with some breakers, whose foam is blown downwind in streaks.	Only for skilled sailors on well-prepared boats. Staying dry is impossible; lunch is all wet.
8	34–40	Gale	Moderately high waves with edges of crests breaking into *spindrift* (heavy spray); foam is blown downwind in well-defined streaks.	Time to head home, no matter who you are.
9	41–47	Strong gale	High waves with dense foam streaks and some crests rolling over; spray reduces visibility.	Time to rent the movie, *The Perfect Storm* and make some popcorn . . . at home.
10	48–55	Storm	Very high waves with long, overhanging crests. The sea looks white; waves tumble with force; greatly reduced visibility.	Time to put the movie on pause and make sure your pets are all safely inside the house.

(continued)

Table 8-1 *(continued)*

Force	Wind Speed (Knots)	Description	Water-Surface Conditions	Dummies Fun Meter
11	56–63	Violent storm	Exceptionally high waves that may obscure medium-sized ships. All wave edges are blown into froth, and the sea is covered with patches of foam.	Better hope you used some good knots on the dock lines of your boat.
12	64–71	Hurricane	The air is filled with foam and spray, and the sea is completely white.	I want my blankee!

This relationship between what the surface of the water looks like and the wind speed really works. Guessing the wind speed every time you go out on the water is fun — and good practice, too. For example, one of the tips that always seems to come in handy is the one for Force 4. At around 12 knots, a few whitecaps are definitely apparent on the surface.

Of course, these descriptions of the water's surface apply only in areas where the wavelets and waves have a long enough distance to build up. For winds up to about 20 knots, that means you need at least a half mile of open water in the direction the wind is coming from. The water can be glassy smooth right next to a beach, yet the wind can be blowing 25 knots from an *offshore* (from the land toward the water) direction. Places with this unique orientation to the wind are ideal for setting high-speed sailing records, because waves usually slow boats down.

Knowing the wind direction is crucial for any sailor. For the many ways to find the wind direction, see Chapter 5. Wind direction is defined in terms of magnetic degrees, using the 360-degree compass. If the wind is forecast to be *westerly,* the wind is expected to come from the west. If you turn toward the western horizon, a westerly wind blows straight on your face. You can look at your compass to determine that direction is 270 degrees. (Find more about using a compass in Chapter 9.) By paying attention to the wind speed and direction, you become more aware of the overall weather picture — especially when you combine that information with the weather forecast.

Getting the Scoop on the Weather

Sailors get their weather information from a variety of sources, and none is more accurate than their own observation of present conditions. Because the weather is bound to change while you're sailing, being concerned with what's coming next pays off. Here are some ways to obtain the *local marine weather forecast* before you set sail:

- ✔ **The Internet:** The Internet has a vast supply of weather information; you can find everything from satellite photographs to the local marine forecast — if you know where to look. For forecasts in the United States, a good place to start surfing is the National Weather Service's home page (www.weather.gov). From there, scroll down to find your local marine forecast and other good links. An increasing number of nonprofit and commercial weather services are on the Net, some of which specialize in marine weather. You can find a good list of these links for the United States and around the world at www.Iexpedition.org/Weather.htm. Some services (such as www.iwindsurf.com) even provide marine weather information to an Internet-capable cellphone. For nearly anywhere on the planet, the Internet has resources or links that provide everything from the wind forecast to the tides. You can try your luck on a search engine, or start out at www.weather.gov/om/marine/internet.htm, which provides many links to the Net's marine weather resources.

- ✔ **VHF radio and telephone:** Throughout the United States, the National Weather Service distributes a marine weather forecast on special VHF channels reserved for these broadcasts. *Wx* normally identifies these channels on the radio dial. The forecasts are updated every few hours and repeat continuously. In extreme weather, the information may be broadcast live or updated more often. Valuable information includes expected wind speeds and directions, warnings regarding fog or large waves, and weather observations from various stations around the region. Some National Weather Service offices provide the same marine forecast on a telephone recording. Surf to www.weather.gov/om/marine/noaatel.htm for phone numbers.

  Outside the United States, check with a local marine business or search the Internet to find the various Internet, radio, and other sources for marine weather information.

- ✔ **News media:** Newspapers, television, and AM and FM radio stations all have some sort of weather information. Many report a marine forecast for the local waters and show the weather map. Certain satellite radio stations have excellent marine weather information services as well.

The marine weather forecast is the butt of as many jokes among sailors as the TV weather forecast is around the water cooler at the office. But every little bit of information helps, and as you gain more experience in a given area, you develop what sailors call *local knowledge* — the ability to look at the clouds and present conditions to forecast the weather.

Ever wonder how sailors on extended offshore voyages outside the range of VHF radios and cellphones get their weather information? Technology continues to evolve quickly in this area, but sailors basically rely on two sources for this information (and for communication and safety, as we mention in Chapter 7) when in a remote area: radio and satellite.

- ✔ **Single Side Band (SSB) radio:** The U.S. National Weather Service and other organizations distribute weather information via the SSB. Broadcasts are by voice, Morse code, and data transmission to a fax machine. Offshore sailors often use a computer with special radio-fax decoding software or a stand-alone weather fax receiver that prints out weather maps and satellite pictures. Surf to `http://weather.noaa.gov/fax/marine.shtml` for more information and good links to this technology and to `www.weather.gov/om/marine/home.htm` for information and links about high-seas radio (voice) forecasts. With the addition of some hardware and a computer, you can use the SSB to receive low bandwidth data transmissions, such as e-mail. Some services allow you to subscribe to receive weather information via e-mail (`www.sailmail.com` is Peter's favorite). Check with your local marine electronics store or surf to `www.weather.gov/om/marine/internet.htm` for links to various providers of this technology.

- ✔ **Satellite:** Sailors have an increasing number of satellite communication options available to them (normally at a higher cost but higher bandwidth than SSB). With these devices, sailors receive e-mail — including subscribed weather forecasts. Data bandwidth on a sat phone is slow, but with newer (and more expensive) satellite technology, mariners can surf the Internet at moderate speeds. Again, the National Weather Service's Web site (`www.weather.gov/om/marine/internet.htm`) is a great resource for links and information, as is your local marine electronics store.

When planning a long ocean trip, a *pilot chart* (available at marine stores) can be invaluable. These neat ocean charts show wind information averaged over long periods of time.

Whither the Weather

Although you can use all this weather information at face value, you get more out of it if you understand some basic principles of why the wind blows.

Many variables affect the weather on both a global and very local basis, making the science of meteorology quite complex. But the primary forces that shape weather are *temperature differences* and *air-pressure differences*. In this section, we first look at the big picture of the weather over the planet and then at the small picture, which is important for your day on the water.

The big picture: Temperature and pressure differences

If everywhere on Earth's surface was the same temperature, you'd see very few changes in the weather. But because the sun's rays strike the equator at a more perpendicular angle than at the poles, a temperature differential results. On a global scale, this surface temperature differential (hotter near the equator, colder near the poles), combined with the *Coriolis force* (a global centrifugal force that we discuss in the sidebar "The Coriolis force," later in this chapter), creates belts of weather ringing the globe. Near the equator are the *doldrums* — a belt of light, shifty, and unpredictable weather. The *tropics* enjoy relatively steady easterly winds (northeast winds in the northern hemisphere, southeast in the southern hemisphere), dubbed the *trade winds*. The midlatitudes on both sides of the equator are home to the *westerlies* (winds from the west), interspersed by waves of low-pressure areas circling the globe.

Visual warnings

Some marinas and yacht clubs in the United States display small-craft warning flags (in nighttime hours, they may use lights). These flags, shown in the following figure, are based on the marine weather forecast and indicate expected wind strength. The gray-shaded areas are red in real life.

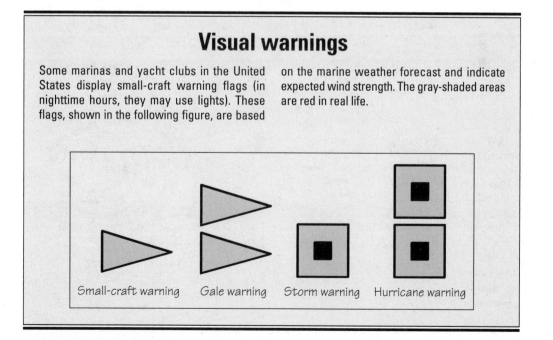

Small-craft warning   Gale warning   Storm warning   Hurricane warning

The Coriolis force

The fact that the wind doesn't simply roll straight down that high-pressure "mountain" can be disconcerting — and the reason why it doesn't is the *Coriolis force*. Because the Earth is a huge spinning ball (a very, very huge spinning ball), air molecules heading "downhill" from a high-pressure area get pulled into a curve.

No, the Coriolis force isn't why a baseball pitcher's curve ball frustrates batters, and it isn't even the reason water spins down a toilet or sink drain (although your science teacher may have used that as an example). The Coriolis force comes into play only on a massive, planetary scale causing the wind to spiral around high- and low-pressure areas.

Another factor in creating weather is pressure differences. Wind is simply air in motion trying to get to a position of equilibrium by moving from an area of high pressure to one of low pressure. On a weather map, pressure is depicted by lines called *isobars,* which connect points of equal air pressure. Think of a weather map like a topographic map, with the areas of high pressure being mountains, and the places with low pressure being the valleys. Wind flows around high- and low-pressure areas, moving downhill at a small angle to the isobars, spiraling clockwise (in the northern hemisphere) out of a high-pressure area and counterclockwise into a low-pressure area, as Figure 8-1 shows. In the southern hemisphere, the direction of rotation is opposite.

Figure 8-1:
Isobars on a weather map indicate air pressure, and their spacing and orientation help predict wind strength and direction (for which we've added arrows).

The closer together the isobar lines, the steeper the mountain or valley, and the faster the wind blows. The weather map of a hurricane shows incredibly tight isobars ringing this immensely deep low-pressure area.

A _barometer_ — a good piece of equipment for a larger cruising boat — measures air pressure. By paying attention to the changes in pressure, you can get a better idea of what will happen with the wind, especially if you're armed with weather maps and professional forecasts. Here are a few general rules regarding air pressure and weather:

- ✔ **If pressure is very high or is going up, the weather is or soon will be nice.** High pressure is associated with clear, dry weather.

- ✔ **If pressure is very low or is going down, batten down the hatches; you're in for a storm.** Low pressure is associated with cloudy, rainy weather.

In the temperate midlatitudes on both sides of the equator, weather usually comes from the west. Even when the local wind is blowing out of the east, the huge weather system (high- or low-pressure area) causing that wind is traveling from west to east, usually around 10 to 15 knots, because the upper atmosphere in these latitudes is moving quite fast from west to east. The _jet stream_ (a band of very fast moving air high up in the atmosphere) is part of this feature. Therefore, pay special attention to the weather on your west side for an indication of what to expect.

Low-pressure areas and fronts

Nasty, windy, rainy weather is associated with low-pressure areas. A complex process that involves the meeting of two air masses of different temperatures creates a low-pressure area, or a low. Emanating from the center of the typical low on a weather map (and in real life) are often two fronts, a _warm front_ followed by a _cold front,_ as Figure 8-2 shows. A _front_ is a line separating two different air masses (warm and cold, moist and dry) and often is distinguished by a large (more than 20-degree) shift in the wind direction when it passes. Cold fronts typically pack the most punch and are often the site of the most extreme sailing weather. _Squalls_ (smaller-scale storms packing incredibly strong winds delivered down from the upper atmosphere) and even tornadoes and _water spouts_ (waterborne tornadoes) can occur just before the passage of the cold front, where warm and cold air meet.

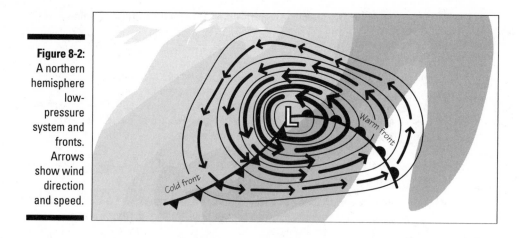

Figure 8-2:
A northern hemisphere low-pressure system and fronts. Arrows show wind direction and speed.

The weather around a typical northern-hemisphere low has three distinct sectors:

- The weather in the area to the north of the warm front is usually described as "dismal," where a thick layer of *stratus* clouds blankets the entire sky (see "More than cloud gazing," later in this chapter). If the air cools enough, you get a steady drizzle or rain.

- The weather in the sector between the warm and cold fronts is warmer and more humid. A warm, moist wind comes from the south. When the sun begins to heat the ground, the air near the ground begins to rise, forming cumulus clouds and, if the conditions are right, thunderstorms.

- The western sector behind the cold front is usually cooler and drier. The wind is from the west to northwest and can be quite blustery.

In the northern hemisphere, if you stand facing the wind, the center of the low-pressure system is to your right. In the southern hemisphere, this orientation is the opposite due to the effect of the Coriolis force.

The small picture

Most sailing takes place over the course of a few hours on an area smaller than 10 square miles (26 square kilometers). A sailor going for an afternoon cruise is concerned with a much smaller slice of the weather pie than a crew heading off to set a record sailing around the globe, but both sailors must look for signs of changing weather. The western sky (in the midlatitudes) is often the sailor's most valuable weatherman. This section contains some important tips to help you predict a change in weather in a few minutes to an hour.

The following signs indicate a future shift in wind direction or speed:

- **A change in the sky.** More clouds, fewer clouds, or different kinds of clouds foretell a shift.

- **Sailboats on the horizon.** The angle of their sails and their heeling show the new wind.

- **Flags or smokestacks on shore.** They provide definitive evidence of a new wind.

- **A rapid change in temperature.** Maybe a front is passing through.

- **A change in the visibility.** For example, in California, if the sky starts to clear on the horizon, then the wind will come from that direction.

- **A change in the water surface.** Darker water means waves and more wind (see the Beaufort Scale in Table 8-1, earlier in this chapter).

- **A changing barometer reading.** As we describe earlier in this section, changing air pressure foretells a change in the weather.

The following are the signs of stormy weather approaching:

- Dark, cumulonimbus clouds approaching on the horizon (see the next section, "More than cloud gazing").

- Thunder and/or lightning.

- A falling barometer reading.

- A change in wind speed — especially when the wind dies off or blows gently toward the big, dark clouds.

More than cloud gazing

Clouds are important to a sailor because they can presage a weather change. Clouds come in all sizes and shapes, but fall into three categories:

- **Cirrus:** The highest clouds, wispy and thin. They signify fair weather — for the next day at least.

- **Cumulus:** Puffy clouds like cotton balls. The associated weather depends on the clouds' color and size. Cumulus clouds mean fair weather when their bases are high in the sky or when they're relatively thin and bright white at lower altitudes. The taller (thicker) and darker ones with low-altitude bases are the *cumulonimbus* variety, which foretell ominous weather, including sudden thunderstorms.

✔ **Stratus:** Layered clouds, very even looking from underneath. *Stratus* comes from the Latin word for "spread, stretch out, or cover," which is what these clouds do. Their associated weather depends on their color, thickness, and altitude — the lower, thicker, and darker, the more they're associated with rain, wind, and (sometimes) low visibility.

Squalls

Thunderstorms, or *squalls,* are sudden, sometimes severe storms that are usually localized in size. Although they may precede the passage of a cold front, they can also be caused by a landmass heating up (with hot air rising into cooler air aloft) during a sultry summer day. Winds can build to over 60 knots quickly and come from any direction, and lightning is common. Squalls are relatively unpredictable (unless you have access to weather radar, which is available on the Internet — for the United States, start at www.weather.gov and drill into your local area). But dark cumulonimbus clouds, a noticeable drop in temperature, and distant thunder are all signs that a squall may be near. Some old salts claim they can smell squalls. We talk more about preparing for squalls in Chapter 14.

Because sound travels about one-fifth of a mile per second, you can tell how far away the lightning is by counting the seconds between the lightning and the thunder and dividing by five. Five seconds means the lightning is about 1 mile away. If you're metrically inclined, count the seconds and divide by three to get the distance in kilometers. For example, three seconds means the lightning is 1 kilometer away.

Facing Up to Fog

Nothing can strike fear (or at least a sober thought or two) in the heart of an experienced sailor like being caught in a strange area in dense fog. Sure, a GPS can tell you where you are within a hundred feet, but only if you have the ability to accurately translate that information onto a nautical chart. When a bank of fog as thick as pea soup surrounds you, the visibility can literally drop to less than a boat length, making safe navigation extremely difficult regardless of your skill and the available navigation aids.

Fog occurs when air contains more moisture than it can hold. When the temperature drops below the *dew point* (the temperature at which the air becomes saturated with water vapor), the excess water vapor becomes visible. Fog comes in several different types, but the same condition occurs in every kind: Moist air gets cooled (usually by water, which is why fog is more likely over cold water) until the air temperature drops below the dew point, and fog appears.

Because fog usually rolls in from the sea slowly, you generally have enough time after first spotting it to turn around and hightail it back to the shore before the fog "socks in" completely. For more information about navigating in fog, see Chapter 9.

Going with the Tide and the Current

The *tide* is actually a giant wave that circles the globe roughly twice a day. The gravitational effect of the moon (and, to a lesser extent, the sun) pulls on the Earth's oceans and causes two humps, or wave crests — one directly under the moon and the other on the exact opposite far side of the globe — that follow the moon in its 24.8-hour path around the Earth, as Figure 8-3 shows.

When the moon lines up with the sun, as it does twice every 29½ days (at the full moon and the new moon), those global wave crests get even bigger — and the corresponding *trough* (low part of a wave) gets even lower. In between, at the moon's first and last quarter, the tides are smallest.

Ten golden rules of sky watching at sea

Sailors have been watching the sky for centuries. Before the days of weather forecasts, the seaman that could foretell the weather by paying attention to Mother Nature's signs had a big advantage. Here are some of those golden rules that have been passed down over the ages:

1. Red sky at night — sailors delight; red sky at morning — sailors take warning.

2. When the sky changes, so will the weather.

3. Mackerel sky — 24 hours dry (high clouds that look sort of like a bunch of fish scales).

4. Dew on decks — wind from the sea; no dew on decks — wind from the land.

5. When the wind speed exceeds the temperature, sailors should head for home.

6. A halo around the moon means rain or snow. The larger the halo, the nearer the precipitation.

7. Rainbow to windward means rain is coming. Rainbow to leeward means rain has ended.

8. The higher the clouds, the finer the weather. (A lowering ceiling foretells rain.)

9. When smoke descends, good weather ends.

10. Seagull, seagull, sit on the sand; it's a sign of rain when you're at hand.

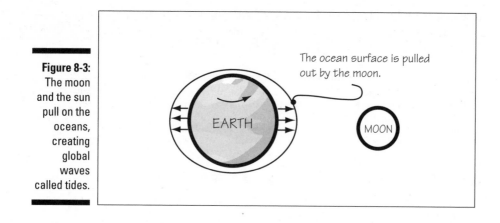

The ocean surface is pulled out by the moon.

As this global wave girdles the planet, it creates water motion called *tidal current,* or simply *current.* Current is moving water, and currents that reach 3 knots or more, rivaling the speed of a small sailboat, aren't uncommon. That much current definitely gets your attention! In some narrow bodies of water, such as the Bay of Fundy in Canada, the current comes in and out like a big tidal wave at speeds in the teens.

Flood tide is tidal current coming inbound as the tide is on the rise; *ebb tide* is the outbound tidal current when the tide is going down. You can discover tons of information about tides and currents by looking at a nautical chart of an area. Focus on the underwater topography, because the current runs strongest where the water is deepest. These general rules about tides and currents can help you while out on the water:

✔ **Current changes on the beach first.** In a confined area like a bay, the direction of the tidal flow changes with the changing tide near the shores first and in the middle last.

✔ **Current is visible by watching the water flow past buoys and other anchored objects.**

✔ **Deep water — stronger current; shallow water — less current.**

✔ **A knot of current counteracts 10 knots of wind on an anchored ship.** If you see a big ship that's anchored pointing 180 degrees to the 20-knot wind, you know that at least 2 knots of current are flowing against the wind out there.

✔ **Strong winds can overpower weak tidal flows causing them to run contrary to their predicted direction.** Strong winds can even create windblown current on lakes that have no discernible tide.

✔ **When the wind opposes the current flow, waves get steep and choppy.** This makes for a fast but bouncy ride heading upwind.

✔ **When the wind is with the current flow, the waves get smoother and more elongated.**

The motion of the ocean

If the moon's pull is constant as it orbits the Earth, why is the tidal range 15 feet (5 meters) or more in some parts of the world and only a few inches in others? The mathematical answer can make a university student's head hurt, but in practical terms, these differences are due to the shape and proximity of land masses, the underwater topography, and the wind.

Fortunately, most regions of the world have tidal predictions readily available in local publications, so you don't have to do the math to know whether the harbor is deep enough for your boat. In the United States, link to www. co-ops.nos.noaa.gov for tidal information, or listen to the marine-weather radio.

One more type of current is of interest to sailors — the huge continental boundary currents flowing along coastlines. Two great examples surround North America. On the west side is the cold, south-bound *Alaska current,* and on the eastern Florida coast is the warm, north-bound *Gulf Stream current.* These two currents act like strong rivers within the ocean, with average speeds up to 3 knots. In small, local areas, the speeds can be much higher. A combination of the Coriolis force, the prevailing winds, and the orientation of the coastlines cause these two currents.

Understanding Sea Breezes

Temperature differences can also cause changes to the weather on a local scale. *Sea breeze* is the name associated with a family of winds generated on sunny and partly sunny days, when the extra heat of the land causes a cool breeze to blow inland from the water. In certain parts of the world, the sea breeze is so predictable during the summer months that you can almost set your watch by it. Summer sea breezes are common in nearly every coastal town in the midlatitudes.

Here's how sea breezes work: As the land heats, the air rises (sometimes creating puffy, cumulus clouds), and an area of low pressure is created over the land by midday. Meanwhile, the water remains cooler, and so does the air above the water. Cool air from the water blows (or, really, is sucked) into the low pressure over the land. If the conditions are favorable (a light offshore wind up at cloud level and a large temperature difference between land and water), the sea breeze can build fairly quickly to 15 knots or more. Figure 8-4 depicts the classic sea breeze.

As the sun drops, the heating of the land diminishes, and so does the sea breeze. In the northern hemisphere, watch for the sea breeze to build until midafternoon and then slowly die away, shifting to the right (clockwise) in response to the ubiquitous Coriolis force (it shifts left in the southern hemisphere).

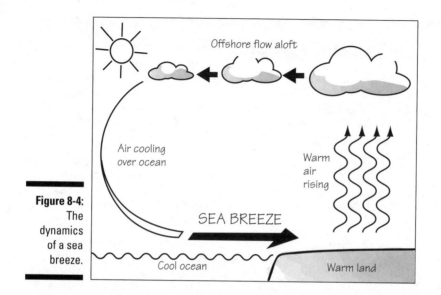

Figure 8-4:
The
dynamics
of a sea
breeze.

Recognizing Wind Shifts

Airflow over water is always a bit turbulent, so even the "steadiest" conditions have little *wind shifts,* or changes in the wind's speed and direction. When you're sailing near shore in an offshore wind, the wild shifts in the wind speed and direction can be downright maddening (although the racers in Chicago's downtown Belmont harbor claim they can predict the wind shifts by watching the doorman open the door at the waterside hotel!). The following are some common types of wind shifts:

- ✔ **Persistent shift:** A *persistent shift* is one where the wind moves in one direction either very quickly (as in the passage of a front) or progressively (as in the case of a sea breeze gradually trending to the "right" over the course of the afternoon). The shifts, which weather forecasts describe, are persistent shifts.

- ✔ **Oscillating shift:** When the wind slowly shifts back and forth around an average wind direction, you call it an *oscillating wind.* These sorts of shifts usually have a period ranging from less than a minute to ten minutes or so and are below the scope of a weather forecast.

- ✔ **Geographic shift:** A *geographic shift* is a shift in direction or speed caused by land. For example, when the wind channels and accelerates through a valley or bends around a hill.

Because the crucial first leg of an America's Cup race can be less than 20 minutes, an America's Cup team focuses its weather experts on trying to predict very short-term shifts in the wind, which are below the radar screen of most meteorologists.

Every time the wind changes, the opportunity arises to sail faster or a shorter course to your destination. A clever sailor can take advantage of wind shifts, as you see in the next section.

Using Your Weather Knowledge

For safety, know the weather forecast before you sail to avoid going out when conditions are too windy or stormy. But you can also use your knowledge of the weather, current, wave conditions, and performance of your boat to pick the fastest route. The whole process can become quite complicated for a racer or serious ocean sailor, but here are some good general rules for anyone trying to get to their destination faster:

✔ **When sailing upwind, sail on the longer tack first (if you have one).** The more "skewed" the course to the destination is relative to the wind direction, the more important this rule becomes. For example, if the course to the destination is 10 miles (16 kilometers) on starboard tack and .5 miles (.8 kilometers) on port tack, definitely go on starboard first because any wind shift will help you, as Figure 8-5 shows.

✔ **If you expect a wind shift when sailing upwind, sail toward the new wind first.** If your destination is more directly upwind and you expect a right-hand (clockwise) wind shift (either a persistent or geographic shift), sail on port tack first. See Figure 8-6.

✔ **Sail on the lifted tack in an oscillating wind.** If the wind is going back and forth, you want to sail on starboard tack when the wind is in its "right/clockwise" phase and on port tack when the wind is in its "left/ counterclockwise" phase.

Figure 8-5:
Sailing on the longer tack first helps you get to your destination quicker no matter which direction the wind shifts.

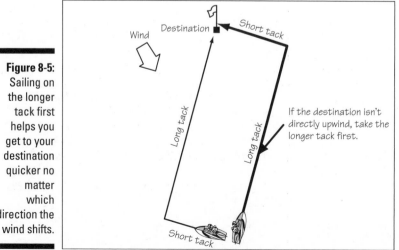

✔ **Get out of the waves:** In strong winds sailing upwind, take the tack toward the windward shoreline (or an area that's more protected) first to get out of the waves, which slow your progress sailing upwind.

✔ **On a reach, sail a straight line for your destination, unless**

- If the wind is strong and ahead of the beam. Then steer slightly below (to leeward of) the destination if you expect the wind to decrease or shift farther behind.

- If the wind is light and behind the beam. Then steer slightly above (to windward of) the destination if you expect the wind to increase or shift farther ahead.

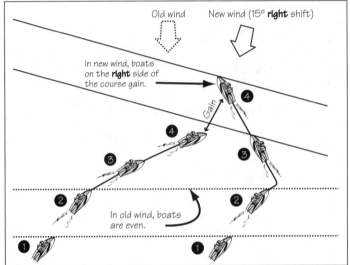

Figure 8-6:
In a right wind shift, the boat on the right can cross ahead.

In the northern hemisphere, the stronger wind is normally associated with a shift to the right (clockwise). In the southern hemisphere, the stronger wind is associated with a shift to the left.

When I'm navigating in an ocean race (say, Los Angeles to Hawaii), I use weather-routing software to calculate the optimum route to take. This software takes the forecasted wind and current (available on the Internet as a digital "grib" file), the boat's *polars* (predicted boat speed at various wind speeds and angles), and the desired destination and then "tries" hundreds or even thousands of possible routes to figure out which one is fastest. New grib files are available every six hours, so throughout the race I continually run my route-optimizing software and study the forecasts to determine the best way to go. Route planning is part art, part science, and part luck.

Chapter 9

Navigation: Holding Your Course

O we can wait no longer,
We too take ship O soul,
Joyous we too launch out on trackless seas,
Fearless for unknown shores.

— Walt Whitman

Navigation, as defined in one of Peter's favorite books (the encyclopedia of navigation, *The American Practical Navigator,* by Nathaniel Bowditch, first published in 1802 and revised periodically by the U.S. Navy), is "the process of directing the movement of a craft from one point to another." The history of navigation is rich with fascinating stories of sailors who crossed oceans with limited knowledge of where they were and even less of where they were going. Yet, however crudely, they did successfully direct their crafts from one point to another and often back again. The lore of navigation spans the globe. For example, ancient Polynesian navigators had a rich oral tradition of sailing directions that enabled them to sail to islands well over the horizon without any instruments.

Advances in timekeeping, technology, basic sciences, and mathematics enable today's sailors to direct their "crafts" from one place to another much more easily and accurately. But despite the satellites in the sky that tell you where you are, the link with this rich history of navigation isn't totally severed. Many of the skills that you will find most practical and easy to use are ones developed centuries ago.

Using Common-Sense Navigation

Whether you're sailing across the pond or across the ocean, you need to use certain basic skills to help you get there. These basic skills involve being attuned to the elements and using your senses and your judgment to get where you want to go quickly and safely.

Here's how navigation skills can help you, even if you're just heading out for a short sail:

- **Knowing where you are:** Asking the birds or fish for directions isn't easy.

- **Getting to your destination:** We're not saying you must always have a destination — sometimes it's fun to be spontaneous.

- **Getting there as fast as possible:** We cover some of the getting-there-fast issues in Chapters 11 and 12, but the navigator has major input into this subject. In Chapter 8, we cover ways to use weather knowledge to plan the fastest route.

- **Getting there as safely as possible:** Safety always comes first, and again the navigator may play a role — by avoiding the dangers marked on the nautical chart to avoid the ignominy of running aground (see Chapter 14) and by recognizing shipping channels where large commercial vessels have the right-of-way (see Chapter 4 on the rules of the road).

Although this section is crucial for sailors on a boat with no compass or chart, these techniques can be equally valuable on bigger boats with all the navigation goodies.

Judging laylines

When the destination is upwind, so you have to make at least one tack (see Chapter 5 for more on tacking) to get there, you have to be able to judge the *layline* — the line beyond which you can *lay* (sail to the destination on a close-hauled course with no more tacks), as Figure 9-1 shows. Sailing past the layline to your destination isn't bad — you simply sail extra distance. In Chapter 8, we discuss the strategy of which tack to take first when sailing in shifting winds. But after you choose your course (of a series of long tacks or many shorter ones), eventually you have to make that final tack. In order to know where the layline is, you need to know how many degrees your boat tacks through — the difference between your port and starboard close-hauled headings. In moderate air (10 to 14 knots), most boats tack through 90 degrees or a little less. If there is current, you must allow for its effect too (see Chapter 8 for more about currents).

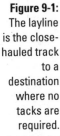

Figure 9-1:
The layline is the close-hauled track to a destination where no tacks are required.

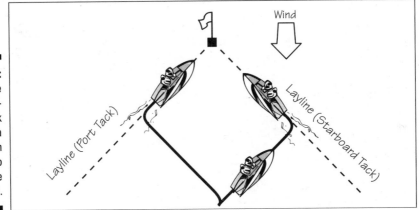

When sailing upwind and your destination is *dead abeam* (perpendicular to the boat's heading), tack over and see whether you've reached the layline.

Holding a steady course

If you can see your destination, steering a straight-line course is usually a simple matter. But if current is pushing you sideways or your boat is sideslipping excessively due to too much *heel* (too tipped over, see Chapter 11), your course over the bottom, or *course over ground (COG),* is different than your boat's *heading,* or the course the boat is steering. If you're sailing on a reach, then you can alter your heading so that the boat "makes good" the course you want — the straight line to the destination. If you're sailing close-hauled and slowly drifting downwind of your desired course, then you aren't yet on the layline, and you need to tack at some point to reach your destination.

If land lies behind the destination, you can use it as a *range* (two objects in a line) to stay on track, as Figure 9-2 shows. A visual range enables a sailor to determine whether current or wind is pushing the boat sideways and how much to alter course to counteract that effect.

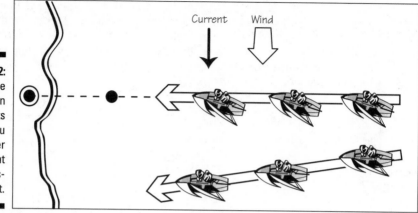

Figure 9-2:
A range
between
two objects
helps you
steer
straight
in cross-
current.

Avoiding shallow water

If the water is clear and the wind calm, the bottom looks amazingly close through the magnifying glass of the water. But this visibility decreases when waves kick up. Use the following tips for avoiding potentially dangerous shallow spots:

- ✔ **Follow another boat.** By using another boat (hopefully with a similar or deeper draft than your boat) as your guinea pig, you can follow directly behind (at a safe distance so you can turn if it runs aground) and stay in deep water. This technique is especially helpful when entering a strange harbor or following a narrow *channel* (deep water lane).

- ✔ **Look at the bottom.** In the tropics, sandy bottoms get brighter white as the depth decreases, and coral heads become darker.

- ✔ **Pay attention to the markers and buoys.** Hang on — we discuss the markers that signal deep and shallow water in the next section, "Relying on Buoys: Aids to Navigation."

- ✔ **Slow down.** If you're in an area where you think that your keel or centerboard may touch bottom, take some pace off. You may not avoid grounding, but at least the contact will be less severe.

- ✔ **Stay away from the shoreline.** By definition, the bottom comes up at the shoreline, so stay away from the shore unless you're sure (from looking at a chart or past experience) that the water is deep enough.

- ✔ **Watch for waves.** As every surfer knows, waves break when they reach shallow water. Beware of an area with breakers or with waves that seem to "mound up" bigger than the surrounding waves.

Relying on Buoys: Aids to Navigation

Sailors have used visual aids to navigate since time immemorial. A big willow tree may mark a good fishing spot; a promontory, the entrance to a harbor. An *aid to navigation* is any device (not on board) designed to assist you in determining position or a safe course or to warn of dangers. Around the world, you find millions of man-made aids to navigation; the most common are *buoys*. A buoy is any floating, albeit anchored, object that can be used for a variety of purposes, including navigation.

Depending on where you are, navigation buoys are laid out in one of two different systems (or a combination of the two):

- ✔ **Cardinal system:** Buoys of specific shapes and colors are laid out to indicate the compass direction to the hazard. The *cardinal points* of the compass are north, south, east, and west; hence the name. Most European countries use the cardinal system in combination with a lateral system.

- ✔ **Lateral system:** Buoys of specific shapes and colors are laid out along the edges of the channels or areas of safe navigation. The United States primarily uses the lateral system, which the U.S. Coast Guard manages.

Not only do buoyage systems vary somewhat from country to country, but they also vary from region to region in the United States. Fortunately, most of the country is governed by the U.S. Aids to Navigation System (which uses the lateral system), with notable exceptions being the western rivers, intracoastal waterways, and smaller bodies of water lying totally within a single state. Conveniently, even those areas use most of the key elements of the U.S. system, which we outline in the next sections. You can ascertain all the important characteristics of a buoy from a nautical chart, as we describe in "Charts: A Sailor's Roadmap," later in this chapter. If you want more details about all the variations in buoyage systems in the United States, surf to www.uscgboating.org.

Knowing your colors

The most important characteristic of a lateral-system buoy is its color. You may already be familiar with the three "Rs" in the expression "red right returning" (from the sea), which describes the basic rule of the U.S. (lateral) buoyage system: When you're coming inbound, entering a harbor, or moving along a channel toward an area that can be considered more protected, you keep the red buoys on your right side. Conversely, you keep the green buoys on your left side. By convention, the red buoys have even numbers painted on them, and the green ones have odd numbers.

Most experienced boaters use the words *port* and *starboard* while afloat. In their terminology, in the United States, a red buoy should be "left to starboard," which means passed on your right side. A green buoy should be "left to port."

Interestingly, in most of the rest of the world, including Europe, the convention is exactly opposite. Green buoys have even numbers, and you leave the green buoys on your right side when entering a harbor.

The concept of red buoys being on the right side when you're returning from sea implies that a safe passageway, or *channel,* is bounded by buoys. If the "returning" direction isn't obvious, ask yourself which body of water is most protected by land or farthest from a bigger body of water. Along the Gulf of Mexico and the Pacific and Atlantic coasts of the United States away from harbors, the red buoys mark shallow spots close to shore.

Identifying the types of buoys

Buoys come in a variety of shapes, which can indicate their meaning, as Figure 9-3 shows. At night, some buoys display lights to help the mariner find his way. Typically, the solid red and green buoys, so important in defining a channel, are lit with corresponding red and green lights. Lighthouses and midchannel fairway buoys often feature a white light. In the "Navigating at Night" section, later in this chapter, we discuss how, with a chart, you can identify a specific buoy from its unique light pattern.

You may encounter the following types of buoys when you're out for a sail:

- **Nuns and cans:** The most common buoys (used to mark the edges of the channel) are the red *nuns* (named for their pointed, conical top) and the green *cans* (named for their cylindrical shape).

- **Lighted buoys:** Lighted buoys are usually taller than nuns or cans, have a floating base and a superstructure supported by an open framework, display a light signal at night, and often emit a sound signal (bell, gong, whistle, or horn) as the buoy rolls in the waves. If they're painted solid red (with a red light at night) or solid green (with a green light), they signal the edges of a channel, just like their unlighted brethren. Check out "Navigating at Night," later in this chapter.

- **Junction buoys:** Junction buoys can be shaped like a nun, can, or lighted buoy, but they're horizontally red-and-green striped. These stripes indicate the junction of two channels, with the color on top indicating the deeper, or preferred, channel. Red on top means that the bigger channel is to port (in other words, pass the red-topped buoy on your starboard side).

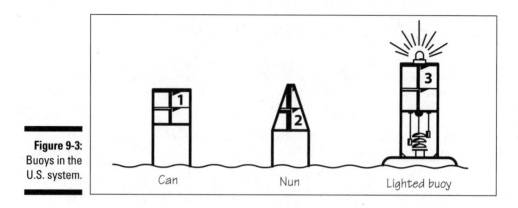

Figure 9-3:
Buoys in the
U.S. system.

Can   Nun   Lighted buoy

- **Midchannel fairway buoys:** If unlighted, these buoys are round balls; otherwise, they're the shape of a lighted buoy and indicate safe water at the center (often the beginning) of a channel. They're vertically striped red and white.

- **Danger buoys:** By definition, all navigation buoys mark some sort of danger. An isolated danger (such as a rock or other hazard) in relatively open water may be marked by a lighted buoy with red and black stripes and two black balls at the top. When unlighted, danger buoys can be either nun- or can-shaped and are white with thin orange horizontal stripes at the top and near the water level.

  Other government buoys can signal an anchorage, quarantine area, fish nets, dredging operations, or special purpose. Refer to the U.S. Coast Guard's Boating Safety Hot Line (800-368-5647) or www.uscgboating. org for any updates to the description of these buoys.

- **Daymarks:** Sometimes, in areas protected from waves in relatively shallow waters (like rivers and man-made channels), *daymarks* are used in lieu of buoys. Daymarks are displayed on poles pounded securely into the bottom. As with buoys, color is the most important feature. Pass a triangular red marker with a red reflective border on your *right* side when returning from the sea; pass a square green marker with a reflective green border on your *left* side when returning from the sea.

With all this talk about red right returning, don't forget that when you're leaving a harbor, you pass the red buoys (or daymarks) on your left side!

You may think that this spot is a logical place to talk about GPS and other electronic aids to navigation, but because these electronic aids require the use and understanding of a chart, we hold off a few more pages. And the great thing about buoys is that after you understand the system, buoys help you navigate even if you don't have a chart aboard (although navigating is much easier if you have a chart).

Charts: A Sailor's Roadmap

Charts are maps for mariners, providing a variety of useful, sometimes invaluable information. Anyone can make a chart — even you. But the indisputable authority of charts in the United States is the federal government. You can purchase paper charts at most marine stores.

Digital charts (charts that you can display on a computer-type device) are also available from a variety of sources in a wide variety of formats. We cover digital charts in more depth in the "Using GPS: Electronic Navigation" section, later in this chapter. This section discusses good ol' paper charts, including how to read them and how to establish a course and range on a chart.

Lining up your latitudes and longitudes

Charts come in a variety of *scales* (coverage areas). To orient yourself to the scale of a particular chart, refer to the scale of *latitude* (horizontal lines on a chart or globe indicating angular distance — 0 to 90 degrees — north or south of the equator), which bounds the vertical (right and left) edges of every chart, as Figure 9-4 shows.

Figure 9-4: The right and left edges of a nautical chart are bounded by a scale indicating latitude, which you can use to measure distance.

No matter where you are on the planet, one degree of latitude equals 60 nautical miles. (Hang on — we have more about the difference between nautical miles and statute miles in a minute.) Each degree is divided into 60 minutes, and each minute is further carved into either 60 seconds or decimal minutes. You can use this catchy phrase to help you glean distances from the edge of your chart: "A minute's a mile the world around."

Be careful: The same isn't true of a minute of *longitude,* which varies in distance depending on how close you are to the equator. Vertical lines on a chart or globe indicate longitude, which designates the angular distance (0 to 180 degrees) east or west of the *prime meridian.* The prime meridian is the line of longitude (or *meridian*) that has been arbitrarily given the value of 0 degrees. The prime meridian passes through Greenwich, England — so guess which country established it!

Latitude and longitude are the navigator's equivalent of streets and avenues in Manhattan (where they run north to south and east to west in a grid). Running at right angles to each other, they provide a universal way of describing your position. For example, in my chair right now, I am at 32 degrees 43.28 minutes north latitude and 117 degrees 13.26 minutes west longitude, or 32°43.28'N, 117°13.26'W. Anyone with the correct chart can determine where I am from those two values.

Deciphering a chart

In addition to latitude and longitude, charts display an enormous amount of information, often coded by a plethora of symbols and abbreviations. Chart No. 1 (http://nauticalcharts.noaa.gov/mcd/chartno1.htm), published by NOAA, explains every one of these symbols and abbreviations — from the symbol for a pagoda to water depth. Chart No. 1 is an indispensable aid in finding out how to read a chart and a valuable reference for the saltiest seafarer. You can purchase a paper version of Chart No. 1 and all U.S. government charts from most marine stores. If they don't have a particular chart, they can order it. Most marine stores also sell CDs featuring digital charts that can be viewed on a computer. You can download digital charts at http://chartmaker.ncd.noaa.gov/mcd/raster/download.htm.

Here are some of the most valuable pieces of information displayed on a nautical chart:

> ✔ **Buoys and other aids to navigation:** As we mention earlier in this chapter, buoys come in a huge variety of different colors, numbers and letters, shapes, lights, and sound signals. All those details come clear when you understand the code.

For example, "RW 'SD' Mo (A) WHIS" written next to a little black circle surrounded by a solid magenta circle with a split trapezoid peaking out clearly identifies the location of a red and white whistle buoy, with the letters "SD" on top, which displays a white light flashing the Morse Code signal for the letter "A" at night and indicates the middle of the entrance to the channel coming into San Diego Harbor. See why you need Chart No. 1!

- ✔ **Compass rose:** The compass rose on the chart helps the navigator orient the chart to his or her compass. The compass rose is so useful that several usually appear on a single chart. A compass rose consists of two concentric circles, each graduated in degrees (0 to 360 degrees) running clockwise from a reference direction (magnetic or true north). The magnetic compass rose is the one navigators usually use, and it's always the smaller, inner one. The true compass rose surrounds it. Farther inside the circle is information about the *variation* (the angular difference between true and magnetic north) as well as how the variation changes over time (slowly).

We have to introduce you to a fact that may shake your belief in Santa Claus. The earth has two north poles. *True north* sits properly atop the globe (at 90°N and 0°E). *Magnetic north* (which magnetic compasses think is north because of the earth's magnetic field) is a few thousand miles away and wanders around a bit because of the molten iron in the earth's core. Luckily, because navigators use compasses, they need to concern themselves only with magnetic north (unless they're performing the art of celestial navigation, where true north is king; check out "Wishing on a Star: Celestial Navigation," later in this chapter, for more tidbits on this subject). Unfortunately, some navigators don't feel the same way, so when discussing compass directions, always indicate which reference system you're using (270°T indicates true degrees, and 270°M indicates magnetic degrees).

- ✔ **Date of printing:** Because important things (such as the position or description of a buoy) change, having a current chart is important. You can find the printing date near the corner of the chart, outside the perimeter of the longitude scale. Old charts make great posters, wallpaper, and gift-wrapping paper!

- ✔ **Depth of the water:** Given a navigator's aversion to running aground, this is the biggie. Depth at a particular spot appears as a number that indicates depth below a fixed *datum* (base value), which is normally *mean low water* (the average level of low tide). This number is usually given in units of feet, *fathoms* (one fathom equals six feet), meters, or some combination. The datum and measurement scale (feet, fathoms, and so on) are indicated somewhere on the chart near the label that identifies the chart by name. The units of depth measurement are so important that they're repeated in magenta ink along the perimeter of the chart. Contour lines joining places of equal depth help provide a picture of the underwater topography.

Using a chart on deck

When you're navigating your way along a coastline, you may find having the chart on deck quite helpful. The downside is that the wind may blow the chart overboard (not a good thing), and writing and taking measurements on the chart can be cumbersome at best. Marine stores often sell a collection of local charts on water-resistant paper bound together in a spiral binder that are more convenient to use on deck (see large chart booklet in the following figure). But

keep in mind that nothing but a current official government chart is guaranteed to be up-to-date and accurate.

Nowadays on racing boats, I use a waterproof computer screen on deck running a navigation program that's interfaced with the boat's GPS and instrument system (see the screen in the following figure). But I still make sure I have all necessary paper charts on board as a backup.

> ✔ **Hazards:** Shallow water is a major hazard, and charts often depict shallower water as a different color than deeper water. Other danger areas, like rocks that are awash at low tide, have their own special symbols. Even military target ranges are clearly noted!

> ✔ **Land:** Because most of your sailing is near land, you can take advantage of the physical characteristics of the shore and any major, charted landmarks like radio towers and mountaintops indicated for reference.

If you haven't figured it out by now, we think that charts are pretty cool, because they possess so much information. Here are some tips on working with and reading charts:

✔ **Bring Chart No. 1 along.** Hey, you can't tell the players without a program, can you?

✔ **Fold the chart to size.** Charts are usually much bigger than your chart table or work space, so fold the chart so that you can easily see the area you're interested in. If that area is too big or too small, get the chart that's the next size up or down in scale. Make sure that you can see a compass rose and a portion of the latitude scale (for measuring distance) when the chart is folded.

✔ **Get the right chart.** Before embarking on a trip, go to the local marine store and check the *NOAA Nautical Chart Catalogue* for your area. If you're traveling some distance, make sure that you have large-scale (close-up) charts of potential harbors you may want (or be forced) to visit.

✔ **Orient the chart for ease of use.** Some people like to rotate the chart so that the direction they're traveling is straight up. Peter prefers keeping true north up, but that's just his taste.

✔ **Use a pencil.** When writing on your chart (perfectly acceptable), use a pencil so that you can erase your scribbles and reuse the chart.

Measuring a course and range

With the help of a nautical chart (and a tool or two), you can determine the distance and compass course between any two points on a chart. Our favorite tools for this job are *parallel rulers* (two straight-edged plastic slats connected by two hinges) and *dividers* (an adjustable metal tool with two sharp points, like an adjustable "compass" that's used to draw circles).

To obtain the course and distance between two points, use your tools and chart, and stick to the following steps:

1. **Pick out the two points.**

   If you like, draw a straight line between them. If you plan on sailing along this course, make sure your line doesn't cross any land or other obstructions.

2. **Lay one long, outer edge of the parallel ruler on the chart so that it touches both points.**

   Use the edge farthest away from the compass rose.

3. **Find the closest compass rose printed on the chart.**

   Doing so minimizes your "walking" distance in the next step.

4. **With two hands, "walk" the parallel ruler to the compass rose, moving one plastic slat at a time and being especially careful that the "other" (nonmoving slat) doesn't move at all.**

   Firmly hold down the nonmoving slat.

5. **When the first slat reaches the compass rose, set it so that its long outer edge crosses the plus sign in the center of the compass rose, and then read the course in magnetic degrees indicated on the inner, magnetic compass ring.**

   Be careful to read the course in the direction you want to travel and not the "reciprocal" course in the exact opposite direction.

   If you think that the nonwalking slat slipped during the walking process, do it again. Make sure that the chart surface is absolutely flat and that the rulers have enough "elbow room" to walk around.

6. **Measure the distance.**

   Use your dividers to compare the distance between the points to the distance indicated on the latitude scale. Remember, 1 minute of latitude equals 1 nautical mile. And for marine navigation, we always employ nautical miles rather than statute miles. A nautical mile equals 6,076 feet (roughly 6,000 for easy mental calculations), 2,025 yards (roughly 2,000), 1.852 kilometers, or 1.15 statute miles.

Now that you have determined the range and bearing between the two points, you can use this information for a variety of purposes. But the most common is to establish a course to steer and to calculate the time it will take to sail to the destination.

Using a Compass

A compass is a device that feels the pull of the earth's magnetic system and provides a reference direction relative to magnetic north. Sailors use several common types of compasses for navigation and steering:

✔ **Steering compass:** Steering compasses are mounted permanently in the boat, usually in a position so that the helmsman can refer to them when steering. They come in two basic varieties:

   • **Binnacle or dome compass:** Mounted on a horizontal surface such as a pedestal or on deck, these are easiest to read and are popular on boats with steering wheels.

   • **Bulkhead compass:** These are mounted on a vertical surface such as the back wall (bulkhead) of a cabin and are used on boats that have no convenient location for a dome compass.

✔ **Hand-bearing compass:** Hand-bearing compasses are small, portable compasses that aren't meant to replace a boat's primarily steering compass. They make taking a *bearing* (measuring the compass course from your boat to an object, which we discuss later in this chapter) easier than with a bulkhead compass.

✔ **Electronic compass:** Electronic compasses use the principles of magnetism and electricity. They're popular in autopilots, in some high-end sailing instrument systems, and even in some hand-bearing compasses. Of course, never rely solely on an electronic compass — what happens when the battery runs down?

Accounting for deviation

Unfortunately, all compasses don't agree as to the direction of magnetic north. Metal objects (or electrical current) affect the compass's internal magnets and cause the compass to *deviate* from magnetic north. To minimize this divergence, mount the compass far away from potential problems (like the engine) and never use iron-based fasteners or fittings nearby (within a few feet). You can determine if a fitting has magnetic properties that would affect the compass by touching the fitting with a magnet.

No matter how careful you are, some deviation (5 degrees plus or minus) is inevitable. So if you plan on using your compass for any sort of serious navigation, get your compass *swung* (calibrated for deviation error) by a professional. In practice, this involved process is usually reserved for larger boats (more than 30 feet, or 9 meters) that require compass accuracy to the degree. Most electronic compasses have instructions on how to calibrate them in their manuals (calibration usually involves driving the boat around in fixed-length laps).

Reading a compass

As you may notice, the *compass card* (rotating piece on which the numbers are written) is divided into increments. The four biggies are the cardinal points: north (000°), south (180°), east (090°), and west (270°). Sometimes on larger compasses, the four other points — NE (045°), SE (135°), SW (225°), and NW (315°) — are also indicated by their initials. On a really large compass, the smallest increments (indicated by a hash mark) can be a single degree. Smaller compasses may have a hash mark for only every 5-degree increment, which is why the bigger the compass, the better!

If you're sitting directly behind a dome compass, you can determine your boat's heading by lining up the center *lubber line* — fixed vertical post(s) around the edge of the compass card — with the markings on the compass card. The lubber line indicating your course is the center one in the direction of the bow. You can read your boat's heading on a bulkhead compass in a similar fashion, but notice that the center lubber line is on the back side of the compass. Keep in mind that regardless of the compass type, it needs to be mounted "straight" for the lubber line to accurately reflect the boat's heading.

Steering a compass course

When the navigator sets a course to sail, he announces it to the helmsman, expecting him to follow that heading like a railroad track. Hey, dream on. Holding a compass course is difficult, especially at night in really wavy conditions. Getting accustomed to the natural movement of the compass card takes a little while.

Sometimes, like when sailing close-hauled in shifty winds, holding a compass course is just about impossible (refer to Chapter 5 for more on sailing close-hauled). However, at other times (such as in thick fog), holding a steady course is crucial. The following tips can help:

- ✔ **Pick a spot on the horizon.** Steering while looking down at the compass is difficult. Try to pick a spot on the horizon that seems to line up with the desired compass course, and then rotate your eyes down to the compass only periodically to confirm your heading with the lubber line.

- ✔ **Steer an average heading.** In big waves, when the compass card is swinging all around, try to bracket the desired heading by steering no more than, say, 5 degrees on either side.

- ✔ **Pay attention and be honest.** In tricky conditions, pay attention to your average heading and report it to the navigator in periodic increments (say, 30 minutes — more often if the conditions and situation warrant).

Basic Navigation — Piloting

Now you're in for the really fun part of navigation, using the skills of piloting. *Piloting* involves frequent determination of position (or a line of position) relative to geographical points. As you discover in the section "Using GPS: Electronic Navigation," at the end of the chapter, an affordable electronic device called a Global Positioning System (GPS) makes navigation so easy that many people never see the need to figure out these "old-fashioned" skills of piloting.

Like any electronic device, however, a GPS can go on the blink, or the batteries can run out. Even when a GPS is working well, the skills of piloting are sometimes easier and more accurate. We strongly urge you to first master how to navigate the old-fashioned way and then — and only then — turn to the alluring GPS. With this in mind, take a look at the fine art of taking information and then plotting it on a paper chart to find your position.

Using a speedometer and a depth sounder

We rely so much on a boat's electronic speedometer and depth sounder that we think of them as "traditional" instruments, but they deserve a little more explanation.

A *speedometer* serves the same function on a boat as on a car — telling you how fast you're going. A tiny paddlewheel fitted under the belly of the hull drives most boat speedometers. ***Note:*** A speedometer only tells you your speed through the water, not speed over the ground, because it doesn't factor in current (see "Figuring in current and leeway," later in this section).

Meanwhile, a *depth sounder* simply uses sonar waves to tell you how much room is underneath the boat and displays this measurement on a dial or digital readout. You can then compare the depth indicated to the information on a chart to help determine your location (and to avoid sailing into shallow water).

Taking a bearing

Unless you're right on top of a known point, such as a government buoy (which is illegal, by the way), you have to determine your position by establishing a series of LOPs, or *lines of position* (lines through some point on which you presume your boat is located as a result of an observation or measurement). The most common measurement in piloting is taking a compass bearing, as Figure 9-5 shows. To help you pinpoint your location, you must take a bearing of an object of known position, such as a buoy or the peak of a mountain, not a moving object or object that isn't on your chart.

The procedure for taking a bearing changes a bit depending on the type of compass you use. (For example, bulkhead compasses don't lend themselves to taking a bearing, because you can't look through them.) However, the basic principles remain the same; just follow these steps:

1. **Pick out the object on which you intend to get a bearing.**

   For example, if you're close to the shore, you might pick a mountain. Make sure the object appears on your nautical chart! Buoys are okay, but they can move slightly. Fixed objects (lighthouses and objects on land) are the best.

—Ship

Figure 9-5:
Taking a
bearing: The
ship in the
distance
bears about
253°.

2. **Situate your eyes so that an imaginary line from the object to your eyes passes through the center of the compass (which you're close enough to read).**

3. **Read the compass bearing on the far side of the compass that's crossed by that imaginary line.**

Taking a bearing requires a good imagination — and sometimes several readings. The key is to visualize the imaginary line from the object to the compass.

4. **With the compass course of the bearing now known, go to your chart and find the object or point that you measured.**

5. **Take the parallel rulers and lay them on the compass rose so that the outer long edge rests on the (magnetic) compass course of your bearing and the center point of the compass rose.**

6. **Carefully "walk" the parallel rulers over to the observed point.**

Use the same one-step-at-a-time technique we describe in "Charts: A Sailor's Roadmap," earlier in this chapter.

7. **Draw a line along the edge of the rulers going through the point.**

Note this line of position with the time of day. Your actual position is (theoretically) somewhere on this line. You may draw this line shorter on the chart if you have a fairly good idea of where you are (see Figure 9-6).

To get a highly accurate line of position, try this cool (albeit uncommon) method. Whenever you visually line up two points that are on the chart, you can plot them as a line of position. This type of observation is called a *range*. Long Island Sound, where I grew up, has a great range that occurs when two huge smokestacks line up on the Long Island shore. Because I sailed up and down the Sound quite a bit, I drew a line on the chart for this range and always watched for it.

Figure 9-6:
Using
two LOPs
(left), your
position
fix is where
the lines
intersect.
With three
LOPs (right),
your posi-
tion fix is
within the
triangle.

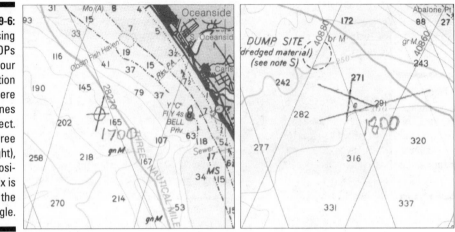

Fixing your position

Where two lines of position taken at the same time cross, you can *fix* your position on the chart, as Figure 9-6 shows. An accurate fix is every navigator's goal, but error can creep in and degrade accuracy in many ways. To minimize error, remember these tips:

- ✔ **Take bearings on objects at right angles to each other.** You can get the most accurate fix from two given LOPs when they're at 90 degrees to each other. When two LOPs cross at a shallow angle, even a small error in one of the bearings can lead to a large error in the fix.

- ✔ **Three is better than two.** By taking bearings on three objects (ideally about 60 degrees from each other), you further minimize the chance of error. Of course, your fix probably ends up looking like a triangle rather than a cross, but you can simply assume that you're in the middle of that triangle, as Figure 9-6 shows.

- ✔ **Take bearings on nearby objects.** The nearer the object, the less effect an error in bearing has on your fix.

- ✔ **Take two or three readings for each object.** Multiple readings minimize any error you may make in taking the bearing.

- ✔ **Use ranges whenever possible.** Ranges are really accurate.

- ✔ **Cross-check your fix with the depth sounder (if you have one that you know to be accurate).** Don't forget to account for the height of the tide above (or below) mean low water. Comparing the depth measured with the depth on the chart is akin to getting yet another fix.

- ✔ **Write down the time of the fix adjacent to it to aid in *dead reckoning* (covered in the very next section).**

Don't dally when taking bearings. This method of position fixing with multiple lines of position assumes that the LOPs are all taking concurrently. If it takes five minutes to get your second and third bearings, and your boat is moving the whole time, then the fix's accuracy will be degraded.

Dead reckoning

Dead reckoning, or *DR,* is the process of determining position by advancing a previous position for courses and distances. (It's also one of Peter's favorite CDs by the Grateful Dead.) By definition, DR isn't as accurate as fixing your position with some accurate lines of position; however, many times you don't have an acceptable object (or only one of dubious value) on which to take a bearing.

To be able to perform dead reckoning calculations, you must understand the important relationship between speed, time, and distance. Speed (always expressed on a boat in *knots,* or nautical miles per hour) is simply distance (nautical miles) divided by time (hours). If you're good at basic math, you'll have no problem remembering the following equations:

$$S = \text{Speed (knots)} \quad D = \text{Distance (nautical miles)} \quad T = \text{Time (hours)}$$
$$S = D \div T \qquad\qquad D = S \times T \qquad\qquad\qquad T = D \div S$$

If you know two of the three quantities, you can determine the third. You use this principle most commonly to calculate distance traveled. If you know your average speed (from your speedometer) and the time you traveled, then you can calculate the distance. Furthermore, if you know the average compass course that you steered, you can advance your position on the chart from your last known (or estimated) position.

For example, suppose that you fix your position on the chart with three bearings taken at noon. You then steer an average heading of 090° at 6.8 knots for 25 minutes. You can calculate the distance traveled as follows:

$$D = S \times T \qquad D = 6.8 \text{ knots} \times (^{25}\!/_{60}) \qquad D = 2.83 \text{ nautical miles}$$

Therefore, you can establish your DR position at 1225 by measuring 2.83 miles along a course of 090°M from the noon fix, using the same techniques of operating the parallel rulers and dividers we outline in "Charts: A Sailor's Roadmap," earlier in this chapter. The updated location is your *dead reckoned position,* and you should mark it on the chart as such with an encircled dot, the letters "DR," and the time.

Use the six-minute rule: When determining distance traveled, you must often use a time interval of less than one hour, creating a cumbersome math problem. But because six minutes is one tenth of an hour, you can use this increment of time to ease your calculations. For example, a boat going 6.8 knots travels 0.68 nautical miles (nm) in six minutes, or roughly 1.4 nm in 12 minutes, and so on.

Figuring in current and leeway

When advancing your position with DR, you may also need to consider two types of movement not measured on the speedometer and compass. *Leeway* is the sideslipping motion that occurs when a boat sails a close-hauled course. The impact of leeway varies from boat to boat. Current has a similar "invisible" effect on the boat's progress. For more on currents, see Chapter 8.

Keeping a log

Given the importance of staying on top of your speed (or distance traveled) and heading, you can see why all serious navigators keep logs. A *log* is simply a historical record of various pieces of information. You can design your log to include whatever information you think is important. Common items of entry include

- **Average heading since the last entry:** Whenever the boat changes course (say, after a tack), make a new entry.
- **Average speed since the last entry:** Make your best guess.
- **Given course:** Course desired by the navigator.
- **Log reading:** Most instrument systems have a *log,* which is simply a distance-measuring device, a nautical odometer (as opposed to your written log).
- **Time:** Normally recorded in the 24-hour format (6 a.m. is 0600).
- **Weather information:** Wind speed and direction, cloud cover, barometric pressure, and so on.
- **Other comments:** For example, what sails are up, who is driving, when the boat tacked or jibed, what was for dinner, and so on.

When should you keep a log? Obviously, you don't need one when you sail a dinghy in familiar waters (nor do you have a place to store it) or when you go on a short harbor cruise. If you're crossing the ocean, definitely keep a log. In between, use your judgment. Keep a log any time doing so can add to the boat's safety.

Grasping Special Piloting Techniques

The key to safe navigation is to make navigating as easy to perform as possible. We began this chapter with the "common sense" section, because you sometimes (such as in your home waters) can perform the necessary tasks without fiddling with parallel rulers and dividers.

However, rigorous dead reckoning and frequent fixing of your position have their time and place. Navigating at night in a new location with many shoals and hazards is an example. Much of the time, your task requires a level of navigational effort somewhere in between the two extremes. This section provides some helpful techniques.

Danger bearing

Often a narrow entrance channel to a harbor is marked by two navigational aids (one on land and one farther away) that, when aligned, indicate a safe course, sort of like landing an airplane on an aircraft carrier. Sometimes lighthouses display a different color light (red instead of white) in a sector of their sweep. The edges (where those colors meet) are *danger bearings:* On one side the boat is safe; on the other could be shallow water.

The navigator can also determine a danger bearing from information gained from the nautical chart. For example, if your present course requires you to sail around an island with rocky shoals on one side, you can plot a line of position (LOP) as a danger bearing tangent to an obvious landmark or navigational aid of which you want the boat to stay outside, as shown in Figure 9-7. By monitoring the bearing to this object and comparing it to your danger bearing (measured in the normal manner on the chart), you can avoid the hazard without having to constantly run down to the chart table and plot your position.

Add some "padding" to the danger bearing. For example, if a bearing of 350 degrees to a buoy just skirts a shoal, add (or subtract, depending on which side of the line is safe water) 5 degrees or so, especially as you get close to the danger.

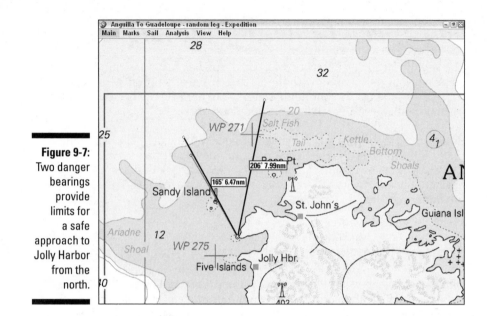

Figure 9-7:
Two danger
bearings
provide
limits for
a safe
approach to
Jolly Harbor
from the
north.

Distance off

You can fix your position on a chart with two LOPs you obtain from bearings, but you can also fix your position if you have one LOP and know your distance, or range, away from that object. You simply find the point at which the LOP crosses the *circle of position* marked by a circle whose radius is the distance you are away from its center. You can obtain a circle of position in many ways. Two of the most helpful are by judging distance and by doubling the relative angle.

Judging distance

Every top navigator likes to think that he or she has the ability to judge distance equal to a pro golfer (or her caddie). The skill comes from practice. Any time you're out on the water (or on the shore), you can practice by making a game of judging distance. All you need is a nautical chart (and knowledge of where you are) to be able to check your guesstimate.

I like guessing distance, and I do it all the time. I've stored away in my "mind's eye" a catalog of what certain distances look like. For example, I know that the distance across Skaneateles Lake (New York) from our dock is 2 miles, and I know what that distance looks like by heart. So when something is about 2 miles away, I ask myself whether it's closer or farther than the other side of the lake. My brain has also stored away what 6 miles looks like from all the time I've spent staring out of jet airplane windows. And of course, 100 yards is ingrained from my early years playing around on a football field. You see, your brain already has a catalogue of what certain distances look like.

Here are some other pointers we've gleaned over the years:

- ✔ If you can discern individual trees, you're less than a mile away.

- ✔ If you can make out house windows, you're less than 2 miles away.

- ✔ If you can't see the true edge of the land and water, you're more than 3 miles away.

Doubling the relative angle

You can find plenty of tricky ways to judge distance by using the science and magic of geometry. The easiest one to remember is "doubling the relative angle," but you have to be steering a straight course for it to work. When you pass an object of interest (say, a lighthouse), note the time when it's 45 degrees (relative angle) off your bow. Pay attention to the average speed, and when the lighthouse is dead abeam (90 degrees to the bow), you've "doubled the angle," so note the time again. Through the wonders of geometry, the distance you travel between the two readings equals your distance away from the object at the time of the second reading. Now you can plot a circle of position, take a bearing on that object, and you have a fix.

Navigating in the Fog

By definition, you can't see anything in fog, so the skills of dead reckoning can become crucially important to avoid getting lost or worse. Here are some good rules to keep in mind when fog descends:

- ✔ **Be aware of the potential for fog.** See Chapter 8 where we discuss how and when fog forms.

- ✔ **If fog starts to roll in, react.** It won't totally blanket you without some warning, so quickly figure out your compass heading back to the harbor.

- ✔ **Assuming you have a chart, immediately fix your position as accurately as possible.** If you don't have a chart or are simply day sailing, immediately set your course for a safe haven (like home).

- ✔ **Follow the procedures for keeping an accurate dead reckoning.** If you have a depth sounder, use it, especially if you're passing areas with steep transitions in depth that can help accurately provide a fix of position by referring to the depths indicated on your chart.

- ✔ **Listen for buoys and foghorns.** The nautical chart (and good ol' Chart No. 1) indicates what navigational aids make certain sounds.

- ✔ **Listen for other boats.** Every boat is required to post a "lookout." Keep in mind that sound does weird things in fog, so pinpointing the location of a sound can be difficult.

✔ **Make sound signals.** The rules of the road require a sailboat (39 feet, or 12 meters, or longer) to make one long horn blast followed by two short blasts every two minutes or less. For the other rules of the road, see Chapter 4.

Remember when we advised you to master the traditional skills of navigation before using a GPS unit? Well, fog is a good time to disobey us!

Navigating at Night

When night falls, you lose some, but not all, of the visual information important to a navigator. Even in familiar waters, the arrival of night is a good time to break out the nautical chart and increase the level of your navigational efforts. One of the most important aspects of coastal navigation at night is your ability to identify lighted buoys, lighthouses, and other boats.

Lighting up the nighttime sky

At night, certain buoys, daymarks, and other navigational aids such as lighthouses display lights to help the mariner find his way. To prevent confusion, navigational aids are lit in a variety of ways, utilizing color, pattern, and *period* (the time interval between flashes) to help identification at night. Typically, the solid red and green buoys, so important in defining a channel, are lit with corresponding red and green lights. Lighthouses and midchannel fairway buoys often feature a white light. On a nautical chart, abbreviations such as "F" for "fixed, unblinking," and "FL Xsec" for "flashing at X-second intervals" indicate the characteristics of each light.

Chart No. 1 can help you decipher the abbreviations defining the characteristics of the light. You usually need to view two or three cycles of the light sequence to be sure that you've positively identified it. Realize also that the lights on buoys have a much shorter range (about 2 miles, or 3 kilometers; even less in big waves) than lighthouses. You may have an easier time identifying a buoy or lighthouse if you first calculate (on the chart) its expected bearing and then look in that direction.

Recognizing other boats at night

All boats are required to have navigation lights (also called *running lights*) at night (including dusk and dawn) and whenever visibility is reduced (such as in fog, heavy rain, or haze). Power boats, larger commercial ships, and other seagoing craft all have required lighting configurations that vary considerably depending on the type of boat (or barge or submarine). But most vessels have red and green lights to identify port and starboard and have some kind of white stern light while underway. Larger ships often use really bright fore-and-aft range lights that help you determine which way it is heading. See Figure 9-8 for the running lights on a typical sailboat and on a larger ship (more than 164 feet, or 50 meters). You definitely want to get out of the way if you can see both the red and green bow lights of any vessel coming at you.

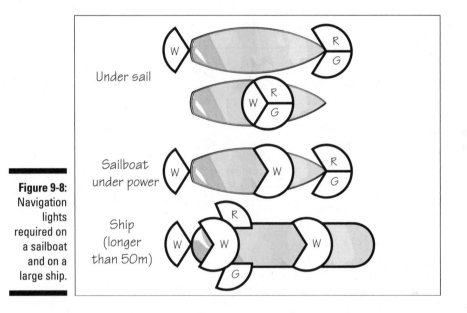

Figure 9-8: Navigation lights required on a sailboat and on a large ship.

At night, keeping interior (and deck) lights to a minimum helps the night vision of those on deck (especially the navigator, who may be going back and forth between the chart table below and the cockpit). Many boats have lights with red bulbs for night operation, because red light doesn't affect night vision like white lights do. Keep in mind that red lines and symbols on the chart look faint and gray in red light.

Using GPS: Electronic Navigation

Understanding and being proficient at the "traditional" skills of piloting and dead reckoning on a paper chart are absolutely crucial before trusting your boat (and your safety) to a machine. But after you master those traditional skills, using a *Global Positioning System (GPS)* unit makes the navigator's job a breeze.

The GPS unit is a satellite navigation device that uses information from a bevy of U.S. Department of Defense satellites to give you your current latitude and longitude. Like your TV set, you don't need to know how it works to use it. GPS units have revolutionized the art of navigation.

Many different GPS models are available, so read the instruction manual for specific instructions on how to turn on and properly configure your GPS. When you configure your device, set the GPS to display magnetic degrees (not true degrees); nautical miles and knots (not kilometers or statute miles); your local time (not Greenwich Mean Time); latitude and longitude units in degrees, minutes, and decimal minutes; and to use the WGS 84 datum (the standard datum, or theoretical global shape — remember that the earth isn't round) used for most nautical charts in the United States. These conventions make navigating by using your own watch and nautical charts easier, because then all the parts are in synch.

The features of different marine GPS units vary, but here are a few common tasks that are helpful to the navigator that virtually all marine GPS units perform:

✔ **Create a waypoint** (the latitude/longitude coordinates of any point you desire) or even a route made up of many waypoints, and then a GPS helps you follow that route by displaying helpful information like course to steer, range to the waypoint, estimated time of arrival, and cross-track error (how far you've drifted off the rhumb line, or straight-line, course).

✔ **Save a man-overboard position** (usually with the push of one button) and immediately switch the GPS into a mode where it helps you navigate back to that position.

✔ **Give you very accurate SOG (speed over ground) and COG (course over ground) reports,** which can help in your navigation or even calibration of your compass and speedometer (if there isn't much current). We like to set the damping of the SOG and COG variables quite low so they update quickly.

✔ **Keep a digital log** so you can determine how far you've gone over a certain period, which can be helpful in navigation or just for knowing whether you just set the world sailing speed record for a 24-hour run. You need to sail more than 700 miles in a 24-hour period at an average speed of more than 30 knots to be close.

But having a GPS doesn't mean you can throw away those paper charts. One thing you need to know is how to plot the position (latitude and longitude) given by your GPS onto a chart as a fix. Here's the most accurate way:

1. **Write down the indicated latitude and longitude from the GPS and find them on the appropriate scales bounding your chart.**

   Make a small tick mark with a pencil at each of those points.

2. **Line up the outer edge of the parallel ruler with a nearby latitude or longitude line.**

   Those lines are either at the edge of the chart or somewhere in the middle, marked by a thin black line running horizontally (latitude) or vertically (longitude) across the chart.

3. **"Walk" the parallel ruler to the tick mark for that value (either longitude or latitude) and draw an LOP.**

   We cover this walking technique earlier in "Measuring a course and range."

4. **Do the same for the other value (either longitude or latitude).**

   Where the two LOPs cross was your location at the time you wrote the coordinates! Refer to Figure 9-6 for how to mark this fix on the chart.

Chart plotting with GPS

We don't need to tell you how fast technology changes the way people do so many everyday things. The art and science of navigation isn't immune to this whirlwind either. For example, the GPS system that seems so ubiquitous now wasn't even available to the general public when Peter won his first America's Cup (in 1987).

We recommend knowing the basic skills of navigation and piloting before relying completely on a gadget comprised of lasers and silica chips that runs on a battery. That said, we love digital navigation technology and the additional information and ease of use that it provides. Although being able to use a computer (or fancy GPS) for navigation offers plenty of benefits, by far and away the most valuable one is chart plotting — being able to plot or display your exact position on a digital chart. With that accurate position plotted on a good chart, you can much more accurately plan your course and avoid dangers — all without taking the time to take bearings and transpose them to a paper chart.

No matter how many GPSs you have on board, never head into unfamiliar waters without the basic tools required for coastal piloting (especially a paper chart) and never ever make a major offshore passage (like crossing an ocean) without having a sextant, instruction book, and either the requisite books (tables and almanacs) or a calculator or PC with all that information stored inside.

You have basically two options for chart plotting technology:

✔ **GPS display:** Some GPS have a built-in chart-plotting feature. The resolution and accuracy of the chart displayed by the GPS varies greatly depending on the technology of the unit. So does the ease of operation of the unit for simple tasks like calculating a range and bearing to a waypoint. Your local marine store has a variety of chart-plotting GPS units that use a variety of technologies.

   If you need the accuracy and ease of chart-plotting technology, but your boat is so small that you don't have a good (and dry) place to work on the computer down below, then you may consider a handheld chart-plotting GPS.

✔ **Computer display:** We generally prefer using a laptop computer to run the chart-plotting software, because the computer already has the computational horsepower to handle the graphics end of things quite easily. Then all you need is to connect your GPS (assuming it has data-out capability) to your computer. We find a computer has a bigger screen, is much easier to operate, and runs much more powerful and versatile software than a GPS. If you go this route, you need to purchase some navigation software (check out your marine store), connect it to the GPS and the sailing instruments, and find a good place to work on the computer where it will stay dry and secure. If your boat is very wet down below, consider a ruggedized (waterproof) laptop.

To keep your computer from sliding around every time the boat tacks, get some sticky-backed Velcro and attach some strips on the bottom of your laptop and on the chart table where you want to work.

When I'm the navigator, I love using a computer interfaced with the instruments, because it helps me make better decisions and do a better job. Over the past few years, I've enjoyed working on the development of special sailboat-racing software (`www.iexpedition.org`), as Figure 9-9 shows, that combines the features of basic chart plotting and navigation with weather analysis and routing and performance optimization. As all this technology continues to evolve so fast, being on the cutting edge is fun.

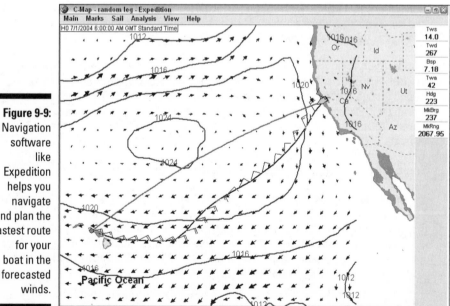

Figure 9-9: Navigation software like Expedition helps you navigate and plan the fastest route for your boat in the forecasted winds.

How accurate is GPS?

You may wonder how accurate GPS is. A basic GPS receiver should be accurate to less than 328 feet (100 meters). As long as the U.S. government cooperates, a GPS fix is currently accurate to 49 feet (15 meters). You see, somebody pushing a button at the Pentagon can degrade, improve the accuracy of, or even turn off the signals sent down by the satellites. But assuming no military reason exists to mess with the information coming to the public, then the GPS accuracy can be enhanced (as long as you have the compatible hardware) in the following ways:

- **Differential:** Mostly around the U.S. coast, more than 60 U.S. Coast Guard–serviced radio stations send a "correction" signal to compatible GPS receivers, which enhance their accuracy. Only differential-capable GPS units within range (100 miles, or 161 kilometers, or so) of the differential radio beacon can benefit from this enhancement, which brings GPS accuracy into the 33-feet (10-meter)10-meter range.

- **WAAS (or Wide Area Augmentation System):** Overseen by the Federal Aviation Administration (FAA) in the United States, this is an even more accurate system, which provides corrections to the GPS signal. But unlike differential technology, the WAAS enhancement is delivered by satellite to the WAAS-enabled GPS units. Accuracy improvements to position fixing surpass even the differential technology. Although primarily aimed to benefit the aviation community (how would you like to land a 777 by computer?), sailors like knowing where they are too!

If you really love all this stuff, then head to the Internet to get the latest information on this evolving technology. Check out the Web sites of GPS manufacturers or surf to www.navcen.uscg.gov/dgps/Default.htm for the USCG's info and http://gps.faa.gov for the latest from the FAA.

Wishing on a Star: Celestial Navigation

From high-tech to really traditional, *celestial navigation* (navigating by celestial bodies like stars, the moon, and the sun) is the coolest form of navigation. Using this system puts you in a league with the greats, like Galileo, Copernicus, Magellan, Columbus, and Cook. Well, maybe that's a bit of a stretch, but the fact that you can determine where you are in the world (to an accuracy of less than a mile) with a *sextant* (device that accurately measures the angular height of a celestial body over the horizon), a watch, and some books of tables is pretty amazing. Oh, yes, you need one other thing — a clear or partially clear sky during daylight, dawn, or dusk hours. Nighttime and clouds put a real damper on celestial navigation, because you need to see the celestial object and the horizon.

A general book like this one is too small to do justice to celestial navigation. Fortunately, you can find many good books on the subject. Peter's favorite is *Kindergarten of Celestial Navigation,* by Joseph Sellar.

The basic principal of celestial navigation is easy to grasp. If you can measure the angle between the horizon and a celestial body of known position at a certain time (thank you, Copernicus and friends), you can generate a circle of position. You are somewhere in that circle of position. Get another reading from a different celestial body or the same one at a different time, and if you haven't moved, the two circles of position cross at your location (and also at a point on the other side of the planet, where you obviously aren't). See an example of celestial navigation geometry in Figure 9-10.

Figure 9-10:
By celestial navigation, you generate a circle of position on which you're located. Two celestial sights give you two circles and thereby narrow down your possible position to two points.

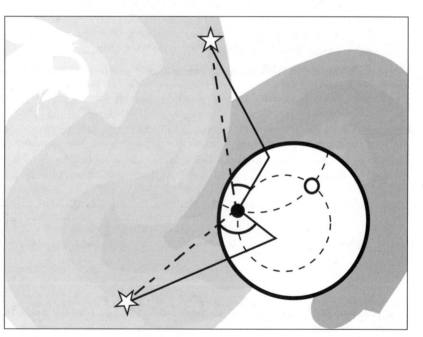

Chapter 10

Anchors Away: Anchoring Your Boat

Anchors aweigh, my boys,
Anchors aweigh!
Farewell to college joys,
We sail at break of day.

— Alfred Hart Miles

Although nowadays many quiet little coves that used to be perfect for a peaceful night at anchor are filled with mooring buoys and marinas, knowing how to anchor is important for those times when you run out of wind or want to try to find a special spot that's all your own. Before reading this chapter, you may want to refer to Chapter 6, which covers the basics of tying up (securing your boat) to a dock and mooring (a permanently anchored buoy).

Anchoring your boat is more involved than tying it to a mooring because you're responsible for lowering the anchor and making sure that it's secure. This chapter focuses on everything related to anchors, from dropping and retrieving your anchor to choosing the best anchor and gear.

Looking at a Basic Anchor

How do you keep a floating object anchored? One way is to find a really heavy rock, tie a strong rope to it, and throw it overboard. But what happens when you want to leave that spot and go someplace else? Hauling that enormous rock on board may be impossible. You can just cut the rope attached to the rock, but then what would you do if you want to anchor the next night (plus you'd be littering)?

Another problem with the rock method is wind or current. A strong wind pushes very hard on your boat, which, in turn, pulls very hard on your rock — so hard that it may simply slide or roll across the bottom. Fortunately, you have a better way — thanks to the invention of properly designed anchors.

Most anchors share the following characteristics, as Figure 10-1 shows:

✔ **They sink!** (An anchor wouldn't work very well if it floated, would it?)

✔ **They have holding power, thanks to one or more prongs or points called *flukes*.** These flukes act like the blade of a shovel to dig into the bottom. Because the flukes help grip the bottom, the anchor can weigh less, making it easier to bring on board.

✔ **They have a long arm, or *shank*, providing mechanical advantage to help the flukes dig in.**

✔ **They have some sort of feature to help keep the flukes dug in when the wind or current shifts and the boat pulls from a different direction.**

✔ **Despite their holding power, they can be "unstuck" relatively easily.**

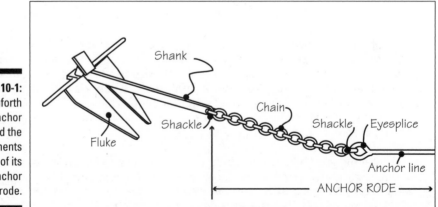

Figure 10-1:
A Danforth anchor and the components of its anchor rode.

If the wind and/or your engine die, knowing how to anchor is an important safety skill. The anchor is typically stored down below deck, usually just forward or next to the mast, but on some bigger cruising keelboats, it may already be rigged and ready to go up on the bow. When stored below deck, the anchor line should be nicely *flaked* (neatly folded), with the anchor and chain on top. *Ground tackle* is the term for the entire package — the anchor plus the *anchor rode* (the line and chain that attach the anchor to the boat).

Adding chain: Why it helps

Attaching several feet of chain to the anchor ensures that the pulling force on the anchor comes from the all-important horizontal direction, parallel to the bottom, so the flukes stay dug into the bottom (check out Figure 10-1). In addition, chain doesn't chafe if dragged over sharp rocks on the bottom. In extreme anchoring conditions (strong winds or a long stay) or for a really big, heavy sailboat, the entire anchor rode needs to be chain.

The scoop on scope

In the cartoons, Popeye simply drops the anchor and rope over the side until it hits bottom and then cleats it off. In the real world, you need to let out much more rope than the depth of the water.

Scope (the ratio between the length of anchor rode you let out and the water's depth) is an important concept to understand when anchoring. Too little scope, such as Popeye's 1:1 scope, is impractical and dangerous — the pull on the anchor is vertical, and your boat dislodges the anchor at high tide or on the top of any wave. Increasing the ratio of scope allows the anchor to be pulled in a more horizontal direction, which greatly increases its holding power.

The basic rule is to use 5:1 scope (five times as much anchor rode as the distance to the bottom at high tide) for average conditions. For example, if your anchorage is 20 feet deep at high tide, then you let out 100 feet of anchor rode before cleating it (roughly 10 feet of chain and 90 feet of nylon anchor line for a 30-foot sailboat).

The more scope (that is, the more rope you let out), the better the holding power of your anchor, as Figure 10-2 shows. When in doubt . . . let out more rope for more scope. Some anchor manufacturers recommend 7:1 scope. As long as you have plenty of room for the boat to swing if the wind or current shifts direction, you rest easier knowing your boat is better secured.

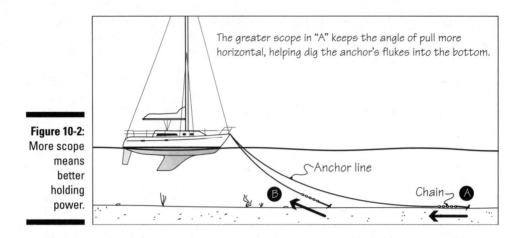

The greater scope in "A" keeps the angle of pull more horizontal, helping dig the anchor's flukes into the bottom.

Figure 10-2:
More scope
means
better
holding
power.

Anchor line

Chain

If the conditions are very mild and you plan on stopping for only a short break and staying on board, you can probably get away with laying out less scope (not less than 3:1) or using a lighter anchor with less chain. Less scope means less work hauling in that soggy wet rope when you want to get under way. Check out the section called "Choosing the right anchor line," later in this chapter, for tips on marking your anchor-line length.

Picking a Good Place to Anchor

To know where to anchor, you need to familiarize yourself with a chart of the area. From the chart, you can determine the water depth and the type of bottom to find a suitable anchorage. You also need to know how much (if at all) the tide will rise and fall. (See Chapter 9 for more on charts and tides.) On a trip, you can buy a local "cruising guide," which points out special considerations about various anchoring spots.

For comfort, you want to find an anchorage protected from the prevailing wind and wave direction. For safety, you need to find an anchorage that features the following:

- ✔ A suitable bottom for securing your anchor
- ✔ Enough depth to avoid the danger of grounding but not so much depth that with a 5:1 or more scope, retrieving the anchor is a back-breaker
- ✔ Sufficient room for your boat to swing in all directions (imagine the anchor is the center of a circle around which the boat swings)

    ✔ A quiet location out of any channel

    ✔ A location protected from waves and strong winds

Spending enough time choosing the best anchorage *before* you drop anchor is much easier than having to pull up your anchor and move.

Finding the lee

Very few anchorages are protected in all wind directions, so your first step is to note the current wind direction and review the marine weather forecast. (See Chapter 8 for more information about weather and marine forecasts.) A good, protected anchorage is in the *lee* of the wind — that is, the adjacent land blocks the force of the wind and waves. If the forecast is for strong, easterly breezes, for example, you want to anchor just to the west of the protecting landmass.

Alongside a *lee shore* (shore facing the oncoming wind and waves) is the most dangerous place for an anchored boat. If the anchor slips at all, you can find yourself getting washed up onto the beach or worse. Anchoring along a lee shore is like standing in the middle of the road — you may be safe for a while, but your odds aren't so good. The tricky part about picking a good place to anchor is that with a 180-degree wind shift, your nice, protected anchorage can become the dreaded lee shore.

Avoiding underwater hazards

You can never go wrong by dropping the hook in some medium-soft mud. Avoid a rocky bottom, because the flukes of the anchor can't dig in. A chart, as shown in Figure 10-3, indicates bottom type and shows you underwater hazards to avoid such as rocks, cables, and shipwrecks. Nothing is worse than getting your anchor so stuck on an object that you have to go swimming or cut your anchor line away.

Fortunately, the world is becoming more ecologically aware. For example, in the Virgin Islands (where you can enjoy some of the nicest cruising in the world, as we point out in Chapter 17), the local authorities now place mooring buoys at popular anchorages. Because tying up to a mooring is infinitely easier than anchoring, life is now much easier for those of us above the water's surface. But the reason for the moorings is to protect the creatures underwater. Dropping an anchor onto a coral reef is a big environmental no-no and causes irreparable damage to this priceless feature of the tropical oceans. Don't do it. If you must anchor near coral reefs, find a sandy spot or even put on your mask and snorkel to help find the best spot before crash landing your anchor.

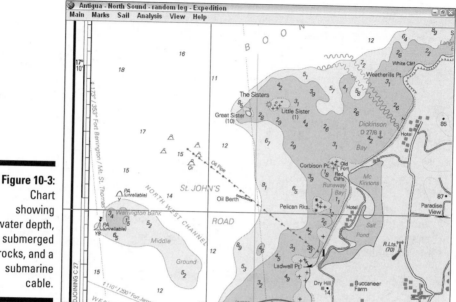

Figure 10-3:
Chart
showing
water depth,
submerged
rocks, and a
submarine
cable.

Keeping an eye on depth and current

Because charts indicate the water depth at *mean low water* (average low tide), seeing spots that are deep enough for your boat is easy. In big waves or a swell, allow a few more feet of clearance for when the boat is down in the trough. Better yet, avoid anchoring in waves; the idea of anchoring is to relax and get a break from the open-water conditions. Use the chart and/or tide books to ascertain the local currents. Avoid anchoring in places with strong current. For more on currents, see Chapter 9.

Staying away from crowds

Avoid crowded anchorages, where you're restricted in the amount of scope you can let out. In a squall, one of these neighboring boats may drag its anchor — possibly into your boat! A boat at anchor swings with the wind and current, so make sure your boat is free to swing in a circle around the anchor (see Figure 10-4).

If you must choose a spot in a crowded anchorage, check out your potential new neighbors. A large powerboat may run a noisy generator all night. Netting on the lifelines and Mickey Mouse swim floats signify the delights of small children on board. So that you aren't the chief noisemaker, remember that in strong winds, halyards can beat a very loud tune, so tie them off away from the mast.

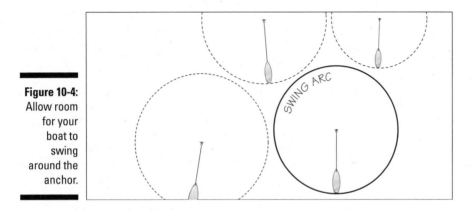

Figure 10-4:
Allow room
for your
boat to
swing
around the
anchor.

Getting Ready to Anchor

After you study the harbor carefully and find the perfect spot to anchor, you want to put that anchor in securely on your first try. Anchoring can be stressful, and knowing that the folks on nearby anchored boats are watching your every move doesn't help.

The key to anchoring is waiting to drop the anchor until the boat is stopped dead in the water and just beginning to drift backward — similar to picking up a mooring (refer to Chapter 6). Keep in mind that the easiest way to go backward on a sailboat is under power. Anchoring under power also has the advantage of letting you clear the *foredeck* (area on deck in front of the mast) of sails before you get started so the crew has space to prepare the anchor and rode without stepping on or dirtying the sails. (Because sometimes you must anchor without using an engine, we have an "Anchoring under Sail" section later in this chapter.)

The most common anchoring mishaps are caused by not preparing the anchor rode to run out smoothly. Murphy's Law is definitely in force during anchoring. The knots and tangles that a long piece of rope can get into are amazing. We hope you check that the anchor line is neatly flaked before you leave the dock, but checking it again after it's on deck while the skipper is finding the ideal anchorage is still a good idea.

When the skipper selects a spot, make sure that the crew dropping the anchor knows the depth so that they can prepare enough anchor rode.

Take the time to lay out (*flake*) enough line so that it can run out smoothly until the anchor can touch the bottom, and neatly coil the remainder (with the part closest to the anchor on top) so that it's ready to run. If your boat has a *chain locker* (compartment in the bow that holds the anchor rode "pre-flaked"), you need to pull out and arrange only enough line for the anchor to hit bottom. As long as the rope in the chain locker was stored correctly, the rest of the rope in the locker pays out cleanly as the boat is backed away from the anchor to add the necessary scope.

Make sure that you lead the anchor line over an anchor roller or through a *fairlead* (also called a *bow chock*) and under the *bow pulpit* (the metal frame surrounding the bow to which the forward ends of the lifelines attach), as Figure 10-5 shows. Always tie the end of the anchor line to a secure point on the boat, such as a deck cleat or the mast, before dropping anchor. The ocean floor is littered with anchors from boats where the deck crew let out "just a little more line" before tying it off.

Before anchoring, make a final inspection of the anchor line for chafe, check that any shackles are tight, and make sure that the bitter end of the anchor rode is tied securely to the boat (if not, you're in for an expensive "oops").

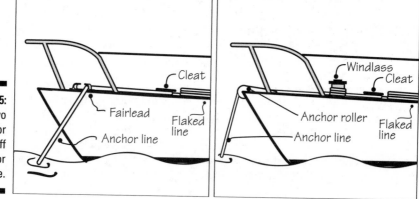

Figure 10-5:
Two systems for tying off your anchor line.

Follow these steps when you're preparing to drop the anchor:

1. **Approach the spot from several boat lengths to leeward and then turn the boat head-to-wind.**

2. **Slow the boat down and stop right over the desired spot for your anchor.**

   This spot isn't where the boat sits; it's where the anchor sits. The boat lies downwind (or *down current*) of this spot. As the wind or current shifts, your boat needs to swing around this spot (hopefully without dislodging the anchor) in a 360-degree circle.

3. Give the signal.

The key to anchoring is waiting to drop the anchor until the boat starts to go backward. Because the best judge of boat speed is the skipper, the crew members on the bow wait to drop the anchor until they see a hand signal (pointing down quickly works) or hear a hail such as, "Drop the hook, mateys." *Hook* is sailor slang for anchor.

Hails can be difficult to hear in a strong wind.

4. Drop the anchor.

See the next section.

Dropping the Anchor

The safest way to lower the anchor and the chain over the side is to slowly lower it hand over hand or under the control of an anchor *windlass* (if your boat is so equipped). A windlass looks like a winch drum mounted near the bow in line with a bow-mounted anchor roller that allows the anchor rode to smoothly drop over the rail of the boat. Figure 10-5 shows an electric windlass that lowers or raises the anchor with a push of a button. A manual windlass gives your muscle power some mechanical advantage, but most only help with raising the anchor.

If you don't have a windlass and are letting the anchor down by hand, try not to let it or the chain touch the hull. As soon as the anchor and chain are safely in the water, you can let the anchor line slide out through the bow chock (a pair of gloves can come in handy here).

Keep your body (especially your feet and fingers) away from and out of the loops of anchor line or chain as it pays out.

You can tell when the anchor touches bottom — either the rope stops paying out so fast, or you feel the weight of the anchor disappear as it settles in. The foredeck crew's job isn't over when the anchor hits pay dirt; you need to let out sufficient *scope* or extra rope (see the section "The scoop on scope," earlier in this chapter). When enough line to achieve the desired scope goes out, the foredeck crew cleats off the anchor line and gives the signal to the helmsman that you're ready to *set* (dig in) the anchor.

Digging In for Awhile

You can ensure that your anchor is set and holding in a couple of ways:

> ✔ **By touching the anchor rode with your hand, you can sometimes feel the anchor bounce over the bottom, similar to taking someone's pulse.** When the anchor digs in, the bouncing stops, but you can feel the line stretching as the boat surges in waves.
>
> ✔ **With the boat in reverse, you may be able to see the bow dip when the flukes of the anchor take a grip on the bottom.**

If you feel jerking motions, the anchor is dragging along the bottom. If your anchor keeps dragging, you can try any of the following techniques to get the anchor to set:

> ✔ **Let out more scope.** The anchor is probably skipping along the bottom, and with more scope, the anchor can dig in.
>
> ✔ **Give the anchor line a quick tug.** This tip works best on a smaller boat.
>
> ✔ **Speed up the engine in reverse.** Try this on a bigger boat.

If you keep dragging, you may have to pick up your anchor and try again.

When your senses tell you that the anchor is holding, try to confirm it by watching landmarks or a range. By sighting through two objects, you can establish a line sight and watch your position to ensure that you're not dragging, as Figure 10-6 shows.

Figure 10-6:
Sighting through a buoy to a large tree to ensure your anchor is secure.

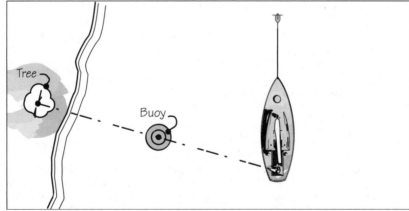

To be doubly sure that your anchor keeps on holding, try the following:

> ✔ **Make sure you have enough scope.** Consider the expected conditions, your type of anchor and rode, and the anticipated length of stay.
>
> ✔ **If a convenient range isn't available, take a few compass bearings on some distinctive landmarks.** You can also use buoys (especially in the

direction perpendicular to your anchor line) for reference. For more information about taking bearings, see Chapter 9.

✔ **Share the range with your crew.** Then they can double-check that you're securely anchored.

✔ **Write down these safety bearings so that when your insomnia kicks in at 2 a.m., you can reassure yourself that your boat is okay.** Remember that your range and bearings change if the boat swings with wind or current shifts.

✔ **Listen to your GPS system.** Your electronic navigation system may have an "anchor watch" alarm that rings if the boat moves out of a set area. See the "Tackling Anchoring Problems" section, later in this chapter, for more tips on using your GPS while at anchor.

✔ **If you're still concerned, dive down with a mask and inspect the anchor, chain, and rope.** Of course, this advice is easiest to follow if you're anchoring in the tropics.

✔ **Follow Coast Guard regulations.** The Coast Guard requires anchored boats to display a black ball up in the mast during daytime and a 360-degree fixed (not flashing) white light at night.

Retrieving Your Anchor

The key to picking up the anchor is teamwork between the crew and skipper. After assigning positions, including the key role of the foredeck crew, follow these steps:

1. **Slowly motor directly toward the anchor.**

   The helmsman probably needs the crew (who is performing Step 2) to occasionally point left or right to help keep on track.

2. **As the boat is moving toward the anchor, the crew pulls the slack out of the anchor line.**

   Moving up on the anchor creates slack in the line. This task shouldn't be physically difficult, because you're simply pulling in limp line.

3. **When the boat is directly over the anchor, the crew signals for the helmsman to stop.**

   We use a closed fist hand signal.

4. **Shift into neutral while the crew securely cleats the anchor line after pulling out all the slack so the anchor line is vertical.**

5. **When the line is cleated, the crew signals that the helmsman can start slowly going forward again until the anchor comes free.**

Because the anchor line is pulling up and forward (the opposite direction it was dug in) on the anchor, the flukes usually lift out of the muddy bottom easily.

Don't blow out your back — let the boat's engine do the tough work of getting the anchor free of the bottom.

You can tell when the anchor is free because the bow bounces up slightly and the anchor line has less pressure on it.

6. **When the anchor is free, put the engine back into neutral and begin the hardest part of the exercise — raising the anchor to the deck.**

   If you're lucky enough to have an electric windlass, you may not even break a sweat. A manual windlass gives you the mechanical advantage of a winch, but you still need muscle power to crank it; otherwise, get ready to pull and pull and pull some more.

   If your boat has an anchor windlass, make sure you understand exactly how it works before using it. Keep your hands clear of the moving parts and treat its operation as you do any powerful power tool — slowly and carefully.

   Regardless of the equipment on board, let the engine do all the work until the anchor breaks free from the ground. Take extra care to keep from dragging the chain (and anchor) along the hull.

7. **Before you bring your trusty anchor back on board, take a look at it as it clears the water and clean it if necessary.**

   Chances are that the anchor has some remnants of its temporary home still attached to it. Mud or sand may come off with repeated dunkings. If not, grab the old standbys — a bucket and a brush — to clean the sticky stuff off the anchor and chain before storing them.

8. **Put the anchor away.**

   If your anchor gets stored on a bow roller, make sure that it's safely lashed in place before setting sail. If your anchor, chain, and line get stored in a compartment on the bow, make sure the anchor line is neatly flaked back and forth in long sections so it stays untangled. If storing down below, see Chapter 4 for how to coil a rope.

Anchoring under Sail

Anchoring under power is much easier than anchoring under sail — the sails are out of the way, the boat is easier to control, and the entire crew can concentrate on the task at hand. But if you don't have an engine, anchoring under sail is certainly possible and may be necessary if the wind dies.

We recommend dropping, folding, and stowing the jib (or furling if your boat has a roller furler) before approaching the drop spot so that the anchor team has room to do its work.

The key to anchoring under sail is boat control — slowing the boat to a stop at your desired anchor drop spot and then *backing* the mainsail (pushing the boom out so that the main fills backwards) to go in reverse until enough scope is out to get the anchor to set. When you first back the main, put the tiller or wheel in the center. After you start sailing backward, you can swing the stern to the left (to port) by turning the helm to the right (to starboard), and vice versa. Be careful not to oversteer — a little rudder movement goes a long way. Practice going backward out in the open with no anchor involved until you get it right. After you master sailing backward, the steps to dropping the anchor are the same as in the preceding section.

All boats are less maneuverable at low speeds — and sailboats can be tricky to get going again. So the toughest part of anchoring under sail is that, for a moment, you intentionally stop the boat, and you lose steerageway until you pick up speed in reverse. This loss of maneuverability is why we recommend practicing first in open water. Leave your mainsail up (and luffing) until you're sure that you're safely anchored so that you can easily escape under sail if you have any problems.

If you do lose steerageway and are stopped, pointing straight into the wind, you're simply in irons. As in the case of anchoring under power, you want to drop the anchor and begin going backward to add scope. But if you aren't yet to your desired anchoring spot — you need to get out of irons and get moving forward again. Put the tiller or wheel to one side until the boat is pointed on a reaching angle, and then you can trim your sail and get going again. (See Chapter 5 for more information.)

Tackling Anchoring Problems

As the preceding sections illustrate, you need to consider many factors before anchoring. Whether you plan to leave your anchored boat for a picnic on the beach, go for a quick snorkeling trip, or you just want some peace of mind so you can fall asleep down below while at anchor, here's our "what-if" section. We take the most common anchoring problems and provide you with solutions.

 ✔ **You start swinging too close to another boat.** Some boats "sail" around quite a bit under anchor, powered by the force of the wind on the mast and hull. You can't do much to prevent this movement. But if you're swinging too close to another boat, either due to "sailing" or a shift in the wind, one or both of you has to pick up anchor and move farther away or put out a stern anchor to keep the boat from swinging (for more on setting a second anchor, see "Looking At Advanced Techniques," later in this chapter). Etiquette says the boat that anchored last has to move, but if no one is aboard the other boat, then you just pulled the short straw.

✔ **You think your anchor starts dragging several hours after you anchored.** Keep in mind that your boat swings around the anchor (in a circular arc) depending on changes in the direction of the wind and current. The compass bearings that you took to double-check that you were securely anchored won't be valid if your boat swings 180 degrees because the current switches direction. If everyone in the anchorage seems to be in the same positions relative to one another, but they're all pointing in different directions, you've probably swung. Before going to sleep, make sure that you have a strong mental picture of the anchorage and your boat's position — you can even mark your position on the chart, or your GPS may have an "anchor watch" feature.

If I have a GPS with a chart plotter or a computer with a charting program attached to the instruments, I zoom in the chart to the maximum resolution after anchoring. By watching the trace of the boat's track over time (you may have to enable this feature on your GPS or computer), you can often see if you're dragging or simply moving in an arc around your anchor.

✔ **The weather starts getting nasty.** The added load from increased wind, waves, and current in a storm may cause the anchor to start dragging. If you know that more wind is coming, consider seeking better shelter. If you decide to stay, let out plenty of additional scope (in rough conditions, you may need as much as 10:1 scope). In rough weather, pull in or let out several feet of anchor rode every few hours to minimize chafe on the line where it goes through the bow chock or roller. If you have a second anchor, you may want to set it (see the section "Doubling up: Two anchors," later in this chapter).

✔ **You can't pull up your anchor.** First, make sure that you start directly over the anchor with all the slack pulled out and the anchor line securely cleated. If the wind shifts and your boat swings during your stay, you may not be motoring in the right direction to get the flukes to pull out. Try other directions, slowly increasing the engine power to apply more force.

If you're having a problem getting the anchor on deck after you get it off the bottom, (and your boat isn't equipped with an anchor windlass on the foredeck), you may need to take the anchor line to a winch and grind the line up. Make sure that the anchor line has a good lead through the bow chock and back to the winch, without chafing on anything, and stop grinding before the chain starts rubbing on the side of the hull. Pulling up an anchor can take heaps of strength, so make sure that you're using the strongest people on the boat for the job.

Choosing the Right Anchor

Most keelboats come equipped with the anchor package (but you may have to search a lot of compartments to find it). In case you need to buy an anchor, chain, or line, this section helps you shop like a pro. Various anchors perform differently, depending on such factors as the type of bottom (sand, mud, grass, or rock). The following are the two most common anchors on sailboats:

- The **Danforth anchor** (refer to Figure 10-1) takes its name from the company that invented it. It's also called the *lightweight anchor;* because the large flukes bury so well, the anchor can be lighter than a plow anchor.

  The Danforth needs a soft sand or mud bottom (two of the most desirable bottom types for anchoring due to their holding potential) to grip properly. This anchor is especially popular on dinghies and small keelboats because of its light weight and low profile on board. This anchor isn't perfect, however; the sharp points on its flukes can be troublesome in storage. Some larger keelboats (longer than 30 feet, or 9 meters) may carry an undersized Danforth as a "lunch hook" for easy temporary anchoring in calm conditions as well as a heavier, primary anchor such as a plow.

- The **plow anchor** looks like the farm implement — hence the name. It's also called by the trade name "CQR." The plow is secure on most bottoms and is arguably the best all-around anchor for larger sailboats (longer than 30 feet, or 9 meters). Although heavier than a Danforth with the equivalent holding power, the plow can get the job done in most conditions. As Figure 10-7 shows, the plow is often kept secured up forward on a roller with the fluke hanging over the bow. You never see this sight on a racing boat — too much weight up forward!

Figure 10-7:
A plow anchor set in its roller on the bow, ready to go to work.

Table 10-1 gives you a quick rundown on what weight the anchor needs to be based on the boat's size, although a live-aboard cruiser picks a bulkier anchor package than the average day sailor.

Table 10-1	Anchor Weight	
Boat Length	**Danforth**	**Plow**
20 ft (6 m)	5 lb (2 kg)	15 lb (6 kg)
30 ft (9 m)	12 lb (5 kg)	20 lb (8 kg)
40 ft (12 m)	20 lb (8 kg)	35 lb (13 kg)
50 ft (15 m)	35 lb (13 kg)	45 lb (17 kg)
60 ft (18 m)	60 lb (22 kg)	60 lb (22 kg)

Adapted from Earl Hinz, The Complete Book of Anchoring and Mooring (Centreville, Maryland: Cornell Maritime Press, 1986).

Table 10-1 is a rough guide to anchor size. If your boat is especially *beamy* (wide) for its length, use a heavier anchor. Also, if you're going to anchor for a long time in extreme conditions, such as very strong winds, consider a heavier anchor.

Securing the anchor and rode

The chain is usually connected to the anchor with a *shackle* (a U-shaped metal fitting) and to the anchor line with an *eye splice* (a permanent loop woven into the end of the rope) and another shackle instead of a knot. Knots can come untied — and need we point out that the last thing you want is to have your anchor line come untied?

Another anchor rode worry is chafe, and with an eye splice, you can use a *thimble* (teardrop-shaped metal fitting that fits tightly inside an eye splice) to cut down on chafing. (To find out more about eye splices, see Chapter 15.) If you must use a knot, tie a round turn and a couple of half hitches or a fisherman's bend. (See Chapter 19 for the lowdown on these knots.) Regardless of the knot, you may want to further secure the bitter end from untying by *seizing* it — using a needle and thread to sew it.

With two strong shackles, you can attach the chain to the anchor line and to the anchor. Use a pair of vice grips or pliers to really tighten the shackles and then *mouse* them — run a few loops of galvanized wire or small line through a hole in the shackle pin to keep it from loosening. Grease the shackle threads first so that they don't freeze up. A galvanized steel (which doesn't rust) or bronze shackle is best.

Chain provides an important role in keeping you safe at anchor. The general rule is to have chain that weighs as much as your anchor. For example, a 30-foot boat with a 12-pound Danforth anchor needs roughly 16 feet of chain attached to the anchor. Table 10-2 shows the recommended diameter of rope, diameter of chain, and length of chain to use for different sizes of boats. Again, shifting up in size and chain length is best if you're anchoring in extreme conditions or if your boat is heavier or beamier than average.

Table 10-2	Anchor Rode Specifications		
Boat Length	**Nylon Rope Diameter**	**Chain Diameter**	**Chain Length**
20 ft (6 m)	⅜ in (1 cm)	¼ in (6 mm)	6–33 ft (2–10 m)
30 ft (9 m)	⁷⁄₁₆ in (11 mm)	¼ in (6 mm)	16–46 ft (5–14 m)
40 ft (12 m)	½ in (13 mm)	⁵⁄₁₆ in (8 mm)	18–48 ft (6–15 m)
50 ft (15 m)	⅝ in (16 mm)	⅜ in (1 cm)	21–46 ft (7–14 m)
60 ft (18 m)	¾ in (19 mm)	⁷⁄₁₆ in (11 mm)	27–44 ft (9–13 m)

Note: The two numbers in the right-hand column indicate the range in chain length for use with the lightest (Danforth) and the heaviest anchors.

Adapted from Earl Hinz, The Complete Book of Anchoring and Mooring (Centreville, Maryland: Cornell Maritime Press, 1986).

Choosing the right anchor line

Don't use just any rope for your anchor line. Here are a few characteristics of a good anchor rope:

- ✔ Long enough for anchoring properly
- ✔ Resistant to chafe
- ✔ Stretchy enough to absorb the surging load without yanking the anchor out
- ✔ Strong enough to hold your boat in expected conditions

Nylon rope is recommended for anchor lines because it provides the best balance of performance in these key areas.

So that you can easily tell how many feet or meters of line you've let out (crucial for figuring out your scope), you can sew or insert small fabric markers into your anchor line at set intervals. Never tie permanent knots in a line for this purpose, because knots weaken the line.

Remember that the basic rule is to use 5:1 scope. So assuming your boat has 15 feet of chain and you must anchor in water depth of 30 feet, you need 135 feet of line for average conditions and more line in severe conditions.

Resist the temptation to go up in anchor rope diameter. You get better strength, but you get less stretch, which is important in keeping the anchor hooked in rough, surging conditions. Plus, anchor lines take up enough space on board already without increasing their diameter unnecessarily.

Maintaining the anchor and rode

A good freshwater hosing after use is important to keep your anchor gear from smelling like the dumpster behind your local fish restaurant. Because your anchor and rode spend most of the time stored in some dark compartment, inspecting this vital equipment from time to time is important. Check your chain for rusty or weakened links and examine the anchor line for chafe or wear. If you notice a rusty or weakened link, make sure you replace it immediately.

The most common place for chafe on an anchor line is where the line has to turn a corner to come on board your boat. A good way to minimize wear is to build a makeshift chafe guard by slicing a short piece of garden hose and wrapping it around the anchor line where it turns the corner over the bow chock. If you're at anchor in rough conditions, periodically pull up (hard) or let out (easy) several feet of anchor line to prevent chafe in one spot.

Anchoring with all chain

Some bigger cruising boats (60 feet [18 meters] or more) have all-chain anchor rodes (and electric windlasses to pull up all that heavy chain). Obviously, these rodes are much heavier, but chain is also stronger and more durable than nylon rope. A total chain anchor rode enables you to use less scope for given conditions. Although chain doesn't stretch, it can provide that critical shock absorption for the anchor because the rode arcs down to the anchor. A pulse of wind or wave pushing on the boat simply pulls some of this arc out of the rode, absorbing some of the energy.

Looking At Advanced Techniques

Sometimes you need to get creative and use two anchors. Or you may need to secure your boat to a sea wall (a common method in Europe). The anchoring chapter isn't complete without showing you these two advanced techniques.

Doubling up: Two anchors

Securing your boat with two anchors can help decrease dragging and swing-ing. One common example is setting two anchors in front of the boat so that when they dig in, the anchor lines create an angle of about 45 degrees (see Figure 10-8). This method is good for really rough weather coming from a fixed direction, because each anchor takes about half the load of the boat's pull. A side benefit is that you can use less scope for the same holding power (but keep in mind that the more scope, the better for rough conditions). The benefit of two anchors disappears, however, in a big wind shift.

Figure 10-8:
Left: For increased security from dragging, two anchors are better than one. Right: A stern anchor keeps boats in a crowded anchorage from swinging around.

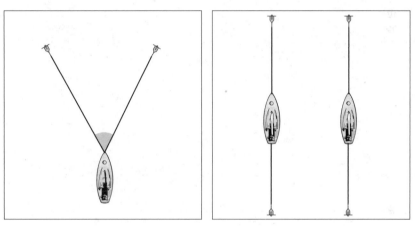

Another common use of two anchors is to set a stern anchor directly opposite the bow anchor to keep your boat from swinging in a crowded anchorage — but only where the weather conditions are quite stable and calm.

Setting double anchors is kind of tricky. You can set them from one boat, but another way, arguably easier, is to set the first anchor normally and then send a crew of volunteers in the dinghy out with an anchor and rode to set the second one. Make sure that the bitter end of this second anchor rode is attached to the anchored boat first!

PETER SAYS

When I was with a television documentary team cruising around Cape Horn and the Beagle Channel, we used a variation of this anchoring system. Of course, no man-made docks or dredged-out harbors were around, but often the water was fairly deep right up close to shore. To get nestled in as cozily as possible and out of the icy blasts of the *williwaws* (sudden gusts of cold air from the mountains), we dropped an anchor well offshore and then took the inflatable dinghy into shore with two lines attached to the back of the boat on big spools. When we got to shore, we found the two strongest nearby trees and attached these stern lines to them (see Figure 10-9). This trick certainly was easier than setting out two more anchors!

Figure 10-9:
Skip
Novak's
charter boat
Pelagic
nestled into
a cozy
anchorage
near Cape
Horn.

Anchoring Mediterranean style

Guess where this system is popular? Docking in the Mediterranean style, also referred to as *stern to,* enables you to tie up with your *stern* (back end) close to the shore, man-made bulkhead, or dock — when the water is deep enough. "Stern-to" is the way the mega-yachts tie up in Saint-Tropez. Of course, many places on the Mediterranean Sea have mooring buoys to facilitate your docking. If no moorings are available and you must use the anchor, simply pick your spot on the shore where you want the stern to end up, and drop the hook the appropriate distance straight out from shore. Then back the boat in slowly (under engine power, please), until you get close to the shore or dock. Secure two stern lines (one from each corner of the back end) to the dock and adjust the tension of the anchor so that you don't hit the dock but are (hopefully) close enough to easily step on shore, possibly with the help of a plank to bridge the short gap.

Part III
Sailing Fast: Taking Your Sailing to the Next Level

The 5th Wave   By Rich Tennant

OF COURSE I KNOW THERE ARE NO DIRECTIONAL SIGNALS ON A SAILBOAT. THAT'S WHY I USED A RIGHT TURN ARM SIGNAL!

HARBOR POLICE

In this part . . .

Are you hooked on sailing yet? We hope so, and Chapters 11 and 12 get you focused on speed — sailing your boat faster. Even if you're not a speed freak, some of the tips in these chapters can make your sailing experience more comfortable. And the final chapter introduces you to sailboat racing — the part of this huge sport that we love the most. So humor us and at least glance at that chapter. The racing bug may bite you, too.

Chapter 11

The Need for Speed: Sailing Fast

. . . .

In This Chapter

▶ Recognizing apparent wind

▶ Using steering methods to go faster

▶ Hiking out and trapezing

▶ Roll tacking and jibing

▶ Planing and surfing waves

▶ Delving into special catamaran techniques

. . . .

> *I wish to have no connection with any ship that does not sail fast; for I intend to go in harm's way.*
>
> — *John Paul Jones*

*S*ailing fast — a powerboater may think that this is an oxymoron — but we've gone sailing with a few professional car drivers, and they've been surprised at how fast sailboats can go. Especially on a boat that's low to the water and gets plenty of spray over the deck, you always feel like you're going faster than you really are.

This chapter looks at ways to drive faster and use your weight to get more performance out of your boat. On all dinghies and small keelboats, how and where you and your crew put your weight can improve your boat's performance. This chapter also shows you how to sail fast boats like catamarans.

Understanding Apparent Wind

Chapter 5 covers the importance of knowing the wind direction. And many of the "go fast" tips in this chapter reiterate the importance of feeling the wind. However, before you try and sail faster, you need to examine more closely the wind that hits your moving sailboat. The wind you feel on board your boat, when your boat is moving, is the *apparent wind,* which is different from *true wind,* or the wind felt by an anchored boat or a flag on shore.

To illustrate the difference between apparent and true wind, imagine jumping on a bicycle and pedaling down the road. If the day is calm, you feel wind in your face (apparent wind) — the faster you pedal, the more wind, right? And if the day is windy, the wind you feel in your face — your apparent wind — is the combination of the *wind of motion,* the wind blowing directly into your face that you create by pedaling fast, and the *true wind,* the wind blowing over the road.

The same phenomenon happens aboard a sailboat: As you move forward, you create a wind of motion that combines with the true wind blowing over the water, resulting in the wind you and your sails feel — the sailboat's apparent wind, as Figure 11-1 shows.

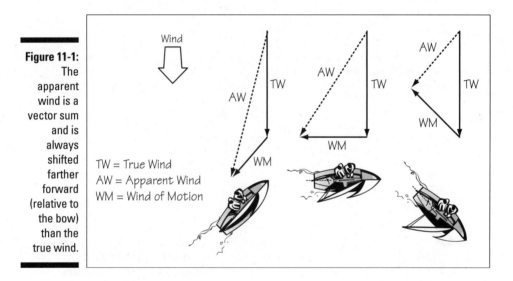

Figure 11-1:
The apparent wind is a vector sum and is always shifted farther forward (relative to the bow) than the true wind.

TW = True Wind
AW = Apparent Wind
WM = Wind of Motion

On very fast boats, this capability to "make your own wind" can have some really amazing results. For mortal monohull sailors, the difference between the apparent wind and the true wind is more subtle, except when you accelerate rapidly, such as when you catch a wave. Here are the key features of apparent wind:

- ✔ **The faster you go, the more effect your wind of motion has on the apparent wind's direction and velocity.**

- ✔ **Apparent wind is always lighter (less velocity) when you're sailing away from the true wind than when you're sailing toward it.** That's why sailing downwind feels warmer than sailing upwind.

- ✔ **Sailing straight downwind can be slower.** Super speedy boats such as catamarans actually sail directly downwind (on a run) more slowly than if they head up and sail on a *broad reach* (deeper than perpendicular to the wind) and then jibe over.

Don't let apparent wind versus true wind confuse you; the sailor's universe still revolves around the wind that he feels. Just know that, as long as your boat is moving, the wind that you and your sails feel is technically called the apparent wind.

Sailing Faster: Go-Fast Tips

A gust of wind hits a beginner's boat and the boat speeds up, but then the puff goes away and the boat slows down again. Keeping your boat fast and getting the most speed out of the conditions requires practice. The following list includes many of the ways to get any boat zooming along and keep it sailing fast:

- ✔ **More wind = more speed.** Wind is like boat speed — more is better, but only to a point. Each boat is different, but most boats benefit from increased velocity up to about 15 knots. At that wind speed, beginning sailors should head back to the dock. Going downwind, most boats respond favorably as the wind picks up to 20 knots, but with more wind than that, control becomes a concern. For more on estimating wind strength, check out Chapter 8.

- ✔ **In light air, sail for the puffs.** Look for the *dark water,* where the ripples and other signs of more wind are. See Chapter 5, where we discuss that darker water means more wind.

- ✔ **Sailing on a reach is fastest.** To review reaching and the other points of sail, refer to Chapter 5. If you had a particular destination in mind and could make the wind blow from any direction, you'd make your course a reach. By sailing on a reach, you can sail on your boat's fastest point of sail and steer a direct course.

- ✔ **Sailing to a point straight upwind takes longer than it looks.** Because you have to zigzag your way back and forth to reach a destination directly upwind (as we discuss in Chapter 5), you end up sailing extra distance.

- ✔ **Waves matter.** Waves slow you down when sailing toward them and can speed you up when sailing with them.

- ✔ **Wind shifts matter.** Check out Chapter 8 to figure out how to use wind shifts to get to your destination faster.

- ✔ **Some boats are faster.** Lots of components determine a boat's speed. As a general rule, a longer boat with more sail area is usually faster, but catamarans and other boats that can *plane* (skim along) are the exceptions to this rule.

- ✔ **Adjust your sail shape for changes in wind speed and direction.** Chapter 12 shows you which ropes to pull to get the perfect sail shape to harness the wind.

Steering Faster: Driving Tips

Just as golfers work on their basic swing, you can improve your driving with practice. To steer faster, try some of the following tips:

- ✔ **Steer straight to steer fast.** When most boats are close-hauled or reaching, they exhibit a tendency, called *weather helm,* to turn toward the wind. Weather helm relates to the balance of all the forces pushing and pulling on the boat, its sails, and its foils (see Appendix C). Weather helm is like driving a car that has its front end out of alignment — the tiller or wheel "pulls" to one side. If you were to release the helm, the boat would turn up until it pointed directly into the wind — dead-center in the no-sail zone.

  But here's something that surprises every new sailor and takes some practice to master — you have to make small steering changes to keep a sailboat going straight. As the wind changes in velocity or the boat changes its angle of heel, the amount of weather helm changes, forcing you to alter the rudder slightly to keep going straight. Although disconcerting at first, a little weather helm is natural, and a skilled helmsman develops a good feel of how to make the smallest steering corrections to keep the boat going straight through the changing conditions. Keeping your corrections small also minimizes the speed-robbing drag caused by turning the rudder. Check out Appendix C for more on drag.

- ✔ **Look around.** Find a point (a tree or building) on the horizon where you're headed to make sure you're steering straight, and look at the sails to make sure they aren't luffing (Chapter 12 shows you how to use an early warning system called *telltales*). Then look at the water ahead for approaching wind and waves. Also look around for boats (from all directions), then back at your point on the horizon, then up at the telltales, and so on. Spend 10 to 20 seconds looking at each station.

  Buddy Melges, the "Wizard of Zenda, Wisconsin," is one of my all-time heroes in sailing. He's won the America's Cup (America[3] in 1992) and an Olympic Gold Medal (Soling class, 1972), but, more important, he is a great person who loves to share his knowledge. One time I asked him how he keeps a boat in the groove going upwind in a breeze. He said that he watches the horizon up ahead of the boat and keeps it at a constant angle to the bow and luff of the jib.

- ✔ **Practice "zen and the art of steering."** When the boat is in the groove, the wind hits your face at a certain angle, the mainsheet tugs with a set force, the rudder pulls on your steering hand just so, and the boat heels a certain amount. Practice keeping the boat at that optimum heel angle, and you're sailing like a pro!

- ✔ **Find that groove.** *Pinching* the boat (sailing too close to the wind) is obvious because the sails start to luff and lose power. As your boat slows down, it slips sideways to leeward more because the rudder and keel (or centerboard) are stalled. If you do stall out and get slow from pinching, ease the sails slightly, bear off 3 to 5 degrees wider of a close-hauled course, and get the water flow going fast again. But you don't want to bear off too far (called *footing*) or you'll be sailing extra distance and away from your upwind destination. Between *pinching* and *footing* is the magical *upwind groove,* providing the best compromise of speed versus angle to the wind.

Trying to reach a point upwind is a balancing act. By pinching, you sail less distance to your destination (because you tack through fewer degrees, as track A in Figure 11-2 shows), but you sail slower. Track B, the intermediate course, provides the best trade-off of boat speed versus distance sailed.

When it's windy, a keelboat's angle of heel can help find the groove. Each boat has a maximum heel angle for optimum performance (see Chapter 12). When it's windy, sailing too wide to the wind *(footing)* can cause the boat to heel too far, which can also cause a stall in your rudder (extreme weather helm) unless you let out your sails — but then you're sailing on a reach and not getting closer to that upwind destination (Track C in Figure 11-2). So ease the sails slightly and then head back up to get to that magic groove (and heel angle).

✔ **React to wind shifts.** All these go-fast tips would be a lot easier if the wind never changed. But the wind is never perfectly steady for very long (see Chapter 8). On a sailboat, shifts are named for the effect they have on your sails and the angle your boat can sail (see Figure 11-3). In a *header,* the wind shifts forward. If your sail starts to luff and you're still pointed in the same direction, then the wind has shifted so that it's coming from farther ahead (a *header*). In a *lift,* the wind shifts aft. In either case, you have to alter course (or retrim your sails) to get back in the groove.

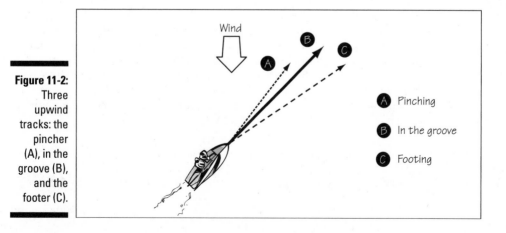

Figure 11-2: Three upwind tracks: the pincher (A), in the groove (B), and the footer (C).

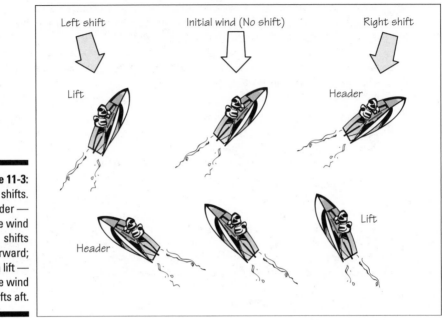

Figure 11-3:
Wind shifts.
A header —
the wind
shifts
forward;
a lift —
the wind
shifts aft.

✔ **Minimize heel.** In Appendix C, we describe how a sailboat can sail toward the wind — because the water flowing over the centerboard (or keel) creates "lift" like a wing that's balanced by the forces of the wind on the sails. As the boat heels over, the centerboard or keel tilts with it, so less lift is generated. The sails also tilt, becoming less efficient.

Bottom line: Too much heel is very slow, so try and limit it any way you can. One way is by moving your weight as far to windward as possible, a technique called *hiking*, as the next section describes. In Chapter 12, we discuss how to adjust the sail trim if shifting your weight isn't enough.

✔ **Fine-tune your sailing skills on a dinghy.** Because dinghies are much more responsive than keelboats, you develop your "feel" more quickly sailing a dinghy. In Chapter 5, we cover the basics of sailing a dinghy — an agile, tippy boat. But because dinghies can capsize (some more easily than others), make sure you review small-boat safety in Chapter 7 and can move your weight quickly. Knowing how to swim is important for dinghy sailing too, and don't forget your life jacket!

Sailing Flat Is Fast: Ease, Hike, and Trim

The best small-boat sailors can anticipate the changes in wind speed by reading the wind as it comes across the water. They keep their boats as flat as possible (not heeled over by the wind) when sailing *close-hauled* (toward the wind). Keeping your boat flat is easy in light winds, but to sail like a pro in more breeze when a *puff* (an extra bit of breeze) hits, take one or more of the following three actions to keep the boat from heeling:

- ✔ **Hike out:** Lean your weight over the side. Read the next section for tips on hiking your hardest in windy conditions.

- ✔ **Ease the mainsail:** Let out the sail slightly to bleed some power from it. When the puff is over, *trim* (pull) the sail back in.

- ✔ **Pinch:** Steer the boat a little bit closer to the wind so that the front of the sail begins to luff (flutter).

Hiking out

Even on keelboats, moving your weight to the "high side" helps coax a little more speed out of your boat. The right photo in Figure 11-4 shows a racing crew with all their weight on the rail.

Figure 11-4:
Dinghy sailors hiking hard, and a keelboat crew using its weight for added speed.

Right photo © Tim Wilkes, www.timwilkes.com

On a dinghy, hiking hard means a workout. If your butt is on the rail, you aren't hiking very hard. If your thighs are the last part of you touching the rail, as the left photo of Figure 11-4 shows, you're really maximizing the leverage of your body. The following tips can help you hike your hardest in a dinghy:

✔ **Hook your feet under the hiking straps** (after checking that they're secure and a comfortable length). If you skip this tip, you're going for a swim.

✔ **Make sure that the *tiller extension (hiking stick)* is long enough.** The steering stick or handle connects to the end of the tiller so that you can still steer as you hike out.

✔ **Make sure that your *mainsheet* (the rope you use to control the trim of the mainsail) is as easy to hold as possible.** Consider adding a ratchet block (see Chapter 5) and/or a cleat (one that's easy to uncleat in a puff!).

✔ **If you're trimming the jib, hold onto the jib sheet while leaning outboard.** Now you're using arm and leg muscles to hike and getting a great workout.

Trapezing for speed

Imagine that you're sailing on a dinghy in windy conditions and are hiking as hard as you can. A really tall person of equal weight would be able to keep his boat flatter, because he has more leverage. Because flatter is faster, off he goes. But what if you hike out so far that you're standing on the side of your boat? Then you can pass that guy like you're being shot out of a cannon.

A *trapeze* lets you do just that — stand on the side of your boat to maximize the effect of your body weight. Trapezing is like "superhiking." Whoever invented the trapeze must have really hated to hike out or been a really smart person. A trapeze system includes a support wire *(trapeze wire),* which runs from near the top of the mast to a ring just above deck level. It also includes a *trapeze harness,* which you wear with a hook at belly-button level in front, enabling you to "hook in" to the trapeze wire, as Figure 11-5 shows.

Many dinghies and catamarans are designed to have one or more crew members ride on a trapeze. Trapezing requires athletic ability, balance, and sailing skills (to anticipate wind shifts and to keep from being dragged in the water or flung around the bow by a wave).

JJ SAYS

The trapeze artist in Figure 11-5 is my 1992 Olympic teammate, Pamela Healy. You're probably wondering how Pam can tack while on a trapeze. As the boat begins the turn, she swings into the boat and unhooks, supporting her weight by holding onto a small handle on the trapeze wire. Then, with her other hand, she uncleats the jib sheet as the boat turns through the no-sail zone. When the boat is on the new tack, she leaps out over the water on the new side, holding onto the handle of the new trap wire (yes, the boat has two wires — one on each side). In her other hand, she trims in the new jib sheet. Finally, she hooks in, and off she goes. An excellent dinghy crew like Pam can go from tack to tack in less than two seconds.

Figure 11-5:
Pam Healy
(JJ's
Olympic
teammate
in '92) on a
trapeze.

Positioning for Proper Fore-and-Aft Trim

Sitting in the wrong position *athwartships* (across the boat) on a dinghy is pretty obvious, because it dramatically heels one way or the other. *Fore-and-aft weight position* errors (such as sitting too far back) don't give you an instant indication that something is out of whack, but they're very important if you're looking to maximize speed.

Make sure that the boat is sitting *on its lines* — that is, level in the water when you view it from the side, with neither the bow nor the stern sitting abnormally low or high in the water. Keeping the boat on its lines usually means sitting somewhere near the boat's *center of buoyancy* (the central point of all the buoyancy forces on the boat). If you could push your boat down with a huge finger, the center of buoyancy would be the point where downward pressure evenly sinks both ends of the boat.

Keep the following basic guidelines in mind to fine-tune your weight position for proper fore-and-aft trim:

✔ **Stay out of the "ends" of the boat.** Generally, if you sit near the centerboard or keel, you're close to the right spot.

✔ **If you have more than one person on board, sit close together.**

✔ **In light air, shift your weight forward one or two body widths.** Look at your *wake* (the disturbed water behind your boat) to make sure you're not dragging your stern.

> ✔ **When hiking out or trapezing while sailing upwind, position yourself at the widest point of the boat for maximum leverage.**
>
> ✔ **In strong winds, when reaching or running or if the waves start to come over the bow, move back one or two body widths.** This action keeps the bow out of the water and floats the boat more on the back end, which has a flatter shape, resulting in less drag for high-speed sailing.

Rockin' and Rollin' the Boat

You've heard the expression *don't rock the boat,* right? Well, in most dinghies, if you want to go fast in a straight line, then lose the word *don't.* Kinetics are techniques for flapping your boat's "wings" (both above and below the water). Kinetics include *rocking* (repeatedly rolling), *pumping* (repeatedly trimming and easing) the sails, roll tacking, roll jibing, and *sculling* (repeatedly turning the rudder back and forth). In windy and wavy conditions, some of these techniques can give you that extra burst of speed that enables the boat to start *planing* (skimming along the surface of the water) and surfing waves.

This section provides several tips to help you master some rocking and rolling in your boat. (Just no head banging, please.)

Roll tack

Kinetics are so fast that the racing rules restrict them. However, intentional rocking is legal during tacking and jibing maneuvers. Experienced dinghy racers have turned this technicality into an art form, rolling the boat during tacks and jibes so effectively that the boat actually accelerates during the turn.

Follow these steps for a successful *roll tack,* as Figure 11-6 shows:

1. **Begin the tack by leaning in slightly, adding about 10 degrees of leeward heel.**

2. **Start turning the rudder just like in any tack.**

3. **When the boat points nearly directly into the wind, hike the boat hard to windward (windward on the original tack) to begin the roll and trim the mainsheet in tight at the same time.**

   Keep turning!

4. **When your butt is about to get wet, quickly change sides to the new windward side.**

   Normally, you change sides when the turn of the tack is about 75 percent complete (that is, you're almost on the new close-hauled course).

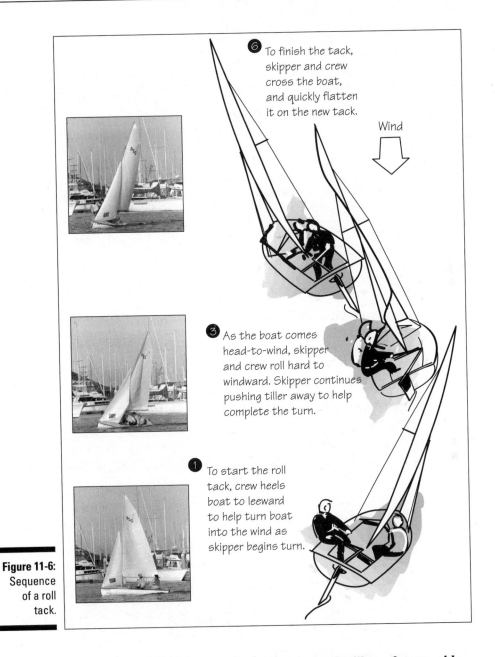

6 To finish the tack, skipper and crew cross the boat, and quickly flatten it on the new tack.

Wind

3 As the boat comes head-to-wind, skipper and crew roll hard to windward. Skipper continues pushing tiller away to help complete the turn.

1 To start the roll tack, crew heels boat to leeward to help turn boat into the wind as skipper begins turn.

Figure 11-6:
Sequence
of a roll
tack.

5. Ease the mainsheet about 1 foot and trim the jib on the new side.

6. As the boat turns onto the new close-hauled course, the skipper and crew hike (in unison) the boat flat on the new side, trimming the mainsheet back in the amount that you eased it in Step 5.

The boat squirts forward on the new tack!

Be careful — too much roll and over you go in a capsize.

In light air, the skipper's weight alone may be enough to flatten the boat on the new tack. So the crew just moves to the centerline of the boat or whatever position brings the boat level.

Roll tacking takes a great deal of practice and coordination between skipper and crew, because you get the biggest roll when the whole crew moves together. Timing is crucial. Starting the roll too early or not hiking hard enough results in a lame excuse for a roll tack that may even slow the boat down.

Because of its keel, you and a bunch of your biggest friends won't be able to get much roll out of a keelboat. But by using the preceding rolling tips and keeping your weight on the old windward side until the boat is through the tack, you can still slightly improve the speed of your keelboat tack — especially in light air.

Roll jibe

Roll jibing is very similar to roll tacking and requires just as much practice. Here are the steps to a successful roll jibe:

1. **Heel the boat to windward an additional 10 degrees by hiking out.**

2. **Begin your smooth turn downwind with the rudder.**

3. **Grab the mainsheet and fling the mainsail quickly across.**

   Alternatively, the crew can grab the *boom vang* (sail control rigged between the boom and the mast) to fling the main onto the new jibe.

4. **Just before your butt drags in the water, quickly switch sides and gently but forcefully flatten the boat by hiking out with your weight.**

5. **At the same time as you switch sides, give the mainsheet a quick pull in to help acceleration.**

6. **Return the boat to its optimum downwind course and let the mainsheet back out.**

The initial change in heel for both the tack and the jibe helps start the turn so that you use less rudder motion (which is less drag, as you see in Appendix C). The second, more forceful roll gives you that kinetic boost of speed, as if you're flapping the "wings" (sails and underwater foils) of your boat!

As the wind comes up, all this rocking and rolling can be a quick ticket to capsize — so be careful. Rocking and rolling techniques work best in light to medium wind. In fact, in heavy air, you may need to hike to windward as the mainsail fills out of a jibe to keep the boat from capsizing. And you may need to steer into the turn, as the next section describes.

S-turning in heavy air

An S-turn jibe is the opposite of a roll jibe but is the key to staying under control during a jibe when the wind picks up. Follow these steps for a successful S-turn:

1. **Start on a very broad reach.**

   This angle minimizes the turn needed to complete the jibe.

2. **When the crew is ready, bear away (gently) to jibe.**

   Now is the time to pull in the mainsheet fast.

3. **Reverse the helm about 15 degrees at the split second in the turn when the boom catches wind on the new side and begins to blow across the boat, steering the boat back toward the old jibe, as Figure 11-7 shows.**

   This "S-turn" counteracts the momentum of the boom and keeps the boat from heeling too far when the mainsail fills on the new jibe.

4. **A second later, just after the mainsail fills with a bang on the new jibe, reverse the helm again and steer straight (or wherever you need to steer in order to be on a very broad reach on the new jibe).**

   Have your crew keep the boat flat throughout this maneuver — everyone may have to hike out right out of the jibe to keep the boom from touching the water.

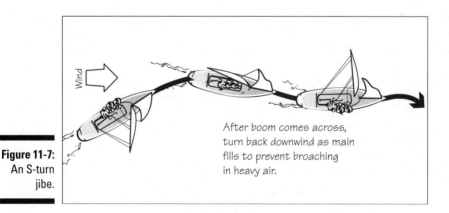

Figure 11-7: An S-turn jibe.

Wind

After boom comes across, turn back downwind as main fills to prevent broaching in heavy air.

You've gotta rock it

You can actually rock your sailboat back and forth to generate a good head of steam when absolutely no wind is blowing, as Figure 11-8 shows. On a light dinghy, rocking works better than paddling.

Here's how to rock your boat to generate your own wind:

1. **Put the centerboard/daggerboard all the way down.**

2. **Set the sails to a loose close-hauled trim.**

3. **Have the skipper hold the tiller straight or, if single-handing, let the tiller go where it pleases.**

   Or the skipper can practice *sculling,* repeatedly turning the tiller hard to one side and then the other, propelling the boat forward.

4. **Violently rock the boat one way.**

5. **Right before the boat begins to capsize (which is always a risk if you aren't careful), violently rock the boat back the other way.**

   Having the primary "rocker" stand up and hold the mast helps.

6. **Continue until you reach your destination or collapse from exhaustion.**

Figure 11-8:
No wind?
No problem;
rock your
boat home.

Planing and Surfing the Waves

Nothing compares with the thrill of sailing a small dinghy on a high-speed reach, with water spraying off the bow like a fire hose. You may be going only 10 or even 20 knots, but the sensation of speed is greater than going four times that fast in a car — really!

Most heavy keelboats are stuck within the bow and stern waves that they create as they cruise through the water. But given enough power from the wind, light dinghies can jump over those waves and skim over the water, similar to a speedboat or a surfer.

If you have enough wind, this skimming action, called *planing*, doesn't require any special action on the part of the crew. As soon as you begin to plane, you know it — because of the huge smile that spreads across your face as you realize that you're going faster than you'd thought possible.

A close cousin to planing is surfing. Technically speaking, planing occurs any time the boat breaks free of its own bow and stern wave and rips along, regardless of the texture of the water's surface. Surfing only happens when a wave *crest* (top) grabs the boat and gets it speeding along, sliding "downhill" on the face of the wave.

When we talk about surfing the waves, we're not talking about going in close to the shore break. You have a mast overhead, a mast that would get crumpled if you capsize in the surf close to shore — not to mention what would happen to you and your boat.

The great thing about surfing waves is that you can surf ocean swells, power-boat wakes — anything with a slope to it. Because waves usually run the same direction as the wind, your best chance to catch them is when sailing on a broad reach or a run.

Any surfer can tell you that to catch a wave, you need to be going close to the wave's speed. On a sailboat, you may need to use kinetic techniques (such as rocking and pumping) to accelerate your boat when the wave starts to pick up your transom.

In order to start your surfing career, follow these easy steps:

1. **Get the boat pointed on a broad reach with the sails perfectly trimmed.**

   If the boat has a spinnaker, use it for extra horsepower. See Chapter 12 for how to use a spinnaker.

2. **If you have a centerboard or daggerboard, pull it up partway.**

   This reduces the drag underwater and is good practice anytime you're sailing off the wind.

3. **When your boat is pointed downhill on the wave and is starting to accelerate, give a good pump to the mainsheet by pulling it in 3 feet (1 meter) or so very fast and then immediately releasing it.**

   If you're reaching with a spinnaker, you can pump it, too. The boat scoots forward and starts to shoot down the face of the wave.

4. **Quickly slide your weight back in the boat to raise the bow out of the water and enable the boat to sit on the flatter (more surfboard-shaped) back half of the hull.**

Now you're surfing, and you can steer the boat straight down the face of the wave. You need to trim your sails, because your apparent wind moves forward the more you accelerate. See "Understanding Apparent Wind" at the beginning of this chapter.

Don't get greedy! Don't stay surfing one wave so long that your bow plows into the back of the wave ahead of you, flooding the cockpit with water.

5. **As you get near the bottom of the wave (the *trough*) and the bow starts to point uphill, turn to windward about 10 to 20 degrees to try to stay riding on the downhill portion of the wave or at least build speed so that wave passes under you.**

6. **When you feel the boat slow down, slide forward to your normal position again.**

Sailing on a Catamaran

If you know how to sail a keelboat or dinghy, then you can sail a catamaran, because a catamaran, also commonly referred to as a *cat,* is simply a sailboat with two hulls instead of one. Figure 11-9 shows a basic cat. Sure, some multi-hulls are big, heavy cruisers, but we're talking about the kind you launch off a beach, around 20 feet (6 meters) or smaller. Note that a cat has some features you don't find on other sailboats, including a crossbar to hold its unique twin hulls in place; the *trampoline* — rope mesh or fabric surface between the two hulls; full-length battens in the mainsail; and a rotating mast to optimize sail shape.

Because the principles of sailing a catamaran are the same as for any boat, this section focuses on some areas where you run into significant differences.

Making your own wind

The big difference between cats and dinghies is their speed. Cats are faster on almost every point of sail, in every wind condition. The reason for the speed is twofold: The narrow hulls cause very little drag, and the "wide wheelbase" enables the crew to sit very far away from the sails, providing great mechanical advantage to keep the boat from heeling. The added width is sort of like having a supertrapeze — in fact, many cats have trapezes, too!

Figure 11-9:
A catama-
ran flying
a hull.

Although catamarans, like any other boat, can sail directly downwind (with the wind dead astern), the faster way to get downwind is to broad reach one way and then jibe and broad reach the other way, in a zigzag route. Although you sail a longer distance than when you steer straight downwind, the extra speed generated by reaching up and making some of that magic apparent wind is usually well worth the trouble.

Flying a hull

A catamaran doesn't heel over — it flies — which is certainly the feeling you get the first time the windward hull (which you're sitting on) lifts up out of the water. *Flying a hull* is the same thing as *heeling* on a monohull; it just looks cooler, because the windward hull is so high above the water. If you go too far, you invite a capsize (reducing your cool factor to zero).

For maximum speed, you want to have the windward hull just kissing the waves, which minimizes the drag of the craft going through the water but maximizes the efficiency of the sails and foils. You can get the hull back down closer to the water the same way you reduce heel in a dinghy, by

- ✔ Hiking out harder (or using your trapeze)
- ✔ Easing the mainsheet a few inches to bleed power from your biggest sail
- ✔ Turning the boat toward the wind to bleed power from the sails by pinching

Pinching works fine in most conditions. But if conditions are windy, you can fly a hull when sailing very close to a dead-downwind course. In this case, turning the boat toward the wind adds power into the sails, and the boat heels even more. The correct reaction, then, is to bear away more to slow the boat down. The only way to know which way (toward or away from the wind) will depower you best is by paying attention to your heading relative to the true wind direction.

Fully battened sails

Almost all catamarans have a fully battened mainsail — that is, the battens in the sail go all the way from *leech* to *luff* (back edge to front edge). The extra support from the long battens enables the sailmaker to build more area onto a given mast-and-boom combination. Fully battened sails aren't unique to catamarans; some monohulls, such as the America's Cup–class boats, have them too.

Watching the leading edge of the sail for the small "bubble" that indicates slight undertrim can be difficult on fully battened sails, because they don't luff as dramatically as "soft" sails. Make sure that your mainsail has *telltales* (see Chapter 12).

Tacking made easy

Not all catamarans are created equal, and some can be a real chore to tack. If you find yourself on one of those cats that has trouble tacking, try these steps:

1. **Make sure that you're going as fast as possible on a close-hauled course.**

   Do this before starting your tack.

2. **Pick a smooth spot in the waves to begin the turn.**

   Hitting a big wave in the middle of the turn can stop your boat.

3. **Turn the boat in a fairly sharp arc.**

   Catamarans lose momentum quickly so keep that tiller hard over.

   If the boat has a jib, keep it cleated on the old tack and let it *backwind* (fill backward) as the boat turns through the wind. At the same time, release the mainsheet so that it's free to run. The "backing" jib and eased mainsail combination helps spin the boat down onto the new close-hauled course.

   If the boat doesn't have a jib, completing the tack can be difficult. Often, the boat loses too much momentum and ends up stopping as it comes on a course pointed directly at the wind direction. Congratulations — you're now in irons. Check out Chapter 5 on getting out of irons. Next time, try jibing instead.

Recovering from a capsize

When catamarans capsize, you can be in for some real excitement. If you aren't careful, you can get catapulted from the high side and land on the sail or the mast. See Chapter 7 for the basics on righting a capsized boat, but this section has tips just for cats.

The following steps can help you recover from a catamaran capsize.

1. **Rig your cat with a *righting line*.**

   This inventive piece of equipment is a fairly thick (mainsheet-size) piece of rope rigged for easy access in the event of a flip.

2. **Avoid falling off the boat, if at all possible, by holding onto a *shroud* (wire that supports the mast) or some part of the trampoline or hull.**

   If you do fall, try to land feet first (presuming that you have shoes or booties on) with your knees bent.

3. **Prevent the boat from *turning turtle* (flipping over all the way so that the mast is pointed straight down).**

   Recovering from a turtle is much harder than recovering from a regular capsize, when the mast stays horizontal on the water. If you're clever enough to still be high and dry on the upper hull, get off: Your weight on the upper hull isn't helping the situation and may, in fact, be adding more pressure to sink the mast. Fortunately, most production cats have sealed mast sections or a float attached to the top of the mast that inhibits the boat turning turtle.

4. **Lean your weight (and your crew's) out on the extended righting line (as Figure 11-10 shows) to pull the boat upright.**

Figure 11-10:
Using a righting line to add leverage and right a capsized catamaran.

Release the sheets first so the sails don't fill when they do get dry again. Then try to get the boat to rotate around so that the bow points into (or close to) the wind direction. You may be able to rotate the boat simply by standing on the "lower" bow, adding drag so that the stern blows downwind more. If that strategy doesn't work, you can try swimming the bow upwind — a tiring task! Popping the battens in the mainsail so that they're convex (looking down on the boat) can also help you right the boat, because as the sail begins to come out of the water, the wing shape of the mainsail helps lift the mast farther out of the water.

5. **When the boat begins to come upright, the cat reaches the critical point of balance, where the upper hull falls down fast.**

Watch out for falling hulls! Stay clear of the hull and the *dolphin striker* (the support strut mounted to the front cross beam below the mast) if your cat has one. As the boat comes upright, have the crew hold on to the lower hull to prevent the boat from continuing to roll over and capsize the other way.

If you capsize on a boat that doesn't have a righting line, you may be able to create a makeshift one by tying a rope (the jib sheet may work well) to the mast or "upper" trampoline support bar. The mainsheet is also a possible righting line, but first make sure that it's long enough and rigged in such a way that you aren't pulling up a sail full of water and that the sails will still be fully eased and luffing as the boat is righted. Otherwise, the sails may fill with air as the mast comes up, and the boat may flip back over again.

Chapter 12

Trimming Your Sails for Speed

· ·

In This Chapter

▶ Making sure your sails aren't stalled

▶ Adjusting the sail shape

▶ Controlling the power in your sails

▶ Going fast downwind with spinnakers

· ·

A wet sheet and a flowing sea,
A wind that follows fast,
And fills the white and rustling sail,
And bends the gallant mast.

— Allan Cunningham

*I*f your sails are the engines of your boat, then the lines you use to adjust your sail shape, also known as the *running rigging,* are your throttle. Because the wind and seas are rarely perfectly steady, the optimum shape of your sail changes according to the weather conditions, just as the wing of a fighter jet is different in shape from the wing of a glider because of their dissimilar speed and lift requirements.

To optimize boat speed, some boats use different sails for different points of sail or different wind strengths. For example, for the best downwind speed, you may fly a *spinnaker,* a parachute-like sail. In this chapter, we discuss how to adjust the shape of your sails, how to control the power in your sails, and how to utilize spinnakers — all to garner more speed.

When in Doubt, Let It Out

After you get your sails trimmed perfectly at the beginning of the day, you can just *cleat* them (tie them off) and ignore them, right? Wrong. The angle of the sails to the wind can easily change if

✔ **The wind shifts.** A number of factors can cause a change in the wind direction; check out Chapter 8 for more on wind shifts.

✔ **You turn the boat.** Every course change requires a change in sail trim.

When the angle of the sails to the wind is wrong, the boat slows down or may even stop. So how can you tell if your sails are *trimmed* (pulled in) just right? Looking up at the sails is your best and fastest indication of improper trim. In simple terms, sails can either be undertrimmed, overtrimmed, or perfectly trimmed.

✔ An **undertrimmed sail** — one that isn't pulled in enough — is fairly obvious: The sail *luffs,* which means that it's spilling air and thus losing power.

✔ An **overtrimmed sail** — one that's pulled in too much — is a more devious animal. It also slows you down, but it's harder to see because it still appears full of wind. If you could see the air molecules as they travel over an overtrimmed sail, however, you'd see that the airflow is *stalled* (turbulent, not smooth), as Figure 12-1 shows. As you know from any air disaster movie, a plane that has stalled can't fly because the wings can't generate *lift* — and you know from Appendix C that lift is what makes a sailboat move.

✔ A **perfectly trimmed sail** is constantly adjusted to maintain that perfect trim. "When in doubt, let it out" is the first rule. Ease the sheet out until the sail just starts to luff, and then trim it back in an inch. Repeat often (unless you're out for a relaxing cruise, then just cleat the sheet and grab a refreshing beverage instead).

Figure 12-1:
Wind flow over a properly trimmed sail (left) and stalled flow over an overtrimmed sail (right).

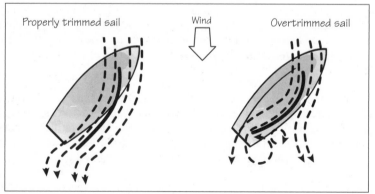

Properly trimmed sail   Wind   Overtrimmed sail

Relying on Telltales

Another way to tell if your sail is stalled is to use telltales as an early warning system. *Telltales* are little strands of yarn or cassette tape that are attached (usually with tape) to the sail. Telltales are more sensitive to changes in the flow than the sail is, so they luff sooner than the sailcloth does. See telltales in action in Figure 12-2.

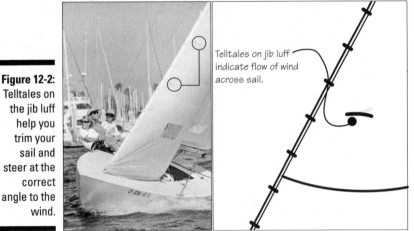

Telltales on jib luff indicate flow of wind across sail.

Figure 12-2: Telltales on the jib luff help you trim your sail and steer at the correct angle to the wind.

Telltales placed on either side of the forward-most sail (the jib, if you have one) about a foot back from the *luff* (front) of the sail give an excellent indication of whether the sail is undertrimmed or overtrimmed. If the sails are perfectly trimmed for your course, both telltales (on either side) flow straight back. If you turn toward the wind, the sail becomes undertrimmed, and the inside, or *windward,* telltale starts to rise and flutter as the flow is disturbed. Because the sail is already trimmed tight, this flutter is the helmsman's cue to turn away from the wind *(bear away).* If you turn too far away from the wind, the air flow starts to get disturbed on the back *(leeward)* side of the sail as the sail gets overtrimmed, so the leeward telltale starts to flutter and then droop. You can either ease the sheet out enough to get both telltales flowing again, or the helmsman can head up until both telltales flow.

When sailing close-hauled, you don't really have to keep the telltales flowing perfectly all the time. In fact, a little rise by the inside telltale occasionally is okay, especially in stronger winds. That little movement just means that you're sailing a very fine line, and you don't want to sail any closer to the wind.

On a mainsail, telltales on the luff are less accurate because of the turbulence caused by the mast. Therefore, keep looking for an occasional slight "bubble" in the front of the mainsail, indicating that the sail is just on the verge of luffing, rather than relying on telltales. However, a telltale placed on the leech of the mainsail (by the top batten is best) gives you a quick indication when the mainsail is overtrimmed (and therefore is stalled) because the telltale no longer flows straight back.

Shaping Your Sails

The most important speed control — your boat's throttle — is the sail's sheet, which controls the angle of the sail to the wind. But if you want to eke out another few percent of power from your sails, then you must delve into the subject of sail shape a little deeper. Come on in. The water's fine!

You discover in Appendix C that your sail is really a wing, generating lift as the wind flows past it. Figure 12-3 shows a horizontal cross section of that sea-going wing with the following measurable attributes:

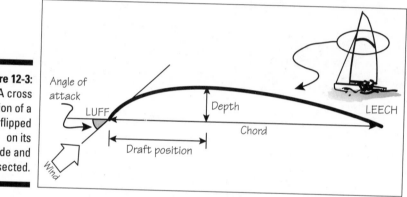

Figure 12-3: A cross section of a sail flipped on its side and dissected.

- ✔ **Angle of attack:** This is simply a technical term for the concept you already know as the "angle of the sail to the wind." You measure angle of attack as the angle of the wind to the sail's chord; the sheet controls it. Check out "Controlling the power," later in this chapter, for more on the angle of attack at various points of sail.

- ✔ **Chord:** The straight line between the leading edge (luff) and the trailing edge (leech).

- ✔ **Depth:** The fullness of a sail, expressed as a percentage of the depth at the sail's deepest point to the length of the chord.

- ✔ **Draft position:** The position of the sail's deepest point, expressed as a percentage of the distance the point is back from the luff to the length of the chord.

- ✔ **Twist:** The amount the angle of attack changes vertically in the sail, from bottom to top, as Figure 12-4 shows.

No one except a sailmaker is concerned with the absolute quantities of depth, draft position, and twist. From a practical standpoint, sailors are mostly interested in the relative quantities — making a given sail deeper or flatter or more or less twisted.

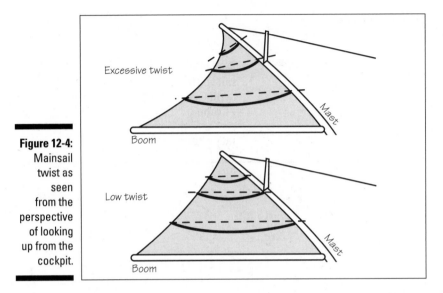

Figure 12-4: Mainsail twist as seen from the perspective of looking up from the cockpit.

Pull That Line — No, THAT Line

We've stated it before, but it's important enough to repeat ourselves: By far and away, the most important aspect of sail trim is the angle of attack, which a sail's sheet controls. Pull the sail in until it just stops luffing, and when in doubt, let it out!

Of secondary importance are a variety of fine-tuning controls. Follow our tuning suggestions in this section to get the sail shape in the correct range for the wind conditions. From there, you can experiment with small adjustments to see whether you can get more performance out of your boat. Here are the basic mainsail controls (and see them in Figure 12-5):

✔ **Mainsheet:** The mainsheet is the biggie — the most adjusted piece of running rigging on the boat — because it controls the sail's angle of attack. When sailing upwind, the mainsheet also controls the twist. Read more about twist in the "Controlling the power" section, later in this chapter.

✔ **Outhaul:** The *outhaul* controls depth in the bottom of the mainsail. Again, getting the outhaul tension in the ballpark is most important, and you can do so by using the same visual cues as you use to determine luff tension (except that the stress or looseness is seen along the foot of the sail). If the wind is moderate or strong, err on the tight side. Increased foot tension flattens the bottom section of the mainsail.

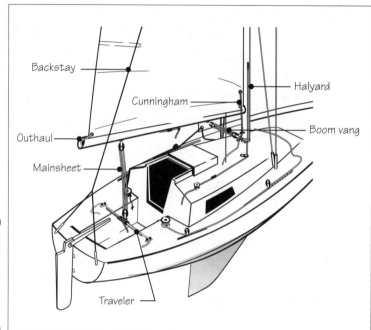

Figure 12-5:
The sail
shape
controls on
a basic
keelboat.

✔ **Boom vang:** Most boats have a *boom vang* (also called a vang) system to control the twist of the mainsail when sailing downwind. Usually the vang is a system of pulleys connecting the boom to the mast to hold down the boom. The vang takes over primary twist control from the mainsheet when the sail is eased out on a reach or a run.

A great starting point is to set the vang when you're sailing close-hauled. With the mainsail perfectly trimmed, pull the slack out of the vang rope and cleat it. Then, as you bear away (turn downwind) and ease the mainsheet, the vang takes up tension. The tighter the vang, the less the twist on reaches and runs. A good rule is to put enough boom vang on so that the top batten is parallel to the boom.

✔ **Traveler:** A secondary control for changing the mainsail's angle of attack is the *traveler,* but not all boats have a traveler. It moves the lower mainsheet attachment point (on the boat) from side to side, thereby changing the angle of attack without changing the sail's twist. When sailing to windward in light air after the mainsheet is trimmed for the right amount of twist, pull the traveler to windward so that the boom is on centerline for maximum upwind power. In heavy air, you can reduce power by dropping the traveler to leeward.

✔ **Backstay:** The *backstay* is the support wire between the top of the mast and the back of the boat. Some smaller boats (and most dinghies) don't have a backstay, and some bigger boats don't have convenient means to control the backstay tension. But if your boat has a backstay control that's easy to use, you'll love the backstay because it gives you more control over mainsail shape than any other control line except the mainsheet. As you tension the backstay, the mast bends. This bend dramatically decreases the depth of the mainsail.

✔ **Halyard and cunningham (that clever pig):** The *halyard* is primary and the *cunningham* secondary in controlling the tension in the luff of the sail. Some boats don't even have a cunningham (also called the *downhaul*), a control rope that pulls the luff downward at or near the tack. (In Chapter 4, we discuss the two visibly obvious extremes of luff tension.) Proper luff tension depends on the design and shape of the sail, your point of sail, and the wind velocity. To eke out that last inch of speed, you need to tighten your luff sailing upwind and loosen it downwind. Increased luff tension usually moves the draft position forward and decreases the depth of (flattens) the sail slightly.

You may think that a smooth sail is fastest. However, a few loose wrinkles along the lower luff are called *speed wrinkles*. In my experience, most sails in most conditions like to have the luff tension set a little loose. But beware of stress lines parallel to the mast — these lines show that your halyard or cunningham is too tight.

Powering Up Your Sails

One great way to picture what variations in sail shape do is to think in terms of power. More power makes you go faster in a race car (until you have to go around the curve), but in a sailboat, it's not quite that simple. When a wing shape generates the all-important lift, it also generates drag (see Appendix C). Therefore, designers of airplane wings and sailors trying to optimize their sail shape are looking for the same thing — optimizing the ratio of lift to drag. That ratio varies depending on many variables, including the depth of the wing (sail), draft position, angle of attack, twist, and the speed of the air flowing past. Every wind speed has an optimum wing shape that maximizes the lift-to-drag ratio. (That's why some fighter jets have wings that change shape and angle, depending on how fast the plane is flying.)

Generally, in light and medium winds, you need full sails for maximum power; at higher wind speeds, you flatten your sails because you need less power (and because full shapes become "draggy" and slow as the wind speed increases). In Figure 12-6, the better shape for strong winds is the flatter sail on the bottom.

Controlling the power

We can use this concept of power to describe the effect of variations in sail shape. We start with the most important variations, moving to the least important.

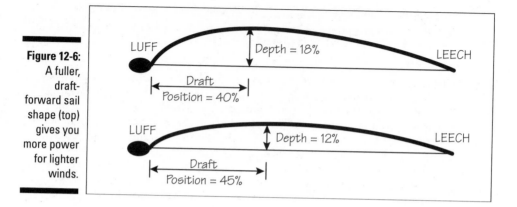

Figure 12-6: A fuller, draft-forward sail shape (top) gives you more power for lighter winds.

✔ **Angle of attack:** Imagine that your boat is pointed on a *reach* (with the wind coming across the boat) and your sail is luffing — this is 0-degree angle of attack. As you trim the sail in with the mainsheet, you increase the angle of attack until the point where the sail gets overtrimmed and stalls, as Figure 12-7 shows. The traveler can also change the angle of attack.

✔ **Twist:** If the top of the sail has a 0-degree angle of attack to the wind (then it's luffing!) and the bottom of the sail is perfectly trimmed to the wind, then the sail has a very *twisty* shape. Power increases with less twist — to a point (see the "Why twist at all?" sidebar in this chapter). You can power up the sail by decreasing twist to the point that both the top and the bottom of the sail are perfectly trimmed (best angle of attack). The vang and the mainsheet affect twist. For an illustration of twist, see Figure 12-4.

✔ **Depth:** Power increases with depth — at least until the winds get stronger, when a deep shape has quite a bit of drag. You can change the depth by adjusting the outhaul, backstay, and mast bend.

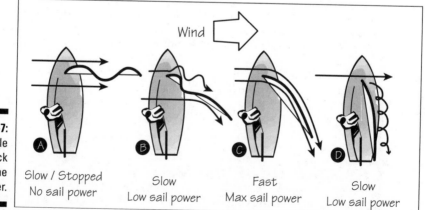

Figure 12-7: The angle of attack controls the sail power.

Why twist at all?

You may think that zero twist has the most power, but that's rarely the case, because of a phenomenon related to friction. At and near the water's surface, friction noticeably slows the true wind as the wind rubs against the water and waves. Moving up toward the top of the mast, the true wind speed increases. This vertical variation in true wind speed causes a situation of great interest to sailors — the apparent wind felt at the bottom of the sails is farther forward (more from the bow) than the apparent wind felt at the top of the sails. (See Chapter 11 for a discussion of apparent wind.) The fact that the wind shifts in direction up and down your sails (as long as you're moving and creating apparent wind) explains why zero twist is usually slow — because at some height, the sail is overtrimmed and stalled. In most conditions, to get your sail at the optimum angle of attack at every level from top to bottom (for maximum power), you want to set the sails with a moderate amount of twist.

✔ **Draft position:** Draft position primarily affects the sail's capability to accelerate. Draft farther forward (about 45 percent or so) is a great accelerating shape — good for light or moderate air and waves that are constantly slowing the boat down. Draft farther aft (50 percent or more) is a better shape for straight-line speed in constant conditions. You can move the draft by adjusting luff tension and secondarily by adjusting depth.

Reducing the power

On windy days, when you're sailing close-hauled or close reaching (see Chapter 5 to review), the boat wants to heel way over, indicating that it's overpowered. In this situation, you don't want full power from the sails. When the boat reaches its maximum heel angle (for optimum sailing speed, as Table 12-1 shows) and the crew weight is outboard as far as possible (see Chapter 11 for good stuff about hiking out), then you must reduce the power in your sails. Here are five ways to do so:

✔ **Ease the sheets.** The quickest, fastest, and best way to "depower" your sails is by easing the sheet and decreasing the angle of attack. Slowly ease the mainsheet (or the traveler, if it's easier to handle, but keep the jib in unless conditions are really windy) and feel the heel decrease. Stop easing when the heel is at the optimum maximum angle, as Table 12-1 shows. Don't worry if your sail luffs a little bit — you don't want that extra power.

✔ **Pinch.** Slowly turning the boat toward the wind also decreases the angle of attack. The danger here is that you slow down and stall out your centerboard or keel, so pinching is usually most effective when done subtly and combined with easing the mainsheet.

✔ **Add twist.** Adding twist is really just decreasing the angle of attack up high, and depowering the top of your sail first is good to do. Add twist by easing the mainsheet and jib sheet slightly. You can also move the jib lead back an inch or three to add twist in the jib, as we describe in the next section.

✔ **Make the sails as flat as possible.** Bend the mast (tighten the backstay), tighten the luff tension (with the halyard and cunningham), and tighten the outhaul.

✔ **If you're still overpowered, reef your sail.** See Chapter 7 on how to *reef* (reduce sail area).

Table 12-1	Optimum Heel Angles
Type of Boat	*Maximum Efficient Heel Angle*
One- and two-person dinghies	0 to 5 degrees heel — essentially upright
Larger, heavier dinghies	0 to 10 degrees
Scows (flat-bottomed dinghies with two rudders)	About 20 degrees — to the point where the leeward rudder is straight down
Catamarans	Just enough that the windward hull "kisses" the water
Keelboats	10 to 25 degrees, depending on the design — you heel more on a keelboat so that the ballast in the keel fin can get some leverage to prevent further heeling

Heel too far and your rudder and keel will stall and slow you down. When conditions are windy, especially on a dinghy, you have another good reason besides speed and balance to limit your heel angle — if you're heeled over too much, the boom will hit the water when you ease the mainsheet. Check out the "Rounding up" section, later in this chapter, to see what happens next in this ugly scenario.

Trimming the jib

The principles of sail shape and trim apply similarly to the jib. But some of the controls we cover in the preceding section apply to the mainsail only. Because your jib is the first sail to "see" the wind when you're sailing close-hauled, take a closer look at some of its controls.

The sheet is the most important control, because it affects the angle of attack of the sail. Get the sheet right, and you're doing better than most sailors on the water today! Simply ease out the sheet until the sail begins to luff, and then slowly pull it in until the luffing just stops. When in doubt . . . ease it out! As we discuss earlier in this chapter in "Relying on Telltales," telltales can be a very effective trim aid on a jib.

The halyard usually controls luff tension on the jib, just like on the mainsail, and the same rules apply. However, the jib doesn't have an outhaul to adjust foot tension or a boom vang to control twist. The jib sheet does all that work, with a little help from the *jib leads.* The jib leads, or *jib cars,* are the first fittings (usually a pulley or fairlead) through which each jib sheet (one on each side) passes as it comes from the sail on its way to the cockpit. (You can check out Chapter 4, where we describe the rigging process of the jib and the jib sheet, if you're feeling a bit confused at this point.)

Jib leads are typically adjustable fore and aft and affect the jib's twist. Move a lead too far forward and, as you trim the sheet, it pulls down on the jib leech too much, acting more like a boom vang and less like an outhaul. Move a lead too far aft and, as you trim the sheet, it pulls out on the foot excessively but doesn't pull down on the leech enough. The correct setting is in between these extremes, as Figure 12-8 shows.

Figure 12-8:
Left, lead too far forward, center, too far aft, and right, perfect. The illustration (far right) shows the same lead positions.

As the wind increases, you move your lead back to twist and decrease power in the jib. Some boats, mostly larger keelboats, have several jibs in varying sizes and strengths. In general, you want to use the biggest sail in light winds and the smallest sail in strong winds (for reduced power).

Sailing Fast Downwind

All of the principles of trimming sails apply equally well on all points of sail. The only difference is that, on the broadest points of sail (when the wind is coming from behind), the boat is heeling less. So to sail faster downwind, you often can increase the power of the sails, or put up a bigger, more powerful sail, such as a *spinnaker* (a large, lightweight, balloonlike sail). But if you don't have one, or if your crew is on a coffee break and refuses to put up the spinnaker, you can try some of the following trimming tips for getting more speed from your boat and sails while sailing downwind.

- **Make sure the mainsail (and the jib, if it's set) is sheeted properly, right on the verge of luffing.** If the wind is coming from too far behind (broad reaching or running), the mainsail can't luff because the boom hits the shrouds, and you may need to *wing out* the jib to get it to fill, as we describe in Chapter 5.

- **Ease the luff tension (halyard and/or the cunningham) to make the sails as full and powerful as possible.**

- **Ease the outhaul to deepen the lower section of the mainsail.**

- **If the jib is still being trimmed on the leeward side, move the lead forward and outboard (about 1 foot on a 30-foot boat).**

- **On a dinghy, pull up the centerboard halfway to reduce drag.**

- **Set the boom vang to limit mainsail twist.**

Setting a symmetrical spinnaker

Now for the fun sail — the spinnaker. Setting a spinnaker when going on a reach or downwind can be like lighting up the afterburners on a jet aircraft. Sailing with a spinnaker is fast, but because it's attached only at the corners, you can easily get into a love-hate relationship with this potentially unruly sail. Fortunately, you have this book, so get ready to love this big, fat, colorful, nylon parachute. Two types of spinnakers exist: symmetrical and asymmetrical, as Figure 12-9 shows. Asymmetrical spinnakers are also called *gennakers,* because they're designed to be flown like a big jib (*genoa*) but have the sail area of a spinnaker. They're popular cruising sails because of their ease of use.

We start with the symmetrical spinnaker, because as soon as you master that big sail, the asymmetrical is a breeze (bad sailing pun). But, in fact, many of the techniques in this section apply equally to both types of spinnakers.

Figure 12-9:
Two
America's
Cup boats
on San
Diego Bay.
Left: asym-
metrical
spinnaker;
Right:
symmetrical
spinnaker.

Gathering your spinnaker equipment

Before you can set a spinnaker, you need the following equipment. (Check out Figure 12-10 for a clear illustration.)

- ✔ **Spinnaker pole:** A lightweight pole that attaches to the mast and supports the tack of the spinnaker when set.

- ✔ **Topping lift (also called the *pole lift* or *topper*):** Halyardlike control rope running from the mast, used to lift the outboard tip of the spinnaker pole into position.

- ✔ **Foreguy or downhaul:** Rope coming from the foredeck area, used to keep the outboard tip of the spinnaker pole from lifting too high.

- ✔ **Spinnaker halyard:** Rope used to hoist the spinnaker.

- ✔ **Spinnaker sheets:** Control ropes on either side of the boat used to adjust the sail's angle of attack. When the spinnaker is flying, these sheets change their names — the sheet on the windward side that goes through the fitting at the end of the spinnaker pole is called the *guy* or *afterguy*. The sheet on the leeward side is still the sheet. Of course, when you jibe, they swap names, because now the wind is blowing on the opposite side of the boat. The number of spinnaker sheets you use depends on the boat's deck layout, size, and jibing method. Some boats employ just one sheet per side while others use two sheets (a dedicated guy and sheet) on each side (lazy guy and sheet method) as shown in Figure 12-10.

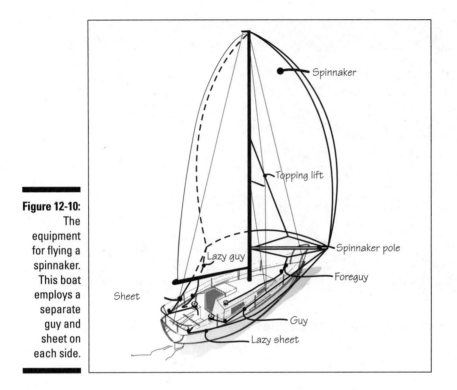

Figure 12-10:
The equipment for flying a spinnaker. This boat employs a separate guy and sheet on each side.

Preparing to hoist

Because spinnakers are made of ultra-lightweight cloth, they're most easily stored stuffed into a sail bag, or *spinnaker turtle*. Like its close cousin the parachute, a spinnaker must be meticulously prepared so that it deploys correctly. Nothing is more frustrating than expecting to see a big, powerful sail fill with air and, instead, seeing a twisted mass of nylon.

One of the most embarrassing moments in sailing is when a crew hoists a sail sideways. Don't laugh, because all of us have done it by mixing up the sail's corners when rigging. To save your pride, write each corner's name on the sail in permanent marker — that works well on a spinnaker, because it has no bolt ropes.

You can choose from several methods of packing the *chute* (sailor's slang for spinnaker), but they all have one thing in common: When the sail is stuffed back into its bag, all three corners are clearly separated, ready for attaching to their respective sheets and halyard, with no twists in the body of the sail. Some racing crews on boats over 35 feet (11 meters) go one step further and compress the body of the spinnaker with yarn or rubber bands so that it can be fully hoisted before it fills. This extra effort is nice but not necessary in all but the windiest conditions, as long as you use the *cruising hoist,* which we describe in the "Hoisting: The 'cruising set'" section, later in this chapter.

As you see in Figure 12-11, packing the chute is easiest on a nice big lawn, where you can stretch the sail out, untangle any twists, and stuff it in the bag carefully, starting on its centerline and working toward the head and the two clews (until a chute is flying, it's said to have two clews and two leeches). The three corners of the sail (the head and clews) should be on top.

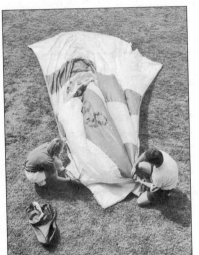

Figure 12-11: Packing the chute the easy way, spread out on a lawn.

Sometimes a nice big lawn isn't available for packing — such as while you're afloat — but, fortunately, you can pack the chute within the confines of the boat's interior, with some creativity. Try tucking the head of the sail under a bunk cushion and make sure the chute doesn't twist!

If you're in a rush, your spinnaker still stands a very good chance of setting cleanly if you run one of the leeches (sliding your hands from one edge to the other and making sure there aren't any twists) and then don't twist the two corners attached to that edge when stuffing the sail into the bag. Your odds get even better when you run both leeches.

Hooking up the spinnaker

In preparation for the set, the three corners of the spinnaker need to be attached to the three control ropes — the halyard and the two sheets. You may think that hooking up the ropes to the corners is a simple task, but, for some reason, this chore is the source of many problems. Here are some tips to make this job easier:

- ✔ **All three ropes should follow the same path to the sail.** If the sheets come in under the jib, then the halyard should too.

- ✔ **Attach the halyard and sheets securely and to the correct corner.** Writing "head" on the head of the sail and so on really helps.

✔ **Make extra sure that your sheets and halyards are led properly.** Check that you haven't made any loops around stanchions, spreaders, and other paraphernalia in their paths.

Hoisting: The "cruising set"

Being deliberate with each stage of setting the spinnaker pays off. Nothing is worse than a spinnaker filling when it's halfway hoisted, because then the halyard has tons of load as you haul it to the top. Here are the steps to a conservative spinnaker-setting procedure that Peter calls a *cruising set*. The beauty of this set is that the sail doesn't fill until you're ready for it.

1. **Make sure that the spinnaker is attached to the sheets and halyard properly and that the bag is secured to the boat.**

2. **Connect the inboard end of the spinnaker pole to the mast, attach the topping lift and foreguy to the outboard end, and then raise the pole.**

   The correct height depends on your boat and the wind conditions. Make sure that the guy is running through the outboard end of the pole.

3. **Turn the boat onto a very broad reach or run.**

   Be careful not to accidentally jibe. Turning the boat onto a broad reach or run lets you hoist the spinnaker behind the mainsail — protected from the force of the wind.

4. **Make sure the crew is ready, and call for the sail to be hoisted.**

5. **As the sail is being hoisted, pull the guy until the clew of the spinnaker touches the pole.**

   If you're using winches, make sure that you have enough wraps on the guy's winch drum to take the load when the sail fills. For more about winch use, see Chapter 5.

6. **When the halyard is fully hoisted and cleated, set the guy to its proper position, drop the jib, carefully turn the boat onto the desired course, and trim the sheet as required.**

Trimming the spinnaker

Trimming a spinnaker is similar to trimming any other sail. Get the angle of attack correct, and you're off and running. Your spinnaker will inevitably collapse, because it's a relatively finicky sail that requires constant — and we mean constant — attention.

The key to trimming the spinnaker is working through a basic cycle. First, set the guy, then the sheet, then the pole height. Like every other sail, the control rope that gets the most work is the spinnaker sheet. Here are the rules of spinnaker trim:

1. **Set the guy so that the pole is about 90 degrees to the apparent wind when broad reaching or running, and ease it forward so the pole is almost touching the forestay on tighter reaches.**

2. **Trim the sheet so that the luff of the sail has a small curl in it.**

   If you trim just a little bit more, the curl disappears, and the sail looks completely full. If you ease just a little bit more, the curl gets larger and ultimately causes the sail to collapse.

3. **Set the outboard end of the pole height so that the tack of the spinnaker is level with the clew.**

4. **Set the height of the inboard end of the spinnaker pole (if it's adjustable) so that the pole is horizontal.**

Avoiding a spinnaker collapse

If you get a wind shift, or your helmsman changes course suddenly, or if you just neglect it for a moment, your selfish spinnaker will collapse. Unfortunately, the spinnaker doesn't luff gently when it collapses; it flaps in a loud manner that makes you feel like something is very wrong. The spinnaker can collapse in two ways:

- ✔ **Downwind collapse:** In this case, the sail falls into itself, usually caving in on top and ultimately hanging like a limp mass. The cure for a downwind collapse is to turn the boat up toward the wind (about 20 degrees) until the sail fills and/or bring the pole aft (trim the guy) and ease the sheet.

- ✔ **Upwind collapse:** When the wind comes too far forward for the trim of the chute (too little angle of attack), the spinnaker luffs completely. The cure is to turn the boat away from the wind until the sail fills and/or trim the sheet.

Jibing the spinnaker

Any maneuver with a spinnaker can be a trial, but thanks to the cruising set (and the *cruising takedown,* which we outline in the next section), the most difficult maneuver is, without question, the jibe. You know you've jibed successfully when

- ✔ The sail fills cleanly on the new jibe with the pole set properly.
- ✔ The sail stays full during the entire jibe.
- ✔ Nothing (and no one) falls in the water.
- ✔ The crew member on the bow comes back into the cockpit with a big smile on his face.

Here are the steps to a successful jibe (and check out Figure 12-12):

1. **Make sure the crew is ready and in position.**

2. **Turn the boat down to a very broad reach (so that the turn during the jibe isn't very sharp) and retrim the chute accordingly.**

   Work hard to keep the spinnaker full throughout the jibe.

3. **Announce the turn into the jibe by saying "Jibe-ho," "Jibing," "Here we go," or anything else that makes sense.**

4. **As the boat turns, keep trimming the guy back and easing the sheet forward so that the spinnaker stays trimmed perfectly.**

   Because the boat's angle to the wind is changing, this step is crucial throughout the maneuver. In a good jibe, you must continue to rotate the spinnaker so that it stays full.

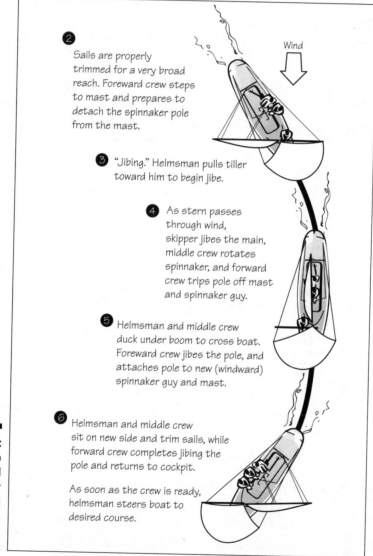

Wind

2 Sails are properly trimmed for a very broad reach. Foreward crew steps to mast and prepares to detach the spinnaker pole from the mast.

3 "Jibing." Helmsman pulls tiller toward him to begin jibe.

4 As stern passes through wind, skipper jibes the main, middle crew rotates spinnaker, and forward crew trips pole off mast and spinnaker guy.

5 Helmsman and middle crew duck under boom to cross boat. Foreward crew jibes the pole, and attaches pole to new (windward) spinnaker guy and mast.

6 Helmsman and middle crew sit on new side and trim sails, while forward crew completes jibing the pole and returns to cockpit.

As soon as the crew is ready, helmsman steers boat to desired course.

Figure 12-12:
The steps to a successful spinnaker jibe on a three-person boat.

Switching the pole: Dip pole versus end for end

Depending on the type of boat, your *bowman* (foreward crew) can use one of two methods for shifting the pole. The *end-for-end* jibe is common on dinghies and smaller keelboats. During the jibe, the two pole ends are disconnected from the mast and old guy and reattached so that the old inboard end is attached to the new guy, and the pole is pushed out so that the old outboard end can be attached to the mast.

The *dip-pole* jibe is common on keelboats longer than 40 feet (12 meters). During the jibe, the pole's outboard end is disconnected from the old guy, lowered so that it can swing behind the forestay, and then connected to the new guy and raised up into position on the new windward side.

5. **Turn the boat through the jibe while shifting the pole from the old windward side to the new windward side by *tripping* (detaching) the pole ends from the mast and old guy and then reattaching the pole on the new side.**

This step is often the hardest part of the jibe, because it requires fancy footwork on the foredeck and coordination on the part of the foredeck team, trimmers, and helmsman to facilitate the switch. And during this step, the mainsail must be jibed too. Stop the turn when you're on a very broad reach on the new jibe.

6. **When the pole is attached on the new windward side, the spinnaker is properly trimmed on the new jibe, and the crew is ready, you can turn up to a sharper reach (requiring further trimming of the spinnaker) if you desire.**

Think rotation! One of the most common errors in spinnaker jibes is not rotating the spinnaker around as the boat is turned through the jibe. The result is a tangled mess, with the spinnaker often blowing between the forestay and the mast. Practice jibing the spinnaker without the pole to get the feel of rotating the sail with the sheets. In light air, pull the mainsheet in tight (overtrimmed) or even drop the mainsail completely to facilitate this drill.

Whether you have a spinnaker up or not, a jibe can be a pretty wild maneuver in windy conditions. The force of the mainsail swinging across and filling with a BANG on the new side can generate a major turning force that can lead to a capsize on a dinghy and a *broach* (rapid, out-of-control turn up toward the wind) in a keelboat. In windy weather (more than 12 to 15 knots), the helmsman can perform an *S-jibe* to counteract the momentum caused at the moment the mainsail fills after a jibe, as Chapter 11 shows.

Taking the spinnaker down

The key to a calm and successful takedown is to plan it early enough that the helmsman can keep the boat pointing downwind — hiding the lowered spinnaker behind the mainsail until everything is cleaned up. Here are the steps to a *cruising takedown:*

1. **Turn the boat onto a very broad reach and hoist the jib.**
2. **Collapse the spinnaker by easing the guy forward and pulling in the sheet.**

   The sail collapses and is docile, protected from the wind behind the mainsail.

3. **Grab the sheet and begin pulling the sail on board.**
4. **Ease the halyard in concert with the sail being pulled in so it doesn't fall into the water (drops too fast) or require a struggle by the take-down team (drops too slow).**
5. **Stuff the spinnaker into the forward hatch (if you have one) or into the back hatch or spinnaker bag on a smaller boat.**
6. **Lower the pole and secure it and the spinnaker sheets.**

When Peter raced in the America's Cup, his team had four different varieties of takedowns. Dinghies and smaller keelboats often take the spinnaker down on the windward side in races. You can also find several other types of racing spinnaker sets. But those methods all require tons of practice, whereas the good ol' cruising set and takedown work on any boat and are the easiest way to get that colorful sail up and down.

Setting an asymmetrical spinnaker

Asymmetrical spinnakers, or *A-sails,* are a great evolution of the spinnaker. Configured correctly, they have all the spinnaker's advantages (more speed for downwind sailing) but are easier for the crew to manage.

A-sails have a luff longer than the leech and, unlike the spinnaker, always are set with the same edge (the luff) forward — just like a jib. An asymmetrical spinnaker usually doesn't have a guy; it simply has a tack line that holds the *tack* (front corner) of the sail down to the bow or a built-in bow pole called a *sprit.*

At the clew are two sheets, one for the left side and one for the right, just like a jib. For sets and takedowns, you can still use the cruising method of bearing away to hide the sail behind the mainsail to avoid problems. Jibes are easy because you don't have a pole to shift (except on the few boats that fly these sails from spinnaker poles — more about that in a minute), and the sail is meant to collapse as it jibes, blowing around in front of the boat.

The techniques for preparing the sail for the set are similar to a spinnaker, and, when hoisted, the trimming techniques of an A-sail are also analogous. Some racing keelboats use both A-sails and spinnakers and therefore set the tack of their A-sail on a spinnaker pole. Other racing keelboats use only

A-sails but employ a spinnaker pole rather than a sprit. In either case, jibing the A-sail becomes a major production and very labor intensive. For this A-sail with pole combination, you have a plethora of rigging methods available for setting up the two guys and for the procedure for shifting the pole from one side of the headstay to the other during the jibe. The bottom line is that these boats are giving up the ease-of-use advantages of an A-sail in the quest for a bit more speed. The trade-off may be worth it on some bigger racing boats but not for cruisers and recreational sailors.

Losing Control in Strong Winds

Before you read this section, we urge you to read the "Reducing the power" section, earlier in this chapter. If you feel like keeping the power on and finding your boat's limits, then you can use all the go-fast tips in this chapter (and Chapter 11) in stronger winds and bigger waves. But we should warn you about two kinds of wipe-outs: rounding up and rounding down. The other name for rounding down is the *death roll* — see why we wanted to warn you? But don't worry. You'll survive and have a great story to tell later.

Rounding up

Broaching, or *rounding up,* can occur on any type of boat on any point of sail, but it's most common when you're sailing off the wind. Rounding up occurs when a massive amount of weather helm (which we describe in Chapter 11) from all the forces acting on the boat causes the boat to "round up" swiftly toward the wind. In a round up, you feel as though the rudder is gone, because you have no steering control. Actually, the rudder is just stalled. Telltale signs — increasing weather helm and increasing heel — precede a round up. The following list provides a few ways to avoid this embarrassing (and potentially hazardous) fate when sailing on a windy reach:

- ✔ **Ease the boom vang.** This tip is especially important when the boat is heeling so much that the boom is close to the water.

- ✔ **Move the crew weight back.** This action keeps more of the rudder in the water. Make sure the crew is hiking, too.

- ✔ **Play the mainsheet aggressively.** In big wind and waves, you must play the mainsail to keep the boat "on its feet." The helmsman should ask the trimmer (sometimes one and the same on a dinghy) for a quick ease if he starts feeling weather helm building.

- ✔ **"Pump" the rudder.** By rapidly jerking the helm from "straight" to "bearing away sharply" and then back to "straight," you may avoid stalling and help the rudder stay gripped to the water.

- ✔ **Reduce heel.** See Chapter 11 and this chapter for ideas such as flattening your sails and pulling up your centerboard partway (if you have one).

If you do broach, make sure all the crew is still aboard and hanging on tight. Then put the helm to center, ease all the sails, and try, with what little forward motion you have left, to coax the boat back away from the wind again by jerking the rudder hard to bear off. If you're flying a spinnaker or an A-sail, you may need to take it down to get the boat back on its feet. Keep the guy (or tack rope on an A-sail) on tight and let the sheet out all the way so the sail luffs. You may have to drop the halyard and then pull the sail in from that remaining corner.

Rounding down

The *round down,* or *death roll,* is probably the most spectacular crash. It occurs most commonly on dinghies, resulting in a capsize, although keelboats aren't totally immune. The round down starts with the boat sailing on a very broad reach, run, or by the lee (Chapter 5 covers the points of sail). In strong winds, if you let the spinnaker fly too far to windward of the boat, or if you heel the boat to windward with too much twist in the main, the boat can roll dramatically to windward while it turns "down," away from the wind direction. The forces start to multiply, and soon you've lost steering control. *Rounding down* can result in a dangerous accidental jibe.

The following preventive measures can help you avoid the death roll when sailing on a broad reach or run:

- **Don't let the mainsail out too far and keep the boom vang on tight.** On this point of sail, you want to minimize mainsail twist.

- **Don't sail too low.** Turn the boat toward the wind until you're clearly on a broad reach. The higher the better — to a point, because as you turn up you now risk a broach and may be steering way off course.

- **Keep your spinnaker pulling the boat forward, not to windward.** If your spinnaker seems to have a mind of its own and is unstable, pull in on both the sheet and the guy to fly the spinnaker closer to the boat.

- **Keep the crew weight in the middle of the boat.** Keep the crew weight balanced, and have your crew be ready to move quickly to leeward if the boat rolls that way.

If you do capsize in a dinghy, then we hope that you read all about getting out of this predicament in Chapter 7. On a keelboat, you end up on your side, like in a broach.

You don't have to jibe, ever; you can always turn the other direction by tacking and then bear off again (take down the spinnaker or A-sail first, please). In heavy air, try to minimize any jibes — planned or not. And if you do decide to jibe, remember to employ the S-turn technique, which we describe in Chapter 11.

Chapter 13

Racing Sailboats: Going for the Gold

> *O Captain! my Captain! our fearful trip is done,*
> *The ship has weathered every rack, the prize we sought is won,*
> *The port is near, the bells I hear, the people all exulting.*
>
> *— Walt Whitman*

As you read this chapter, one fact becomes obvious, so we may as well state it upfront — we love sailboat racing. It's our passion, so this chapter is very biased. But hey, at least we're warning you.

We've competed at all levels, and sailboat racing has enriched our lives in many ways. Through our racing, we've traveled and made friends around the world. JJ represented the United States in two Olympics, winning a Bronze Medal in 1992 with teammate Pamela Healy and a Silver Medal in 2000 with Pease Glaser. Peter was navigator for the Dennis Conner–skippered *Stars & Stripes* boats that won the America's Cup in 1987 in Perth, Australia, and again in 1988 in San Diego, California. The victory tour included a trip to the White House and a New York City ticker-tape parade. Peter has set several records in distance races, such as from Los Angeles to Hawaii in a little more than six days! JJ has been racing sailboats since she was 8 and Peter from age 13. If not for sailboat racing, we wouldn't have met and had the opportunity to write this book. (Of course, editing each other's writing has been an interesting challenge. We've needed *Marriage Counseling For Dummies* occasionally.)

Whether you plan on embarking on a racing career or just want to know what the boats are doing that you see racing on the water or on television, this chapter introduces you to the incredibly diverse sport of sailboat racing — everything from the top trophies in racing to the types of sailboats that race to what you can do if you're interested in competing.

Winning the Top Trophies in Sailing

Sailboat racing comes in many forms, from casual weekend racing to grand prix professional racing with television coverage and even prize money. In the 1800s, the sport of *yachting* — a formal name for sailboat racing — began to develop. This section looks at the world's most prestigious and competitive sailboat races: the America's Cup and the Olympics.

Which race is more important in the world of sailing: the America's Cup or the Olympics? Certainly the Cup garners more public attention, but if you take a poll of racers, the Olympics would probably come out on top. Maybe the Olympics wins out because individual sailing skill is a bigger part of an Olympic Gold Medal. But for a top professional racer, the America's Cup does have something going for it — competing in it's a real job.

The America's Cup

The America's Cup is the oldest international sporting event in the world, and today it's the biggest event in sailing (as measured by media and general public interest). The event started in 1851 when a group of clever Yankees sailed their quick schooner, *America,* over to England looking for some suckers to race (and wager). They were unsuccessful in drumming up a challenge for money, so they entered a race around the Isle of Wight in southern England, and the rest is history. *America* beat 14 British boats around the course (although some controversy stirred over whether the Yankees had skipped a mark of the course) and took home a sterling silver ewer, renamed the America's Cup after the boat that won it.

For 132 years, the America's Cup trophy was in the possession of the New York Yacht Club — the longest winning streak in the history of sports. But in 1983, a team of Aussies with a very fast boat with a winged keel carried the Cup down under. A U.S. crew led by skipper Dennis Conner (with Peter as navigator) representing the San Diego Yacht Club went to Perth, Australia, and won the Cup back in 1987. The winner of the Cup gets to host the next event, so in the early '90s the Cup races took place off our home of San Diego. Since then, the United States, New Zealand, and Switzerland (with Valencia, Spain, as the Swiss team's host city) have won the Cup. Teams from France, Italy, Canada, Japan, Sweden, Spain, China, and South Africa have tried to win the Cup and bring it to their home waters. The America's Cup is a match-racing competition (see the following sidebar, "Facing off head-to-head: Match racing," for more information) that typically features a several-month-long elimination series among the challenging teams to decide who races the defending team in the America's Cup match — often a best-of-nine race series.

Over the years, the America's Cup has attracted its share of characters. Around the turn of the century, Sir Thomas Lipton tried, unsuccessfully, five times to win the coveted trophy. He did, however, win America's tea business in the process. Other notable players over the decades include Sir Thomas Sopwith (of Sopwith Camel biplane fame), Cornelius Vanderbilt (yes, one of those Vanderbilts), Baron Bic (you probably have one of his pens), Ted Turner (you probably get a few of his channels on cable), and Larry Ellison (owner of Oracle and one of the world's wealthiest men). Dennis Conner, "DC," shown in Figure 13-1, has won the Cup four times, lost it twice, and has been at the forefront of the increased professionalism in the competition.

Figure 13-1:
Dennis
Conner
holding the
coveted
America's
Cup.

In recent years, the Cup races have taken place every three or four years, and for most of the last century and a half, the fastest boat has usually won. Over the years, a variety of large monohulls have competed for the America's Cup. The massive 135 foot J-boat *Reliance* won in 1903. After the 1988 Cup, the IACC (International America's Cup Class) rule was created. See the "Box rules and development classes" section, later in this chapter. The IACC boats are between 80 and 85 feet in length. As in any sailboat race, boat speed is ultra-important in the America's Cup, and teams spend millions of dollars on their design efforts in the quest of a small edge.

If you have to ask how much vying for the Cup costs, you can't afford it. In winning the Cup in 1992, Bill Koch's America3 team spent a record $64 million over three years. Most of the money went into the design and construction of an armada of boats, masts, sails, and other equipment. In 2003, Swiss billion-aire Ernesto Bertarelli spent at least that much and (to the dismay of New Zealand) hired away New Zealand's top sailors, including skipper Russell

Coutts. Bertarelli was rewarded for his raiding efforts with an America's Cup victory and the opportunity to host the first ever America's Cup in Europe. For the latest America's Cup news online, check out www.americascup.com.

The Olympics

Most sailors consider the Olympics to be the premier sailing competition and the purest test of sailing skill, because the boats are strictly *one design* (built to very strict measurements to ensure their equality). Sailing has been a part of the Olympics since the Paris games in 1900.

Olympic sailing awards Gold Medals to the winners in 11 different classes of boats, from a three-person keelboat to a sailboard. When JJ competed in the women's double-handed event, she competed in a 470, which is a two-person trapeze dinghy with a spinnaker (see Figure 13-2).

Sailors often try for many years to first earn a spot at the Olympics for their country (by finishing at or near the top at world championship qualifying events), and then earn a spot for themselves because the Olympics allows only one team per country per class of boat to compete. JJ and Pam Healy trained in the 470 class for seven years before achieving their dream of being on the U.S. Olympic team. JJ's teammate in 2000, Pease Glaser, spent 15 years training in four different types of Olympic boats before she stood on the podium. Luckily, experience often trumps youth in sailboat racing!

At the Sydney Olympics, the sailing competition took place all over Sydney harbor, even right in front of the famous Sydney Opera House. But in land-locked Olympic cities, the sailing usually takes place at a nearby lake or harbor.

Facing off head-to-head: Match racing

When just two boats are in a competition, the race is called a *match race*. The premier match-racing event is the America's Cup. Match racing is tremendously exciting to participate in. And, unlike watching other sailing competitions (which some compare to watching paint dry), match racing can be thrilling to watch. Before the start of the race, the boats vie for control, circling each other in an elaborate game of cat and mouse.

Match racing has its own set of rules, which are slightly different from the regular racing rules, creating very close, aggressive competition in which collisions are certainly not rare. Match racing also has on-the-water judging, with umpires doling out "instant justice" on the water.

A world circuit of professional match-racing regattas is the training ground for the America's Cup hopefuls. Races are sailed close to shore in identical boats, providing plenty of excitement for spectators. Events take place around the world, and most have prize money and television coverage.

Figure 13-2:
JJ and Pam Healy planing at high speed in big waves — on their way to the Bronze in the '92 Olympics.

Racing Sailboats All Over the World

Boats come in thousands and thousands of different types, and you can race any type. Additionally, races take place all over the globe, from Cape Horn to the fjords of Norway. You can race model boats on ponds and ice boats on frozen lakes. Some races are around *buoys* (anchored, floating turning marks), and other races go offshore from point to point. Here's a look at the many different types of racing.

Fleet racing: All together now

Races can be as short as ten minutes, or they may last for months. You can race *one-design* (in which all the boats are identical) or under a *handicap* system (in which boats of different types race together with the faster boats owing time to the slower boats). The majority of sailboat racing is done in fleets (hence the term *fleet racing*, in which many boats compete together).

One-design racing

Maybe the most competitive sailing in the world is in the incredibly diverse world of one-design dinghy, keelboat, catamaran, and sailboard racing. Races are hosted literally around the globe, and many of the more popular classes (both Olympic and non-Olympic) have exceptionally well-organized regional, national, and international circuits. Because the competing boats are almost identical, one-design racing provides the purest test of a sailor's skill. Figure 13-3 shows a typical one-design world championship. One-design racing is the backbone of the sport of sailboat racing, and virtually all the world's top sailors have spent most of their sailing lives in one-design competitions.

Figure 13-3: More than 100 boats blast off the starting line at the Melges 24 World Championships.

© Tim Wilkes/www.timwilkes.com

Handicap racing

Handicap (rating rules) racing allows boats of different types to race against each other by calculating how much time the faster (usually bigger) boats owe to the slower boats. Fully crewed yachts more than 36 feet (11 meters) long race in a variety of grand prix–level events around the world. Some crews are professional, and many top international sailors travel from race to race, living out of a duffel bag. Popular major events are in Sardinia, Kiel, Palma, San Francisco, Newport, Bermuda, Sydney, Key West, Chicago, and the Caribbean.

Box rules and development classes

Box rules allow boat designers to exercise some creativity as long as the boat fits into a "box" of parameters (usually length, width, and sail area). Then the boats compete evenly with no handicap. Some classes, often called *development classes,* encourage design and construction creativity. Development classes have produced some wild types of boats, including boats with hydrofoils,

Racing through the school years

Many junior sailing programs start kids racing soon after they master the basics of sailing. Kids race certain types of boats, like the Optimist dinghy, the Laser, and the 420, around the world. More than 100 kids compete in the annual world championships in these classes. In the United States, high school sailing teams are growing in popularity, and many colleges have varsity sailing programs and recruit top sailors. College sailing is generally a series of short races in two-person dinghies provided by the host school. Teams rotate boats and combine the scores of two divisions. Both of us were collegiate All-Americans at Yale University, and Peter was named College Sailor of the Year after a stellar sophomore year.

amazing catamarans, and skiffs. (One popular type of development-class boat is affectionately known as the 18 footer [pronounced eyedeen-footer] skiff in its home waters of Australia.) Figure 13-4 shows a 49er — the Olympic skiff.

Figure 13-4:
Two agile sailors trapeze off the racks on an Olympic 49er.

Team racing

Team racing is extremely exciting. Usually sailed in two-person dinghies, team racing's most common format has six boats racing, three boats per team. Tactics and boat handling are crucial to this exciting sport, as competitors try to hold back their opponents to enable their teammates to catch up.

Around the world in less than 80 days

In a modern-day take on Jules Verne's classic novel, French multihull sailor Bruno Peyron created the Trophee Jules Verne. The course is simple: Start between England and France, head south around Antarctica, and then finish back at the English Channel. The winner must finish in less than 80 days. In 1993, *Commodore Explorer,* a fully crewed 80-foot (24-meter) catamaran with Peyron on board, just broke the barrier in 79 days. Since then, several boats have lowered the time by using faster boats and waiting for the optimum weather window to start. In 2005, Peyron and crew cut the record to 50 days (making planet Earth seem quite small). Also in 2005, Ellen MacArthur, a petite 28-year-old Brit, captured the world's attention when she sailed the same route by herself on a 75-foot trimaran in only 71 days. She also drew the admiration of the British Royals, who promptly named her England's youngest Dame.

© Benoit Stichelbaut/DPPI/Offshore Challenges Sailing Team

Distance racing: Point to point

Distance racing from point to point harks back to the clipper ships of the mid-19th century. The desire in Europe and the eastern United States for goods such as tea from China forced shipping companies to build faster ships. The clipper ships, probably so named because they moved at such a fast clip, were sleek, narrow ships with enormous sail area and lengths up to 300 feet (91 meters). Trips from the Far East that had taken five months now only took half that long. The discovery of gold in California and Australia heightened the need for cargo space and delivery speed, yet the trip from New York to San Francisco was an arduous 15,000-mile route around stormy Cape Horn. *Flying Cloud*'s record-breaking trip of 89 days in 1851 was front-page news, and the fastest clipper ship captains were heroes.

Many famous distance races today follow the same trade routes as the clipper ships of the 19th century. Transatlantic races run from Cape Town to Rio de Janeiro, Los Angeles to Hawaii (the famous Transpac race), Chicago to Mackinac Island, and Newport to Bermuda, to name a few. Yet today, the fastest boats carry as little cargo as possible, and the crews eat freeze-dried food and make drinking water (with a desalinating machine run off an onboard generator). Following transatlantic races on the Internet is fun, because tracking software shows you the boats' courses, and crew reports let you feel like you're on board (except you get clean clothes, fresh food, a dry bed, and warm showers).

Another major offshore race is the Volvo Ocean Race. Seventy-nine-foot (21-meter) boats with ten crew members race around the world with stopovers in various ports. These boats are fast, as you can see in Figure 13-5. The longest and most grueling legs are in the Southern (Antarctic) Ocean, blasting downwind at full speed dodging icebergs. That part of the race makes for some great television coverage. Check it out at www.volvooceanrace.org.

Figure 13-5:
Full speed around the world in the Volvo Ocean Race.

© Oskar Kihlborg/Volvo Ocean Race

The exceptionally rugged (and possibly antisocial) sailor can compete in a nonstop around-the-world race — alone! It takes a really special person to want to be in a high-tech, 60-foot sloop, racing as fast as possible around the globe solo for more than 100 days. Needless to say, doing so is very dangerous, but check out the Vendee Globe race (www.vendeeglobe.org). The Mini Transat class, 21 feet long, provides popular (and lower-budget) single-handed offshore racing to a mostly European fleet of sailors.

Racing with the pros

One of our favorite regattas is the Pro-Am at the Bitter End Yacht Club in Virgin Gorda in the British Virgin Islands. The resort invites top sailors (such as Paul Cayard, Russell Coutts, and, lucky for us, ourselves) to come race for a week with the hotel guests.

We've attended several regional charity regattas that auction us off as crewmembers to raise money for a worthy cause. So check out your local sailing magazine — you may have a chance to sail with the biggest names in the sport of sailing and raise money for a good cause too.

Trying Sailboat Racing: Why Do It?

No doubt sailors have been racing against that boat nearby since man first put to sea. Racing is a fantastic sport for many different reasons. This section covers a few of them.

Racing is for everyone

Racing sailboats is for people of all sizes and all ages. Although some crew positions on certain boats are very physically demanding (such as the grinders on the America's Cup boats), the most important characteristics of a good racer are mental — concentration, quick reactions, analytical skills, and a desire to learn. Even individuals with physical disabilities can participate in sailboat racing. (See Chapter 2 for more info.) Sailing has been part of the Paralympics since 2000, and sailors with disabilities have raced several distance races, including the Transpac race from Los Angeles to Hawaii.

Men and women compete equally in sailing at all levels. In 1995, JJ had the opportunity to be a part of an all-women's America's Cup team, America3. The race marked the first time that women competed head-to-head against men at the top level of a professional sport. In any given local sailing race, you can find women and men racing against each other.

Racing teaches sportsmanship

Sailboat racing encourages fair play because the sport is self-policing, relying on a set of right-of-way rules (see the section "Knowing the Rules of the Game," later in this chapter). A few competitions have on-the-water referees, but most sailboat races rely on the competitors' sense of sportsmanship to obey the rules.

Racers are at one with nature

Sailboat racing can have all the intensity of NASCAR racing without the noise, the burning rubber, and the burning fossil fuel. You're out in the middle of nature just like an off-road racer, yet you're not tearing up the tundra. After your boat goes past, the only thing you leave behind is your wake.

To win a sailboat race, you must let all your senses work for you, from feeling the wind on your skin to reading the water for clues to the wind shifts. When racing, you have to sail your boat as fast as possible while looking around and planning which way to go.

Racers always discover something new

Imagine a football game that takes place on the water, where the waves and wind constantly change the playing field — that's sailboat racing. It's like a three-dimensional chess game in which the board and the competitors are always moving. Some compare match racing, the one-on-one racing format used in the America's Cup, to aerial dog fighting. In any type of sailboat racing, you discover so much about the weather, the current, the hydrodynamics and aerodynamics of the boat and sails, tactics, how you perform under pressure — and the list goes on and on.

PETER SAYS

Sailboat racing in cold weather

Some people are so keen on sailboat racing that they continue to race all year round — even in frigid climates. Sailboat racing in cold climates is called *frostbiting* — for good reason. Personally, I think that any time you have to break the ice out of a boat to go sailing, you should make the trip very short and follow it up with something hot to drink in front of a blazing fireplace.

In college, I raced in a dinghy regatta on Lake Michigan in late November. My crew and I used rock salt (the stuff they throw on roads to melt the ice) to keep the deck from turning into a skating rink and the ropes from freezing solid — now that's frostbiting!

Iceboats are incredibly fast sailboats that skate across the ice on runners similar to ice skates. Iceboats can fly at incredible speeds — over 100 miles per hour (161 kilometers per hour). If you get a chance to go iceboating, don't forget your helmet.

Racing takes place in nice places

Sailboat racing has taken each of us literally around the globe. We have been to some of the nicest places in the world, such as Bermuda, Denmark, New Zealand, Australia, and Sardinia. And, unlike most of the other visitors, who are shore bound, we get to go sailing. Now that's what we call a great sport!

Understanding a Sailboat Race

This section has the big picture of what you need to know to race in the most common type of sailboat race — a *fleet race* (many boats competing together) around a course defined by *buoys*. Don't worry — you'll be back at the dock in time for dinner and a nice hot shower!

Preparing the boat

Anyone with a boat can find a race to enter. But to maximize your chances of performing well, you need to prepare your boat and crew. One of the most important aspects of racing is boat speed. If your boat is slow, you can still win a race by using clever tactics and maneuvering better than the competition, but winning is much easier with a fast boat. Boat speed comes through preparation — refining your equipment so that it's fast and easy to sail. Making sure that your boat can handle the stress of heavy winds and big waves can help you avoid the agony of a breakdown. Even the little things, like polishing your boat's bottom, can make the difference between winning and losing.

Preparing the crew

Some boats are sailed single-handed; others you race with a large crew. No matter how many people are on board, the abilities, motivation, and teamwork of the crew are critical to success. A blown maneuver, like a spinnaker takedown at a mark rounding, can cost dearly, but a good crew can make an average *helmsman* (driver) look like a superstar. The crew constantly feeds the helmsman information about wind shifts, wave conditions, and boat-on-boat positioning so the driver can steer as quickly as possible without looking around too much. The more competitive the racing, the more important it is that the entire crew work smoothly as a team.

Entering the race

Local sailing or yacht clubs run most races. A document called the *Notice of Race* explains the basic details of the *regatta* (a series of races scored together as a whole): when the racing starts, what type of boats can enter, if you need to pay an entry fee, when you can register, who is organizing the event, and so on. You can usually find a club's upcoming race schedule on its Web site with links to registration materials and a downloadable copy of the NOR.

After you register, you receive a copy of the *Sailing Instructions* (SIs). The SIs cover important details, such as a schedule of races, a chart of the race area, and the type of race courses. Figure 13-6 shows you a windward-leeward course typical for an around-the-buoys race. The starting and finishing lines are imaginary lines between an anchored race-committee boat and a buoy.

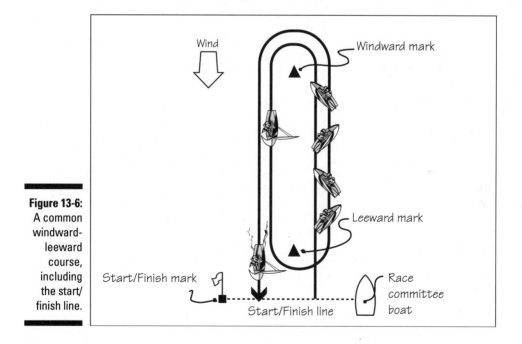

Figure 13-6:
A common windward-leeward course, including the start/finish line.

A skipper's, or competitor's, meeting may precede the first race. The meeting is a good chance to ask questions and learn more about the upcoming event.

As soon as you know what time the first race starts, figure out when you want to leave the dock and make sure your team arrives early. You need time to check the notice board (the SIs describe its location), pack your gear bag or change into your sailing clothes, and rig your boat. On race day, it may take

Preparing for your child's first race

If the racing bug bites your child and you don't know port from starboard, usually your child's sailing instructor can help you make her first race a success. Probably the most common mistake kids make is to forget some key piece of equipment at home, so feel free to run through a checklist (sail, mast, parts, gloves, hat, and sunglasses) and ask their instructor about racing-specific gear, such as a watch, gloves, and a rules book. Also, your child may be too nervous in the morning to remember to bring a dry change of clothes and a towel for after sailing.

The key is making sure your child has enough time in the morning for all the pre-race preparation. Even if the start isn't until noon or 1 p.m.,

you may have to get to the boat at 9 or 10 a.m. If the race area is several miles away and the winds are generally light in the morning, the race committee or the coach may offer a tow for the boats. For more on towing, see Chapter 7. Your child may not have room on the dinghy for extra gear or even for lunch, so pack food, water, and a light jacket in a plastic baggie or small duffle bag. Bring another plastic baggie for Sailing Instructions, and tape the page with the course diagrams into the boat where your child can easily refer to it.

And you can remind your child to apply sunscreen and go the bathroom — he or she will thank you later.

longer to launch your boat than normal, with everyone leaving at the same time. In deciding when to meet, factor in how long it will take you to get to the race course area and give yourself close to an hour at the racing area before the start for the first race of the day.

Before the start, crews develop their racing strategy by carefully monitoring the changes in the wind direction and velocity and watching for variations in current. Based on their observations, crews may develop a game plan to favor one side of the course because it has more wind or some other advantage. Crews also may use the time to practice maneuvers.

Getting a good start

The start is often the most important part of the race. A good start can propel you into an untouchable position — or at least give you a better shot at a top finish. A series of sound and visual signals from the race-committee boat counts the time down to the start.

The goal is to be just behind the starting line at full speed, just as the countdown clicks to zero and the starting gun fires. Sounds easy, but all the other boats are trying to do the very same thing. Another prestart consideration is which end of the line is "favored" with respect to the wind conditions and your competitors (see Figure 13-7). Sail to the middle of the starting line and point your bow into the wind. If your bow is pointing toward one end of the line, that end is favored (assuming the first mark is upwind).

Basically, the five minutes or so before the starting gun fires is a massive free-for-all in which boats randomly zig and zag around until *boom!* At the start, the mayhem magically becomes a spectacular water ballet, with all boats lined up and heading for the first mark. If the mayhem doesn't subside and boats start prematurely, the race committee can recall specific boats (using flags and hails), or call the whole fleet back for another try.

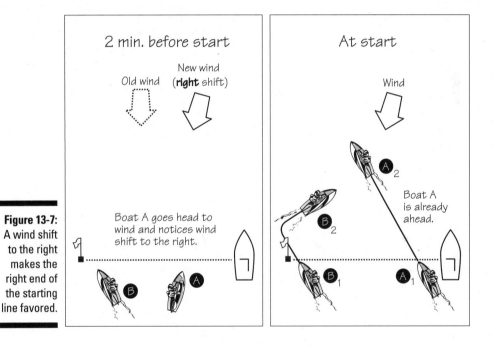

Figure 13-7:
A wind shift to the right makes the right end of the starting line favored.

Against the wind: The first leg

The first turning mark is commonly positioned directly upwind of the starting line. As you discover in Chapter 5, no sailboat can sail straight into the wind, so on the first leg the fleet works its way to the top mark tack by tack. Of course, a boat can reach the mark by tacking only once, but often, because of wind shifts and other competitors, boats must make more tacks. Strategic considerations include wind shifts — even a small five-degree wind shift affects the positions in the race. Boats that head to the right side of the race course (by first sailing on port tack) benefit greatly from a clockwise shift, as Figure 13-7 shows. But if the wind goes counterclockwise, those same boats lose out — which is why you try, before the start, to figure out what the wind will do and, during the race, you keep looking for clues to what the wind will do next.

While racing upwind, you must also focus on keeping clear wind in your sails and avoiding the exhaust (disturbed air) coming off a competitor's sails. The boats ahead often try to "cover" their competition and force them farther back. While employing these various tactics, the crew tries to keep the boat sailing at maximum speed, adjusting the sails and the crew's position on the boat to stay in perfect tune with the changing wind conditions.

Around the mark

On the open course, the boats spread out across a mile or more, and then they all converge at the mark before turning the corner. Mark roundings provide an opportunity for the crews to strut their stuff as they set and drop sails (when turning the first mark to go downwind, many boats set the colorful spinnaker; see Figure 13-8). A well-practiced crew can gain valuable boat lengths with deft boat and sail handling. Luckily, universal sailing rules cover which boat has the right-of-way, or crowded mark roundings would be complete chaos.

Figure 13-8: On the downwind leg, the crews try to get every ounce of speed out of their spinnakers.

With the wind: The downwind leg

Many race courses have two buoys: a *windward* (top) and a *leeward* (bottom) mark near the starting line. On the second, downwind leg, the boats continue to focus on boat speed while keeping an eye on the puffs of wind and the position of the competition. The boats in the back now have the opportunity to attack by using their wind shadows to slow down the leaders.

The finish gun

Like the starting line, the finish is an imaginary line between two objects, usually a buoy on one end and a flag on the committee boat on the other. No sound is sweeter than the blast of the gun as you cross the line in first place, but you don't need to win every race to win a regatta. You just need to be in the top group consistently.

Knowing the Rules of the Game

In order to play a game with other people, you have to agree on the rules. The governing body for the sport, the *International Sailing Federation* (ISAF), writes the *Racing Rules of Sailing*. Every four years, ISAF updates the rules.

If you want to race, buy a copy of Dave Perry's book, *Understanding the Racing Rules of Sailing*. Dave's well-written book covers the most common racing situations and helps you understand the tactics of racing while teaching you the rules. You can download a copy of the racing rules at `www.isaf.org` or `www.sailing.org`, or purchase a printed copy at your local marine store. To give you an idea of how the rules work, we outline the seven most basic rules in sailboat racing in the following list:

- **Avoid collisions with other boats and any buoys or turning marks.** Sailboat racing isn't bumper boats.

- **You must start properly.** The starting line is meant to be crossed after the starting gun. If you cross before the gun fires, you have to go back and restart.

- **Starboard tack has the right-of-way over port tack.** This rule and the following two rules are in force under the rules of the road (for nonracing sailboats) and the Racing Rules (for racing sailboats only). See Figure 13-9.

- **The leeward boat has the right-of-way over the windward boat.** This rule applies when two boats are on the same tack; if they're on opposite tacks, then the preceding rule applies and starboard tack has the right-of-way over port tack. See Figure 13-9.

- **The overtaking boat must keep clear.** Makes sense, doesn't it? The boat that's passing must stay out of the way of the boat being passed.

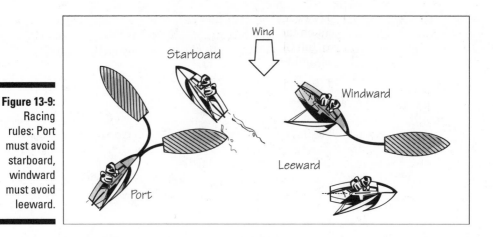

Figure 13-9:
Racing
rules: Port
must avoid
starboard,
windward
must avoid
leeward.

✔ **When rounding marks, the inside boat is king.** If two or more boats approach a turning mark or some sort of obstruction while overlapped, the boat on the inside of the turn has the right-of-way.

✔ **You can make amends — sometimes.** The penalties in sailing vary depending on the Sailing Instructions. Some regattas allow you to exonerate a foul (when you break a rule) by immediately sailing two complete circles (two tacks and two jibes) or by accepting a percentage penalty to your finish score. However, in many races, if you foul another boat, don't take a penalty, and are found guilty in a post-race hearing, you're disqualified from the race — ouch.

How to Win — or at Least Get Started

This section contains our advice for mastering the basics of sailboat racing:

✔ **Become a student of the sport.** You can read a number of outstanding books on sailboat racing, including *Expert Dinghy and Keelboat Racing* by maybe the best sailboat racer ever, Paul Elvström, winner of four Olympic Gold Medals; the *Sail To Win* series (from Fernhurst Books in the United Kingdom); and *Winning in One Designs* by Dave Perry (the author of the other must-have book *Understanding the Racing Rules of Sailing*). You can also find great magazines on sailboat racing, such as *Sailing World, Sail, Seahorse* (U.K.), and *Yachting*. For all the latest sailing news, check out www.sailingworld.com, www.sailing.org, and www.sailingscuttlebutt.com.

✔ **Enroll in a racing seminar.** Check with your local marine store, sail loft, or sailing club for local seminars. If your local college has a sailing program, it may offer racing classes too. Here are our favorite racing seminars in the United States:

- **North U** (www.northu.com)**:** North U offers a variety of seminars for racers on tactics and boat speed and weather and cruising seminars too. Bill Gladstone and a host of instructors (occasionally one of us) hold North U seminars in a classroom setting.

- **J World** (www.jworld-sailing.com)**:** J World runs on-the-water clinics on both U.S. coasts.

✔ **Find the right boat.** Most racing venues feature active fleets of boats. Some popular fleets even have casual races on weekday evenings. Many dinghies (like the Snipe or Lido 14, Lightning, 470, and Tasar) are great for husband-wife and parent-child racing teams. Make the effort to race different types of boats and to learn all the different jobs on board.

✔ **Know the rules.** Successful tactics are dependent on using the rules to your advantage. For example, as you get close to a mark, the boats converge. So being on starboard tack (which has the right-of-way) on the approach gives you a tactical advantage.

✔ **Practice, practice, practice.** In order to succeed on the race course, you must do many things well. You must sail fast, work well with your team, handle your boat and your sails smoothly, and acutely perceive the strategy and tactics of the race. The best racers spend much more time practicing than racing.

✔ **Sign on as a crew member.** You can't improve your sailing skills unless you get out there and sail. Many local sailing magazines (you can find them at your local marine store) publish lists of interested crew. Put your name on the list. Certain regions have on-line crew lists. Join the local racing fleet and go to its dinners — most people like to race with friends rather than strangers. And go to the marina where the boats dock and introduce yourself to the racers. Sometimes a boat needs a last-minute replacement, or if the weather is windy, racers may want to bring more crew on board to keep the boat from heeling too much.

Part IV
Sailing Away for a Year and a Day

The 5th Wave   By Rich Tennant

"That's not what I meant!"

In this part . . .

Remember the owl and pussycat who went to sea in a beautiful pea-green boat in Edward Lear's classic book? They sailed away for a year and a day to the land where the bong tree grows. Haven't you always wanted to see what a bong tree looks like? No? Well, then, have you always wanted to sail away? Yes? (If you aren't familiar with the owl and pussycat, you can read Edward Lear's classic, *The Owl and the Pussycat,* before you head out.) The skills that you acquire by reading this book and practicing on the water have you ready to embark on an adventure.

In this part, we first cover how to deal with mishaps, such as running aground and fixing broken equipment, and then focus on the basics of boat maintenance. But then we move to cheerier topics. You can daydream in earnest as we introduce you to the world of cruising. Find out about chartering (renting) a boat in beautiful vacation destinations around the world. And if you have kids, we show you tips for making sure that they enjoy the sailing trip, too, and we introduce you to some of our favorite boats — sailboards.

Chapter 14

Encountering Sailing Emergencies (And How to Handle Them)

Give me a spirit that on this life's rough sea
Loves t' have his sails filled with a lusty wind,
Even till his sail-yards tremble, his masts crack,
And his rapt ship run on her side so low
That she drinks water, and her keel plows air.

— George Chapman

This chapter covers what to do when bad luck strikes and unfortunate mishaps happen. Most sailors have their own great disaster stories — the time they were aground until the next high tide, or how the mast broke and bits of sharp aluminum rained down on the deck, missing them by inches. The best sailors have fewer exciting stories, because they're prepared for most situations and can fix any minor problem before it turns major.

When something unusual goes wrong, you're under stress. Because you can't walk away and ignore the problem, you have to deal with it. Keeping your cool under pressure is very valuable when you have to make important decisions that affect the safety of your boat and your crew.

PETER SAYS

Planning ahead

Having a clearly defined game plan for the crew to follow, with one person who is ultimately in charge, really helps in emergencies. A great example was during the America's Cup races in windy Perth, Australia.

During one practice race, a jib blew out, and most of the crew (myself included) rushed up to the pitching bow to help drag it down and set a new one. The waves were throwing the boat all around, and conditions were definitely "one hand for yourself and one for the boat." Despite the talent and years of experience of the crew on the boat, we bungled the recovery so badly that Dennis Conner finally turned downwind to give us a break, giving up the practice race.

On the way in, we discussed the problem. Everyone knew that we had to get the tattered sail down, but some of the crew stuffed pieces down one hatch and some down another, creating a hopeless mess. We agreed that in any subsequent situations like that, we'd let one person, Scott Vogel, our bowman, decide the plan for solving the problem.

Ultimately, that meeting won us a race, maybe even the America's Cup, because another jib exploded in the Challenger Finals while we were racing against *New Zealand.* Not only did we get the pieces of the old sail down, but we got the new sail up so fast that we retained the lead!

Chapter 7 discusses basic safety preparedness on a sailboat, including practicing a man-overboard rescue and recovering from a capsize. This chapter addresses the not-so-common emergencies that you can't practice but that can happen to you while out in a sailboat. Don't worry — these mishaps are rare. But just in case your lucky day was yesterday, read through this chapter so that you can be the one who stays calm, knows just what to do, and saves the day.

Running Aground

When any part of your boat touches the shore or the bottom, you've *run aground*. Usually your underwater fin (keel or centerboard — see Chapter 1) is the first to hit, although we've seen boats run aground with their masts — when they capsize in shallow water and stick the tip of the mast in the mud. A grounding can be (hopefully) a gentle kiss or an ordeal in which you're really stuck with the tide dropping, or even worse. Most experienced sailors run aground at some point — often in their home waters on a warm, sunny afternoon when they aren't paying attention.

Prevent those groundings

In order to prevent a grounding, you need to do more than just pay attention. The following tips can prevent the majority of groundings:

- **Brush up on your navigational skills.** Be familiar with the nautical chart of your sailing area, and if you're in unfamiliar waters or have shallow, tricky home waters, be able to *fix* (determine) your position on a chart and perform piloting skills (see Chapter 9).

- **Know how to raise your centerboard and rudder.** On a dinghy, you can often pull up the foils and slide over shallow waters. Just make sure that you're headed to deeper water!

- **Know how to "read" the bottom.** Chapter 9 covers how the color of the water and shape of the waves can help you spot shallow waters.

- **Know the depth of the water under your boat.** A good depth sounder is helpful for larger keelboats with electronics.

- **Know the exact depth *(draft)* of your boat.** How deep is your keel?

- **Know the shape of your keel.** Some keelboats get deeper when all the passengers are in the stern or when the boat is under power. If you do run aground, knowing your keel shape is crucial for making the right assessment of how to get free, as we discuss in a minute.

- **Understand the local tides.** See Chapter 8 on tides. Have a local tide book, which predicts the estimated range of tides, on board (available at marine stores), but use this information with a grain of salt. You can cross-check the predicted current direction with the wakes on buoys.

Don't push it — but if you must sail over a shallow area to get home, sail slowly (at half speed or less). Doing so makes it easier for you to get free if you do get stuck.

When you go aground

So you're out on a nice, sunny day for an afternoon sail and you run aground. What do you do? (No, don't cry into your coffee.) This section looks at the ways to free your boat from a nice, soft bottom. Later in this chapter, in the "Halting Hull Damage" section, we tell you what you should do in the rare event that you hit rocks and sustain serious damage.

In order to free yourself from a soft bottom, try these tips:

✔ **If you hit softly, slow down and immediately turn the boat to deeper water.** Hopefully, you can sail free.

✔ **Send someone below to check for damage.** Look in the *bilge,* where the keel attaches inside the hull, for water leaking into the boat.

✔ **If you have a centerboard (lucky you), immediately pull it up partway.** A *centerboard* is the center, retractable fin on a dinghy.

✔ **Try to make the boat less deep.** Heeling works for all sailboats, except for those with a twin or winged keel, because it reduces the boat's draft. When you hit, immediately move all the crew weight to leeward, as Figure 14-1 shows. If you're on a reaching heading, overtrim the sails to generate heel from the wind.

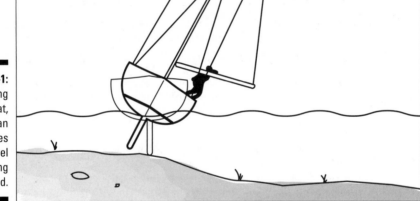

Figure 14-1:
By heeling the boat, you can sometimes free the keel from being aground.

✔ **Consider using the engine, but only in combination with some of these other remedies.** First, check that the rudder isn't stuck — you can break it by moving the boat. Depending on the situation, you may want to try forward or reverse gear. Watch the temperature gauge — silt can clog the water intake and cause overheating. And never put the engine in gear before ensuring all lines are out of the water.

✔ **Take the sails down if they're driving you farther into the shallow area.** First let them luff.

Obviously, you should perform the preceding procedures as quickly as possible. If you're aboard a keelboat and still not afloat after trying these tricks, try one of these more involved actions:

✔ **Really heel the boat.** Drop and secure the mainsail. Then release the mainsheet and push the main (supported at the outboard end by a halyard or other secure line) all the way out to the side the boat is heeling toward. Next, have some crew members climb up on it and slide as far outboard as they can. Lashing the boom to a shroud or tying it off to a forward cleat can free a crew member for other duties. Falling into the water is easy to do while performing this trick, so this act is only for the acrobatically inclined. Have the crew don life jackets first, and leave at least one person on board.

✔ **Get creative on ways to heel.** If you have a rowing dinghy, maybe you can suspend it (filled with water if necessary) from the end of the boom to increase heel.

When a boat is heeled further than normal, check for leaking fuel or other potential problems.

✔ **Lighten the ship.** Offload extra crew and heavy gear into a dinghy to reduce draft. If you don't have a dinghy, try moving all the crew to the bow to see if that helps.

✔ **Use the anchor to pull you off.** This system, called *kedging,* or *setting a kedge,* requires sending a rowing dinghy (or other boat) out with an anchor to set. Put the anchor and sufficient anchor line in the boat and head toward deep water, making sure that the end of the anchor line is tied to the dinghy or the sailboat. When the anchor is set (the farther away, the better chance the anchor will hold), start pulling yourself free. Use a winch if you have one. Meanwhile, keep heeling, powering with the engine or sails, and trying other measures.

✔ **Wait until high tide.** Even if you get stuck at high tide (assuming you're on a tidal body of water), you'll eventually float free. Having an anchor set in deeper water hopefully keeps you from getting pushed further aground as the tide comes in. Try to heel the boat toward shallow water so that the incoming tide doesn't swamp your boat. If you're really "high and dry," take heart — most boats are built to withstand lying on their sides. Try to cushion the hull if possible.

✔ **As a last resort, you can accept a tow.** If your boat is hard aground, pulling it off can cause extensive keel and rudder damage. Or the tow line can snap and hurt someone as it recoils. Hiring a professional towing service can be expensive (not as expensive as salvaging a sunken ship, however). In case of a true emergency, contact the Coast Guard on VHF Channel 16. (For more on using the radio and safe towing tips, see Chapter 7.) The Coast Guard may refer you to a towing company.

Biscayne Bay blues

When I was part of a crew delivering a racing boat back to New England from Florida, we went hard aground at night as we were leaving Miami for the long sail north. Fortunately, the keel was stuck in nice, soft sand, and we were in the protected waters of Biscayne Bay. So after trying all the easy tricks, we gave up until morning and went to sleep with the boat on a 30-degree heel.

At dawn, we put up the spinnaker (to heel the boat more), put out an anchor, and ultimately flagged down a passing boat to add some towing power. When the tide rose, we finally clawed our way off and were on our way. Because going aground is kind of embarrassing, we agreed to keep the episode to ourselves — until a friend mailed me a copy of the front page of the *Miami Herald* with our beautiful spinnaker photogenically framing a boat that was clearly very hard aground!

Jury-Rigging Out of a Bind

A body of knowledge called *jury-rigging* (the fine art of replacing broken gear with a temporary fix) covers many possible emergencies. Covering all the possible jury-rig solutions is beyond the scope of this book, but this section provides a list of the equipment and tools that are common to many different solutions — plus some examples of how to use these items. Creativity is the key to effective jury-rigging. Keep in mind that you can't stuff as much equipment into a small dinghy as you can into a big keelboat.

✔ **Duct tape:** Duct tape can fix just about anything, including a boo-boo on your finger when you run out of bandages.

✔ **Knife:** A sailor's best friend. Use a knife to cut a heavily loaded sheet or halyard that's hopelessly tangled.

✔ **Rope:** Sailors can do amazing things with rope. Besides an anchor line, you should have at least one other rope that's long and strong enough to serve as a sheet, halyard, or dock line. A 15- to 30-foot (5- to 9-meter) length of ultrastrong, small-diameter rope (³⁄₁₆ inch, or 4 millimeters) can be nearly as valuable as duct tape in an emergency. Braided rope with a low-stretch core is best for this (see more on rope in Chapter 15). *Sail ties* or *webbing* (strong, ribbonlike straps available at sail lofts) can also fit through some tiny holes and provide great lashing material.

✔ **Spare parts:** The list depends on your boat. However, no matter how big the boat, bring a few shackles (matching the size of common ones on the boat) and some clevis pins or machine screws with nuts. A couple of medium or large pulleys *(blocks)* are also great in your *ditty bag* (a bag for good jury-rigging items).

✔ **Sticky-back:** This stuff is also called *insignia cloth.* A wide (3-feet, or 1-meter) roll of sail-repair material with adhesive backing can repair holes in boats and in sails.

✔ **Tools:** A dinghy may have only a screwdriver and vice grips (although we recommend a multipurpose tool), while an ocean-circling keelboat may carry several tool boxes. Sailors often pull bottle openers (hey, jury-rigging is thirsty work), hammers, adjustable wrenches, wire cutters, and hacksaws out of the box first in an emergency. Don't forget a few good sailmaker's hand-sewing needles, thread, and a *palm* (leather device that fits over your palm, enabling you to push a needle through many layers of sailcloth — sort of a super thimble).

So what do you do with all these good things? Use your imagination, because that's what jury-rigging is all about.

Overcoming Sail Problems

Without functional sails, you can't do much sailing. Sails can blow out and rip — sometimes from misuse, sometimes from simple wear and tear. If your sail does blow out or tear, take it down right away, before any further damage can occur. Depending on the size of the rip, you may be able to fix it, sometimes as good as new. Your best friend in this procedure is that roll of sticky-back cloth you brought aboard after reading the previous section about jury-rigging.

If you need to repair one of your sails, follow these easy steps:

1. **Make sure the area you're operating on is clean, dry, and salt-free.**

   You may have to rinse the sail in freshwater before it will dry completely.

2. **Lay the repair area on as flat a surface as possible.**

3. **Try to position the torn edges into their original positions.**

   Getting the edges into position may take several hands.

4. **Calculate the size of the sticky-back bandage (make sure you overlap the edges sufficiently) and cut it.**

5. **Apply the sticky-back.**

   Start at one edge of the tear and work slowly to the other, trying to keep the sail as smooth and as close to its pretear position as possible.

6. **Press the applied tape firmly to the repaired area.**

   Use a solid object and press hard on the repair, sandwiching it to the table or work surface. Really work the sticky-back onto the repair, especially any stitched seams that are covered up. For most sails, this repair is enough. But if the repair is in a high-load area, like the leech of a jib or mainsail, consider stitching the tear through the sticky-back.

Furling blues

Although roller furlers are a convenient way of handling a big headsail, they aren't foolproof. One common problem occurs when furling the sail after use. If a light amount of tension isn't retained on the jib sheet while furling, the sail can end up with an uneven or unbalanced roll. The protruding edges of the sail can catch the wind and cause the sail to partially unroll and flap, damaging the sail. Always make sure your jib is furled smoothly.

Can't get your sail down

Occasionally a sail gets "stuck" when hoisted. Often, this is because the halyard has jumped the *sheave* (rolling part of a pulley) at the top of the mast. The best way to solve this problem is to haul a person up the mast in a bosun's chair to inspect and hopefully fix it. (See Chapter 15 for the proper use of a bosun's chair.) If the problem is a jumped sheave, then disconnect the sail from the stuck halyard so you can pull it upward to try to get it unjammed. If that doesn't work, you may need to carefully remove the sheave and then replace it with the halyard led correctly over the top. But if a halyard jumps a sheave once, it can happen again. After you get to shore, you may want to have a marine rigger help you figure out a more permanent solution (such as getting a bigger halyard).

Fouling the Prop

Sailors sometimes must use their boat's engine. A mishap known as "fouling the prop" proves that power and sailing don't mix all the time. Getting a rope tangled up in the propeller is a drag; when it happens on a boat with an inboard engine, the engine stalls and the propeller gets stuck, unable to turn. Next thing you know, someone (probably you) has to jump in the water (probably cold) and untangle the prop. Usually the culprit is a halyard or sheet (or dock line or tow line) from your boat.

Preventing a fouled prop is simple. Keep your lines out of the water, and always look around the boat before turning on the engine.

Unfortunately, people aren't as vigilant as they should be, so here's how to deal with tangled ropes on an inboard engine propeller. (If you have an outboard, what are you waiting for? Pull it up and unwrap the rope!)

1. **Turn off the engine immediately (it may have already stalled out).**

2. **Find the transgressing rope and gently pull it with the shift in neutral.**

   Pull harder and pray, because if the rope doesn't release, you're swimming.

Cutting your losses

Have you ever noticed in the old pirate movies that every sailor carries a knife? Well, that knife isn't just for coaxing the good guy to walk the plank; it's a valuable tool for every sailor to have, especially in an emergency. A very sharp knife, with a blunt point to avoid any accidental perforation of boat or body parts, can cut through a highly loaded halyard or tangled sheet in a second, often saving the mast or the boat in an emergency, such as a sudden squall.

3. **Consider whether you really need the engine.**

   If you don't really need the engine, or if the conditions are too rough and dangerous to go in the water, then you just have to sail. Keep in mind that in big waves, the boat is going up and down fast, so swimming underneath it, near the propeller blade, is no fun. If you delay the swim until later, tighten the fouled rope and tie it off on deck.

4. **You can try, as a last resort, putting the engine in reverse (dead slow) just for an instant and then pulling hard on the line.**

   We've never found this trick to work, but you never know.

5. **If the conditions are safe, or after you return to shelter, you can jump in.**

   Before swimming, stop the boat and make sure that it's dragging a line that you can grab. A mask, snorkel, and fins are nice.

6. **Using the wrapped rope as a guide, swim down to the prop (engine's off, right?) and try to untie the knot down there.**

7. **If untying the knot is impossible, get your knife so that you can chop that stupid rope into tiny little pieces.**

   Hey, be careful with that thing!

Steering Problems

Once every blue moon, the same fate befalls a rudder on a keelboat. The steering system feels stuck because a rope is wedged between the top of the rudder and the hull. Usually you can get out of this situation with a good tug on the infringing line from the right direction. If not, turn the helm hard one way and try again (you may have to drop the sails in strong winds). That usually works. If not, did you bring your swimsuit?

Surviving a Storm

Chapter 7 covers preparing yourself and your boat for strong winds. After following the safety steps in that chapter, here are some additional tips for a really big blow:

✔ **Feed the crew.** Going into battle against the elements with the fuel tank full is a good idea. If the crew has eaten recently, have someone prepare the next meal, even if it's just sandwiches. It may be tough to find a volunteer for galley duty in the middle of a storm.

✔ **Fix your position.** Consider increasing the level of your navigational energies, too. See Chapter 9 to find out how to fix your position.

✔ **Set a watch system.** If you're on a longer passage, you may already have established a rotation of the crew so that everyone can rest. A common rotation divides the crew up into two *watches,* or groups (of equal ability), with each watch being "on" for three or four hours (you decide) and then "off" to get some rest down below in a bunk.

Safety harnesses

A safety harness works like an extra hand to help keep you on board as you move around the deck on bigger keelboats. Wearing a safety harness leaves your hands free for handling sheets, lines, and so on.

Never use a safety harness on a dinghy, which can capsize. Safety harnesses are only for keelboats.

Pick a safety harness that fits snugly and is the proper size (they're often rated by body weight). The harness attaches to a tether that clips onto any solid object, including *jack lines.* Jack lines are ropes, webbing, or cables that run along the deck on either side of the cabin the length of the boat, specifically for use with safety harnesses (see Figure 14-2). Never attach a harness to a lifeline; lifelines put you closer to the edge of the boat and can break. Rig a jack line so that you can clip your safety harness onto it before you leave the cockpit and never have to unclip it as you move around on deck.

Wear a harness during the following times:

✔ Any time a man-overboard rescue would be difficult

✔ When on deck alone

✔ When sailing at night — especially if you leave the cockpit

✔ When sailing in rough conditions

Figure 14-2:
By clipping your safety harness onto a jack line, you can have both hands free to work anywhere on deck.

— Harness tether

— Jack line

Safety harnesses can be great for kids; for more, see Chapter 16.

Heaving-to and running before it

If you're ever in really heavy weather — like when the wind is blowing the dogs off their leashes — you may need to use an extreme technique for survival. *Heaving-to* is a technique for extreme conditions that also works (on boats with jibs) any time you want to "park" your boat, even in light air, as Figure 14-3 shows. It involves *backing* your jib (filling it backwards with wind) while filling your main partially on a close-hauled or close-reaching course. If conditions aren't too windy, the boat stays balanced, moving forward and to leeward very slowly. You can get into the heaved-to position by sailing along close-hauled and tacking over while keeping the jib cleated. Then adjust the mainsail until the boat "feels" comfortable. Heaving-to is a great way to take a break.

Look at the jib while you heave-to, and if it seems impaled on the windward *spreader* (the strut that holds the shrouds away from the mast), ease the sheet some to keep the sail from ripping, or you'll have to cancel your lunch break.

Figure 14-3:
Heaving-to:
Cleat the
jib on the
windward
side and let
the main
luff. Now
you can
take a
break.

Running before it is a heavy-weather tactic for when it's too windy to sail in any direction, upwind or downwind, without getting into trouble. This technique entails slowing the boat down until it has minimal headway (just enough to keep steerageway). In really strong winds, this means taking all your sails down and even dragging ropes or any sort of object that slows the boat down enough to be safe.

Avoiding thunder and lightning

In the Midwest and on the East Coast, the summer sailing season coincides with thunderstorm season. Sudden summer storms bring strong winds and lightning — a huge danger for sailors, because that aluminum mast on your sailboat puts you at risk for getting hit by lightning. Check the weather forecast before you go sailing (see Chapter 8). If you ever see a storm brewing or see lightning, head for shore as soon as possible. If getting to shore isn't feasible, you can anchor your boat. Go in the cabin, stay low, and stay away from any metal objects. Turn off the VHF radio and other electronics while the lightning is close.

JJ SAYS

When my five-woman team was preparing for the start of the J-24 World Championships on Lake Ontario and a big storm hit, we anchored the boat. One crew member suggested attaching the spinnaker pole to the wire shroud and letting the other end dangle in the water. She felt that the pole would help dissipate the electrical current if we did get hit by lightning. Luckily we didn't get hit, so I'd probably try that again if caught in a similar situation.

Breaking the Mast

Breaking a mast is a real drag. Not only does a broken mast mean that you (or your insurance company) are out a good chunk of change, but it can be dangerous, especially in strong winds and big seas. Clearly, the best cure is an ounce of prevention. We cover the basics of spar care and maintenance in Chapter 15, but even with the best care, seemingly perfect fittings can fail for no apparent reason. When this happens, the next thing you know — bang — a gravity storm. Another cause for a *dismasting* is a violent capsize and subsequent *turtling* (a capsized position when the mast points straight down) in shallow water.

To avoid breaking the mast, keep out of shallow water when sailing dinghies in strong winds.

Every dismasting is a little different. Masts can break at a fitting or at some other weak point. The broken mast may fall in the water, or it may dangle from the remaining stump. On a dinghy, you may be able to pick up and secure the broken pieces with one hand, whereas even lifting the standing rigging is a task for more than one person on a 40-foot (12-meter) keelboat. Therefore, no one "right way" exists to deal with a broken mast. You must use your common sense and creativity to solve the unique problem it creates. That said, here are some general rules to keep in mind:

- ✔ **Save the crew and the boat first.** If the process of retrieving and securing the broken pieces of the mast is endangering the safety of the crew or the boat, cut it away as fast as you can.

- ✔ **Don't run the engine while rigging and stuff are in the water.** See the "Fouling the Prop" section, earlier in this chapter, if you don't believe us.

- ✔ **Be conscious of the loads.** Consider the direction of forces on things. As you clean up the broken gear, you're like a lumberjack cutting a tree; cutting one thing may have a domino effect on other things.

- ✔ **Get the boat downwind of the mess.** If the mast falls into the water, try to maneuver the boat so that the mast is upwind. That way, the waves don't drive the hull onto the mast. Fortunately, Mother Nature should be on your side, because the mast and sails want to drag upwind like a sea anchor.

- ✔ **Recover all the wreckage, if you can.** If you're way out to sea, you may find that those pieces of mast, sails, and rigging come in handy in jury-rigging a new sail so you can get home.

If you must jettison the broken pieces for safety, being able to do so quickly is nice. Sharp hacksaw blades (several) and heavy-duty wire cutters are invaluable tools. Often, the easiest way of freeing the rigging is by removing the clevis pins at one end. See Chapter 15 about shackles with clevis pins.

The race isn't over until . . .

In a famous incident in the Transpac Race (from Los Angeles to Honolulu), the 70-foot *Cheval* was 25 miles from the finish and in first place with a nice lead when the unthinkable occurred: The mast broke during a jibe.

As the disheartened crew rushed to clean up the mess before the boat blew onto the reef, the owner climbed on deck after doing some calculations at the chart table. "Hey guys," he said, "we can still win this race — all we have to do is average six knots the rest of the way!" Rekindled with enthusiasm, the crew cut away the broken pieces and began jury-rigging halyards to the 15-foot mast stump sticking out of the deck. Soon they had a small sail hoisted and were doing five knots — hardly the 20 knots or better the boat was capable of doing in the conditions, but movement, at least.

After some more macramé and creative use of spinnaker poles and booms, the crew had managed to set another, bigger sail sideways. The crew added more "canvas" as the boat began surfing the swells in the Molokai Channel. *Cheval* did win that race, and this story is a great example of how human creativity (and probably a fair amount of duct tape) can solve most any problem.

Halting Hull Damage

Serious hull damage below the waterline can be a major problem. It can happen when you run aground, especially in rocks or coral, or if you run into a solid object floating just under the water's surface. Fortunately, this misfortune taken to its extreme is rare, but minor or medium-size leaks caused by a keel jarred loose in a grounding or a collision are more common. Here are some ways to stave the flow and save your boat:

- **Plug the hole with any available material.** Clothing or cushions can work well, and so can a life raft or a rubber dinghy. You can use a paddle or convenient brace to secure the plug, as Figure 14-4 shows. You can use a sail as an external bandage, and we're sure you aren't surprised to hear that we've used duct tape to plug holes.

- **Use heeling to your advantage.** This situation is one time when more heel can be good. If the hole is near the waterline along the side of the boat, you may be able to sail the boat on a particular point of sail (using the reverse of all the tips to limit heel, which we discuss in Chapters 11 and 12) so that the hole comes partially or completely out of the water. This direction may not get you to safety, but at least this tactic gives you time to repair the damage.

- **Get out the pumps.** If leaking water is a problem, everybody should be bailing. Buckets work great.

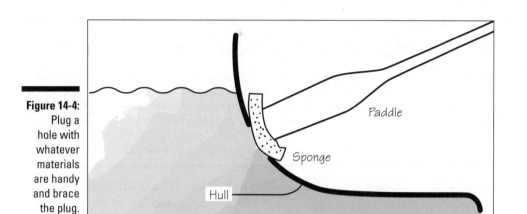

Figure 14-4:
Plug a
hole with
whatever
materials
are handy
and brace
the plug.

✔ **Radio for help.** For information on using your VHF radio, see Chapter 7. To get the attention (and assistance) of nearby boats, use the basic distress signal — stand and wave your arms.

✔ **Get to safety as soon as possible.** This may mean sailing to a different port than the one from which you started. In an extreme case in which the boat is truly sinking, you may have to intentionally ground the boat (or beach your dinghy). If you must use this tactic, pick a spot that's as sheltered (especially from waves) as possible and has a nice, soft sand or mud bottom.

Abandoning Ship

Between the two of us, we've been on boats that have run aground, blown out sails, been towed to safety, fouled a prop, been holed, been dismasted, and sunk (in shallow water — Peter's cellphone was the only casualty). But neither of us has ever had to activate an EPIRB or abandon ship into a life raft. Hopefully, you can say the same thing after thousands of miles have passed under your keel. But, remembering the Boy Scouts' line, it doesn't hurt to be prepared.

EPIRB stands for *Emergency Position Indicating Radio Beacon.* Marine stores sell these incredible devices, which are directly responsible for saving hundreds of sailors' lives. When activated in an emergency, an EPIRB emits a distress signal on a frequency that's monitored by satellites and airplanes — which makes finding you much easier for rescuers! Check with your marine store to see whether you need to register your EPIRB.

Abandoning ship means abandoning your claim

Don't give away your boat! The law of the sea says that if someone finds an abandoned boat drifting along and tows it home ("salvages" it), it's his! So don't abandon ship. If you must leave your boat, leave a note saying that you intend to return. Even if you're aboard and in need of help, you don't want to risk any outrageous salvage claim, so clearly establish the terms of the helper's aid *before* you get too far along in the rescue process. Also, it looks better in the eyes of the law if you pass your rescuer a line (indicating a voluntary acceptance of aid) rather than having your rescuer pass a line to you.

You can't abandon ship into a life raft if you don't have one. They're big and bulky, but carrying one when sailing significant distances out of sight of land is wise. Obviously, we're talking about keelboats; no one should sail a dinghy out of sight of land. Make sure the raft is rated for the number of people you have on board and has been recently inspected. If not, or if you're unsure, check with your local marine store to find a company that specializes in inspecting and "refreshing" your life raft.

An old adage says, "Don't abandon ship into a life raft until you have to step up to get into the raft."

This saying highlights an important fact. The situation has to be pretty darn desperate before you exchange your big sailboat for a glorified air mattress with K rations. Don't take this the wrong way — we believe in life rafts; the modern ones are marvelous pieces of technology. But still, things have to be pretty bad before you're safer in a life raft than aboard your boat.

A modern life raft is packed into a hard plastic case and is very heavy to lift. Therefore, you want to be sure that the raft is up on deck in a very accessible spot (and tied down securely) if abandoning ship is in the cards. Peter did inflate and get inside a life raft once, for a TV show, and he remembers a few things about that experience worth relating:

- ✔ You can find a cartoon-style description of how to deploy and inflate the life raft on a life raft's case.

- ✔ Tie the life raft's bow line (which is apparent outside the case) securely to the boat before throwing the raft into the water and inflating.

- ✔ The K rations taste kind of like vanilla wafer cookies — and the water comes in cans.

For a great true story about this subject, check out Steve Callahan's best seller, *Adrift.*

Fighting Fire

Fire is one of the most serious dangers a sailor can face. Fire can occur by any number of means, but most start in the *galley* (kitchen), around the engine, or in the electrical system. Needless to say, put out fires immediately.

The U.S. Coast Guard requires that all boats with motors carry fire extinguishers (except boats shorter than 26 feet, or 8 meters, with outboard engines, as long as that boat doesn't have permanently installed fuel tanks or spaces where fumes can collect and isn't carrying passengers for hire). With all fire extinguishers, having the right type for each fire, keeping them in good working order, and storing them in a convenient spot are imperative.

Table 14-1 can help you sort out the USCG regulations regarding fire extinguishers.

Table 14-1	Fire Extinguisher Requirements	
Boat-Length System	Without Fixed Extinguishing System	With Fixed System
Under 26 ft (8 m)	1 B-I	None
26–40 ft (8–12 m)	2 B-I or 1 B-II	1 B-I
40–65 ft (12–20 m)	3 B-I or both one B-II and one B-I	2B-I or 1 B-II

Fire extinguishers are rated by both the types of fires they extinguish and the amount of extinguishing material. A letter, A, B, or C, indicates the type of fire, while the fire volume is a number. A is for alcohol and wood, B for gasoline and grease, and C for electrical. For example, a B-II has twice as much chemical as a B-I. Purchase fire extinguishers for your boat at your local marine store and buy enough extinguishers to fulfill Coast Guard regulations, but then consider the special needs of your boat. If you have electronics on board, you may want a Halotron 1 extinguisher nearby or the new Aqueous foam extinguishers.

Depending on the type of fire, your best strategy and equipment for extinguishing the fire varies. Table 14-2 covers the action to take for the most common types of fires on board. Remember to aim at the base of the fire, and shoot the spray in a sweeping motion.

Table 14-2	Putting Out a Fire
Problem	*Action to Take*
Gasoline, diesel, or grease fires	Use a Type B fire extinguisher — *not* water.
Engine fires	Turn off the engine, and use a Type B fire extinguisher. Be careful not to "blast" the fire to other areas.
(LPG) Propane — liquid gas fires	Turn off the fuel supply at the tank (not just the stove) and then let the fire burn out. Prevent the fire from spreading by dousing surrounding area with water.
Alcohol, wood, and textile fires	Flood with water.
Electrical fires	Use a Type C fire extinguisher designed for electrical fire or flood with water.

Chapter 15

Caring for Your Craft

· ·

In This Chapter

▶ Maintaining your boat, all its parts, and the sails

▶ Checking the engine

▶ Storing your boat

· ·

Mothlike in mists, scintillant in the minute brilliance of cloudless days, with broad bellying sails.

They glide to the wind tossing green water from their sharp prows while over them the crew crawls.

— William Carlos Williams

*I*n the grand old days of Admiral Horatio Nelson's British Navy, the crew of a square rigger would *holystone,* or scrub, the decks every day at dawn in all but the most extreme conditions. Unused sails had to be furled with a military precision rivaling the beds of today's U.S. Marines. This tradition of keeping your boat looking good, with everything in its proper place and stored absolutely correctly, is still in place today. Part of the tradition is simply good seamanship, and part is pride of ownership. Your boat and your sails are a reflection on you — and you don't walk around town with seagull poop on your head, do you?

Regular inspection of your boat for wear and tear helps avoid problems on the water. Many parts of the boat show signs of rust or stress cracks prior to breaking. The key is knowing where to look to find signs of a worn-out part — and remembering to look. In this chapter, we start by looking at the areas requiring the most regular maintenance and replacement (the ropes, rigging, and sails) and then cover the mast, hull, and engine (if you have one).

Forty years ago, this subject of maintenance was a much bigger part of boat ownership, but as builders have shifted from wood to fiberglass, maintenance has become much easier. For those who prefer to leave the grunt work to others, you can choose from a virtual plethora of boatyard and marine-maintenance professionals. Plus, you can rent boats from charter companies and sailing clubs and avoid any maintenance work. (Check out Chapter 17 for more on chartering and Chapter 2 for more on finding sailing clubs.)

Doing basic maintenance on our own boat is fun, and we hope that this chapter makes you feel the same way. When it comes to the major repairs, however, we usually turn to the pros, not because we can't do the job, but because that kind of project takes forever and never seems to come out as nice when we do it ourselves.

Rapping about Running Rigging

Running rigging, as we cover in Chapter 1, is all the control *lines* (ropes) and gear you use to adjust the sails and includes the sheets and halyards. Because running rigging gets a real workout every time you sail, you need to keep it in top condition — you can't sail a sailboat with a broken mainsheet.

In this section, we first talk about something every boat has plenty of — rope. We then focus on the blocks, winches, and cleats that help you work with those ropes and how to keep them functioning effectively.

A few lines about line

Line is "rope with a purpose." Because most of the millions of ropes on a sailboat have some use, they're usually called lines, although in this book we both use the word *rope* often and interchangeably — with no ill effect! When selecting or replacing a line, consider the following characteristics in determining what's appropriate for the task at hand:

- **Strength:** All lines used as running rigging should be made of some sort of synthetic material because of its superior performance. Most of the rope we use on racing boats has a space-age Vectran, Spectra, or Kevlar core — very light and incredibly strong.

  Different sailing parts have different strength needs, depending on their application. A jib sheet must be stronger than a mainsail cunningham. An anchor or tow line should be strong but very stretchy. Your man-overboard retrieval line should float, as we discuss in Chapter 7. A dock line should be strong and very resistant to chafe. Some storage applications may call for incredibly stretchy rubber-filled rope called *bungee cord* or *shock cord.*

- **Diameter:** A line increases in strength with its diameter. Some high-tech fibers are stronger than the same diameter of wire. Comfort is most important in a line that you hold onto constantly — that's why you want a relatively thick, fuzzy mainsheet. If a line must pass through several pulleys and is usually kept cleated (like a block-and-tackle backstay adjuster), you should opt for thinner line for less friction (and smaller, less expensive blocks).

✔ **Color:** If every rope on the boat is white, life gets pretty confusing (not to mention boring).

✔ **Cost:** Check out the rope department in your local marine store (most hardware stores don't stock good sailing rope), and you see why so many boats have white polyester line — all those fancy colors and high-tech materials are *expensive!*

✔ **Feel:** A rope that's softer and smoother is easier to hold — but more expensive (and you may wear gloves anyway).

Comparing laid and braided rope

Rope that has three visible, primary strands twisted in a spiral is called *laid* rope. Laid rope, which is usually less expensive than its braided cousin, is common in dock lines and tow lines. However, for the running rigging in your boat, *braided* rope is far superior. As the name implies, braided rope looks like the tiny fibers are braided together. Braided rope often has an inner core (where those space-age fibers can be used) that carries most of the load. You can see laid and braided rope in Figure 15-1.

Figure 15-1: Laid line (left) and braided line (with core, on right) with their component parts exposed.

Using splices

In Chapter 19, we show how to put a loop in a line by tying a bowline knot. Another, much more permanent way to make a rope loop is an *eye splice.* Eye splices are neater, less bulky than knots, and are commonly found at the working end of a halyard (where the rope attaches to a shackle) and at the end of an anchor line. They're time consuming for a beginner to create, but a professional rigger can whip one up in less than five minutes (but probably charges for an hour!). If the splice will have a major load (like an anchor line), you must insert a *thimble* (metal or plastic teardrop-shaped fitting) into the loop to distribute the load and prevent chafe. Figure 15-2 shows an eye splice at the end of a braided line halyard attached to a snap shackle (on the left) and an eye splice at the end of a laid-line anchor rope with a thimble inserted to prevent chafe (on the right).

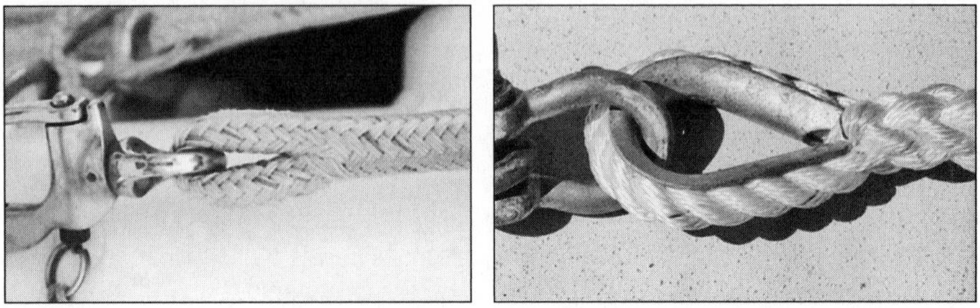

Figure 15-2:
Eye splices
(left: braided
line; right:
laid line).

Your local marine store should have a book about knots and splices. (In it you discover that more types of both exist than you can ever imagine!)

Going to the bitter end

No matter what kind of rope you use, the very end of it can be a problem area if it starts to fray — because the usable part of the line gets shorter and shorter. The easiest solution for most ropes is simply to melt the end with a butane lighter, some matches, or a special *hot knife* (commonly found in the rope department of a marine store). With braided rope, sometimes the inner core won't burn. So pull out and cut off a few inches of the inner core. Then slide the cover over and melt the end of the cover, as the right photo of Figure 15-3 shows.

If burning doesn't work, you can always tie an overhand knot in the end (a temporary fix), wrap tape around it, or *whip* it. *Whipping,* the old-fashioned way to secure a splice or the end of a rope, requires the use of a special sail-maker's needle and strong synthetic thread. Wrap the thread tightly around the rope to hold it together, and then stitch the thread securely through the rope so that it doesn't unravel during use, as the left photo of Figure 15-3 shows. Melting the rope's end "outside" the whipping is still a good idea.

Caring for your lines

When not using a line, securely coil and store it. (We discuss how to coil a line in Chapter 4.) If you sail in saltwater, flush the wet lines with freshwater after sailing. Hang wet line where it can dry and try to store it (whenever practical) out of the incredibly damaging rays of the sun. Check them periodically for wear, especially where they commonly load up on a pulley or other corner. To extend the life of your lines, consider switching your halyards and sheets end for end occasionally — sort of the yachting equivalent of rotating your tires.

Figure 15-3:
Left: A
whipping at
the end of a
laid rope to
keep it from
unraveling.
Right: Melt
the end of a
braided
rope's cover
to keep it
from fraying.

Whipping

Figure 15-3: Left: A whipping at the end of a laid rope to keep it from unraveling. Right: Melt the end of a braided rope's cover to keep it from fraying.

Sailing gear

This section focuses on the fittings that help your lines do their work — the winches, blocks, shackles, and cleats. Remember that a key part of caring for this gear is visual maintenance — looking for hairline cracks in metal parts, signs of corrosion, or other indications that something isn't quite right.

Blocks

Your boat has many *blocks* or pulleys; they're probably hanging from the boom, bolted to the deck, and built into your mast (see Chapter 4). Blocks come in all different sizes and shapes and must be matched to the task at hand, or they may cause problems. The key considerations include

- ✔ **Strength:** The manufacturer provides information on the working load. Usually (but not always), the bigger the block, the stronger it is. The size of the metal or fiber strap or shackle used to attach the block to the boat indicates the block's strength. A block that's too weak starts to deform. Often, a sticky *sheave* (the moving wheel-shaped part that the rope turns over) is the first sign of problems.

- ✔ **Proper use:** Some blocks are designed specifically for wire; they often have metal sheaves. If you put wire on a block intended for rope, the sheave can crack or chafe and develop a groove in it. Also, don't use too thick a rope in a block. Err on using too small a rope diameter, and you have less friction.

Most sailing blocks are very low maintenance. Rinse any block with freshwater after a day of sailing in saltwater, and all blocks appreciate being stored out of those ultraviolet rays. Some blocks require occasional lubrication; however, check with the manufacturer's directions first, because the lubricant may gum up the works. Often, the way the block is attached to the boat — by its shackle — is the weak link.

Shackles

Shackles (the metal fittings used for attaching different parts of the boat, mast, and sails) are everywhere on your boat, just like blocks. Your boat may have twist shackles, snap shackles, brummel hooks, and/or captive pin shackles, to name a few. Keep the following considerations in mind when picking out, installing, and maintaining shackles:

✔ **Strength:** The shackle's manufacturer specifies the safe working load; however, you can get a good idea of its strength by looking at the diameter of the metal.

✔ **Accessibility:** A *snap shackle* is the easiest type of shackle to open, but it can be large and expensive. The *D-shaped shackle* is by far the most common, but it's more difficult to open in a hurry.

✔ **Security:** Shackles, especially the ones attached to the corners of the sails, can really get flapped about when the sails are luffing. Wrapping plastic tape around a snap shackle keeps it from opening accidentally. D-shaped shackles are often secured by a screw pin; tighten the pin securely with a wrench. As with any nut and bolt, be careful not to cross-thread these shackles.

D-shaped shackles and other fittings can have a *clevis pin* with a *cotter pin* or *ring ding* securing it, as Figure 15-4 shows. Ring dings are easier to put on and take off, but you must tape them so that they don't catch something and open up. Cotter pins shouldn't be too long and should be spread open, with the ends bent out just enough to facilitate removing the pins in an emergency, and taped, because their points are very sharp.

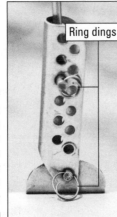

Ring dings

Cotter pins

Figure 15-4: Clevis pins secured by ring dings (left) and by cotter pins (right).

Winches

In Chapters 4 and 5, we discuss winches and the techniques for using them. Because of their many moving parts, they need more attention than pulleys. The manufacturer's literature or the folks at the local marine store can help you pick out a winch (although most keelboats already have plenty) and maintenance supplies. In the following list, we provide the keys to maintaining your winches:

- ✔ **Clean your winch:** Take the winch totally apart at least once a year (doing so is sort of like playing with an erector set — just don't forget where each piece goes!) and clean all the internal metal parts. A big bucket with an inch or so of gasoline or paint thinner in it and a toothbrush make a great washtub and scrubber. Lay out a huge drop cloth and have plenty of rags for this very messy job.

- ✔ **Keep your winch salt free:** Flush it with freshwater after use and make sure that all the drain holes around its base are open so that any rainwater can escape.

- ✔ **Lubricate your winch:** Check for any special instructions from the manufacturer. After taking the drum off and setting it aside, inspect and lubricate all the moving parts and bearing surfaces. Pay special attention to the *pawls,* which allow the winch to spin one way and not the other, shown in Figure 15-5. The pawls should swing easily with the touch of a finger, with the spring providing sufficient power to return the pawl to the "open" position. If they don't move freely after cleaning and a lube, replace both spring and pawl. Inspect and lubricate your winches at least twice a year (and more if you use the boat frequently).

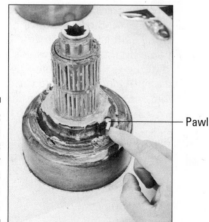

Figure 15-5:
Checking the pawls and their springs inside a winch.

— Pawl

Don't forget — regular visual inspection is important. When sailing, pay attention to how well the winch works, and be especially concerned about any jerking under load or weird noises. Also, when you have the winch apart for lubrication, take a close look at all the internal parts for wear or signs of fatigue.

Inspecting the Mast

A mast is supported by wires called, as a group, the *standing rigging,* which we introduce in Chapter 1. And in Chapter 14, we discuss the potential hazardous consequences of one of a sailor's biggest nightmares — a dismasting.

First make sure that your mast is straight (or *in column*) by sighting up the mast from the bottom. On a boat with shrouds, you can adjust the *turnbuckles* (devices used to adjust shroud tension) to get the mast straight. This "tuning," or getting the mast in column while at the dock, is pretty easy. But you should also sight up the mast when sailing upwind in moderate winds and make further adjustments as needed. If you're having trouble, ask a local rigger to help.

Depending on your use of the boat, you may have to inspect your mast and components twice a year, every month, or even more often — especially after sailing in heavy weather, when things get stressed to the maximum. On a dinghy or small boat, you can take the mast down to inspect it. For a larger boat, you have to send someone up the mast.

To hoist someone up the mast, you need a *bosun's chair* — a harness-type device that provides a "seat" and can be attached to the halyard, as Figure 15-6 shows. A winch will be necessary if the person going up is heavy. Never trust your safety to a halyard shackle; always tie the halyard rope with a bowline to the bosun's chair. The person going aloft should be ready for a wild ride if you're under way, especially if you're in the midst of waves, because the motion of the ocean is accentuated at the top of the mast. Always ensure that any tools or hard objects (which can put a major dent in the deck if they fall) are secure when going aloft. For that same reason, never stand beneath anyone who's working up in the rig.

Whenever possible when going aloft, use a second halyard as a backup. You don't want to find out about a worn halyard when you're up the mast!

Examine the following areas for signs of stress or damage:

✔ **Mast section:** Dents and cracks are bad — so are missing rivets.

✔ **Sheaves:** Every halyard has a sheave that you need to examine and possibly lubricate.

✔ **Spreaders:** Try moving the spreaders by shaking them at the end. Movement is bad, unless they're clearly designed to move laterally (fore and aft at the tip). Look for fatigue at the inside end and check the attachment to the shrouds.

✔ **Standing rigging:** The ends of the standing rigging, where they're terminated into some sort of fitting for attachment, are the first places to look. Check carefully, because a broken stay is a sure way to lose a mast. As with all metal fittings, look for cracks, signs of deformation, and corrosion.

✔ **Tangs:** *Tangs* are the attachment points for the standing rigging.

✔ **Turnbuckles:** Some turnbuckles — which are adjustment devices used primarily to tighten rods — are on deck; some may be aloft. You should lubricate turnbuckles when they're tuned under load.

✔ **Water pockets:** Anywhere that water can sit is a prime location for corrosion. Look under taped fittings and anywhere else water may pool.

Figure 15-6: A bosun's chair provides comfort and safety when going up the mast.

Maintaining Your Sails

Sails are your boat's engine, so keep them "well oiled" and in tune. With proper care, your sails will last longer and retain their designed shape when flying in the wind. In this section, we focus on how to fold, store, and care for your sails.

Folding sails

After using your sail, put it away in a manner that's easy on both the sail and you. Some racers roll their sails (from top to bottom) after a day on the water. Rolling may be easier on the sailcloth, but doing so is a cumbersome task. An easier way is folding the sail.

You can easily roll sails that are fully battened, like most catamaran mainsails, because the battens provide support, like a venetian blind. Rolling these sails is preferable to taking out all the battens and then folding the sail.

You can fold sails from bottom to top with creases horizontal to the foot, like an accordion. Mainsails on larger keelboats can be flaked in this manner right on top of the boom for easy storage, as Figure 15-7 shows.

Figure 15-7:
A mainsail flaked on the boom and secured with ropes or sail ties.

Follow these easy steps to fold your sails:

1. **Pick your spot and stretch the sail out to its full size (if possible).**

   Find a spot that's at least as long and wide as a single fold on which to fold the sail. Grass lawns make great sail folding surfaces; parking lots are bad because they're rough and dirty.

2. **Remove the battens from their pockets on the sail.**

   Except for the very short, permanently installed battens sewn onto the leeches of some jibs, remove all the battens so that you can fold the sail into a smaller bundle.

3. **Stretch the foot out and, with one person at the tack and one at the clew, begin folding the sail like an accordion, starting at the bottom, as Figure 15-8 shows.**

   Pull against each other just enough to define the crease of the next fold.

Figure 15-8:
Folding a sail — start at the bottom and work up.

4. **Work to the top.**

   Each fold should be approximately the same width — about 1 foot (30 centimeters) wide for a dinghy sail and 3 feet (1 meter) or more for a 50-foot (15-meter) keelboat sail.

5. **Roll up the sail and bag it.**

   When you reach the head of the sail, begin rolling or folding the sail lengthwise into a shape that fits in the sail bag.

Storing sails

Here are some tips to consider when you're putting sails away after a day on the water:

- **Keep all the pieces together.** If battens or other fittings come with the sail, store them with the sail in its bag.

- **Keep your sails out of the sun.** The sun's ultraviolet light degrades sailcloth and the stitching that holds the seams together. Therefore, cover the sails or store them away from the sun's rays while you aren't using them.

> ✔ **Minimize the creases.** If you don't have to roll them up into a tiny bundle, don't. Try not to crease any plastic windows.
>
> ✔ **Store your sails dry.** If you're going to sail again tomorrow, you don't have to dry your wet sails, but if you plan to store your sails for longer than a few days, make sure that they're dry. A lawn or the deck of your boat can be a good spot for spreading the sails out to dry. If you're storing them for the winter, take the extra effort to rinse the salt off, too.

Caring for your sails

Most sails suffer their worst damage when they're hoisted under sail. You can take a few measures to protect your sails and to keep them looking good and holding together longer:

> ✔ **Don't let them flap too much.** Luffing degrades sails faster than the sun. In the America's Cup, crews actually keep track of the number of times a sail is tacked because it flaps when it tacks, shortening the sail's competitive life. Never leave your sails luffing at anchor or at the dock.
>
> ✔ **Don't sail without battens.** Without their support, the sail becomes overloaded in the region around the missing batten.
>
> ✔ **Don't use sails in too much wind.** Some sails, especially spinnakers, are made out of lightweight cloth that can blow out in strong winds.
>
> ✔ **Inspect the seams, batten pockets, bolt rope or slugs, and corners for wear and tear.** Sails usually rip in these places. If they look questionable, take them to a sailmaker, drag out your needle and thread, or slap on some of that sticky-back tape we discuss in Chapter 14.
>
> ✔ **Protect sails from chafe.** Common chafe locations occur where the sails hit the spreader and the lifelines during tacks. A layer of sticky-back applied over the at-risk location provides sufficient protection.

When your sails do get a rip or a hole, have a sailmaker fix it. However, you can always refer to Chapter 14 if you're underway or in a "do-it-yourself" frame of mind.

Caring for the Hull

As you hose off your boat and fittings after sailing (an important part of boat maintenance if your boat sails in saltwater), take a good look at some of the high-load areas where serious structural problems may be apparent. Keep your eye open for cracks or signs of water leakage that indicate weak areas. Sometimes, supposedly "stainless-steel" fasteners attached to the hull begin to show signs of rust. If possible, apply a light amount of force and "shake" any attached fittings to see whether they're still secure.

The following list includes some parts of the hull and deck above the water line that come under high loads and that you should inspect after each sail:

- *Chain plates* (metal fittings to which the shrouds, forestay, and backstay are attached)

- Jib tracks

- Main traveler and mainsheet

- Mast step and *partners* (the point where the mast leaves the deck)

- Attachment point of other fittings

If your boat is stored in saltwater, its metal parts can turn it into a big battery. If left undeterred, this chemical reaction can result in serious corrosion. To fend off the highly corrosive effect of saltwater on metal, you must provide the saltwater with something even more "edible." If your boat has an inboard engine, you should have a zinc fitting attached to the propeller shaft. When dockside, you can also hang a plate of zinc (attached by a battery-type cable to the chainplates) overboard. Your local marine store has these zincs in stock.

Looking Under Your Boat

If your sailboat is a dinghy, you may be able to flip it upside down on shore easily to look at and work on the underside of the hull. You can most easily inspect keelboats on a trailer or other support on dry land — or you can always don a mask and snorkel. The same principles and guidelines apply under the waterline as above the waterline. Pay attention to the following high-load areas:

- **The attachment point of your foils (keel/centerboard and rudder):** Look for small, horizontal cracks that can develop where the lead keel meets the hull or keel stub, or rust stains around the keel bolts. Ask a professional to look at any problem areas.

- **The steering system:** Check the rudder and its attachment points for signs of wear and tear. If you have a wheel, check the *quadrant* (bracket around the rudder post that connects to the steering cables) and steering cables.

- **The propeller shaft:** If you have an inboard engine, inspect the propeller shaft and its support structure.

Most dinghies and keelboats that are *drysailed* (stored out of the water when not sailing) are happy with their original gel-coat bottom. If your boat lives in the water, it probably already has *anti-fouling bottom paint* on it. This stuff inhibits the growth of barnacles and slimy grass. If you're considering a new coat of anti-fouling bottom paint, check with a local boatyard to find out about any restrictions in your waters. Certain types of these toxic paints are restricted, especially in clean freshwater lakes.

When selecting a bottom paint, consider the manufacturer's information. Certain types of paints work better for different situations. We like to refer to *Practical Sailor* (www.practical-sailor.com) for advice on the best materials to use. Another great magazine for the "do-it-yourselfer" is *BoatWorks,* from the editors of *Sail* magazine (www.boatworksmagazine.com).

Most marinas have divers who scrub the bottom of your boat (and maintain the zinc on the propeller shaft) each month for a reasonable fee (compared to the hassle of donning that dive gear and doing it yourself). Keeping your bottom clean is well worth the investment — a clean bottom is a fast bottom.

Keeping an Eye on the Engine

Hey, isn't this book about sailing? Yes, but most larger (longer than 25 feet, or 8 meters) keelboats have a noisemaker that can come in handy when docking in tight situations, in emergencies, and when, heaven forbid, the wind dies. This section focuses on using and caring for your engine.

Using the engine

Before you do anything with your engine, make sure you read your owner's manual; it's the best source of information on operation and maintenance. You also want to remember the following general operating rules for all types of engines:

- **Don't count on reverse:** We discuss operating a boat under power in docking situations in Chapter 6. Just remember that if you're moving forward at any significant speed, the reverse gear's effect is laughable, so don't count on a blast of reverse to be able to stop the boat.

- **Look for water:** Most inboard engines have water-coolant and exhaust exit holes or pipes visible from on deck, which are often in the transom. When you start the engine, confirm that water is coming out (usually a slow, pulsing flow) of the exhaust — this means the cooling system is working properly.

- **Slow down to shift:** Hey, this isn't a rental car. Idle the throttle down to a bare minimum before shifting gears.

✔ **Ventilate first:** Explosive fumes from all sorts of sources can collect in the bilge of your boat. Make sure that the area around the engine (which can get hot and often has sparks involved) is ventilated before starting. If the boat has a *blower,* a fan in the engine compartment, run it for at least five minutes. Make sure that the cabin of the boat has been open for a while and check below for any funny smells before starting the engine.

✔ **Watch the temperature:** A high temperature tells you that you have a cooling-system problem (maybe a plastic bag sucked into the intake). Avoid operating your engine at maximum throttle — doing so may cause overheating. Watch the RPM meter if you have one, and keep the RPMs at or below the engine's safe operating limit. If your manual doesn't tell you this speed, check with a professional for advice.

Caring for the engine

Like with your car, you probably want to leave the major (and maybe even the minor) stuff to a professional. Maintaining the engine in your boat is very important. The saltwater environment, often less-than-pristine fuel sources, and operation at various angles of heel can wreak havoc on the best power plant. Here are some important points to remember:

✔ **Change your oil.** Check and change it regularly; oil is the lifeblood of any engine.

✔ **Check your filters.** Along with having an adequate fuel filter, you should have a water separator/sedimenter in the fuel line — check and clean it regularly.

✔ **Rinse out that salt.** Saltwater corrodes metal. You can flush the cooling systems of most outboard engines with freshwater by using a special set of ears that attach to a hose. You should flush an outboard after every use. Rinse off all the external parts of the engine with freshwater. For inboard engines, see the section "Caring for the Hull," earlier in this chapter, about attaching zinc.

✔ **Take along spares.** If you plan on making a longer trip, make sure that you have some common spare parts (such as drive belts) and know how to install them. Ask your engine mechanic for a good list and instructions.

Leaving Your Boat

When the sailing is over and the time comes to go home, you want to make sure that your boat is happy and safe while you're away. This short section looks at the short-term and long-term concerns you need to remember.

Short-term

If you'll be back to the boat in the next few days, or even within the month, after sailing you want to put your boat away securely, but not so securely that you need the whole weekend to prepare for your next sail. Here are some tips to help make sure that your boat is ready to go again when you decide to take it out for another spin:

- ✔ **Minimize water collection:** Dinghies can be stored upside down if you take down the mast. If you leave the mast up, try to angle the dinghy so that rainwater drains out quickly. Many dinghies have drain plugs on the stern for this purpose. Most cockpits of keelboats drain automatically, but make sure that all hatches and openings are well sealed. A cover over the boom tied to the rails can also help keep the rain out.

- ✔ **Make no dents, please:** Be careful when storing your dinghy on land. If you store it with the mast up, make sure that the hull is supported in several locations, not a single point where the hull can depress and weaken. If you store your dinghy upside down, consider where the deck is strongest — often at the very bow, near the chain plates, and at the transom.

- ✔ **Protect your boat and its gear from the sun:** Store as much stuff (rope, blocks, sails, and so on) as practical out of those rays.

- ✔ **Protect your gear from the wind:** You know to tie down the hull, but consider other things that can loosen up and blow on a windy day (such as any sail, including a roller-furled jib and halyards, which can cause a real racket).

- ✔ **Secure the hull:** If you store your boat on land, make sure that you tie it down securely. If your boat lives afloat, check the dock or mooring lines. In Chapters 6 and 10, we cover the best way to secure the boat.

- ✔ **Turn off anything electrical other than an automatic bilge pump on keelboats.** You may also need to remove fuel tanks on boats with outboards and/or close fuel valves on any boat with an engine.

Long-term

Unfortunately, in many parts of the world, the sailing season isn't year round. If you're going to leave your boat for longer than a month, consider these further efforts to keep the boat happy:

- ✔ **Covering:** Whenever possible, cover your equipment to protect it from rain, snow, sun, and dirt.

- ✔ **Engine:** Ask your mechanic what, if anything, you should do to your engine, including winterizing to avoid ice forming in the engine block.

Disconnect the battery terminals unless the boat is stored in the water where an automatic bilge pump is necessary.

✔ **Fluids:** Drain water and gasoline tanks and top off diesel tanks.

✔ **Haul out:** Most large keelboats are hauled out at a boatyard, cleaned (especially below the waterline), derigged, and covered with protective tarps for the winter. Make sure that the boat is supported and secured adequately.

✔ **Lubrication:** Consider lubricating all your moving fittings, including parts of the mast, to protect them from inactivity.

✔ **Mildew:** If you live in a wet area and plan to store your boat under plastic tarps, you're going to have a mildew factory under there. Take home for storage anything susceptible to damage. Some bigger keelboats even have a dehumidifier rigged up to drain into the sink.

✔ **Sails:** If rolling your sails is ever worth the time and effort, this is the time — if you have the space to store them. You may want your sailmaker to check out your sails in the loft.

Chapter 16

Cruising with Children

O, well for the fisherman's boy,
That he shouts with his sister at play!
O, well for the sailor lad,
That he sings in his boat on the bay!

— Alfred Lord Tennyson

*I*f you have a family and love to sail, here's an important point: You get to sail more frequently if your family also enjoys the sport. And sailing with your family brings other benefits. Sailing for the day can bring your family closer as you work together to keep the boat moving. On a weeklong cruise, your kids may even discover that some of the "necessities" at home — such as the TV and video games — are really luxuries that they can live without.

In this chapter, we look at how to enjoy a sailing trip with your children. We focus mainly on making the most of an extended sailing trip on a bigger sailboat, but we also include information on planning a daytrip and on sailing with children on smaller boats. Kids come in all sizes and shapes, but we focus mainly on the younger, preteen years.

Preparing Your Family Crew

A big reason why our daughters feel comfortable on a boat is that we feel comfortable having them on board. That comfort level is important. Children are very sensitive to their parents' emotions and can pick up on their fears. If you're afraid to have children on a boat, they're afraid to be there. If you're nervous, try to assess *why* you're concerned and then take concrete steps to conquer those fears.

Probably every parent's biggest fear on a boat is a child drowning. We can't say it often enough: One of the most important steps before taking your family sailing is to *make sure that everyone can swim.* When children are confident of their swimming abilities and are comfortable in the water, they seem to pick up the basics of sailing much more easily because they're more relaxed and more likely to have fun.

When picking a swimming instructor, make sure he or she is properly trained in the techniques *and* knows basic safety procedures. In the United States, look for swimming instructors who have first aid, cardiopulmonary resuscitation (CPR), and Water Safety Instructor (WSI) certifications, which are available from the American Red Cross.

If you sail on the ocean, keep in mind that your children won't enjoy swimming in saltwater as much as swimming in a pool at first. Saltwater tastes "funny," stings the eyes, and often isn't as warm as a pool; the waves are also hard to handle.

Of course, nonswimmers can enjoy sailing, too. In fact, four-time America's Cup winner Dennis Conner can't swim. Nonswimmers (and children) should always wear a life jacket, even on larger boats (everyone should wear a life jacket on a dinghy). Check out the section "Wearing the right life jackets and safety harnesses," later in this chapter, as well as Chapter 3 for more information.

After your kids have mastered swimming class and enjoy the water, check out sailing school options in Chapter 2. Most children grasp sailing very quickly on small dinghies at camp, sailing schools, or with an older friend or relative who sails.

Picking the Right Boat and Trip

While your crew is getting shipshape, you can think about what kind of boat to ship them out on. The most important factor is the *experience level of the adult.*

We do *not* recommend that novice sailors ever take children sailing on boats that they're skippering. Novice sailors should try to go sailing with people who have *more* experience than they do. For intermediate sailors, the most important point is to pick a boat that they feel comfortable in — so that the children feel comfortable and enjoy the experience.

This section provides you with some quick pointers about selecting the right trip as well as the right boat for you depending on your ability level, your crew's comfort level, and the length of your trip.

Choosing a keelboat

Beginning sailors, young and old, usually feel more comfortable on a *keelboat* than aboard a dinghy (see the next section for more on dinghies). A keelboat — check out Chapter 1 — has a heavy, ballasted keel fin under the boat that provides stability and prevents capsizing. Large cruising multihulls (that gain stability from having more than one hull) are also stable and comfortable. Here are some other reasons why these bigger boats are the best choice for families, whether your trip is going to last a week or just an afternoon:

- ✔ Keelboats often have cabins down below that are handy for taking naps, storing snacks, and spreading out toys.

- ✔ Most keelboats have a deep cockpit, where kids can play safely and see the sights without the risk of falling overboard. A boat longer than 25 feet (8 meters) probably has lifelines that provide extra security for the very little ones.

When is your child old enough to sail?

A child is never too young to enjoy a sailing trip as long as you, your boat, and your crew are prepared. We've been taking our daughters sailing since before they were born. Every summer we go to Catalina Island — 20 miles off the coast of Los Angeles — on my parents' boat. Games and books keep them occupied while we're under way, but their favorite time is while we're at anchor.

As toddlers, the girls saw boats as fun jungle gyms, and spent hours turning the winches to hear the sounds of the gears. Feeding bits of bread to the fish (and smart seagulls) kept them entertained as well. Their favorite stuffed animals are all sea creatures: Marly has a beloved shark, and Megan has a family of seals that live on her bed.

If you're adamant about sailing with your kids, but you've only completed a basic sailing course and have little other experience, then your best boat choice is a small keelboat (18 to 25 feet)— but *only* day sailing in light and moderate winds in protected waters.

Table 16-1 offers some general guidelines for the *minimum* age of children on various types of boats, given the experience of the sailor.

Note: The table assumes light to moderate wind and sea conditions in protected waters. For the purposes of the table, a *novice* sailor has the equivalent of one basic sailing course and little practical experience. An *intermediate* sailor has completed basic sailing training and has six months to two years of practical experience. And *advanced* sailors have three or more years of experience in a variety of wind conditions. An "X" indicates that we don't recommend that novice sailors take children of any age on these boats.

Table 16-1	Suggested Minimum Age of Child on Different Boats		
	Skill Level of Adult Skipper		
Type of Boat	**Novice**	**Intermediate**	**Advanced**
Dinghy shorter than 13 ft (4 m)	X	10 years old	5 years old
Dinghy longer than 13 ft (4 m)	X	6 years old	3 years old
Keelboat 18 to 25 ft (5 to 8 m)	10 years old*	6 years old	Newborn
Keelboat longer than 25 ft (8 m)	X	6 years old	Newborn

*For novice sailors, we recommend sailing with children on a small keelboat only if the children are good swimmers and are comfortable in new situations.

Selecting a dinghy

Dinghies are usually smaller than keelboats (shorter than 20 feet, or 6 meters) and have a lightweight, retractable fin instead of a heavy lead keel, and therefore are less stable and can flip over. In our experience, the scariest parts about dinghy sailing for small children are the sudden changes in *heel* — the tipping motion — and the fear of *capsizing* (tipping over). But if you're taking the kids out in a dinghy, here are tips to make the day a success, starting with tips before you leave the shore:

✔ Make sure that the kids dress warmly. A waterproof jacket is nice so they stay warm even if they get wet.

✔ Have a towel and change of clothes on shore so the kids can get dry and comfortable as soon as you finish sailing.

✔ Before you leave the dock or beach, talk with your children about heeling. Put them in the boat and show them how to move their weight to counteract heel.

✔ Run through what to do with your children if the boat capsizes (see Chapter 7). Go on the water and do a controlled capsize (where you pull the boat over) so that the kids can see how easy getting the boat upright is.

✔ Make sure that you and your children are wearing life jackets.

✔ Be prepared to move your weight around often to minimize heeling while sailing.

✔ Hold on tight to the little ones so that they feel secure.

✔ If possible, let your children sit in the center of the boat in a secure spot where they can hold on.

✔ Be confident so that your children feel confident too.

Although dinghies offer the thrill of being close to the water, they have less room, and often each crew member has a specific job. That makes caring for the comfort, entertainment, and safety of a small child difficult, no matter how good a sailor you are.

Practicing Safety on the Water

This section covers important safety matters, including childproofing your boat, selecting the right life jackets and safety harnesses, keeping an eye on your children, and knowing when your children earn the right to be unsupervised.

Childproofing your boat

Sailing safety begins before you get under way. Before your family steps onto a cruising sailboat, keep these safety precautions in mind:

✔ **Weave netting onto the lifelines.** Netting, as Figure 16-1 shows, provides a barrier between your younger child (and toys and pets) and the water. Even with netting, never leave your child unsupervised on deck.

✔ **Don't allow leaning over or through the lifelines.** Netting or not.

✔ **Rule out running.** Especially while under way.

✔ **Establish appropriate safety rules.** (See the section "Keeping tabs on the kids," later in this chapter.)

✔ **Ensure that any lifeline gates have clasps that little fingers can't undo.** Securely close the gates as soon as you leave the dock.

✔ **Look at where a child would land if he fell down the hatch.** Do you need to pad any sharp corners in the cabin?

✔ **Put an awning over the cockpit while at anchor.** Sunburn can ruin a child's (as well as everyone else's) enjoyment of sailing. Awnings provide a shady, cool resting spot.

So after you childproof the boat for your children, your job's over, right? You know better than that. A parent's job is never over, which is especially true while sailing.

Figure 16-1:
Weave netting onto the lifelines of your boat if you have a toddler onboard.

Wearing the right life jackets and safety harnesses

Do you let your small child go for a car ride without getting into a car seat? Probably not. The same consistency can help you get your child to always wear a life jacket on the water. See Chapter 3 for information regarding life jackets. When purchasing a small child's life jacket, look for the following specifics:

✔ **A bright color for visibility.** Reflective tape is great, too. You want to be able to spot your child quickly if she falls in the water.

> ✔ **A strap between the legs.** This strap can keep the jacket from slipping off.
>
> ✔ **A snug fit.** The life jacket shouldn't be so bulky that the child can't put both hands together in front (or else he won't be able to hold on to the lifelines and handrails properly).

If you're still nervous about your child being near the water, even in a life jacket, test the life jacket in the pool first.

Children's life jackets have become so comfortable that we see lots of kids riding their bikes home after sailing class with their life jackets still on. But some families who live aboard a sailboat use safety harnesses (sometimes instead of life jackets) for the kids. A safety harness provides security from falling overboard and allows a child freedom to move around without the bulk of the life jacket. Only used on keelboats, a safety harness should fit a child snugly without falling off the shoulders, and for small children, should have a strap between the legs. You can attach the tether in front or in back and then you clip it onto a solid fitting in the center of the boat, as Figure 16-2 shows. Make sure that the tether is short enough that the child can't reach the water. (See Chapter 14 for more on harnesses.)

Figure 16-2: A safety harness is safe only if the tether is properly clipped on.

— Harness

— Attachment point

— Tether

Keeping tabs on the kids

Watching your child play around a boat is like watching your child play near a busy street — real danger lurks close by, and you must know where your child is at every moment.

When our young children are on a boat, knowing that they can swim reassures us because we know that they won't panic if they fall in. We *never* leave a younger child alone on deck for even a second.

You can use the following safety rules and guidelines to get started when cruising with kids:

✔ Allow children on deck only with an adult; make children have to tell the adult when they're going back down below.

✔ While sailing, don't allow children to go on deck without an adult's permission or without their life jacket and/or safety harness.

✔ Know all the ways that children can get on deck — they may surprise you by opening and climbing through the front hatch by themselves.

✔ Review with your kids the safety information in Chapter 7, especially the information about where the safe areas are on deck.

✔ Know when you're "on watch." We always hand off the caretaker's responsibility verbally.

✔ Watch children just as carefully when you're at the dock as when you're sailing.

Earning the right to go on their own

At some point, a child gains the maturity and the experience to be a valuable member of the crew, and many of the rules in the preceding section are no longer applicable. We don't think this transformation occurs at a set age, but we encourage you to keep this fact in mind: Giving your child more freedom and authority on a boat (at the right time) is another great way to build her confidence and love of sailing.

As a child, getting to go off in the rowboat by yourself or with your friends is a big step. As a parent, watching your older child head off in the rowboat for the first time is as nerve-wracking as letting your child ride his bike to a friend's house a few blocks away for the first time (even though the peace and tranquility after he's gone is well worth it). The key is to teach the kids about safety and to set some guidelines.

Your older children need to master the following skills before heading off on their own:

✔ **Ability to handle the equipment:** Children must know how to operate and get a boat onto and off a beach safely and how to tie secure knots if docking the boat.

✔ **Emergency preparation:** Practice a man-overboard drill, what to do if the boat swamps, and how to propel the boat if your children lose one oar. Review the appropriate safety information we cover in Chapters 7 and 14.

✔ **Responsibility:** Responsible behavior includes being careful with the equipment and continuing to wear their life jackets even when they're out of sight.

> ✔ **Knowledge of wind direction, tides, currents, and rocks in the area:**
> Rowing upwind or upcurrent can be exhausting or impossible. Before
> they go, review Chapter 9 on navigation and look at a chart of the area
> with your children.

Having a second rowing dinghy, kayak, or some other means of transportation while your children are gone is pretty nice for you and can be crucial for safety (in other words, a rescue) if they don't come back.

Essentially, you must make sure that your children feel comfortable and safe in the boat. Then you can trust them while they're off having fun — because, as the Water Rat says in *The Wind in the Willows,* "There is nothing . . . half so much worth doing as simply messing about in boats."

Letting Children Help on the Boat

Even if your children have never had a sailing lesson, they can learn a great deal from a day on the water, especially if you let them help with certain jobs. Children can do almost anything on a boat with adult supervision, but certain jobs, including the following, can always be in the kids' domain:

> ✔ **Making all the lines shipshape.** Both of us spent hours as kids carefully coiling all the ropes.
>
> ✔ **Putting up the flag in the morning.** And taking it down at night.
>
> ✔ **Relaying commands when anchoring or mooring.** With their help, no one has to yell.
>
> ✔ **Scrubbing the decks.** Or else they can walk the plank!
>
> ✔ **Stowing fenders.** And putting dock lines away too.
>
> ✔ **Tying knots.** (Check out Chapter 19 for a quick overview of many knots.)

School stuff afloat

Letting older children help study the chart, plot the course, and dead reckon (all navigational skills we cover in Chapter 9) can be a great way to put your child's math and geometry skills to work while improving map-reading skills. Celestial navigation is also a mind bender. But even if you don't own a sextant, being out on the water is a great time to explore the joys of astronomy. On a boat, you're surrounded by nature, both above and below the water; bring some books along to make identifying your wild companions easier.

Rock-a-bye, baby

At anchor, letting a baby sleep on the floor, up forward so that no one steps on him, is easier than worrying about him falling (or climbing) out of a bunk. Figure out a safe place to leave a wakeful baby in case all hands are needed on deck.

For sleeping under way, make sure that the bunks have *leecloths* — pieces of fabric that create a soft "wall" on the "downhill" side of the bunk, or a *bunkboard* — a removable wood slat that serves as a wall to the bunk — so that a sleeping body doesn't roll out when the boat tips.

Of course, the job your children want most of all is steering. Unlike handing over the keys to the family wagon, steering a sailboat is a safe way for kids to satisfy the "Dad, let me drive" urge. Letting your kids steer is also a great chance to give them an introductory sailing lesson.

Enjoying a Longer Trip

Although keeping children happy on long-distance trips is quite possible, you're better off interspersing short sails with longer periods at anchor or dockside at your destinations — unless you don't mind being asked "When are we going to get there?" a million times. Planning ahead can keep those restless passengers entertained.

The most important item to bring is food. Nothing makes sailors grumpier than running out of food, even on an afternoon sail. With all the new experiences that your children have while sailing, they find eating their favorite foods at mealtime comforting. And although getting back to nature and fishing for your meals is great, assume when you're packing that the fish won't be biting.

Keeping it clean

One of the great aspects of sailing is the way you're in tune with nature. Over the years, we've watched certain bodies of water get cleaner, while others seem to have more junk floating in them every day. Because your children inherit this Earth, set a good example both ashore and afloat.

Keep the waters clean. If you live in the United States, check the Coast Guard's regulations on dumping, which are quite strict if you sail close to the shore. Never throw any garbage overboard. Teach your children at an early age how important clean water is to everyone!

In addition to everyone's favorite food, this section has tips on how to sail with a baby without filling an entire bunk with baby paraphernalia, as well as what gear and books to bring to keep older kids happy on a longer trip. Obviously, you have the best idea of what to bring to keep your kids happy, but these suggestions can help.

Sailing with baby

On a longer sailing trip with a baby, using disposable diapers probably makes sense, because cleaning cloth diapers can run through your water supply very quickly. Disposables take up a great deal of space, though. You need to pack plenty of plastic bags to keep those used diapers sealed well until you can throw them into a trash can on shore.

You can leave the portable crib at home — it takes up too much space, and the cockpit (with a canvas awning to protect baby from the sun) works great as a playpen.

We use a bucket as a portable bathtub for babies while on board. And a *sun-shower* (a black plastic bag filled with freshwater warmed by the sun) (check out Figure 16-3) works well for keeping older kids clean (and adults, too).

Figure 16-3: A sun-shower can be the closest thing to a hot shower on a sailboat.

Sailing for two

So you think pregnancy rules out sailing? Not so. In fact, I sailed in the United States, Japan, and Spain while pregnant. A quick tip for pregnant sailors: Your center of gravity is higher than usual — so be extra careful when you step into a tippy dinghy (especially if you're as big as I was and can't see your feet).

Also, even if you haven't had any morning sickness or don't usually get seasick, the motion on a sailboat may make you feel queasy during pregnancy. Of course, pregnant women can't take seasickness medicine. I tried the acupressure wrist bands, and they seemed to help me. I also kept a supply of saltines, apples, and ginger ale handy and always tried to keep a little food in my stomach. For more tips on combating seasickness, see Appendix B.

Packing the right gear

Even if you're like JJ, and the thought of baiting a hook with a piece of squid makes you gag, the kids may want to spend all day fishing, so don't forget to bring fishing poles and gear. The following are suggestions for other gear to keep the kids entertained when you're at anchor:

- Extra buckets for holding "beach finds"
- Snorkels, masks, and fins, as well as "viewfinders," which are great for watching the creatures on the bottom from a rowboat

Watch out for games and toys with small parts that you can lose on deck — some games may have to remain below deck. Designate a certain area (an out-of-the-way space like an aft cabin) to store toys, games, and invaluable collections of shells and rocks.

Buckets are useful as baby washtubs and hermit crab houses, besides their regular function for *swabbing* (cleaning) the decks. But be careful when trying to fill a bucket by dunking it over the side while under way: The force of the water can pull the bucket out of your hand — or pull a child overboard.

Books to bring for you and the kids

Children on a boat read more than they do at home (especially if you ditch the portable video games). And they may surprise you by reading thicker and older books than you expect. Many good books are available for younger kids about sailing and sea life, including ones in the Magic Tree House and Magic School Bus series. Here are some of our favorites, starting with books for the youngest to the oldest kids:

- *The Owl and the Pussycat,* Edward Lear
- *The Little Sailboat,* Lois Lenski
- *Sarah's Boat: A Young Girl Learns the Art of Sailing,* Douglas Alvord
- *Dove,* Robin Lee Graham
- *Around the World in Eighty Days,* Jules Verne
- *Jonathan Livingston Seagull,* Richard Bach
- *Treasure Island,* Robert Louis Stevenson
- *Island of the Blue Dolphins,* Scott O'Dell
- *The Voyage of the Dawn Treader,* C. S. Lewis

So that you can set a good example, leave the trashy romance novels at home and bring some of these nautical classics for your own reading pleasure:

- *The American Practical Navigator,* Nathanial Bowditch
- *The Kon Tiki Expedition,* Thor Heyerdahl
- *Riddle of the Sands,* Erskine Childers
- *Song of the Sirens,* Ernest K. Gann
- *Endurance,* Alfred Lansing
- *Master and Commander,* Patrick O'Brian (then read the series)
- *The Annapolis Book of Seamanship,* John Rousmaniere
- *The Horatio Hornblower Series,* C. S. Forester
- *Sailing Alone Around the World,* Joshua Slocum
- *Capt. James Cook,* Alan Villiers
- *Moby Dick,* Herman Melville

And some great reads include the following:

- *The Race,* Tim Zimmermann
- *Longitude,* Dava Sobel
- *The Last Navigator,* Stephen Thomas
- *Around the World in Seventy-Nine Days,* Cam Lewis and Michael Levitt
- *Sex Lives of Cannibals: Adrift in the Equatorial Pacific,* J. Maarten Troost
- *Adrift,* Steve Callahan
- *Airborne,* William F. Buckley, Jr.
- *In the Heart of the Sea: The Tragedy of the Whaleship Essex,* Nathaniel Philbrick

✔ *Upset, Australia Wins the America's Cup,* Michael Levitt & Barbara Lloyd

✔ *Blue Latitudes, Boldly Going where Captain Cook has gone before,* Tony Horwitz

✔ *The Shadow in the Sands,* Sam Llewellyn (and his other great sailing novels)

✔ *The Nautical Chart,* Arturo Perez-Reverte

For a list of sailing books, check out www.sailingscuttlebutt.com/ssc/books. And don't forget to pack a few encyclopedia-type books with information about the stars, weather, local birds, fish, rocks, and shells!

PETER SAYS

Spinnaker flying — nature's roller coaster ride

When you and your family are seasoned sailors (and have already mastered using the parachute-like spinnaker sail discussed in Chapter 12), a fun way to spend the afternoon while anchored is to position the boat so that the kids can go *spinnaker flying,* as shown in the following figure. You need moderate winds and warm water, and then follow these steps:

1. **Anchor the boat in the wrong direction — with the stern into the wind.**

   (See Chapter 10 on anchoring.)

2. **Secure a bosun's chair as a seat to slide along a line attached to both lower corners of the spinnaker.**

   (Check out Chapter 15 for what a bosun's chair looks like.)

3. **Hook the top of the spinnaker to the halyard.**

4. **Tie an extra-long safety retrieving line from one clew (lower corner of the sail) to the bow of your boat.**

5. **Have your friends or family members on deck hoist the spinnaker about ¾ of the way — not all the way to the top.**

   Keep it from filling by having someone pull on the retrieving line hard to keep the sail luffing close to the water.

6. **Jump in the water with a friend or family member.**

7. **Climb into the chair and slide it along to the center point of the rope between the two corners.**

8. **Release the retrieving line, and have a friend in the water help spread the corners of the sail so that the wind catches it, and off you go!**

On a puffy day, spinnaker flying can make for a wild ride!

Chapter 17

Chartering: Changes in Latitude

Whenever I find myself growing grim about the mouth; whenever it is a damp, drizzly November in my soul . . . then, I account it high time to get to sea as soon as I can. . . .

— Herman Melville, Moby Dick

*I*magine spending a week's vacation with your closest friends and family in some of the most beautiful spots in the world. Thanks to sailboat charter companies, you can take short vacation cruises in sailing paradises around the world. You can sail in remote areas and spend a week without ever seeing another soul, or you can cruise to hot spots in the Mediterranean and spend your nights surrounded by the Cote d'Azur chic in a local nightclub.

In this chapter, we look at your options for chartering a boat and sailing away. We also help you prepare for the business side of the charter. You need to be able to sail to bareboat charter, and we review the skills you need. Lastly, we look at the top cruising spots around the world. So what are you waiting for? You don't even have to own a boat!

Knowing What to Expect When You Charter a Boat

Thanks to excellent charter companies around the world, chartering a boat doesn't require as much planning as you may expect. Hey, you can go today — just pick up the phone! The larger charter companies, such as Sunsail (www. sunsail.com) or The Moorings (www.moorings.com), can help arrange everything from air travel to hotel stays and side trips to provisioning. You can even schedule a "cruise-and-learn" vacation to brush up on your sailing skills during the whole trip or for just the first part of your trip. Some charter companies also organize *flotillas,* where a lead boat with a professional captain and other staff provide support and organize excursions and parties.

The most common way to book your trip is directly with the charter company, but charter brokers can do the deal on your behalf. You can research the various charter companies by scanning the advertising sections in the back of some sailing magazines or going online.

A great magazine for charter aficionados is *Cruising World.* The magazine has monthly features on different cruising locales as well as an annual readers' survey of the best charter companies. Just to let you know how popular cruising vacations are, more than 90 percent of the respondents to *Cruising World*'s annual surveys feel that the cost was worth the experience and that their sailing vacation went smoothly. We think that the other 10 percent probably never came back from the islands!

This section specifically details what you need to do and what you can expect when chartering a sailboat. Follow our advice, and you should have a memorable experience.

Going bareboat cruising

The most common way to charter is through a *bareboat charter,* in which your group rents a *bare* boat from a charter company, fully rigged but without any skipper or paid crew on board.

Planning the trip

If you want to have a successful bareboat cruise, look into the following when you plan your vacation:

> ✔ **The type of boat:** Chartering enables you to try sailing different boats. The bigger charter companies offer a variety of monohulls and catamarans from which to choose. As you see in Figure 17-1, a catamaran has more space on deck (and that second hull for more space down below) than a monohull of the same length. If having a specific boat is important to you, make sure to get a commitment in writing from your charter company. Ask about the contingency plan if the boat you request isn't available or isn't ready when you arrive. If you're sailing with a large group, make sure that you get a plan of the boat's sleeping arrangements. (Pick the biggest cabin for yourself!)

Figure 17-1:
Sailing in paradise on a chartered catamaran.

© *Sunsail Sailing Vacations,* sunsail.com

✔ **The charter fee and contract:** When you book a charter, expect to pay a deposit (usually 25 percent of the total) upon booking and have the remainder due 60 days before the charter start date. Your charter contract should include a refund schedule, but expect to forfeit the entire charter fee if you cancel within 60 days. The average price of a weeklong bareboat charter (40-foot, or 12-meter, boat) is about $3,000. Prices vary greatly with the season, size and type of boat, and location. And sometimes the smaller charter companies offer more competitive rates — so shopping around can pay. You can also purchase travel insurance to cover you if you must cancel. You may also be asked to prove your sailing ability; often a resume is helpful — or any certifications you've earned at a sailing school.

✔ **Liability coverage:** Each charter company has its own policy for damage and loss. The typical policy is either a large, refundable deposit ($500 to $2,000) or a small, nonrefundable premium ($25 to $40 per day).

✔ **Maintenance and repair services:** Keep in mind that a newer boat is probably less likely to have broken equipment, although the top charter companies have fantastic maintenance programs. Ask about the turn-around time between charters; the boat needs to be at the charter base for at least a day for routine maintenance.

✔ **On-site support:** Make sure that you know how to contact the charter company through VHF or SSB radio (see Chapter 7) and that you know its policy if you need assistance. Cellular phones are becoming more common in popular charter regions. Most charter companies have support bases throughout the cruising area.

Don't forget to pack a good book

We both love a good sea story, and we urge you to check out our list of our favorite sailing books in Chapter 16. JJ can't be pinned down on the subject of her favorite sailing author; she blows with the wind. But Peter's favorite sailing author is Joseph Conrad. The descriptions of storms and adventures at sea in his short stories and novels are true classics. And although your first introduction to them may be in an English class, if you take the time, you can find many gems in his bibliography.

✔ **Boat provisioning:** The charter company can organize partial or full provisioning, saving you a day of shopping in unfamiliar markets. When you get aboard, stow the food yourself so that you know where to find it. Unless cooking in a sailboat-sized galley is your idea of a great vacation, we advise you to keep your menus as simple as possible and plan on eating out a bit as part of your vacation budget.

✔ **Additional gear:** You need a *rowing dinghy* (often an inflatable equipped with a small outboard engine) to get to shore, and the charter company should include one.

Throughout this book, we use the word *dinghy* to describe any sailboat with a centerboard. Here we refer to a *rowing dinghy,* which can be called *dinghies,* too; they just aren't rigged with sails (although some can be). So for the rest of this chapter on chartering, when we say dinghy, we mean a rowing dinghy (that may have an outboard). Okay?

The charter company can organize snorkeling and other watersports gear — even kayaks and sailboards. We usually bring our own masks and snorkels and rent the fins. Make sure to put any specific gear requests in writing and get a confirmed response. Charter companies should also provide navigation equipment, including nautical charts and a VHF radio.

Having a hibachi grill mounted on the stern pulpit is the best way to cook the fish you catch!

✔ **Items to pack:** Pack lightly — the charter company can advise you on expected weather conditions. Space is at a premium, especially if you're chartering with several people. See Chapter 3 for tips on clothing needs afloat. And in the tropics, cover up lily-white skin no matter how warm the weather.

Checking out your craft

After you arrive at the front door of the charter company, ready to go cruising, you need to do the following:

✔ **Inspect your boat.** Make sure that all the required equipment is on board. Check all lines for signs of wear, and make sure that all the winches and blocks are functioning properly. Go over all the equipment with the charter-company representative. Make sure you point out anything you notice is wrong during the inspection. Ideally the charter company should fix any broken equipment before you leave.

✔ **Attend boat orientation.** The charter-company representative should give you a thorough orientation to the boat. Make sure that you understand how the onboard systems work, such as the sails, safety equipment, sun shades, ventilation system, windlass system for anchoring, storage, galley facilities, navigation gear and radios, marine heads and showers, and, of course, use of the rowing (or outboard-powered) dinghy.

✔ **Get to know the cruising area.** Always take the time to sit down with a company representative to look over the nautical chart of the area. You want to be briefed on the local attractions and any hazards. Be sure to ask for help in planning your ideal itinerary as well as backup plans in case of adverse weather.

✔ **Prove your ability to handle the boat.** An old joke in the charter industry goes like this:

> **Q:** What qualifications do you need to be able to bareboat charter?

> **A:** A check that doesn't bounce.

We hope that the charter company has you prove your ability. Certainly, certification to a recognized standard, such as the American Sailing Association or U.S. Sailing Bareboat Charter Standard, is helpful. If, after a checkout, the charter company doesn't think that you possess the ability to handle the boat, it has the right to refuse your business or give you the opportunity to pay for a captain to come along.

Cruising with a skipper

If you need pampering on your vacation, chartering a fully crewed yacht is for you. You can help with the sailing as much or as little as you like. Delicious meals appear at the proper times, and you can just relax and enjoy the sights. Of course, your next bank statement will reflect this first-class treatment. We've seen some truly *awesome* boats, 80 feet (24 meters) in length and longer, in the islands on fully crewed charters. The crew can even rig up the sailboard for you!

One in-between option is to have a partially crewed trip in which you hire a skipper for the first half of the trip. Then, if the charter company feels that you're qualified, you can go the rest of the way bareboat. The Moorings offers a "friendly-skipper" service for free for a half day on your first day out to help you refresh your skills.

Both The Moorings and Sunsail also offer a variety of "learn-to-sail" vacations where you can earn certification while cruising the British Virgin Islands. The introductory courses combine a few nights ashore with a week of cruising with an instructor.

Identifying Important Chartering Skills

What skills do you need to operate a charter boat safely for a week? You should have at least one full sailing season of experience skippering a similar-sized boat in similar conditions. Fortunately, most charter destinations are in fairly protected waters. (Who wants to vacation in the middle of the ocean?) If you've mastered sailing on your lake aboard a two-person dinghy but have never been aboard a bigger keelboat, you need to take some lessons and build more experience.

Not everyone on the crew needs to be an expert sailor, but at least two sailors need to be competent. You need to possess and be able to demonstrate the following ten pieces of knowledge and skills before chartering a boat:

- Experience as a skipper on a live-aboard cruise of at least 48 hours.

- Ability to anchor and pick up a mooring safely, using the equipment provided.

- Ability to obtain and interpret the weather forecast.

- Ability to perform coastal piloting by using a nautical chart and compass.

- Understanding of basic safety procedures for the type of boat you're aboard — including man-overboard rescue routines.

- Ability to handle the boat under power in confined areas. (But always make some practice maneuvers in open water first.)

- Understanding of onboard systems, including navigation equipment, engine, marine head, and galley facilities. Most cruising boats have a roller furler for the jib, a lazy jack system for storing the mainsail, and a windlass to help with the anchor — make sure you understand these systems too.

- Understanding of etiquette when anchoring in a crowded harbor.

- Ability to instruct and advise nonsailors and less-expert sailors on the operation of the boat and basic safety considerations.

- Ability to sail. Just tell the charter company that you've read *Sailing For Dummies!*

Using Your Dinghy

Figure 17-2 shows an idyllic cruising scene. A key component to that fun is the dinghy tied behind the cruising boat. Because your dinghy is often your ticket to freedom on a cruise, you want to make sure that it doesn't float away. The following tips can make life afloat with a dinghy more enjoyable:

✔ **Bring a paddle.** An outboard engine may power your dinghy, but make sure that you have some alternate means of propulsion — just in case!

✔ **Stop that banging.** Assuming your dinghy is a rubber inflatable, you can tie it so the engine can't hit the hull of your sailboat. But kayaks and other water toys have a habit of banging against the hull as the wind shifts in the anchorage at 3 a.m., so you may want to pull them up on the dinghy at night.

✔ **Tie your dinghy securely.** Whether you're towing your dinghy behind the boat or leaving it high and dry on an idyllic beach while you do some exploring, make sure that you tie it up well. Use a bowline knot, or tie your dinghy around a horn cleat, as Chapter 19 shows. Inspect the dinghy's bow line for chafe; if it looks shaky, tie on a new one. On a beach, always secure the dinghy (with an anchor in the sand or a bow line tied to a sturdy object) above the highest possible level that the tide and waves can reach, and keep an eye on it.

Figure 17-2:
Another beautiful day in paradise aboard a bareboat charter boat.

© Sunsail Sailing Vacations, sunsail.com

✔ **Tow your dinghy safely.** If you decide to pull your dinghy behind you from place to place, then take everything out of the boat (oars, fuel tank, engine, swim fins, and so on) before you get under way. Check with the charter company for its recommendations of dinghy towing. The same principles of safe towing that we cover in Chapter 7 apply. When backing or maneuvering the sailboat in close quarters, bring the dinghy close alongside, and have one person watch it so that you don't run over the tow rope.

✔ **Watch out for surf.** Don't try landing your dinghy on a beach with breakers; even small waves can tip your boat. If you must beach your dinghy in waves, try to make your timing so that a wave washes you far up the beach. Then quickly climb out and grab the bow line so that it doesn't drift back. Always land bow first and depart bow out. Avoid standing in the water between the dinghy and the beach because a wave can throw the boat right at you.

Eyeing Popular Cruising Grounds

So you think you're interested in taking a charter. This section provides a list of the ten nicest places we know to go cruising and some close runner-ups. All places have great charter companies, but you can also sail your own boat there.

✔ **Australia's Whitsunday Passage:** Located in the Coral Sea between Queensland and the Great Barrier Reef, the Whitsunday Passage features great diving and a steady southeast trade wind, especially August to October.

✔ **The Bahamas:** The Bahamas are popular and easily accessible from the United States. Some of the most beautiful islands are the Abacos (the Family Islands), Eleuthera, and the Exumas. They have plenty of shallow waters, so be attentive to the visual clues of depth and the reading on your depth sounder as well as being a vigilant pilot, as we describe in Chapter 9. Many safe anchorages in close proximity to each other provide for variety and carefree planning when you're afloat.

✔ **Caribbean Islands:** Without doubt, the Caribbean is the No. 1 charter destination in the world. Especially popular are the U.S. and British Virgin Islands. They feature great year-round weather (although you may want to avoid hurricane season). These islands are especially good for novice charterers because of the predictable winds, deep waters, numerous protected sailing areas, easy navigation, and plenty of beautiful and safe anchorages.

✔ **Florida Keys:** With easy access from the mainland United States to the Sunshine State, the Florida Keys feature warm, shoal waters.

Extreme chartering

Ever dream of rounding Cape Horn or dodging icebergs while sailing to Antarctica? You can on a crewed charter with expert sailors! A few outfits specialize in expedition-style charters. Peter cruised the Beagle Channel and the region around Cape Horn aboard Skip Novak's 55-foot (17-meter) sloop *Pelagic.* Pelagic Expeditions (www.pelagic.co.uk) now has two boats in its fleet and offers a variety of "expedition charters" to remote, high-latitude locations in both hemispheres. Southern California's Orange Coast College School of Sailing Seamanship offers adventure charter opportunities closer to home (www.occsailing.com/pages/eagle.html).

✔ **Great Lakes:** Get out of the nearby big cities, and you'd swear that you're in the middle of nowhere when you're on the Great Lakes. Did you know that the water of northern Lake Huron is crystal clear?

✔ **Mediterranean:** Spain, France, Italy, Croatia, Greece, and Turkey all have plenty of beautiful cruising grounds and lessons in ancient history.

✔ **Mexico:** The waters of the Gulf of California inside Baja, Mexico, can be magical.

✔ **New Zealand's Bay of Islands:** Summer — February and March (remember the southern hemisphere) — is the peak season for the Bay of Islands.

✔ **Pacific Northwest:** Uncrowded, scenic anchorages are the highlight in the Pacific Northwest. The protected waters of Puget Sound are great cruising grounds, but they have strong currents, big tidal ranges, and cold water.

✔ **South Pacific:** Tahiti, Tonga, and Fiji have big charter fleets. Watch out for cyclones in the South Pacific in the summer months.

Here are a few of the runner-ups (fitting the world in a list of ten is hard):

✔ **California:** We love the Channel Islands of California — a pristine cruising ground just offshore from Southern California.

✔ **Chesapeake Bay:** Peter loves the softshell crabs of Chesapeake Bay. Just make sure that you have a shallow-draft boat to get to all the neat little harbors on the Eastern Shore.

✔ **Maine:** Maine has beautiful cruising grounds, but they're not for beginners. Prime sailing months are July to early September, but the weather is fickle. Secluded anchorages are plentiful. Difficulties for cruising include large tidal ranges, strong currents, possibility of fog, and the rocky coastline.

✔ **Scandinavia:** Can you say "fjords"? You may after sailing these waters — plus you have some amazing archipelagos to explore.

The *high season* is the time of the year when a destination is most popular. Weatherwise, high season is the best time to go to a particular place, but be aware that some areas get pretty crowded during this peak season — plus the high season is more expensive. Table 17-1 outlines the high seasons of ten of the most popular charter destinations.

Table 17-1	Charter Destinations' High Seasons
Location	*High Season*
Bahamas	December to May
Florida	December to April
Caribbean	December to April
Mexico	November to May
Tahiti	July to August
Australia	December to March
New Zealand	December to March
California	May to October
Mediterranean	May to September
New England	June to September

Chapter 18

Sailing Sailboards

At the bottom, so, and bent them, gently curving
So that they looked like the wings of birds, most surely.

— Ovid, translated by Rolfe Humphries

In this chapter, we introduce you to our favorite kind of sailboats —
sailboards. An offshoot of surfing, sailboarding developed in the United
States in the late 1960s and now is popular all around the world. Sailboarding
(which some also call *windsurfing,* a trademark of a brand of boards and sails)
requires just what the name says — a board and a sail. Plus, you can go sailboarding just about anywhere. We've even tried it in a swimming pool!

One of the great features of sailing is that after you master the basics on one
boat, you can transfer those skills to other boats with relative ease. But if
you've spent any time trying to sailboard, you may think that these boats are
the exception to the "If you can sail one boat, you can sail any boat" rule. Not
really. Sailboards are a little more difficult to sail than other boats because
they require more balance and coordination, but we show you exercises that
you can do to get comfortable standing on the board. And take it from us —
sailboarding is definitely worth the effort.

Windswimming, Anyone?

Just as with any other type of sailing, we recommend finding a certified instructor to show you the basics of sailboarding. Most sailboard schools have special equipment, such as "simulator" boards, that let you get the feel on shore before heading out and getting wet. And you're definitely going to get wet. This phase of your sailboarding career isn't called *windswimming* for nothing!

A sailboarding vacation may be the best way for you to start. Great vacation packages are available in sailboarding hot spots around the world — *hot* being the operative word. We recommend that you take a good look at these possibilities, because the warmer the water, the easier it is to enjoy and get through the windswimming phase.

The sailing skills that you develop with other sailboats — being attuned to and feeling the wind direction — are just as important with sailboards. The safety rules that we review in Chapters 3 and 7 still apply; make sure that you check your equipment, that you have sufficiently warm clothing (such as a wetsuit and/or a life jacket), and that you aren't heading out in conditions that are too windy or rough. A qualified instructor can make sure that your experience is as safe (and fun) as possible.

Even if you can manage a sailboard in light winds, if you want to take up high-wind sailboarding, we again recommend taking instruction from a qualified instructor. A number of schools and resorts can give you great instruction and expose you to the myriad equipment options you face when you want to get into this end of the sport. Careful, though — high-wind sailboarding is very addictive!

Kiteboarding — the newest craze

You may have seen them on your last trip to the beach — a bunch of crazy wakeboarders attached not to speedboats but to colorful kites that allow them to get launched out of the water and fly in the air (not just the kites but the sailors too). Kiteboarding is the latest extreme craze. To kiteboard, you just need a kite with lots of strings so you can fly it, a harness to help you hold on, a board slightly bigger than a snowboard or wakeboard, and a helmet for safety. All the equipment is easy to carry to the beach. But definitely make sure you get proper instruction from a qualified instructor. New equipment is making the sport safer and easier, but kiteboarding is still a bit dangerous — what goes up must come down (and possibly get dragged down the beach). Your sailing skills can help smooth out that learning curve a bit — especially your ability to sense the wind's strength and direction and to read the waves and water. So put on that helmet, call your local kiteboarding shop, sign up for some lessons, and get ready to fly.

Parts are parts

The parts of a sailboard are similar to the parts of any sailboat, as Figure 18-1 shows. Your arms become the mainsheet; your body becomes the standing rigging. The biggest difference is that a sailboard doesn't have a rudder — you steer a sailboard with the sail and your body weight. The following is a rundown on a sailboard's distinctive parts and features:

- ✔ **Boom (or wishboom):** Wishbone-shaped tubes attached to the mast and sail that allow you to adjust the sail's trim.

- ✔ **Camber inducers:** Fittings in the sail's luff into which the battens sit. (See Chapter 4 to review the parts of a sail.) Their shape creates a three-dimensional, winglike shape for the sail. Camber inducers are used primarily on high-performance (not beginner) sails.

- ✔ **Footstraps:** Straps to secure your feet that are normally used in high-speed and wave sailing. Footstraps aren't on all boards.

- ✔ **Gooseneck:** A fitting (often a clamp) attaching the boom to the mast.

- ✔ **Harness:** A harness you wear with a hook that can connect temporarily to the harness lines, thereby taking the load off your arms.

- ✔ **Harness lines:** Rope loops on either side of the boom into which you hook your harness. Harness lines aren't on all boards.

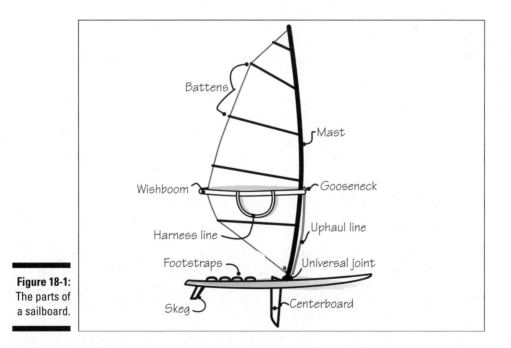

Figure 18-1:
The parts of a sailboard.

- **Mast base:** A fitting at the bottom of the mast that connects to the universal joint.

- **Mast sleeve:** The sailcloth tube along the luff of the sail into which you insert the mast when getting ready to sail.

- **Skeg:** A fixed fin providing directional stability under the back of the board.

- **Towing eye:** A loop near the front of the board for attaching a tow line.

- **Universal joint:** A fitting connecting the rig to the board, enabling you to rotate the rig in any direction.

- **Uphaul line:** A line attached to the gooseneck to help pull the rig out of the water.

The ideal setup

The ideal conditions for beginning sailboarders include flat (no waves), warm water and a steady, light-to-moderate breeze parallel to the shore. Because beginners start out with sailing on a reach (for a review of the points of sail, see Chapter 5), this orientation makes going out and coming in easy. If the breeze is blowing offshore (away from the land), you have to sail close-hauled back to shore, a difficult point of sail for a beginner. When the breeze is blowing onshore, trying to sail away is difficult and frustrating. Sailboarding in too much wind is nearly impossible for beginners.

Fortunately, I began sailboarding in Florida, where the water is nice and warm. I started sailboarding right at the beginning of the windsurfer craze, so no one was really an expert yet. My friends and I sailed out of a marina with lots of boats and very tight confines — not the ideal place to begin. We sat for hours, watching each other struggling through the shifting winds and falling every few seconds — to the glee of the crowd on the dock. Today, you can avoid much of that embarrassment thanks to the much-improved teaching techniques that have evolved over the years.

Bigger is better — at least at the beginning

Start on the biggest, floatiest board you can find — it provides the most stable platform. Make sure that the deck has sufficient roughness to prevent you from slipping off. If not, try wearing rubber slippers (available at marine stores) to increase your traction. The big sailboard manufacturers offer trainer boards especially aimed at the newbie — trainer boards really help facilitate the learning process.

After you master the basics, you'll probably be tempted to try out different boards, including the much less buoyant, high-wind boards that are so popular around the world. The difference in maneuverability and performance will amaze you.

One reason why you may want to take your first few lessons at a school is that its boards are ideal for beginners. And you may want to delay your first purchase until you can handle a slightly more advanced board.

Your instructor probably recommends an undersized "training sail", because beginners fall a lot when learning. A smaller sail is easier to pull back out of the water and lets you get the feel of how to balance without being overpowering.

Rigging the Board

The great part about sailboards is that they're easy to rig. The more high-performance sails, with their long battens and camber inducers, can be a bit trickier to rig, but a beginner's sail should have few (if any) battens. Rigging your sailboard (especially the sail) is similar in many ways to rigging any sailboat (see Chapter 4). Like some dinghies, you don't have a halyard to hoist; the sail's luff sleeve simply slides down onto the mast. The trickiest part can be securing the boom to the mast so that the boom is at a comfortable height (roughly chest height), so have your instructor help out.

Making a Not-So-Dry Run

Have we mentioned that you're going to get wet and look a little foolish when you first begin sailboarding? You can minimize your embarrassment (a little) by getting used to the board and the sail before you put them together.

Getting used to the board

After you assemble the right equipment, leave the sail on shore for a while and familiarize yourself with the board. You can try some of the following drills to get comfortable on your board:

- ✔ **Practice lying on your stomach and paddling the board.** Try paddling in a circle.

- ✔ **Stand up and work on your balance.** Keep your knees bent and your hands out to the side — just like a tightrope walker.

- ✔ **Move your feet out to each side of the board, and practice rocking the board from side to side.** Try to keep your balance!

- ✔ **Walk toward the front of the board, practice turning around, walk toward the stern, and turn again.** You can't do this drill on a small, high-wind board — the board is too small and unstable.

When you feel comfortable on the board, put it back on the beach near your starting point, and get the sail.

Getting used to the sail

Balance is the first tricky part about sailboarding. The second tricky part is that a sailboard doesn't have a rudder. You steer the boat with the sail and your weight.

Your instructor may have access to a simulator. Use it if possible. Otherwise you can get a feel for the dynamics of handling the sail as follows:

1. **Stand the sail up on shore, bracing the mast base with your foot.**

2. **Stand to windward of the sail and hold onto the mast at or near the gooseneck.**

   The sail luffs like a flag with the wind.

   Note: A fully-battened sail doesn't flap like a normal sail.

3. **Face directly downwind, with your back to the wind and the sail pointing downwind away from you.**

   Get comfortable in this luffing, or "safety," position, as Figure 18-2 shows, because you're in this position quite a bit at first.

4. **Try tilting the sail to your left and then to your right.**

   When you're on the water, you turn the board by tilting the sail in this manner.

Figure 18-2:
Standing on the shore with the sail in a luffing position.

Getting Your Feet (And the Rest of You) Wet

After you attach your rig to the board, here are the steps to getting going:

1. **Put the board in deep enough water that the centerboard can be down all the way.**

   Position the board so the wind blows across one side.

2. **Put the sail downwind of the board so that the mast and board form a T.**

3. **Kneel on the board at the mast base and grab the uphaul line.**

4. **Stand up and start pulling the sail out of the water with the uphaul.**

   Use your full body weight. Bend your knees — don't strain your back.

5. **When the sail is all the way out of the water, hold the mast in the luffing position like you practiced on land.**

   Your feet straddle the mast.

6. **Holding the mast with your back hand (the hand that's farthest back when you get under way), cross your forward hand over and grab the boom about a foot behind the mast.**

7. **After grabbing the boom, bend this arm and bring the rig across your body, as Figure 18-3 shows.**

   The sail is still luffing.

8. **Take slow baby steps around to the side of the board as you grab the boom with your back hand about 3 feet behind where your forward hand is.**

   Keep both hands on the boom. Your back arm is the mainsheet. Your front arm is like the *shrouds* (wires supporting the mast). If you pull in your back arm and keep your front arm steady, you trim in the sail and start to move forward.

9. **Pull in your back arm so that you're facing the middle of the sail — perfectly positioned to balance the force of the wind.**

   You're sailing on a reach!

Figure 18-3: (Left) Grab the boom with your forward hand and (right) bring the rig across your body.

Lean your body back away from the rig as much as you need to keep your balance. You can control the trim of the sail by the position of your arms. To trim in, pull in your back hand. To ease out, either push out your back hand or pull in your front hand. To stop, just return to the luffing or "safety" position by first releasing your back hand from the boom and then bringing it forward to hold onto the mast or uphaul line.

Of course, by now you're great at the other method for stopping — falling in.

If you fall, make sure that you always swim back to the board right away, or else it may drift off. Use the board as your swim platform to take a break.

Whether you're in the Caribbean on a learn-to-sailboard vacation, taking lessons at a local lake, or at your friend's beach house on the shore, keep these points in mind as you practice your sailboarding skills:

- ✔ When you fall in, try to fall backward on your butt instead of jumping feet first. Otherwise, if the water is shallow, you can twist your ankle.

- ✔ As you come back to the surface after a fall, put your hands up above your head so that you don't hit your head on the sail or board.

- ✔ If you find that you're constantly sliding off the board, ask the school or rental shop for a different board. The board's original nonskid surface may be worn off. We've also seen boards that have suntan lotion all over them and are as slippery as a seal. For traction, some people swear by those special rubber booties.

Steering the Board

After you master getting moving, you quickly want to know how to turn. Many beginners get the first part right, but then they keep going and going because they don't know how to turn around and get back, or they're so fearful of attempting a tack that they get too far from shore. (If this scenario happens to you, hope that your instructor has a motorboat!)

Practice the leaning techniques you tried on land. With the rig in the safety position, lean it to the right, and the board swivels left — and vice versa (see Figure 18-4). Keep practicing until you can turn the board 360 degrees. As the board turns, take baby steps around the mast base to keep your back facing the wind direction.

Figure 18-4:
With the rig in the safety position, lean it to one side to make the board turn the other direction.

When you pull in the sail and are moving forward, you can steer by leaning the rig forward or backward while keeping the sail sheeted in with your back hand, as Figure 18-5 shows. The key is to stay in balance and tilt the rig without changing the angle of the sail to the wind too much.

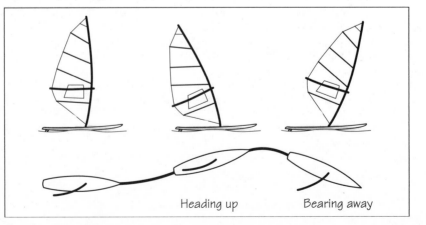

Figure 18-5:
To turn toward the wind, tip the sail back (center); to turn away from the wind, tip the sail forward (right).

Heading up   Bearing away

As you experiment with turning, you quickly discover that sailing upwind and reaching are very similar, but sailing on a run is a real challenge. Therefore, the first maneuver a sailboarder tries is a tack rather than a jibe.

Tacking

To *tack* means to maneuver through the no-sail zone so that the wind is blowing on the opposite side of the boat. Here are the steps to tacking on a sailboard:

1. **Tilt the rig aft (toward the back) and trim the sail to turn the board toward the wind.**

2. **When the board is almost pointed directly toward the wind in the no-sail zone, step your forward foot around the front of the mast so that you end up straddling the mast with your back to the wind.**

3. **With the sail luffing, continue making baby steps to the other side of the board as you lean the rig sideways to get the board pointed on a reaching course on the new tack.**

   The wind is coming over the new side of the board.

4. **As the board bears away, cross your new forward hand over to grab the boom — as we describe in the "Getting Your Feet (And the Rest of You) Wet" section, earlier in this chapter — and pull the sheet in with your back hand.**

   Take your final baby steps so you're facing the sail standing on the new windward side, and off you go!

Going straight on a reach or close-hauled is relatively easy to master because all the forces are pretty balanced, and you can make fine adjustments with your arms. Balancing only becomes a challenge when the board slows down (such as in a maneuver) and when you're sailing downwind. Just like in so many other sports, the best advice is *bend your knees!*

Sailing downwind

When you go downwind, all that nice stability and control goes out the window. With the wind straight behind, you must stand facing the front of the board, counteracting the forward pull of the sail. Any movement to the right or left really rocks the board — this point of sail really tests your balance.

To begin downwind sailing, follow these steps:

1. **Start by sailing on a reach.**

   The wind is blowing across the board.

2. **To bear off on a broader reach, tilt the mast forward to turn the board down (away from the wind), constantly moving your feet and rotating your body to counteract the sail's force.**

   As the wind comes from more dead behind, the force on the sail may feel more powerful.

3. **To counteract the force on the sail, bring both hands closer to you or take a step or two back — thereby tipping the top of the sail backward — until you feel like you can control the sail.**

   If you get hit with a huge puff, you can always release your back hand (the hand closest to the *clew,* or back corner, of the sail) and luff the sail to keep from being pulled forward into the water.

Bend your knees to maintain your balance.

Jibing

When sailing downwind, you may want to try a *jibe.* A jibe is a maneuver where you change tacks by turning away from the wind. Jibing on a short, high-performance sailboard can be downright thrilling — like carving a turn on a slalom water ski or on a snowboard. But on a big *longboard* (trainer sailboard), tacking around and then bearing off is much easier than jibing because the big board is tough to turn.

The easiest way to jibe is simply to unload the sail and revert to the safety position, holding onto the mast near the gooseneck. Then tilt the rig and walk around to the "new" windward side to turn the boat until it's pointed on a comfortable reaching course. Then get going again in the standard fashion.

A cool, exhibition-style jibe maneuver is possible on a longboard. Here's how to pull off one of these maneuvers:

1. **As you sail downwind, step *aft* (back) to sink the back of the board.**

   If your board isn't big and floaty, you can stay forward to keep the board from getting too unstable.

2. **Rotate the sail (keeping it full of wind) so that the board turns onto the new jibe.**

3. **Quickly release your back hand (closest to the clew) and pull in your front hand.**

4. **As the clew of the sail goes winging away from you, cross your old back hand over and grab the boom about a foot back on the new windward side.**

   The momentum of the clew rotating around enables you to grab the boom with your new back hand.

5. Pull the boom in and go!

All the while you're doing this maneuver, you're keeping your balance precariously on the board. If you don't fall in the water, be ecstatic!

Sailing straight downwind in anything but light air is a pain on a longboard. So if I need to get to a downwind destination, I sail on a broad reach across the wind, jibing (or tacking) each time I want to zig or zag back the other way. If conditions are windy, this approach is a really fun way of getting downwind, because your board creates its own wind and flies across the water.

Keeping in balance

Anticipating wind shifts helps you keep the sails trimmed properly — which means you stay drier, too. Here are some tips for staying balanced when the wind changes:

- As a puff of wind hits, lean your weight out more. Be ready to let out your back hand and pull in your front hand to ease the sail slightly so that you stay balanced and don't get pulled over.

- If you anticipate the end of the puff, bring your weight to the center as the wind dies away.

- If the wind dies suddenly, bend your knees and get your torso over the top of the board quickly to avoid falling backward into the water.

If you've ever been skiing, you know how easily you can pick out the beginning skiers coming down the hill. The same principle applies with sailboarding; just look for the guy with his butt sticking way out. If you want to look cool, tilt your hips forward and bend your knees!

Getting Back to Shore in Case of Problems

If you have a problem such as a dying breeze or broken equipment, you can always paddle the board and the rig back to shore. The ability to rescue yourself is crucial to sailboarding safety.

While you're sailing, make sure to keep an eye on your distance away from shore. Try a tack or a jibe after a few minutes so you don't sail too far from shore.

Peter's ten favorite sailboarding spots

I love sailing shorter boards that perform best when the wind is up. So my favorite spots are known for reliably strong winds (except Skaneateles Lake which has other attractions).

1. Perth, Western Australia
2. British Virgin Islands
3. San Francisco Bay, California
4. Columbia River Gorge, Oregon
5. North Shore, Oahu, and Maui, Hawaii
6. Canary Islands
7. Seal Beach, California
8. Cape Hatteras, North Carolina
9. Skaneateles Lake, New York
10. Anywhere the water is warm and the wind is more than 18 knots

Europe also has a number of hot sailboarding spots; I just haven't had a chance to check them out yet!

If you must paddle a short distance, try laying the rig over the stern of the board so that it's partially out of the water, lie or kneel on the board, and start using those arms. The problem with this technique is that the sail is like a big brake dragging in the water. If conditions are windy, or if you have a long distance to go, de-rigging the sail may help. Release the outhaul, roll up the sail along the mast (or if the sail is fully battened, slide it off the mast and then roll it up), fold the boom up against the mast, and start paddling, as Figure 18-6 shows.

Figure 18-6: Self-rescue on a sailboard.

If you need to signal for help, kneel or stand on the board and wave your arms. In an emergency, always stay with your board — it's your primary source of flotation. Staying out of the water on the board keeps you much warmer. If you try to paddle back to shore, but the extra *windage* (drag) of your rig components make forward motion difficult, you can always sacrifice the rig to Poseidon to save the board — and yourself.

Part V
The Part of Tens

The 5th Wave   By Rich Tennant

"Very clever, but how much do you want for the boat without the bottle?"

In this part . . .

So you want to buy a boat? A great Walt Disney video shows Goofy walking to work every day past a boat store. One day, while he's daydreaming about boating, he walks in and buys a boat, no questions asked. He's in a trance as he hooks the boat and trailer to his car and drives to the lake. Luckily, the cartoon ends happily (they always do), and we want to make sure that any boat purchase you make ends happily, too. In this part, we show you ten essential knots so you can keep that boat securely tied, and we cover all the right questions to ask the salesperson (and yourself) to get a boat that fits your needs. We finish with a list of our ten favorite things that keep us daydreaming about sailing just like Goofy.

Chapter 19

Ten Nautical Knots and How to Tie Them

* *

In This Chapter

▶ Securing the most common types of knots

▶ Mastering the more advanced knots

* *

No one but an acrobat or a sailor could have got up to that bell-rope from the bracket, and no one but a sailor could have made the knots with which the cord was fastened to the chair.

— Sir Arthur Conan Doyle

Yes, you can tie the knot on a boat, but we're not talking about marriage. This chapter reviews the basic knots on a sailboat and shows you how to tie them. On most boats, you can find a bowline, a figure-eight knot, a square knot, and maybe a couple of half hitches somewhere.

Knowing how to tie these knots (especially the bowline and the round turn with two half hitches) and using them properly can save you a great deal of time and make your life afloat safer. With a 5-foot length of rope, you can practice these knots at home and master them quickly. Master them, and you're well on your way to becoming an "able seaman."

Overhand Knot

An *overhand knot* is the basic knot that you use to begin tying your shoes and, as you see in the following sections, is the first step of many sailing knots. If your mother only lets you wear shoes with Velcro straps, and you can't make an overhand knot, see Figure 19-1 on how to begin tying your shoes. (You may want to buy *Getting Dressed For Dummies* as soon as it comes out.)

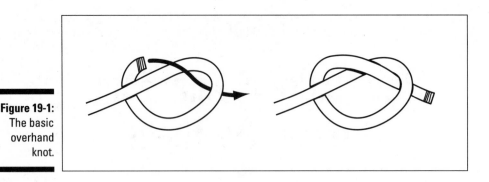

Figure 19-1:
The basic
overhand
knot.

Figure-Eight Knot

The *figure-eight knot* is a lightweight, but it's fun to tie and can save you a great deal of aggravation. While you're sitting in the boat, let your eyes follow the sheets or halyards from start to finish. The "finish" is probably at some sort of cleat. On smaller boats, all these *running rigging* lines should have figure-eight knots, as Figure 19-2 shows, at the very end to prevent the line from getting pulled out of its rigged path (that is, through pulleys and so on). Trust us — when a line "sucks" out of its normal path, it's a hassle, especially if the rope is a halyard!

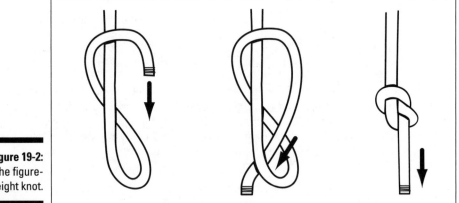

Figure 19-2:
The figure-
eight knot.

Note that with the additional loads on bigger boat lines, you don't want to tie knots in the ends of spinnaker sheets because you may need to let the line run through the block in an emergency.

The reason to use a figure-eight knot instead of a simple overhand knot is that the figure-eight is easier to untie after it has been under load (a characteristic of most good sailing knots), whereas an overhand knot can get very tight. Plus, the figure-eight is a bulkier knot and is thus less likely to slip through a cleat or block.

To tie a figure-eight knot, follow these steps:

1. **Make a loop in the end of the line.**

2. **Pass the end of the line under, back over, and up through the loop so that it looks like a figure eight.**

Bowline Knot

The *bowline* (pronounced *bow-lynn,* so it rhymes with *rollin'*) is a beautiful knot. You can call it the essential sailing knot: It's quick to tie, easy to untie, and a practical knot all around the boat. It forms a loop (of any size you want) at the end of a line, and sailors commonly use it to tie jib sheets onto the sail. On many dinghies, you use a bowline knot to attach the halyard to the sail.

The easiest way to remember how to tie a bowline is the kid's way — by imagining a bunny rabbit coming out of his hole, as Figure 19-3 shows.

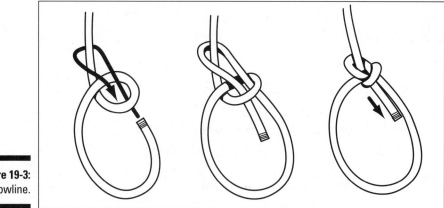

Figure 19-3:
A bowline.

Follow these steps for tying a bowline:

1. **Make the rabbit hole, as Figure 19-3 shows.**

2. **Make the rabbit come up through the hole and around the back of the tree.**

3. **Make the rabbit go back down the hole.**

4. **Pull the three ends to tighten.**

To untie a bowline, bend back the part formed when the rabbit goes "around the back of the tree," and the knot loosens up nicely.

Square Knot

The *square knot* is a knot that you may have practiced in Scouts. It's just two overhand knots with the first tied right over left, and the second tied left over right (or vice versa), as Figure 19-4 shows. (A *granny knot* is when you tie both overhand knots the same way.)

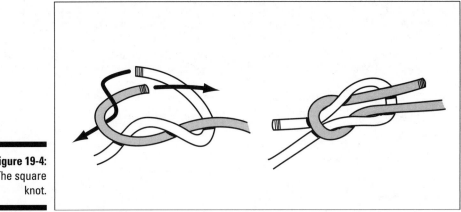

Figure 19-4:
The square
knot.

Tie a square knot like this:

1. **Tie an overhand knot (the first knot you tie when tying your shoes).**

2. **On the second overhand knot, tie it the opposite way.**

    If you put the left piece over the right on the first knot, put the right piece over the left for the second knot.

You've tied it right if the ends of the lines are parallel to the *standing* (working) part of the lines — so that it looks like two symmetrical loops. Use a square knot to tie two lengths of the same type of line together.

Cleat Knot

Use the cleat knot in Figure 19-5 any time you find a horn or t-cleat, such as when you're tying off halyards and tying your boat to most docks. Make sure you loop your line one full turn around the base of the horn cleat before tying this knot. If your dock line is a very small diameter, it can slip off the horn cleat, so in that case, you may want to tie a bowline through the center of the horn cleat instead.

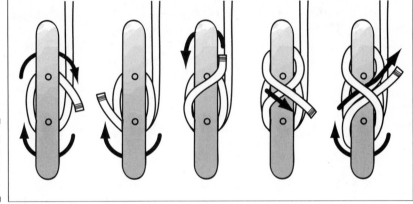

Figure 19-5:
Securing a
line around
a horn cleat.

Two Half Hitches

Two half hitches knot is also called the *double half hitch*. It's really two over-hand knots tied around the standing part of a line. This quickie knot has many temporary uses, including tying a tow line around your mast in a dinghy to get a quick tow. Tying two half hitches is a quick way to temporarily cleat off a line on a winch or other fixed object. If the rope is going to be under load, add the extra friction of a wrap or two around the object before tying the hitches (hence the term *round turn and two half hitches*). That way, you can untie it easily later, even if the rope has been stressed to its limit. Check out Figure 19-6 to tie a round turn and two half hitches.

Here are the steps to tying a round turn and two half hitches:

1. **Make two turns around the mast or object so that you can comfortably hold the line in your hand.**

2. **Tie two half hitches (two overhand knots) around the standing part of the line.**

PETER SAYS

The round turn and two half hitches is, in my opinion, the most underrated of knots. It's the most practical knot there is; it's just so darn useful all over the boat. And the thing I like best is how easy this knot is to tie, even under pressure situations when you need to make that knot fast *now!*

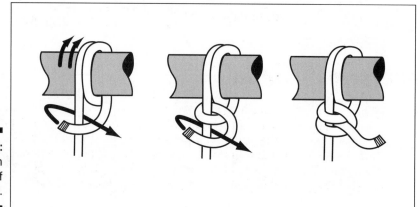

Figure 19-6:
Round turn and two half hitches.

Clove Hitch

You must tie the *clove hitch,* a close cousin to two half hitches, *around* something, such as a lifeline or piling. It's a quick knot for tying on fenders, tying a dock line to a piling, and anything you use temporarily. With the first loop, you can hold the line in place, and then you can tie the second loop to be secure. Unlike a round turn with two half hitches, the clove hitch can get very difficult to undo under pressure. See the step-by-step details of tying a clove hitch in Figure 19-7.

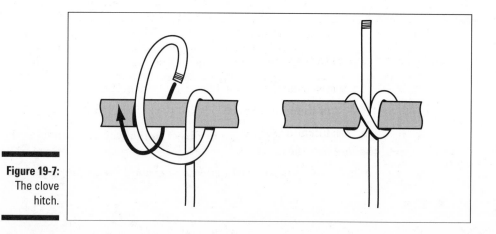

Figure 19-7:
The clove hitch.

Follow these steps to tie a clove hitch:

1. **Make a loop around the pole or object.**

2. **Make a second loop by crossing over the first loop.**

3. **Put the tail under the second loop.**

4. **Pull both ends to tighten.**

Fisherman's Bend

The *fisherman's bend* isn't a common knot because other knots, such as the bowline and the round turn with two half hitches, can also do its job. This knot is less likely than a bowline to loosen but is more difficult to untie, making it a good knot to use when you want to leave the knot in place for a long time. You often use the fisherman's bend to attach an anchor to its line, so it's sometimes called an *anchor bend.* Check out the how-to in Figure 19-8.

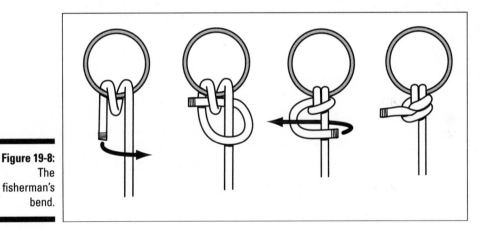

Figure 19-8:
The fisherman's bend.

Here are the steps to tying this knot:

1. **Make two loops around the shackle or anchor chain.**

2. **Pass the end of the line through both loops and tighten.**

3. **Add another hitch for safety.**

Rolling Hitch

This is an all-around great knot, one that can really impress your fans because you can use it to get out of trouble. You use the *rolling hitch* for tying one line to another. It grips so tightly that you can use it to take the load off the end of the other line in an emergency (such as a winch override; see Chapter 5). If you look closely at Figure 19-9, you see that a rolling hitch is a clove hitch with another twist or two.

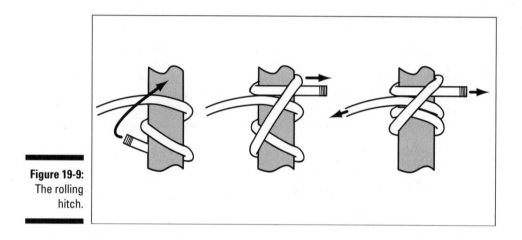

Figure 19-9:
The rolling
hitch.

Tie a rolling hitch like this:

1. **Make two loops around the rope or other item to be attached.**
2. **Put the tail over the two loops, and then make a third loop.**
3. **Put the tail under the third loop and tighten.**

Always wrap the first two loops of a rolling hitch on the side closer to your intended pulling direction. For example, if you're tying a line to a halyard coming out of the mast, wrap around the bottom first, because you intend to pull down. The third loop (the "hitch" that turns it into a real knot) wraps above the first two.

Trucker's Hitch

We used to show the kids at different sailing clinics a great old Warren Miller video that shows a 15-foot dinghy flying off a car and sliding down a ditch. Somehow, the music and Warren Miller's dry humor make the scene hilarious, but having *your* boat fly off *your* car isn't funny. Tying your boat on the car or trailer well is a rare art, but the *trucker's hitch* (a combination purchase system and knot all wrapped up in one) makes the task much easier. For the how-to, see Figure 19-10.

Follow these steps to tie a trucker's hitch:

1. **Make a loop a few feet from the end of the line.**

2. **Tie an overhand knot with the loop and tighten, keeping the loop big enough to pass a line through.**

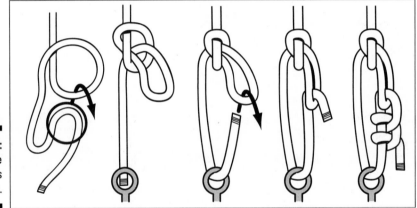

Figure 19-10:
The
trucker's
hitch.

3. **Pass the end of the line around your roof rack or trailer bar.**

4. **Put the line up through the trucker's hitch loop and pull.**

   You've made a quick 2:1 (two-to-one) *purchase* (mechanical advantage) so you can pull that line tight twice as easily. You can tie off the line with two half hitches.

JJ SAYS

Whenever I packed up my Olympic dinghy for a drive up the coast or out to Florida, Peter went around the boat and retied every line before I left. His favorite knot for cinching a boat onto a roof rack (or onto a trailer) is the trucker's hitch.

Chapter 20

Ten Questions to Ask Yourself When Buying a Sailboat

· ·

In This Chapter

▶ Evaluating what a sailboat has to offer

▶ Looking at value

· ·

> *There was a great difference in boats, of course. For a long time I was on a boat that was so slow we used to forget what year it was we left port in. But of course this was at rare intervals.*
>
> — Mark Twain, Life on the Mississippi

*W*e hope by the time you read this chapter that you're hooked on sailing. In fact, we hope you're so hooked that you catch yourself daydreaming of having your own sailboat. You can "window shop" for your dream boat in the pages of sailing magazines, at boat shows, on the Internet, and even just by walking around the local marina.

Shopping for a sailboat can be intimidating, especially if you're new to sailing. However, if you decide to take that next big step and buy your own sailboat, this chapter can help you gather the information and better prepare yourself to make that big decision.

What Do You Plan to Use the Boat For?

Are you planning to go for day sails or on extended cruising trips? Do you want to start racing? Do you need to entertain (and impress) the boss? Are you into athletic exercise, or are you more of a couch potato–type sailor? What other types of activities do you plan? If you're planning on doing some overnight trips, you may want a *windlass,* a mechanical device to assist pulling up the anchor as described in Chapter 10, for easy anchoring. An avid diver may want a large swim step. Do you envision fun outings with the whole family? If so, make sure your family has input in the selection process. Do you plan to make this new boat your "home away from home"? (Sadly, most sailboats spend most of their time tied up at the dock.) If so, then you may require lots of headroom down below. Are you interested in racing? Then check what fleets are popular in your area. The answers to these types of questions can help you narrow your search.

Who Do You Want to Bring Along?

You can comfortably sail many dinghies and even some keelboats (if rigged with an autopilot and roller-furling sails) single-handed. Some high-performance dinghies and large keelboats require a full contingent of expert crew and may not have room for extra bodies.

Lining up a number of expert sailors for each and every sail can become a hassle, so be realistic about how big a boat you need. Make a list of your potential crew members and make sure that you don't need each and every one of them before you can leave the dock. (This fact may surprise you, but some of your crew may have other commitments from time to time.)

Where Do You Plan to Use the Boat?

Are you going to sail in protected waters, such as a small lake, or out on the open ocean? What are the heaviest winds and seas you expect during your sailing? Different boats work better for different locations. In Southern California, for example, a popular cruising destination is Catalina Island, a 20-mile (32-kilometer) sail from Los Angeles. Because sailing to Catalina requires an open-ocean crossing, you need a bigger, better-equipped boat to sail there than if you plan to stay inside the confines of the Long Beach breakwater.

Sailors in Florida need lots of *portholes* (windows) for air flow and a nice big bimini cover to protect them from the sun. Sailors in Maine or the Pacific Northwest need a boat with a *pilot house* (high cabin with lots of windows surrounding the steering wheel) for protection from the rain and cold. If you live near a lake, you may want a boat that's easy to store on a trailer. Many manufacturers have boats with retractable keels for just that purpose.

A related question is "How deep is the water where you plan to use the boat?" Some manufacturers sell two models of popular cruising boats — a "shoal-draft" model, which is popular in shallow areas like Florida and the Bahamas, and a standard, full-draft model, which may be more appropriate on the West Coast.

Where Should You Buy a Boat?

If you're shopping for a used dinghy or smaller catamaran or keelboat (shorter than 25 feet, or 8 meters), your best bet may be keeping an eye on classified ads in the local papers (especially the boating newspapers) and watching the bulletin boards at marinas and yacht clubs. Most often this sort of transaction is handled privately. For a larger, more expensive used keelboat, you probably want to employ the services of a broker, as we describe in this section. If you're interested in a smaller (shorter than 25-foot, or 8-meter) racing class of boat, talk to local owners of the same class to find out your options.

Boat shows are a great place to buy a new boat — especially the bigger, (longer than 25 feet, or 8 meters) more expensive models — because you have lots of boats to choose from, and dealers and manufacturers often offer deep discounts. But whether you want new or used, do your homework before going to the boat show. Your first step is finding a broker. A good boat broker should ask you many of the same questions we do and will have lots of the answers you need to make the right purchase. They get their fee from the seller and, kind of like real-estate brokers, they can help in all aspects of the purchase, including finding dock/storage space and financing.

Most new boats are sold by dealers, similar to cars, but some manufacturers sell their products directly to consumers. Some dealerships even offer personalized instruction in sailing or operating your new boat.

If you like doing research online, check out *SAIL Magazine*'s Sailboat Buyer's Guide (www.sailbuyersguide.com) or search the Web for brokers in your area or specific manufacturers. You can also find a wide variety of boats at some popular Web sites, such as www.boats.com and www.usedboats.com.

Where Do You Plan to Keep the Boat?

Is a place available to launch your boat so that you can keep it on a trailer or put it on your car top and store it at home? If you're planning to store your boat on a trailer in your yard, have you checked with your spouse, neighbors, and/or neighborhood covenants first? Do you have access to a *slip* (in-water dockside storage) at a marina or yacht club? The slip fees at your local marina may cost as much as loan payments on your new boat (and finding a slip can be hard — but boat brokers have good connections here, too).

How Much Can You Afford to Spend?

Prices for a new 12-foot (4-meter) dinghy begin around $3,000, while prices for a new 25-foot (8-meter) keelboat begin in the neighborhood of $22,500. But of course, you can spend many times that price. When you're calculating how much you can afford, don't forget to put together a realistic yearly operating budget, including storage fees, maintenance costs, and some replacement gear. For a dinghy, that jib sheet rope you need to replace may be just a few dollars, but the same part on a keelboat can set you back $50 or more. In northern climes, you have to haul and store boats on land during the winter. Even in warmer areas, you should have a yearly haul-out for most boats for maintenance. Call the local boatyard to get a quote. As a rough guide, remember that the bigger and more active the boat, the more it costs to run and maintain.

For the love of classic boats

Ever since I built a 13-foot (4-meter) Blue Jay wooden dinghy for my sister (during college, when I should have been studying), I've been enamored with wooden boats. We visit Mystic Seaport (the Museum of America and the Sea; check out www.mysticseaport.org) and its fascinating exhibits whenever we get back to Connecticut. And I serve on the advisory board of the International Yacht Restoration School in Newport, Rhode Island (www.iyrs.org). Recently my friend Dennis Conner undertook a full restoration of the 1926 Q boat, *Cotton Blossom* (see the following figure). The finished boat is simply incredible — and is certainly the most beautiful wooden boat sailing on the West Coast. Dennis even races it occasionally!

Are You Getting a Good Value?

Buying a boat with good resale value may be important, especially when you're buying your first boat. One consideration is the taste in your local market. For example, a classic wooden boat has much more value on the East Coast than in the Caribbean. Try to think ahead: As you gain experience, your taste in boats may change, so a rash purchase today may not suit you tomorrow. New boats are like new cars — they can lose a great deal of their value as soon as you drive them off the lot. And make sure that you have a complete inventory of what comes with the boat so you know whether that cool depth sounder is still there when you have the pink slip.

Is the Boat Seaworthy?

An Internet search may link you to articles and/or forums on the merits of various types of boats. But the best way to find out whether a specific boat is seaworthy is to pay to have a marine survey, which includes (for a larger keelboat) a haul-out for inspection. A marine surveyor can give you a comprehensive report on the boat's seaworthiness and is also useful for insuring your new boat. Usually, a marine survey is more applicable to the sale of a keelboat. With a dinghy, you may have to rely on your skills of observation.

A *sea trial* (the nautical equivalent of a test drive) can also help you assess the boat's seaworthiness and whether you like the way it handles various conditions — hopefully you get to test a boat on a windy day. And ask the seller for the maintenance history on the boat.

What Equipment Do You Need?

The local conditions and your sailing plans affect what you need. Check out other boats at the local marina or ask local sailors for gear recommendations. For example, in San Diego, where the wind rarely exceeds 12 knots, you may never use a small, heavy-air jib, but if you're sailing in San Francisco Bay, such a jib is the sail you use a lot of the time. Wait to add equipment (except essential safety equipment) until you sail the boat several times. However, if you know you're planning to sail a larger sailboat short-handed, purchasing an autopilot and a roller furler is a smart investment right away.

What Kind of Boat Do You Want?

As you search for your perfect boat, you hear names such as *sportboat* or *blue-water cruiser*. These names are loose categories that can help you type-cast a particular boat. For example, the following list includes some of the common categories for keelboats:

- **Sportboat:** A sportboat is a fast keelboat (usually 20 to 30 feet, or 6 to 9 meters) with hardly any amenities, such as a *galley* (kitchen) or private *head* (cabin with toilet) down below. But in a sportboat, you get from point A to point B fast (and probably a bit wet).

- **Day sailer:** A day sailer is about the same size as a sportboat and also doesn't have many creature comforts below but is cheaper (and slower) than a sportboat.

- **Blue-water cruiser:** A blue-water, or long-distance, cruiser is a sturdy, well-built keelboat (usually longer than 40 feet, or 12 meters) that's meant to make long passages, say from New York to the Azores.

- **Cruisers:** And then you have all kinds of cruisers in between: from budget cruisers that won't break any speed records or have as many appointments but satisfy that urge to get out on the water, to floating gadget palaces with watermakers, flat-screen televisions, and all the toys.

Admit it — you look at other cars on the highway to find one that you like. The same is true with boats. One day, you may see the perfect boat go sailing past, but how do you know what it is? Many boats have an insignia on their mainsail that indicates their type, as Figure 20-1 shows. Sometimes the insignia is a class logo, and other times it's a manufacturer's logo. Some use stylized artwork (like the Laser in Figure 20-1) that you have to know to recognize, while some logos provide an obvious clue to the boat's type (the Sunfish dinghy, for example, uses a picture of a sunfish as its logo).

Figure 20-1: An Optimist dinghy logo on the left, a Laser dinghy logo in the middle, and a cruiser made by Hunter on the right.

Part VI
The Appendixes

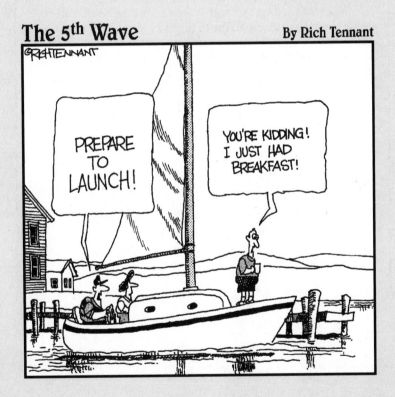

The 5th Wave — By Rich Tennant

In this part . . .

In this part, you can find a handy glossary with all the important sailing terms that we use in this book. You don't need to memorize these terms to go sailing, but you may want to review them from time to time, especially if you can't remember the difference between a jib and a jibe. In Appendix B, we show you some basic first aid in case someone on your boat gets sick. Of course, if someone is really sick, call 911 and contact the Coast Guard on Channel 16 of your marine radio. The final appendix shows you how a boat works — the basic physics of getting your boat to sail. Some people think sailing is like driving — you don't really need to know how that engine works to drive your car, and you don't really have to know how a sailboat works to sail. But we think a better analogy is buying *Driving For Dummies* back when the first cars were invented. Back then, knowing why you turned that starter crank and why you needed a clutch was important when you couldn't just call someone on your cell phone if your Model T stalled.

Appendix A

Glossary

....

They say that when your ship comes in, the first man takes the sails,
The second takes the afterdeck, the third the planks and rails.

— Robert Hunter

*I*n this glossary, you can reference Figure A-1 to see where the different parts of a keelboat are.

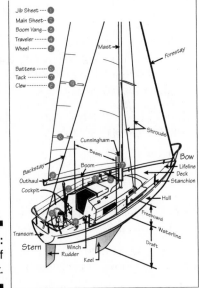

Figure A-1:
The parts of
a keelboat.

abeam: At right angles to the boat's center line.

aft: Toward the *stern;* opposite of forward.

apparent wind: The wind felt on board your boat. A combination of the wind from your forward motion and the *true wind* blowing onto the boat.

athwartships: Across the boat.

back: To *trim* a sail to *windward* so that it fills with wind backward.

backstay: The support wire between the top of the *mast* and the back of the boat.

battens: Slats inserted into pockets along a sail's *leech* to help maintain its shape.

beam: A measurement taken at the widest part of the boat; also the widest part of the boat.

beam reach: *Reaching* on a heading perpendicular to the wind direction.

bear away: To turn away from the wind (or to turn to *leeward*).

bearing: The angle to an object measured in degrees.

block: A pulley through which ropes run.

bolt rope: A rope (often covered with fabric) sewn to the *luff* or *foot* of a sail.

block

boom: The horizontal pole that supports the bottom edge of the *mainsail.*

boom vang: The control *line* system, running from the boom to the base of the *mast,* that controls *mainsail* twist.

bow: The front of the boat.

broach: A sudden, unplanned turning of a boat toward the wind that occurs in strong winds.

broad reach: *Reaching* at a wide or broad angle to the wind (greater than 90 degrees).

buoy: A floating (albeit anchored) object that can be a navigation aid or a *mooring.*

by the lee: Sailing *downwind* with the wind coming over the same side of the boat as the boom is *trimmed,* which can cause an accidental *jibe.*

cam cleat: A cleat with two moving "jaws" that allows for rapid adjustment of a line. Optimized for use on dinghies and small keelboats to secure lines that require frequent adjustment like the mainsheet.

cam cleat

capsize: To flip the boat over so that the top of the *mast* is in the water.

catboat: A *keelboat* that doesn't have a *jib,* only a *mainsail.*

centerboard: The retractable, unballasted center fin on a *dinghy* that keeps the boat from sideslipping (moving sideways).

catboat

chafe: Abrasion; wear.

chain plate: Attachment point of the *standing rigging* on the *hull.*

charter: To rent (as in chartering a boat).

chop: Short, steep waves.

cleat: (1) A fitting used to tie off or secure a *line* under load so that the *line* doesn't slip. (2) To make fast or secure a rope.

clevis pin: A metal pin that secures a *shackle* or other fitting on a boat.

clew: The *aft,* bottom corner of a sail.

close-hauled: The closest course to the wind that you can effectively sail. Also called sailing *upwind, on the wind,* or *beating.*

close reach: A reach at any heading between 90 degrees to the wind and *close-hauled.*

cockpit: The area where the crew sits to operate the boat.

cunningham: The control *line* system near the *tack* of a sail used to adjust *luff* tension.

current: Horizontal movement of water caused by tidal change, gravity, or wind.

cutter: A type of sloop with the mast set farther aft, about halfway back from the bow.

cutter

daggerboard: A *center-board*-type fin that's raised and lowered vertically through a slot in the *hull*.

daymarks: Warning markers displayed on poles used in lieu of buoys, typically in shallower water.

dead reckoning: Plotting your position based on the course and distance from a previously known position.

death roll: A *capsize* to *windward;* generally occurs while sailing *downwind*.

deck: The top of the *hull*.

depth sounder: An instrument that measures depth of water below the boat.

deviation: The angular difference between the real magnetic heading and the one indicated by a compass; compass error.

dew point: The temperature at which the air becomes saturated with water vapor.

dinghy: (1) A sailboat with a *centerboard* (or *daggerboard* or *leeboard*); (2) a small rowboat.

dividers: An adjustable metal tool with two sharp points used in navigation.

downwind: (1) A run, but can mean any point of sail when the wind is *aft* of the *beam (broad reach)*. (2) The direction that the wind is blowing toward. (3) Any point that is farther from the source of the wind than another point.

draft: (1) The distance from the water's surface to the deepest point on the boat. (2) The amount and position of fullness in a sail.

ease: To let out (a rope or sail).

ebb: A tidal *current* flowing out to sea.

fender: Rubber cushion placed between a boat and a dock for protecting the *hull*.

fetch: (1) The distance of open water that waves have to grow. (2) To sail a course that will clear a buoy without *tacking;* to lay.

flood: Tidal *current* coming inbound from the sea; a rising tide.

foils: The *keel* (or *centerboard*), *rudder,* and the sails.

foot: (1) The bottom edge of a sail. (2) To sail slightly lower than *close-hauled* in order to go faster.

forestay: The support wire that runs from the *mast* down to the *bow*.

freeboard: The distance between the *deck* of the boat and the water; the height of the *topsides*.

furl: To roll or fold a sail and secure it.

gaff: The shorter boom at the top of the *gaff rig*.

gaff rig: A traditional type of *rig* with a four-sided *mainsail* attached to two *booms*.

galley: A boat's kitchen.

gaff rig

genoa: A large *jib* that overlaps the *mast*.

gooseneck: The fitting that attaches the boom to the *mast*.

GPS (Global Positioning System): A navigation system that uses satellites to plot location.

grommet: A small plastic or metal ring pressed or sewn into a sail, creating a hole.

guy: The *spinnaker sheet* (control rope) on the *windward* side that attaches through a fitting on the *spinnaker* pole to the *tack.* Also called the afterguy.

halyard: The rope running up the *mast,* used to pull the sails up.

hanks: Snaps or clips at intervals along the *luff* of a *jib,* used to attach the sail to the *forestay.*

head: (1) The top corner of any sail. (2) The bathroom/toilet aboard a boat.

head up: To turn the boat toward the wind (to *windward*).

header: A wind shift that causes the boat to turn away from the old wind direction.

headsail: Any sail that sets up forward, in front of the *mainsail.*

headstay: See *forestay.*

heavy air: Strong winds.

heel: When the boat leans or tips to one side.

helm: (1) The wheel or *tiller* — the steering device. (2) A technical word for the balance of forces on the *rudder.* (3) The position of the *helmsman* on the boat.

helmsman: The driver or skipper of the boat.

hike: To lean over the side, usually to counteract the *heeling* forces.

hiking stick: See *tiller extension.*

hoist: To pull up the sails.

horn cleat: A common *cleat* shaped like a T; also called a *t-cleat or anvil cleat.*

horn cleat

hull: The body of the boat.

in irons: When a boat has stopped moving and is stuck pointing directly into the wind.

jack lines: Ropes, webbing, or cables that run along the *deck* on either side of the cabin the length of the boat, specifically for use with safety harnesses.

jammer: A mechanical fitting with a lever arm that cleats a rope.

jib: The most common *headsail.*

jibe: To change *tacks* by turning away from the wind.

jury-rigging: Temporarily fixing broken equipment.

kedge: To use an anchor to get a grounded boat back to deep water.

keel: A fixed, ballasted center fin that keeps the boat from sideslipping and provides stability to prevent capsizing, or tipping over.

keelboat: A sailboat with a *keel.*

ketch: An old-style *keelboat* with two *masts,* the front one being taller. The mizzen (smaller) *mast* must be in front of the *rudder* post (the attachment point for the *rudder*).

ketch

knot: (1) Nautical mile (6,076 feet) per hour. (2) A rope trick.

lateen: The top *boom* on a *lateen rig.*

lateen rig: An old-fashioned triangular *mainsail* arrangement with two *booms* that pivot the *mast.* The two booms meet at the front corner of the sail.

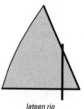

lateen rig

layline: The *line* beyond which you can *lay* (make) the destination on a *close-hauled* course with no more *tacks*.

lee shore: A shoreline to *leeward* of a boat onto which the wind is blowing.

leeboard: A retractable fin like a *centerboard* but attached to the side of the boat.

leech: The back edge of a sail.

leeward: *Downwind;* away from the wind.

lifeline: A wire supported by low poles called *stanchions* that encircle the *deck* to keep crew from falling overboard.

lift: A wind shift that enables the boat to sail closer to the old wind direction.

line: A rope used on a sailboat with a specified purpose.

log: (1) A nautical record of a ship's voyage. (2) A device that measures distance traveled.

longitude: The vertical lines on a chart ǀor globe designating the angular distance (0 to 180 degrees) east or west of the prime meridian.

LOP (line of position): A line through some point on which you presume your boat to be located as a result of an observation or measurement.

lubber line: Fixed vertical post(s) on the front edge of the compass.

luff: (1) The front edge of a sail from the *head* to the *tack*. (2) The flapping motion of sailcloth when a sail is undertrimmed (or not *trimmed* at all).

mainsail: The *aft*-most sail on a boat with one *mast*, normally attached to the *mast* along its front edge.

mainsheet: The adjustment rope that pulls the boom (hence the *mainsail*) in and out.

Marconi rig: The most common *rig*, where the *mainsail* is a triangle shape with one boom. This *rig* became popular in the 1920s. It was called a *Marconi rig* because with its supporting wires *(standing rigging)* and tall height (compared to the *gaff rig*), it resembled the radio towers built for Guglielmo Marconi's invention. This *rig* is so prevalent that no one now refers to it by a special name.

mast: The vertical pole that supports the sails.

mooring: A permanently anchored buoy to which a boat can be tied.

nautical mile: 6,076 feet; 1.15 times longer than a statute (regular) mile; equal to one minute (1/60th of a degree) of latitude.

no-sail zone: Zone where a sailboat can't sail; about 90 degrees wide, with the center point being directly toward the *true wind* direction.

off the wind: Sailing on a *broad reach* or run.

outboard: (1) Out to the side of the boat. (2) A removable engine.

outhaul: The control *line* system used for adjusting the tension of the *foot* of the *mainsail*.

parallel rulers: A navigation tool with two straight-edged plastic slats or rulers connected by two hinges; used to measure and draw compass courses.

PFD (personal flotation device): A life jacket or other buoyancy device.

piloting: Navigation involving frequent determination of position.

pinch: Steering slightly closer to the wind than a *close-hauled* course.

plane: To skim along the water's surface.

pole lift: See *topping lift*.

port: (1) Left side while facing forward. (2) A small, round window on a boat, also called a "porthole." (3) A commercial harbor.

port tack: Sailing with the wind coming over the left side of the boat.

puff: An increase in wind velocity.

purchase system: Block-and-tackle system that gives a mechanical advantage.

quadrant: Bracket around the *rudder* post that connects to the steering wheel cables.

Quick-Stop method: A man-overboard rescue technique in which you instantly stop the boat as close to the victim as possible.

ratchet block: A block that turns freely when you pull the *line* but doesn't turn at all in the other direction.

reaching: Any heading between *close-hauled* and *running*.

reef points: Several horizontal reinforced holes in a row built into the sail to facilitate *reefing*.

reefing: Reducing the exposed area of a given sail.

regatta: A series of races with the cumulative race scores counting for the final results.

relative bearing: A bearing measured in degrees relative to a boat's heading.

rig: (1) The *mast* and *standing rigging*. (2) A term for preparing the boat (or sail or fitting) for use.

righting moment: Leverage provided by crew weight or ballast that inhibits *heeling*.

roller furling system: System of sail storage and *reefing* where the sail wraps up on a narrow spool; most commonly used for *headsails*.

rope clutch: See *jammer*.

rudder: The underwater fin that steers a boat; controlled by a *tiller* or wheel on *deck*.

running: The course you're steering when the wind is behind you.

running lights: A boat's navigation lights.

running rigging: The ropes and pulleys used to raise, lower, and adjust the sails.

schooner: An old-style *keelboat* with two or more *masts*. The front *mast* (foremast) must be shorter than the main *mast*. If the sails are *rigged* in the old-fashioned, *square-rigger* manner (with rectangular sails set on booms crossing the *mast* like a T), then you get into another family of *rig* names, which we will kindly not list here.

schooner

shackle: A metal fitting often used to attach a sail to a rope.

sheave: The moving "wheel" part of a *block* or pulley.

sheet: The primary *line* that adjusts the sail's *trim*. Usually referred to with the sail it adjusts, as in, "Pull in the *mainsheet*."

shoal: A shallow area.

shock cord: Elastic rope; also called *bungee cord*.

shrouds: The support wires that run from the *mast* down to the edge of the *deck* on the left and right sides of the *mast*.

slip: A dockside parking space for a boat.

sloop: The most common type of *keelboat*. Has only one *mast*.

sloop

snap shackle: Fast-opening fitting that attaches the corner of a *spinnaker* to a control rope.

snap shackle

spinnaker: A big, colorful, parachute-like specialty sail used when sailing *downwind.*

spring lines: Additional *lines* that are tied from the middle of the boat at opposing angles to the fore and *aft* dock *lines* to prevent the boat from surging forward or backward.

square rigger: See **schooner.**

standing rigging: All the wires that support the *mast,* including *forestay, shrouds,* and *backstay.*

starboard: Right side facing forward.

starboard tack: Sailing with the wind coming over the boat's right side.

stern: The back end of the boat.

swamp: To fill up with water.

tack: (1) The front, bottom corner of a sail. (2) The boat's heading in relation to the side of the boat that's closer to the wind (that is, on *starboard* or *port tack*). (3) To change tacks by turning toward the wind, entering the *no-sail zone* from one side and exiting on the other.

telltales: Strands of yarn or cassette tape that are attached to the sail or *standing rigging* to help judge the wind angle and whether the sails are *trimmed* properly.

tiller: The lever arm that controls the position of the *rudder.*

tiller extension: A device attached to the end of the *tiller* that enables a person to sit farther *outboard* while steering.

topping lift: *Halyardlike* control rope running from the *mast;* used to lift the *outboard* tip of the *spinnaker* pole.

topsides: The outer sides of the *hull.*

transom: The outer side of the *stern.*

trapeze: A system for adding *righting moment* by standing on the side of a boat wearing a harness with a hook, which is attached to a wire running down from the *mast.*

traveler: A sail-control system that can move the *mainsheet* attachment point on the boat from side to side.

trim: (1) To pull in a rope or a sail. (2) The set of the sails. (3) The bow-up or bow-down position of the boat when not moving.

trough: The low part of a wave.

true wind: The actual wind (as opposed to the *apparent wind*) that would be measured by a boat at anchor (that is, not moving).

turtle: A type of *capsize* where the boat turns all the way over with the *mast* sticking straight down.

variation: The angular difference between true and magnetic north.

waypoint: The latitude/longitude coordinates of a point along your course.

whitecap: Foamy crest on the top of waves.

winch: A revolving geared drum turned by a handle that provides mechanical advantage and increases the sailor's ability to pull on a rope under load.

windward: Toward the wind; the side the wind blows upon.

wing the jib: When sailing on a run, to *trim* the *jib* on the opposite side as the *mainsail.*

wishbone boom: A two-piece *boom* shaped like a wishbone, commonly found on sailboards and some small sailboats.

wishbone boom

yawl: An old-style *keelboat* with two *masts*. The mizzen (smaller) *mast* is behind the *rudder* post (the attachment point for the *rudder*). See *ketch*.

yawl

Appendix B

First Aid Afloat

· ·

Out of this nettle, danger, we pluck this flower, safety.

— William Shakespeare

This appendix is meant to give you an idea of what the most common afflictions aboard a boat are and the basic remedies for those ills. Obviously, anything can happen when you're out to sea, so you may need to help with a wide variety of medical situations. This appendix gives you some presailing advice and then covers the most common illnesses on board a boat, including hypothermia, seasickness, and sunburn.

If anyone on your boat requires prompt medical attention, call the Coast Guard (Channel 16 on your VHF radio). Or your cellphone may work if you're sailing close to shore, so call 911. For more on using your VHF, see Chapter 7.

Preparing for Sailing

Make sure that you and everyone you're planning to take sailing knows how to swim. See Chapter 16 for tips on how to choose a swimming instructor for your children. We also strongly recommend that you know cardiopulmonary resuscitation (CPR), regardless of whether you plan to go sailing. Being on the water increases the amount of time that emergency personnel needs to get to you, and CPR is the best way to keep someone alive while rescue personnel are on their way. Teaching CPR is beyond the scope of this book, but your local Red Cross can teach you the technique in only a few hours.

Be sure to ask your CPR instructor to show you how to use the technique with the drowning-victim recovery position. In addition, smart sailors should strongly consider taking a first-aid course and sailing with a first-aid manual and first-aid kit.

Pick a first-aid manual

Even if you're not planning an extended cruise, investing in a good first-aid manual for your boat makes sense. Ask your doctor and check your local bookstore or marine store for a good first-aid manual. Here are some manuals that we recommend:

- ✔ *AMA Handbook — First Aid*
- ✔ *Advanced First Aid Afloat,* by Peter Eastman, M.D.
- ✔ *Wilderness & Travel Medicine,* by Eric A. Weiss, M.D.
- ✔ *First Aid at Sea,* by Douglas Justins and Colin Berry
- ✔ *Sailing and Yachting First Aid,* by Drs. Bergan and Guzzetta (find at www.store.ussailing.org under cruising education books)

Pack a first-aid kit

On any trip, even a short one, take along plenty of food and water, a good first-aid book (see the list of recommended books in the preceding section), and a well-stocked first-aid kit if your boat has sufficient storage space. Ice is important to bring, and we also recommend those fancy products that become cold compresses when you squeeze or shake them.

Stow a first-aid kit in a dry, watertight compartment with a list of contents on the box for easy reference. Before you sail, familiarize yourself with your first-aid manual for how to use them to deal with burns, cuts, bleeding, and head injuries. If anyone requires medication for an ongoing condition, make sure that medicine is on board. If it needs to be kept cool, place it in a small cooler.

Recovering from Hypothermia

We talk about the danger of losing body heat in Chapter 7. The loss of body heat is called *hypothermia* or *exposure.* Your body temperature cools down 25 times faster in cold water than in the same temperature of air, so hypothermia is most common in people who have fallen overboard, but it can also affect people on deck when they're sailing in cold weather, especially at night. The symptoms of hypothermia start with loss of circulation to the extremities — fingers and toes. As your head gets cold, your mental and physical responses slow down, and you may have difficulty speaking and be disoriented. Shivering is the body's attempt to warm up, and hypothermia is more dangerous when shivering stops.

You must warm hypothermia victims *gradually,* and you need to warm their core area (around the heart) first. If the victim is unconscious without a pulse, contact the Coast Guard and use CPR until medical help arrives.

1. **Remove the victim's wet clothing.**

2. **Place the victim in a sleeping bag with warm blankets.**

3. **Have a crew member (or two) climb in the sleeping bag to warm the victim with body heat.**

   Remember to warm the core (chest area) first. This method of warming up the victim may sound kinky, but it can be a lifesaver.

4. **Give the victim warm (not hot) drinks and high-energy food.**

   Warm soup and warm sugary drinks are better than caffeine or alcohol so the victim can generate his or her own internal heat.

Staving Off Seasickness

Having that seasick feeling can ruin an otherwise great day afloat. To minimize your chances of feeling nauseous, we suggest you try the following actions:

- ✔ **Avoid alcohol (or a hangover).** That "woozy" feeling isn't fun at sea.

- ✔ **Avoid rich, greasy foods.** Choose the bagel instead of the eggs benedict at breakfast.

- ✔ **Focus on the horizon.** Distractions such as steering the boat or helping with a job on deck can help you feel better, too.

- ✔ **Keep some solid food in your stomach at all times.** Crackers or bread are good choices.

- ✔ **Sip small amounts of fizzy drinks.** Maybe just an old wives' tale, but ginger ale and clear soft drinks work best for us.

- ✔ **Stay on deck.** Stay in the fresh air, away from exhaust fumes (if your boat has an engine).

If you throw up, try to do so off the leeward side of the boat, downwind of everyone (including yourself).

Several medicines can help combat seasickness, but you must take most before the symptoms start. Of course, like just about any other medication, don't take any of these medicines if you're pregnant without consulting with your doctor. Even if you aren't pregnant, your doctor may be able to recommend a good remedy. You must take over-the-counter seasickness pills, such as Dramamine, an hour before sailing; however, they can cause drowsiness and a dry mouth. Ask your doctor about a patch that administers Scopolamine, a prescription motion-sickness drug.

Keep an eye on anyone who is feeling seasick. Seasickness can make you weak, disoriented, and extremely sleepy — a danger when on deck. Help people who are seasick to a comfortable spot in the fresh air. If they're just feeling a little queasy, try letting them steer as a distraction. If you aren't feeling well, don't be ashamed; almost all sailors feel queasy at some point.

Steering Clear of Sunburn

The effects of being out in the sun all day, combined with the sun's rays reflected off the water, make sailors prime candidates for sunburn. The following tips can help you avoid having a painful sunburn at the end of the day:

- **Put sunscreen on *before* you leave the dock.**
- **Reapply sunscreen several times during the day — especially in wet conditions.**
- **Always use a sunscreen with a Sun Protection Factor (SPF) of at least 15.** We try to always carry a stick of sunscreen in our pockets so that we can frequently reapply sunscreen to our noses, lips, and ears.
- **Always wear a hat and sunglasses.**
- **If you're fair skinned or are sailing in a tropical locale, wear a long-sleeved, lightweight cotton shirt (one with a collar to help protect your neck) and long pants.** Guarding your skin this way makes your trip much more enjoyable. You'll be amazed at how tan you get even when you're covered up all day.

JJ SAYS

We have a number of friends who've battled skin cancer, and it's not a pleasant fight. So please be careful out in the sun. If you do have severe sunburn, using aloe vera products helps soothe the skin. Drink plenty of cool fluids and try to wear loose-fitting cotton clothes to help your skin heal.

Defeating Dehydration

Dehydration and heat exhaustion are two of the most dangerous illnesses for sailors, because the body rejects the cure, which is to get cool and drink plenty of fluids. With severe dehydration, your body rejects any fluid intake by throwing up, making you further dehydrated. Severe dehydration can result in staying in a hospital hooked up to an IV to rehydrate. So try to drink as much fluid as you can while you're on the water.

In very hot conditions, you can get dehydrated even when you feel like you've been consuming fluids all day. One way to tell whether you're getting dehydrated is by how much you have to urinate. If you haven't had to use the *head* (marine toilet) all day, you need to drink a lot more water.

Appendix C

The Physics of Sailing: Understanding How Sailboats Work

The perfection of a yacht's beauty is that nothing should be there for only beauty's sake.

— John MacGregor

America's Cup teams and the fastest distance racers spend millions of dollars trying to quantify what makes a sailboat move — and move fast (or at least faster than the competition). So know right from the beginning that studying boat movement is a highly complex problem that deals with fluids of vastly different densities (water and air — yes, air is a fluid too), and your boat operates on the confused interface between those two fluids. Although you don't really have to know how a sailboat works to enjoy sailing, finding out how it works can be fascinating — so feel free to dive into this appendix.

Looking at the Basic Forces

Figuring out the best wing shape for supersonic flying at 60,000 feet is much easier than figuring out the best hull, keel, and sail shape for a racing sailboat because, with aircraft, you need to consider only the plane's interaction with very thin air. However, to understand the physical principles involved with sailboat movement, you have to understand the following two basic forces that propel a sailboat:

- ✔ Motion of air over the sails
- ✔ Water flow over a centerboard or keel

The next two sections briefly explain each of these forces in greater depth.

Air moving over the sails

When a sailboat is sailing with the wind behind it, the sails act like a parachute out in front of the boat as the boat moves with the wind. But the dynamics get more interesting when a crew wants the sailboat to sail at an angle to the wind.

First, look at how a simple *airfoil* (wing) generates lift. Put your hand out the window of a moving car with your palm facing forward, and the wind simply pushes it backward. But when you slowly rotate your hand into the wind, twisting your thumb downward, you can feel your hand begin to lift up (in addition to being pushed back). This *lift* is due to the motion of the air that passes above and below your hand. As you begin to twist your hand, the air traveling over the top of your hand speeds up relative to the air streaming under the bottom, as Figure C-1 shows.

Figure C-1: Hands out a car window at different angles to the wind feel different forces.

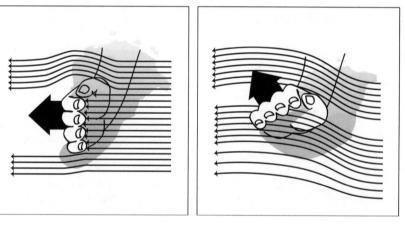

The fast-moving air creates low pressure, so by twisting your hand, you generate a low-pressure area over the top of your hand. The difference in pressure (caused by your hand "wing" and its slight *angle of attack* to the airflow, that is, slightly angled in the wind) results in an upward force that lifts your hand as well as a slight sideways force pushing your hand backwards. Understanding these upward and sideways forces is crucial to understanding lift and why a sailboat moves forward. The same basic principle of wings and air flow works for birds, planes, and sailboats.

So what happens when a boat sails upwind? First, look at the sail. When you pull in the mainsheet and fill the sail with wind, the sail creates a wing shape. That wing has an angle of attack to the wind flow. Just like your hand out the car window (or any airfoil at an angle of attack to the flow), the air over the back side of the sail goes faster than the air on the front side. The resulting difference in pressure creates lift — a force pushing the boat sideways and forward.

Water passing over the underwater wing

If the airflow over the sail was the only force involved, sailboats would slip sideways when they tried to sail close-hauled. A sailboat, however, has wings above and below the water. When a close-hauled sailboat trims in its sails and begins to move through the water, slipping sideways, the underwater wings (centerboard or keel and rudder) also create a force that, when combined with the sail force, moves a sailboat forward. Here's how: Like any other wing, the water passing over the back side of the centerboard or keel goes faster than the water passing over the front side. The resulting difference in water pressure this flow of water creates pulls the boat forward and sideways — but in the opposite "sideways" direction of the sail force. The opposing sideways forces cancel each other out, as Figure C-2 shows, and the forward forces remain.

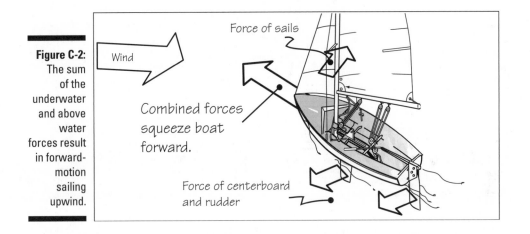

Figure C-2: The sum of the underwater and above water forces result in forward-motion sailing upwind.

Force of sails

Wind

Combined forces squeeze boat forward.

Force of centerboard and rudder

Together, the forces of the wind on the sails and the water on the centerboard or keel (and to a much lesser extent on the rudder) enable the boat to sail at a close angle to the wind. You can't sail straight into the wind, or the sails would flap like a flag, and you wouldn't generate any lifting forces on the sails. Most modern sailboats can sail within 45 degrees (or closer) to the wind direction, a remarkable feat when you consider that the ships in which explorers such as Magellan sailed the world were so inefficient they could barely sail within 90 degrees to the wind.

Balancing the Forces

A main design factor for *naval architects* (boat designers) is to get the sail forces (also called the *Center of Effort* or *CE*) and the underwater forces (the *Center of Lateral Resistance* or *CLR*) in balance.

A sailboard (see Chapter 18) provides a simple example of how these forces interact. First consider the sail when properly trimmed to the correct angle to the wind flow. The CE is the single spot that describes the sum of all the forces from the wind flow up and down the sail — roughly halfway up and one-third of the way back from the front of a sail. Below the water is the CLR — the pivot point of the sailboard (or sailboat) when it turns, as Figure C-3 shows.

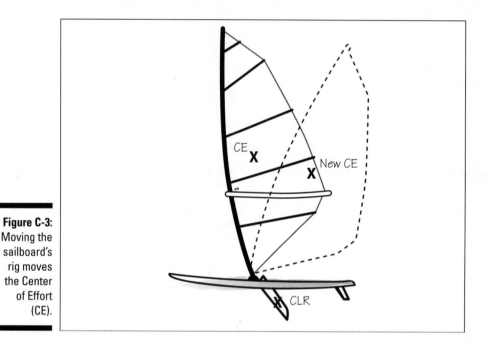

Figure C-3:
Moving the sailboard's rig moves the Center of Effort (CE).

When a sailboard is in the groove (sailing in a straight line), the CE and CLR forces are in balance and the boat tracks straight. But tip the rig back some while keeping it trimmed at the same angle to the wind, and the balance is disturbed. The sail's CE is now behind the board's pivot point as Figure C-3 shows, and the boat turns up toward the wind. Conversely, by tipping the mast top forward, the CE moves in front of the board's pivot point, and the board turns down, away from the wind.

Obviously you can't just tip your mast back and forth on a dinghy or keelboat while underway. But you can change the boat's balance with your heel angle and sail trim. When I was training for the Olympics, my favorite drill was practicing steering the boat without the rudder to improve my feel for the boat's heel and balance. Instead of using our rudder, my teammate and I would steer by

- ✔ **Moving our weight:** By heeling the boat one way or the other, you change the balance of the boat and make it turn. When you (and your crew) heel the boat to *windward* (toward the wind), the boat turns to *leeward* (away from the wind), and vice versa. In order to go in a straight line, the forces above and below the water must balance not only fore and aft, but also sideways. So when you heel the boat one way or the other, you disturb that balance.

- ✔ **Adjusting the sails:** You can also change the balance of a sailboat with a jib and main by filling one sail and luffing the other. When you trim the jib and let out the main, the boat turns leeward. Overtrimming the main and luffing the jib causes the boat to turn windward.

The technique of moving your weight to steer doesn't work as well on a heavy keelboat, because compared to the weight of the boat, your weight is too light to substantially change the heel of the boat.

In Chapter 11, we discuss *weather helm* — the tendency of most boats to want to turn into the wind when close-hauled or reaching. Weather helm results when the CE and CLR forces are slightly out of balance. A slight bit of weather helm is natural and can help you steer "in the groove" by providing a bit of feel. And there are some complicated reasons why it's fast too. But if your tiller or wheel pulls too hard when you're trying to steer straight, you can reduce weather helm by easing the main (which moves the CE forward).

Minimizing Drag

Another force affecting your boat's performance is *drag*. Sailboat racers spend lots of time polishing their hull and underwater foils so the boat slips through the water faster. But because you can't sail in a vacuum, a certain amount of drag is inevitable; in fact, turning the rudder creates drag.

Every time you turn your rudder to steer, you slightly slow down the boat. You see, the rudder is like a huge sea-brake. Imagine the water flow past the rudder when it's straight. Now turn the rudder hard over, and all that flow becomes disturbed and very turbulent. The net result is that the boat turns, but it also slows down.

On a smaller boat, such as a dinghy or sailboard, you can also greatly affect the boat's drag by moving your weight too far forward or aft in the boat. In general, position your weight over the center of lateral resistance, which is usually even or just aft of the boat's centerboard or rudder. (See Chapter 11 for more go-fast tips.)

Less drag by canting the keel

Canting Ballast Twin Foil (CBTF) technology (www.cbtftechnology.com) is now standard equipment on some of the fastest monohulls in the world. CBTF features an innovative underbody consisting of two foils (fore and aft) that are twin rudders to do the steering and a central ballast strut that *cants,* or swings side to side to move the lead bulb where it's more effective. With a push of a button, the bulb can do the hiking for you.

In the late '90s, Peter skippered the first true CBTF design, the 40-foot (12-meter) *Red Hornet* in races in different parts of the United States. The boat was an immediate success and was quite a "giant killer" as Peter and his crew often beat boats that were nearly twice as big. Right before producing the second edition of this book, Peter navigated the 86-foot CBTF design *Morning Glory* to a record-setting run in the Transpac Race (Los Angeles to Honolulu).

Testing the Waters

The description in this appendix of how a sailboat works is, necessarily, simplified. You see, even today, scientists are still fine-tuning the theory of the physics involved in making a sailboat sail upwind. The fact that the physics involved are so complex can make sailing even more fun. You, the sailor, can be a test pilot, fiddling with the various adjustments of sail shape and the boat's angle to the wind to squeeze even more performance out of your craft . . . or you can just go sailing. In the end, sailing is all about balancing out the forces of the wind and water on the boat and its sails. By adjusting the sails, your crew weight, the tune of your mast, and the boat's angle of heel, you can find that magic balance that results in the best speed.

Index